Atlantic History

NATIONAL
HISTORY
CENTER

REINTERPRETING HISTORY
Wm. Roger Louis, series editor

The series Reinterpreting History is dedicated to the historian's craft of challenging assumptions, examining new evidence, and placing topics of significance in historiographical context. Historiography is the art of conveying the ways in which the interpretation of history changes over time. The vigorous and systematic revision of history is at the heart of the discipline.

Reinterpreting History is an initiative of the National History Center, which was created by the American Historical Association in 2002 to advance historical knowledge and to convey to the public at large the historical context of present-day issues.

Atlantic History

A Critical Appraisal

EDITED BY

Jack P. Greene
Philip D. Morgan

OXFORD
UNIVERSITY PRESS
2009

OXFORD

UNIVERSITY PRESS

Oxford University Press, Inc., publishes works that further
Oxford University's objective of excellence
in research, scholarship, and education.

Oxford   New York
Auckland   Cape Town   Dar es Salaam   Hong Kong   Karachi
Kuala Lumpur   Madrid   Melbourne   Mexico City   Nairobi
New Delhi   Shanghai   Taipei   Toronto

With offices in
Argentina   Austria   Brazil   Chile   Czech Republic   France   Greece
Guatemala   Hungary   Italy   Japan   Poland   Portugal   Singapore
South Korea   Switzerland   Thailand   Turkey   Ukraine   Vietnam

Published by Oxford University Press, Inc.
198 Madison Avenue, New York, New York 10016

www.oup.com

Oxford is a registered trademark of Oxford University Press.

Library of Congress Cataloging-in-Publication Data

Atlantic history : a critical appraisal / edited by Jack P. Greene and Philip D. Morgan.
p.   cm. — (Reinterpreting history)
Includes bibliographical references and index.
ISBN 978-0-19-532033-6; 978-9-19-532034-3 (pbk.)
1. Atlantic Ocean Region—Historiography.   2. History, Modern—Historiography.
3. Imperialism—Historiography.   I. Greene, Jack P.   II. Morgan, Philip D., 1949–
D206.A75 2009
909'.09821072—dc22   2008013694

Printed in the United States of America
on acid-free paper

PREFACE

This volume developed out of a session at the 2005 meeting of the American Historical Association in Seattle, which Jack Greene organized, at the request of Roger Louis, on behalf of the National History Center. Rather than putting together yet another session on the promise of Atlantic history, Jack decided that this session might be the occasion for a critical appraisal of that increasingly popular subject and invited scholars of varying opinions to present short papers on its merits and utility. Six of the contributors to this volume participated in that session: Jack served as chair, and Nicholas Canny, Joyce E. Chaplin, Peter A. Coclanis, Philip D. Morgan, and Carla Rahn Phillips presented papers that subsequently developed into contributions to this volume.

The National History Center expected a book to result from this session, and Jack and Phil Morgan assumed the task of putting it together. The editors endeavored to produce a volume that would mirror the contemporary organization and functioning of the Atlantic world as it developed from the fifteenth through the early nineteenth centuries, a volume that would acknowledge the many actors involved in the creation of that world, provide a strong sense of the rich and complex variety of that world, and be as geographically, culturally, and as temporally inclusive as possible. The editors wanted a volume that would assess the impact of the New World of the Atlantic upon the Old Worlds around the Atlantic, and one that would present alternative or complementary frameworks for analyzing that new Atlantic world. To achieve these objectives, we found it necessary to recruit seven new participants: Kenneth Andrien, A. J. R. Russell-Wood, Trevor Burnard, Laurent Dubois, Benjamin Schmidt, Amy Turner Bushnell, and Peter H. Wood, each of whom has contributed a chapter.

The editors wish to thank all the authors for their contributions; several anonymous commentators on the original proposal who made cogent suggestions for expanding and reorganizing the volume; two readers of the first draft of the manuscript who made a number of concise and constructive suggestions, many of which the editors and authors have followed to the letter; and Susan Ferber, whose sharp editorial eye made the volume tighter and more coherent as she shepherded it through the publication process at Oxford University Press. We also thank Susan Danforth, George S. Parker Curator of Maps at the John Carter Brown Library, for suggesting the dust-jacket map, and Joseph Adelman, graduate student at Johns Hopkins University, for completing the index.

Jack P. Greene, East Greenwich, Rhode Island

Philip D. Morgan, Baltimore, Maryland

CONTENTS

CONTRIBUTORS

KENNETH J. ANDRIEN, Humanities Distinguished Professor of History at The Ohio State University, is currently working on a book on intersection of ideas, culture, and public policy in the eighteenth-century Spanish Atlantic Empire.

TREVOR BURNARD, Professor of History, University of Warwick, is working on a co-authored book comparing mid-eighteenth-century Jamaica and Saint-Domingue.

AMY TURNER BUSHNELL, Invited Research Fellow, The John Carter Brown Library, is working on a book about the chiefdom-presidio compact in the eastern woodlands and the concept of a "reconciled" frontier.

NICHOLAS CANNY, Professor of History and Director of the Moore Institute at the National University of Ireland, Galway, and President of the Royal Irish Academy, is currently comparing French with English writing on the natural history of the Atlantic world 1550–1720.

JOYCE E. CHAPLIN, James Duncan Phillips Professor of Early American History at Harvard University, is currently writing a history of around-the-world travel, from Magellan the Spanish explorer to Magellan the GPS system.

PETER A. COCLANIS, Associate Provost for International Affairs and Albert R. Newsome Professor of History at UNC-Chapel Hill, is currently working on the international rice trade between c. 1600 and 1940.

LAURENT DUBOIS, Professor of History and Romance Studies at Duke University, is writing a history of the banjo in the Atlantic world.

JACK P. GREENE, Andrew W. Mellon Professor, Emeritus, Johns Hopkins University, is working on a book on the languages of empire in eighteenth-century Britain.

PHILIP D. MORGAN, Harry C. Black Professor, Johns Hopkins University, is working on a survey of the early modern Caribbean.

CARLA RAHN PHILLIPS, Union Pacific Professor in Comparative Early Modern History, University of Minnesota, is currently working on various projects in transatlantic maritime history.

A. J. R. RUSSELL-WOOD, Herbert Baxter Adams Professor of History, Johns Hopkins University, is working on a manuscript on overseas students at Coimbra University.

BENJAMIN SCHMIDT, Associate Professor of History at the University of Washington, is completing a book on the culture of globalism and politics of exoticism around the turn of the eighteenth century.

PETER H. WOOD, Emeritus Professor of History, Duke University, is researching aspects of French exploration in North America during the decades after La Salle.

Atlantic History

INTRODUCTION: THE PRESENT STATE
OF ATLANTIC HISTORY

PHILIP D. MORGAN AND JACK P. GREENE

Atlantic history is an analytic construct and an explicit category of historical analysis that historians have devised to help them organize the study of some of the most important developments of the early modern era: the emergence in the fifteenth century and the subsequent growth of the Atlantic basin as a site for demographic, economic, social, cultural, and other forms of exchange among and within the four continents surrounding the Atlantic Ocean—Europe, Africa, South America, and North America—and all the islands adjacent to those continents and in that ocean. As people, pathogens, and plants—to mention just three key agents of change—moved ever more intensively across the Atlantic, profound transformations occurred in all spheres of life. Events in one place had repercussions in others. Atlantic history, as John Elliott elegantly puts it, involves the study of "the creation, destruction, and re-creation of communities as a result of the movement, across and around the Atlantic basin, of people, commodities, cultural practices, and values."[1]

If the concept of Atlantic history is fairly new—the first institutional use of the term being traced to the late 1960s, when the Department of History at Johns Hopkins University spearheaded the establishment of its Program in Atlantic History and Culture—the practice is not. As early as the 1870s, Herbert Baxter Adams located the narrative of American history in the Atlantic world, tied to a genetic germ theory that is no longer in favor. During the first half of the twentieth century, Charles McLean Andrews, a specialist on the British Empire, and C. H. Haring, a student of the Spanish Empire, were the most prominent among many historians of early modern empire who took a transoceanic perspective. Through the middle decades of the twentieth century, historians of exploration and discovery, such as

David Beers Quinn, effectively did Atlantic history long before it became fashionable. The same can be said about Perry Miller's analyses of Puritan religious development, Wesley Frank Craven's account of the settlement of Virginia, Bernard Bailyn's study of seventeenth-century New England merchants, James Lockhart's work on sixteenth-century Spanish Peru, and a host of other works by prominent scholars of the early colonial Americas. It is easy to think of key studies, such as Frank Tannenbaum's *Slave and Citizen* (1946), Philip Curtin's *Atlantic Slave Trade* (1969), Ian Steele's *The English Atlantic* (1981), or D. W. Meinig's *Atlantic America* (1986), that took a transatlantic perspective before the term became a buzzword.[2] Jacques Godechot's *Histoire de l'Atlantique* (1947) was perhaps the first to use such a title, although the book was in fact a circumscribed maritime history; Leonard Outhwaite's *The Atlantic* (1957) was also narrowly conceived.[3] If none of these authors thought of what they were doing as Atlantic history or referred to themselves as Atlanticists, few scholars by the early 1950s would have thought that one could adequately study any of the many colonial Americas without an understanding of their European antecedents.[4]

Notwithstanding the success of the Johns Hopkins program, no university replicated its model in the 1970s and 1980s.[5] Since then, however, Atlantic history has emerged as an explicit area of study that, at least in the United States, is challenging the primacy of traditional national or imperial modes of organizing historical understanding. The earliest advocates of Atlantic history thought of it primarily as a *perspective* that would broaden the horizons of specialists in traditional fields by calling attention to the larger contexts and promoting transnational comparisons. Their primary goal was to create not a new field of historical studies, but a group of scholars appreciative of common themes and differences across as well as within national boundaries and language areas, able to put their own specialized works within the larger framework of the loose but cohering Atlantic world. This approach remains an appealing option for Atlantic studies.

By contrast, more recent exponents of Atlantic history, with a measure of missionary fervor, have increasingly begun to think of Atlantic history not merely as a perspective, but as a full-blown *field* of study with the potential to encompass older fields such as European, American, African, or Latin American history, and the imperial and national histories such continental classifications have traditionally assumed. So far, no Atlantic History Association or Organization of Atlantic History has appeared, but existing professional historical organizations, such as the American Historical Association, have shown a growing interest in the topic of Atlantic history.[6]

H-Net now sponsors an online discussion list known as H-Atlantic, and there have been many special issues or forums in a wide variety of journals. Atlantic history has become a subject about which scholars give papers, departments offer employment, and publishers create journals and book series. In 2007 the first Atlantic history textbook appeared.[7]

The institutionalization of the subject in higher education has followed suit. In 1996 Harvard University established its International Seminar on the History of the Atlantic World, which has since sponsored annual seminars and many workshops that have involved the production of over 500 papers and talks by participants from many countries.[8] Other American universities have also established programs in Atlantic history, as have colleges and universities throughout the world—from Galway in Ireland to Sydney in Australia, from Edinburgh in Scotland to Hamburg in Germany—all of which offer courses in Atlantic history.[9]

Although Atlantic history is thriving institutionally and intellectually, much angst can be heard in scholarly circles about the perspective's or field's direction. In one sense, the agonizing is strange, for Atlantic history seems superficially unproblematic. Surely it is simply the study of the ocean, an expanse of water, a geographical expression—the first, in Pierre and Huguette Chaunu's estimation, "to have been regularly crossed"—and of the lands bordering on or connected to it. Yet, despite the seeming naturalness of the subject—simply conceiving of the Atlantic world in D. W. Meinig's terms as "the scene of a vast interaction"—Atlantic history sets some people's teeth on edge. Peter Coclanis, paraphrasing Robert Reich, has characterized Atlantic history as "one of those rare ideas that [has] moved swiftly from obscurity to meaninglessness without any intervening period of coherence."[10]

This critical response seems to be driven by a number of general concerns. Some critics are alarmed by the imperialism of the more exuberant exponents of Atlantic history, who seem bent on absorbing traditional national and imperial fields of study while neglecting those subjects that do not fit neatly into an Atlantic framework. Others see no need to transform Atlantic history from a useful historical perspective into a formal field. Still others find it suspiciously trendy and are doubtful of its staying power.

Whatever the sources of their concerns, critics have raised at least five substantive objections to Atlantic history's popularity that merit serious consideration. First, some critics allege that the Atlantic has little coherence and no real unity, and that it is therefore impossible to speak with confidence of an Atlantic system, region, or civilization in the way that Fernand Braudel spoke of the Mediterranean—and even he might have exaggerated that region's unity. The Mediterranean was, as Braudel conceded, "a complex of seas," but the Atlantic was even more so, and it joined societies with radically different environments and cultures.[11] Thus, the winds and currents of the Atlantic created at least two separate Atlantics—a North and a South; John Elliott, following D. W. Meinig's formulation, identifies three Atlantics: a North European, a Spanish, and a Luso version; others argue that the Atlantic was largely an English or British phenomenon and never meant as much to the Spanish, French, Dutch, or Portuguese; some prefer Atlantics of different hues—white to represent the European migration; black, as in Paul Gilroy's account, to represent the African diaspora; green to describe the Irish dispersal; red to mark a radical international working class; and perhaps tartan for the Scots. And yet others divide the Atlantic world by climate or agricultural use—tropical versus temperate; farm or peasant versus plantation.[12] It seems more manageable, therefore, to think of separate Atlantics rather than an integrated one.

Second, the Atlantic was never self-contained; all seas are joined, and thus the Atlantic was never a bounded entity. Furthermore, the argument goes, focusing on connections across and within the Atlantic risks minimizing the connections outside the region. Descriptions of the Atlantic as akin to an inland sea are deeply misleading, the critics allege. Trade and settlement in the Atlantic, for instance, were clearly linked to simultaneous ventures in Asia. In this volume, chapters 12 and 13, respectively written by Nicholas Canny and Peter Coclanis, present versions of this point of view.

Third, Atlantic history is merely imperial history in a more acceptable guise. It can be characterized, in William O'Reilly's words, as "a neo-colonial, politically correct attempt at re-writing European history with some 'other bits' given deferential treatment." Indeed, for Jorge Cañizares-Esguerra, it privileges an east–west axis over alternative north–south perspectives, so that Latin America tends to get short shrift.[13]

Fourth, students of the indigenous Americas have complained that Atlantic history, by focusing on those land areas bordering on the Atlantic, either deflects attention from inland populations and places or leaves them out of the picture altogether, a point that applies equally well to those areas occupied by mixed peoples, settlers, and traders. To counter this tendency to privilege the history of coastal areas and the spread of European peoples, they advocate, as does Peter Wood in chapter 10 of this volume, what some scholars refer to as a "continental" approach in which each of the continents surrounding the Atlantic becomes a principal site for investigation.[14]

Fifth, as Elliott has complained, much of the work thus far published with an explicitly Atlantic focus has tended to focus upon the connections that tied the many areas of the Atlantic together or, one might add, upon transnational relations within border zones at the expense of developments within discrete areas, and even without much concern about specifying how those connections and transnational relations affected the internal histories of the areas that they connected. By failing, moreover, to advance knowledge about the internal histories of the specific areas that comprised the Atlantic world much beyond what had previously been gained through studies done within national imperial and area studies frameworks, Atlanticists, this line of criticism suggests, have thus shown little concern for pursuing comparative analysis and the identification of commonalities and peculiarities within this highly variegated Atlantic world, surely one of the principal promises of Atlantic history.[15]

These criticisms of Atlantic history contain considerable cogency, but they need not be seen as crippling. Relative to the first, the lands bordering the Atlantic were, of course, remarkably complex and diverse. The Atlantic was multitudinous, comprised enormous variations, and lacked unity. A congeries of entities, each with distinctive features, the Atlantic world was no single system or civilization. But the creation of the Atlantic world increasingly drew many people throughout the Atlantic basin into the colonial project, a vast enterprise in which some people, with or without state help, expropriated the territories, resources, and labor of indigenous and imported peoples in their remarkably successful effort to transform accessible areas of the Americas from indigenous into Europeanized cultural spaces. To be sure, there were profound variations in this transformation, according to differences in physical characteristics and resource endowment; the strength, proximity, and capacity for resistance among indigenous peoples; the cultural proclivities and size of the conquering, trading, and settling populations that constituted the leading edge of that transformation and were its principal beneficiaries; and their access to capital and labor, willing or unwilling, indigenous to the area or imported from Europe, Africa, or other regions in the Americas. Although this phenomenon extended across national spheres of colonizing activity and was far more often competitive than cooperative, it involved people everywhere in parallel, if also distinctive and otherwise largely unconnected, processes that, at the deepest level, linked the new and old societies of the Atlantic basin world into the same general colonial undertaking. Though this development was never wholly confined to the Atlantic world, for over three centuries it did center in it and shape it. This common Atlantic project provides the broad setting for identifying and explaining its many variations.

Moreover, pan-Atlantic webs of association linked people, objects, and beliefs across and within the region. Though always fragmented, the early modern Atlantic world came to be increasingly united through a density and variety of connections. Events in one corner of the Atlantic world reverberated thousands of miles away. As David Eltis notes, "the result was, if not a single Atlantic society, a set of societies fundamentally different from what they would have been without participation in the new transatlantic network." A pan-Atlantic mosaic gradually emerged, with "larger Atlantic circuits binding together four continents," in D. W. Meinig's phrase.[16] The task therefore is to demonstrate connections and explore contrasts. The great virtue of thinking in Atlantic terms is that it encourages broad perspectives, transnational orientations, and expanded horizons at the same time that it offers a chance for overcoming national and other parochialisms.

Of course, this unified maritime region is a modern cultural construction. In the early modern world, few people recognized a single Atlantic, as Joyce Chaplin shows in chapter 1; insofar as anybody thought of the stretch of water now known as the Atlantic, most Europeans saw it as a series of distinct seas. The Atlantic is therefore an anachronistic concept. Rather than simply taking the spatial framework of a given body of water and its surrounding lands for granted, it should be interrogated for its contemporary connotations as well as for the interactions of peoples around, within, and across it. Attention to early modern understandings and to modern cultural constructions should be pursued simultaneously.[17]

As for the second objection to Atlantic history, a web of connections outside of the Atlantic world always existed. Europeans were able to engage in regular Atlantic voyaging only after incorporating such elements as the compass and the sternpost rudder, borrowed from Chinese and Indian Ocean mariners; Asian textiles and Indian Ocean cowrie shells were vital to the Atlantic slave trade; Americans dumped Asian tea into Boston Harbor; American bullion, especially silver, fueled Europe's trade with the Ottoman Empire, India, and China. If vital parts of the story the historian wishes to tell lie outside the Atlantic basin, naturally they should be pursued. Nevertheless, there was an intensity of interaction and activity within the Atlantic world that still merits focused attention. Thus, European overseas migration before the early nineteenth century was primarily across or around the Atlantic, and European overseas settler expansion was largely confined to the western side of the Atlantic basin for more than three centuries, with only a small flow of Europeans into Africa and Asia. Similarly, in the eighteenth and early nineteenth centuries, when the external slave trade of sub-Saharan Africa was at its height, almost nine out of ten African slaves were forcibly transported across the Atlantic rather than across the Sahara or to the Indian Ocean. If Africa's exporting of its people abroad is the focus, then the Atlantic looms largest, even if the full context must always be kept in mind. Thus, while the Atlantic was always enmeshed in a wider world, it has its own coherence and its own importance; it was, after all, the center, as C. A. Bayly notes, of the first global imperial age.[18]

Concerning the third objection, there is nothing wrong with studying empires; they were vital entities in this period, and for some subjects, such as English, Dutch, and French efforts to penetrate or seize portions of Spain's American empire in the sixteenth and seventeenth centuries or the great contest for imperial supremacy over North America and the Caribbean from 1739 to 1763, an imperial framework may be more useful than an Atlantic one.[19] But imperial boundaries were permeable and there was considerable crossing of imperial lines. Of course, much activity occurred within a single imperial entity; illicit trade, smuggling, piracy, and venturing across imperial boundaries were the exception, not the norm. Nevertheless, Atlantic history is not warmed-over imperial history, nor is it simply a combination of imperial histories. Addressing this point, Bernard Bailyn has noted that "Atlantic history is not additive; it is more than the sum of its parts." Benjamin Schmidt's *Dutch Imagination and the New World 1570–1670*, T. M. Devine's *Scotland's Empire*, and Tamar Herzog's *Defining Nations: Immigrants and Citizens in Early Modern Spain and Spanish America* are three superb examples of what can be done by looking at particular imperial worlds in large Atlantic and global contexts. There is also no reason why east–west lines of influence should predominate over those that ran in a south–north direction. All axes need to be considered, although, for some questions, particular directional flows may well be more important than others.[20]

Regarding the fourth objection, Atlantic history does not have to subsume all the societies, polities, and populations living on the continents surrounding the Atlantic. Developments in central and eastern Europe, in central and eastern Africa and on its Indian Ocean coast, and in the interior and western portions of the two American continents and on their Pacific coasts may well be less tightly linked to those in the Atlantic and better approached through other perspectives, including both the continental and, for the Americas as a whole, the hemispheric perspective recommended by Jack Greene in chapter 11 of this volume. Yet, as Amy Bushnell and Philip Morgan show, respectively, about indigenous America and Africa in chapters 7 and 8, it remains an interesting and important question how deeply Atlantic developments penetrated and reshaped the old worlds into which Europeans ventured and how far their interactions with these other old worlds affected Europe itself. If the Atlantic framework cannot explain all of the things that happened on four continents, it can still provide a useful perspective on many of them.

Finally, concerning the fifth objection, in this early stage in the development of Atlantic history, the emphasis on connections and interactions is understandable. These are precisely the questions that were either ignored or confined within national boundaries by older perspectives, and there is no inherent reason why an Atlantic paradigm cannot foster a deeper appreciation of contrasts and stimulate informative work in comparative history.

Atlantic history, then, is not necessarily a flawed, conceptually muddled subject; rather, approached in the right way, it can be a highly fruitful and promising field of inquiry. It is best seen as a framework, an angle of vision, an arena of analysis. For some issues, the Atlantic frame of reference may be too limiting and constraining. In particular cases—following the pathways of silver currency, for example—the goal may well be to connect East and West, the Pacific and the Atlantic. To answer other questions, however, the Atlantic as a whole may be too capacious an entity. Histories *of* the Atlantic world—even if some small slice of it—will always be extraordinarily difficult to accomplish; histories *within* the Atlantic world—invariably slices of it as well—inevitably will prove far more manageable. As further encouragement to both histories *of* and *within* the Atlantic world, we offer six propositions for doing Atlantic history, building upon some of the best ways to approach the vast space that the ocean and its surrounding lands encompass while trying to avoid the many pitfalls. These propositions are not meant to be exhaustive, just useful pointers for future work.

First, the effort to find general patterns in Atlantic history must not exaggerate either the connections or the contrasts. John Elliott's magisterial comparative study of the Spanish and British New World empires offers a model in this regard, by avoiding "a series of sharp dichotomies" while eschewing "an insistence on similarity at the expense of difference, [which] is liable to be equally reductionist." Elliott triumphantly negotiates this complex balancing act by "constantly comparing, juxtaposing, and interweaving the two stories" of Spanish and British enterprises in America. Both empires, for example, legitimated themselves by referring to God's providential design; both experienced the rise of creole communities and local patriotism; both saw metropolitan reforms challenge settler autonomy, leading to reluctant local revolts. At the same time, Spain's American colonies incorporated Indians and accepted interracial mixture, whereas Britain's American colonies sought to segregate indigenous peoples and prohibit or discourage interracial unions; one developed a "culture of show," the other "a culture of restraint"; political independence arose out of a crisis of integration in British America and a crisis of disintegration in Spanish America. The British and Spanish American empires are sufficiently alike, yet significantly different, that they provide intelligent commentaries upon one another. Each entity looks different in light of the other; and understanding of the one is enlarged by knowledge of the other.[21]

Second, some Atlantic history must be interactive and cross borders. Alfred Crosby's *The Columbian Exchange* was a pioneer in exploring the commodities and diseases that circulated back and forth across this intercontinental highway. Since Crosby's pathbreaking work, studies of single commodities—whether sugar, cod, salt, chocolate, tobacco, vanilla, or cochineal—have been fashionable, in part because they can link producers, distributors, and consumers, providing a circum-Atlantic navigation, as it were. In process are studies of coffee, mahogany, pearls, a linked study of chocolate and tobacco; and no doubt other trees, plants, and dyes, such as logwood, brazilwood, sarsaparilla, ipecacuanha, jalap root, cinchona, groundnuts, pineapple, and indigo will not be far behind. And there is still much to learn from studies of commodities that we thought we knew well. Consider Stuart Schwartz's superb edited collection of essays, *Tropical Babylon*, a study of the embryonic sugar industry, which uncovers "a constellation of sugar industries, developing in tag-team fashion, sharing similar technology." Sugar itself determined very little; the form its production took throughout the Atlantic world owed much to decisions, actions, reactions, and interactions made on both sides of the ocean.[22]

Crossing conventional borders is often a feature of Atlantic history. Thus Matthew Mulcahy follows the track of hurricanes, a quintessential Atlantic phenomenon, measuring their impact both in the British West Indies and along the North American mainland, seeing both as part of a Greater Caribbean, a larger plantation complex. Perhaps his work will inspire an even broader trans-imperial investigation of the role and effects of hurricanes regularly sweeping across the Atlantic basin. An extreme example of border-crossing is provided by the diasporic community known as the "Portuguese Nation"—an international group of Portuguese merchants, traders, and mariners, many of Jewish ancestry—who formed a remarkable trading network that spanned the Atlantic. They were, as Daviken Studnicki-Gizbert has shown in fascinating detail, "a nation without a state, a collectivity dispersed across the seas." Despite their mobility, dispersion, and composite religious culture, La Nação constituted a tightly knit and dynamic group, often monopolizing trade in all the major commodities within and beyond the Spanish Empire. They were "a community of circulation rather than one based on permanent attachment to a single territory." Their networks were remarkably decentralized, a spiderweb rather than the typical hub-and-spokes model.[23]

The intense interactivity that can characterize much Atlantic history does not necessarily have to be explored on both sides of the ocean; it can focus, for example, on the crossing of imperial boundaries on just one littoral. Thus one might point, as Nicholas Canny has done, to the development of a common European pool of knowledge about the processes and consequences of colonization. Authors of whatever nationality and religion drew upon the same authorities to justify their involvement in actions that were morally dubious. Or consider April Hatfield's *Atlantic Virginia*, which valuably focuses on intercolonial linkages and foreign borrowings, particularly from the Spanish and the Dutch, while admittedly underestimating other transatlantic connections (to England, Ireland, and Africa) and local innovations. Or there is the international character of fishing on the Newfoundland banks, where Basque, Norman, Breton, and West Country fishermen shared many of the same fish curing techniques, even if some turned more to dry salt cure and others more to wet, depending largely on the market they served. The inhabitants of the seventeenth-century English Shore, on the east coast of Newfoundland, Peter Pope shows, had a mid-Atlantic point of view, with a special relationship to both New England and New France. Newfoundland was a cosmopolitan place which traded with England, Iberia, the Mediterranean, the Atlantic islands, and the Netherlands, as well as New England and New France.[24]

A third proposition is that key sectors—leading edges—of the Atlantic world deserve singular and sustained attention. The Newfoundland cod fishery is just one. As early as 1580, Pope notes, about 500 ships returned annually from Atlantic Canada to Europe with a catch of about 200,000 metric tons—a level of commercial activity that exceeded, in volume and value, European trade with the Gulf of Mexico, usually considered the American center of gravity of early transatlantic commerce. The cod fishery is just part of the most obvious leading edge of the Atlantic world: the maritime sector itself. We need historical studies of all things maritime, from weather patterns to port cities, from sailors to winds and currents. As Michael Person, who has written a synoptic account of the Indian Ocean, notes, it also will help if such studies contain "a whiff of ozone," a sense of what it was like to travel by sea, to experience storms, calms, and anchorages. Such a history must also move easily between land and sea; it must be an amphibious history, as it were. In that regard, Daniel Vickers' *Young Men and the Sea* is wonderfully apt, since it traces the interrelationships between land and sea from an ideal setting: Salem, Massachusetts, one of the "most thoroughly maritime societies" anywhere around the Atlantic rim, which combined an oceangoing fleet, local fishing, and coastal transport. Emphasizing the ubiquitous and unexceptional character of seafaring—no breed apart, these Yankee mariners—Vickers is also at pains to demonstrate that there was no single maritime culture. "It is fashionable now to speak of the Atlantic basin as a fundamentally international world," Vickers notes, "but the evidence from Salem suggests that the maritime labor market in much of that world remained deeply parochial." When most of Salem's mariners went to sea, they went with neighbors, age was the defining feature, cooperation rather than conflict was the norm, moving up the hierarchical ladder was possible, and they returned home when their sailing days were done.[25]

Another key sector comprises all the islands that formed way stations, stepping-stones from one hemisphere to the next. The archipelagos of the Azores, Madeira, the Canaries, Cape Verde, and the islands of São Tomé, Fernando Po, Príncipe, and Annabon in the Gulf of Guinea assumed special importance in the Atlantic world. These islands were hubs for a series of complex commercial networks; they were points of articulation between North and South Atlantic, North and South America and the Caribbean, Africa and the New World, Africa and Europe, and Europe and America. In his study of the Madeira wine trade—an archetypal Atlantic product that was traded largely across imperial boundaries—David Hancock estimates that in the years spanning 1640 and 1815, the number of ships annually departing Madeira increased twelvefold and they took on cargoes for delivery to scores of ports in North and South America, the Caribbean, Africa, Asia, and Europe. Another key island was Bermuda, which, despite its tiny size and limited resources, had a bigger fleet than most mainland North American colonies and sat as a crossroads in the age of sail. The Caribbean islands, another crucial vortex, formed the focal point of European overseas expansion in the early modern world, one of the most heterogeneous social mosaics anywhere, and one of the truly great arenas for interpenetration of African, European, American, and later Asian traditions. John Gillis's *Islands of the Mind* makes the point that the Atlantic world was one linked by chains of islands, and that from the beginning they were also ideas, mythic islands shining like beacons inspiring mariners to venture across the ocean.[26]

Finally, borderland areas, transfrontier regions, places where natives and newcomers collided and often none ruled, formed another vector of Atlantic history. Such places gave rise to entangled histories. These marginal areas, frontier zones, leading edges are extensions of the Atlantic world, often far removed from maritime littorals. In the Great Lakes region, a "middle ground" emerged, at least for a time, due to a military and political standoff in which Europeans and Indians searched for "accommodation and common meaning." Spanish American borderlands were "zones of constant conflict and negotiation over power," but the terms varied from place to place. In New Mexico, where detribalized Indian captives and slaves comprised almost one-third of society, Spanish society sought to incorporate different native groups in relations bound up in class and race identity. In the vast interior of the American West between the Sierras and the Rocky Mountains, the so-called Great Basin, the easternmost groups, principally bands of Ute Indians, were the first to adopt changing strategies of survival in response to imperial intrusions, often by raiding their neighbors for slaves. In eighteenth-century Texas, Juliana Barr demonstrates, Indians largely dictated the rules, and Native American constructions of social arrangements, defined by gendered terms of kinship, held sway in relations with Spaniards. To Native Americans, Claudio Saunt tartly notes, "middle grounds and borderlands were simply homelands," and their experiences were less negotiation and compromise than invasion and destruction.[27]

A fourth proposition is that Atlantic history, which to date has focused primarily on the movement of people and goods, would do well to explore more fully the exchange of values and the circulation of ideas. The balance needs to change—and is changing. One promising line of inquiry is the work of Allan Greer and Kenneth Mills on a Catholic Atlantic, connecting attempts within Europe to Christianize the peasantry—itinerant Jesuits dubbed some regions such as southern Italy "these Indies" or the "other Indies"—with efforts to proselytize natives in the Americas and Africa. As a French Canadianist and a Latin Americanist, their collaboration leads them to appreciate the simultaneous connectedness and autonomy of diverse forms of religious creativity in which indigenous traditions and Christian influences did not so much merge as combine and collide to produce an infinite variety of shifting local variants. More restricted spatially, but also trying to connect both sides of the Atlantic, Dominique Deslandres's investigation of French mission campaigns links the targeting of the peasants of Brittany and native peoples in Canada. Such work needs to connect to the introduction of Catholicism into Catholic Africa, and then follow that west central African diaspora into the New World.[28]

Religious networks can be set alongside others, such as the international information exchange of scientific ideas. Simon Schaffer has brilliantly linked the ways in which "making an Atlantic space of reliable pendulum measures," as part of various Newtonian projects, "was like making an Atlantic space of reliable coin," as in Robert Boyle's attempts to make the hydrometer a widely used assay tool. As Schaffer puts it, "in African trading posts, Akan courts, London counting houses, and Whitehall chambers instrumental dramas were used to get temporary workable agreement about [the] value [of gold]." Atlantic science (a capacious term in the early modern period) was very much part of imperial ventures. Commerce and collecting, mapmaking and maritime exploration, mining and metallurgy went hand in hand; early modern naturalists, Londa Schiebinger notes, sought "green gold." Richard Drayton, for example, has focused on the Royal Botanic Gardens at Kew and shown how botany and empire developed in tandem. In the creation of Spanish scientific traditions, Jorge Cañizares-Esguerra notes, the many metropolitan expeditions and bureaucratic information-gathering campaigns (the *relaciones geográficas*, the detailed questionnaires submitted to thousands of local authorities) of the Spanish monarchy were vital, but partly in response so were the contributions of patriotic provincial elites, indigenous informants, and entrepreneurial settlers and merchants throughout Spanish America. In the British Atlantic, Susan Scott Parrish argues, provincials and local informants also played essential roles in the development of natural knowledge. Distant from centers of learning, anxious at thoughts of "creolean degeneracy," colonists took solace in their abilities to observe and report nature accurately.[29]

Many historians have told the story of the abolition of the slave trade and slavery—the world's first successful movement for human rights—but few have satisfactorily explained it. Mystery surrounds the expression of human empathy, both its timing and its targeting. Why should a large number of people suddenly have become outraged at the loss of *other* people's rights? What galvanized them to translate opinion into action? Christopher Brown's *Moral Capital* avoids the false binaries of humanitarian versus hypocrite, of pragmatism versus principle, of selflessness versus self-interest that have often served as previous explanations. Attending to antislavery's origins and antecedents, Brown makes the point that moral doubts over slavery had a long history. Public disapproval had certainly surfaced by the late seventeenth century; and three local challenges to the morality of slavery occurred in early British America: the attempt to keep slavery out of Georgia in the 1730s, the Quaker expulsion of slave owners in Pennsylvania in the 1760s, and the deterrence against West Indian slaveholders bringing slaves into England in the early 1770s. The key turning point, however, was the American Revolution. It turned the slave system into a symbol, an urgent moral issue. All parties to the imperial contest discovered in slavery an instrument for the validation of their own worth and the denigration of their opponents' character. "By describing complicity in slavery as proof of collective vice," Brown shrewdly observes, "disputants in the Revolutionary era helped define opposition to slavery as proof of collective virtue." It was a way to restore national honor and accumulate "moral capital." No longer would it be possible to locate the roots of abolitionism in either economic determinism or bourgeois humanitarianism. Rather, the shift from sentiment to action was connected to changing views of empire and nation. That three other nations—Denmark, Haiti, and the United States—ended the slave trade in the first decade of the nineteenth century suggests that British abolitionism was no mere historical accident. Brown's story needs to be put into a full Atlantic context.[30]

In the realm of Revolutionary ideas, the urgent requirement is to connect all sides of the Atlantic. For example, two recent approaches within the French Atlantic are pertinent. Emma Rothschild relates how the tragic expedition to French Guyana of 1763–1765 owed much to grandiose, fantastical plans conceived as a way of restoring national honor after the humiliating loss of Canada. The new colony would be a land of enlightenment, not African slavery; it would extend religious tolerance to all, even Jews; it would ensure the freedom of the indigenous population; and it would recruit foreigners, most notably German-speakers. The reality—of 14,000 who embarked, almost all died within a few months—was a catastrophe. The nightmare haunted its victims and its metropolitan promoters. Memories of this exterior, oceanic event invaded interior France, even penetrating remote and mountainous provinces, with ramifications for colonial policy extending into the nineteenth century. Only an integrated French Atlantic can make sense of this event and its repercussions. Similarly, in reflecting on the French Revolutionary era, Laurent Dubois calls for an integrated approach to its intellectual history, bringing together the thoughts and actions of actors on both sides of the Atlantic. For him, debates over the meaning of rights, over universalism, over citizenship reverberate and ricochet back and forth across the ocean. He connects Enlightenment thinkers, colonial administrators, planters, and slaves in a reaction, counterreaction dynamic.[31]

A fifth proposition is that traditional subjects in imperial history, such as the nature of empire and of the legal systems developed within empires to govern intra-imperial relations as well as to sustain the new colonial regimes overseas, can benefit from examination from a broader perspective. Anthony Pagden's study of the imperial ideologies Spain, Britain, and France developed to justify the subjugation of indigenous peoples and the occupation of indigenous lands in the Americas and elsewhere between 1500 and 1800 is a case in point. Tracing the roots of those ideologies in classical and Christian discourse, Pagden contrasts the Spanish Empire's emphasis on conquest, military glory, and the evangelization of indigenous peoples during its first two centuries with the later British and French focus on empire as an instrument for promoting national agricultural, commercial, and demographic resources through settlement of European immigrants in extra-European spaces. Whereas the Spanish "were overwhelmingly concerned with rights over people," the British and French stressed "rights in things," mostly in lands.[32]

From an even wider perspective, Lauren Benton has produced a provocative comparative study of the nature and function of law in the construction of early modern and modern empires. Ranging over a wide number of imperial regimes established between 1500 and 1900, she is mainly concerned to illustrate the emergence of a "global legal regime" evolving out of a transition from the multicentric legal regimes of early modern empires, of which the Spanish Empire serves as her principal example, to the state-dominated and far more unicentric legal regimes of the later nineteenth century, as illustrated by British India and many other cases. Careful not to deny the importance of temporal and spatial variations within and among empires, Benton nonetheless calls attention to the commonalities among imperial legal regimes during the first centuries of political construction, especially the pluralism of those regimes and the degree of indigenous agency in constructing them.[33]

Although Benton's emphasis on the pluralism of early modern imperial legal regimes is at odds with the British experience, which within areas of European settlement witnessed a rather rapid substitution of an English common-law regime for indigenous forms of jurisprudence, her emphasis upon subaltern agency accords well with other recent studies stressing the negotiated character of imperial governance in early modern empires.[34] Elizabeth Mancke's many articles reexamining the dynamics of early modern empire formation represent some of the most penetrating work on this subject, and stress the negotiated character of imperial governance and the agency of European settler populations.[35]

If most of this work derives principally out of the new interest in imperial history and is set within an explicitly imperial context, it is also informed by an Atlantic—and in Benton's case, a world—perspective. But an Atlantic focus has been fundamental to related work on the interactions among early modern overseas empires. Calling for an "Atlantic history of interstate negotiation" and emphasizing the strong "connection between empire and foreign affairs," Mancke treats the early modern Atlantic as a contested space more or less continuously involved with the problem of negotiating a "shifting and ambiguous international order" arising out of the spatial complexities of early modern expansion, beginning with the Atlantic. Ostensibly constructed of sovereign and juridically equal states, an increasingly sophisticated, multilateral interstate system developed that, she argues, was fundamentally shaped by overseas expansion. Also concerned with spelling out the international dimensions of the development of the Atlantic empires, Eliga H. Gould, expanding on Benton's emphasis on the legal pluralism inherent in European expansion, has called for a renewed appreciation of the legal geography of the early modern Atlantic and, more especially, of the emergence of a legal double standard in which Europeans condoned "behavior at a distance that they would have found intolerable on their own doorsteps," thereby acknowledging that the "extra-European Atlantic" was an entangled "zone of conflicting laws, ecological peril," racial and cultural diversity, and "chronic violence" in which "no single power" enjoyed a monopoly of legal force. Benefiting from new insights enabled by a broader imperial, Atlantic, or global perspective, these studies of imperial ideology, law, and governance have reopened subjects that we thought we understood well, and provide a fertile field for further scholarly investigation.[36]

One final proposition is that historians of the Atlantic world must pay close attention to chronology, for sensitivity to time is, after all, the defining characteristic of the historical discipline. The Atlantic world most obviously was not static; it was a place of motion, always in process. Schematic models for conceiving of the development of the Atlantic world seem to come in threes, whether it is Jack Greene's simplification, elaboration, and replication; Allan Karras and John McNeill's implantation, maturity, and transitions; Alison Games's imagination, elaboration, and integration; or Marvin Lunenfeld's discovery, invasion, and encounter. Moreover, quite obviously a uniform chronology cannot be applied across the entire area; there were no neat divisions that were universal in the Atlantic world. Nevertheless, as Bernard Bailyn points out, there was, "despite all the complexities, at least in rough terms, a common morphology, a general overall pattern, however fluid and irregular, of development and change." Bailyn offers his own tripartite schema, as does Elliott. A comparison of the two should prove instructive.[37]

The first phase Bailyn labels an "era of contested marchlands," whereas Elliott uses the more neutral term "occupation." For Bailyn, the first stage of development was a time when life was often literally barbarous, when levels of violence were unprecedented, when everything was "fluid, indeterminate, without stable structures, or identities." It was a time of "pervasive social disorder and disorientation." Only some remarkable utopian projections redeemed the overall bleakness. Elliott, too, pulls no punches, employing terms such as intrusion, exploitation, devastation, and subjugation. Both British and Spanish empires involved an aggressive European reconstruction and renaming of American spaces, harsh confrontations with indigenous peoples, and economic regimes that resorted to plunder and unfree labor. But the differences between the empires complicate the picture. The Spanish settlement of America rested primarily on the domination of peoples, and the British on the commodification of land. The town became the basis for Spanish dominion, whereas British settlements were overwhelmingly rural. The Spanish, partly because of their long experience of mixing with Moors, practiced cohabitation with Native Americans, whereas the English, in part because of their experience of ostensible segregation in Ireland, excluded Indians. Modes of exploitation and subjugation took varied forms.[38]

A second stage of development earns the label "integration" from Bailyn and "consolidation" from Elliott. Pan-oceanic commercial webs drew places together, Bailyn notes; increasingly regular networks of trade, trust, and communications emerged. As places within the Atlantic world became more interconnected and interdependent, forms of human action adjusted and gradually came to resemble each other. A growth in internal complexity occurred at the same time as a trend toward outward uniformity. Elliott, too, notes growing imperial integration, particularly among the British, but the Spanish Empire had always exhibited a more sustained effort to achieve centralization of authority, close supervision from the metropolis, and its colonial societies also exhibited a fair measure of underlying unity and homogeneity (from the role of godparenthood as a force of social cohesion to their three-tier social arrangements of Spaniards, *castas*, and Indians), and a cohesive Roman Catholic establishment and uniformity of faith, at least among the Spanish segments of society. Notwithstanding widespread resistance from both Indians and creoles to metropolitan measures to construct a tightly controlled and integrated empire, metropolitan authority was somewhat stronger during the sixteenth and early seventeenth centuries than later. Elliott emphasizes that as the bonds of empire grew tighter among the British, they moved in the opposite direction from the Spanish. "The difference," he argues, "reflected the divergent trajectories of English and Spanish power during the second half of the seventeenth century." Creole societies in Spanish America gained "new and expanded space for manoeuvre."[39]

The last phase is seen by Bailyn and Elliott in similar terms. It was an era of "creole triumphalism," an age of revolution when new ideals of self-government and freedom from arbitrary power swept across the Atlantic world. Bailyn emphasizes how "reforming plans and programs formed an interactive network," with new ideas "formulated in one area...picked up in others, assessed and absorbed in varying degrees." Elliott terms the era one of "emancipation." He emphasizes "societies on the move," with rising populations and expanding frontiers; he singles out the mid-century wars for empire and the metropolitan efforts at reform which produced similar imperial crises, leading, finally, to the establishment of independence and efforts at state building. Elliott probes why independence came earlier in North, than in South, America. Partly, it was a matter of space: the Spanish Empire was so sprawling that coordinating resistance was difficult. Partly, it was ideology: British Americans had "a more impressive armoury of ideological weapons" and a more extensive communications network than their Spanish counterparts. Partly, it was social composition: British Americans did not have to hold together coalitions of whites, mestizos, and Indians. And partly, it was a matter of language: the two sides of the Spanish Atlantic spoke different *political* languages (defenses of the absolutist unitary state versus claims for composite monarchy), which actually allowed for considerable compromise, whereas Britain and British America, "confusingly, and dangerously," spoke the same language of British liberty and rights, and became "inextricably involved in that most intractable of all forms of conflict, the conflict over competing constitutional rights."[40]

These schemas are open to some cavils, particularly if one tries to apply them to the whole Atlantic world. Arguably, the prehistory of the Atlantic deserves a separate stage. If one wanted to pick a year when Atlantic history of the early modern era began (admittedly a highly arbitrary way to proceed), a good case could be made that it should be 1415, with the Portuguese capture of Ceuta in North Africa, or perhaps 1444, when the Atlantic slave trade began, rather than 1492. Others would go further back in time to the Vikings and the exploration of the North Atlantic.[41] Furthermore, early colonization was as much backward- as forward-looking. A powerful tendency existed to compare the cultures of the New World with those of classical antiquity. Focusing on stages of development can encourage an appreciation of changes wrought by Europeans at the expense of an emphasis on the cost paid for those changes by indigenous and enslaved people. Also, in the first phase, it is easy to exaggerate levels of violence and disorder, whereas the use of terms such as "peopling" and "occupation" can seem too anodyne. The second stage, the process of settling down, is extremely difficult to encompass: a stress on integration may well overlook the degree of autonomy and disconnectedness of many places, and the term "consolidation" may unconsciously minimize the ever-present volatility and explosiveness. Atlantic Africa is largely ignored in all these schemas, nowhere more so than in the last phase, whether labeled "revolution" or "emancipation." Emancipation and revolution must grapple with those places in the Atlantic world, most notably Africa and large parts of the Caribbean, where colonialism deepened rather than weakened.[42]

One last problem deserves consideration here: the temporal boundaries of Atlantic history. Most practitioners seem content to limit the subject matter of Atlantic history to the long period between the European Atlantic discoveries of the fifteenth century and the beginnings of decolonization in the Americas between 1774 and 1825. They see it as essentially ending with the creation of new independent nation-states in the Americas following the American Revolution and the Hispanic American wars for independence, the creation of more powerful centralized national states in Europe during and in the wake of the French Revolution and the Napoleonic Wars, and the powerful turn of European imperialism toward the east during the nineteenth century. The presumption seems to be that the expansion of European imperialism and the spread of commerce after 1800 make a global framework of more utility than an Atlantic one for those who are not content to continue to operate within traditional national and imperial frameworks.

Such limits and considerations aside, however, the Atlantic world constructed during the early modern era continued to exhibit considerable vitality throughout the nineteenth century and well into the twentieth. The Atlantic slave trade did not completely end until the 1880s, and European immigration to the Americas increased steadily throughout the nineteenth century. As the volume of transatlantic shipping increased and sailing times declined in the nineteenth century, commercial, cultural, and political relationships between Europe and the new nations in America strengthened to the point of cordiality, confirming historic ties. Europe's interactions with Africa did not decrease, but became even more vigorous during the late nineteenth century, following the fuller colonization of the continent. Wherever the Atlantic remains a vital, even privileged arena of exchange among the four continents surrounding it, Atlantic history can still be a useful tool of analysis.[43]

This introduction provides a brief and highly selective survey of the burgeoning literature in Atlantic history, and offers guarded enthusiasm for Atlantic history and a few guidelines for how it might best be approached. The thirteen chapters that follow are intended to provide a current survey and to offer critical evaluations of Atlantic history. In chapter 1, Joyce Chaplin analyzes contemporary understandings of the ocean that over the course of the early modern era would come to be known as the Atlantic. We have divided the remaining twelve chapters into three parts.

Some historians have embraced the Atlantic approach as an instrument for breaking down the national boundaries that tended to contain traditional imperial history approaches, but, notwithstanding all the boundary-crossing identified by such historians, the fact remains that contemporaries tended to think of what we now call the Atlantic world as a series of national and competitive spheres of activity in which the language of authority, the system of law, and modes of governance, land occupation, and even religious orientation followed distinctly national lines. Part I, "New Atlantic Worlds," consists of discussions of the five most prominent national Atlantics that Europeans and their auxiliaries created between the end of the fifteenth century and the early decades of the nineteenth century: Kenneth Andrien, treating the Spanish Atlantic; A. J. R. Russell-Wood, the Portuguese Atlantic; Trevor Burnard, the British Atlantic; Laurent Dubois, the French Atlantic; and Benjamin Schmidt, the Dutch Atlantic. These were not, of course, the only European states to participate in the creation of the early modern Atlantic. But they were the principal colonizing powers, all establishing major enclaves of settlement and trade in the Americas and participating heavily in the slave and other African trades. The Swedes and the Danes were also involved in the African trade, but their settlements in the Americas were small and, in the Swedish case, short-lived, and the Russian settlements in northwestern North America never had an Atlantic dimension. These five national chapters focus on four overlapping questions: (1) What is distinctive and what is general about the particular national Atlantic under consideration? (2) Has the growing use of the Atlantic concept produced any advances in our understanding of the nations' activities in the Atlantic or put those activities in a broader perspective that facilitates deeper understanding of them and their distinctiveness? (3) Are there additional questions that might be usefully pursued by historians using an Atlantic perspective? (4) Do we lose anything in the process of incorporating a national Atlantic into the greater Atlantic?

Of course, the emergence of the Atlantic world not only led to the creation of new national Atlantics; it also profoundly altered the Old Worlds of Europe, Africa, and the indigenous Americas. The three chapters of Part II, "Old Worlds and the Atlantic," endeavor to sketch out the differential impact of the new Atlantic world on the old societies bordering on and connected to the Atlantic Ocean, as that impact varied over space and time. In chapter 7, Amy Turner Bushnell looks at Indian societies in both the Americas to analyze those factors that both facilitated cultural and social change in some Indian societies and enabled some to domesticate, and still others to resist such change until long after the early modern era. In chapter 8, Philip D. Morgan looks broadly at Africa's growing involvement with the Atlantic, beginning in the fifteenth century, assessing the impact of the expanding trade in slaves and other goods upon African societies and sketching the extensive role of the African diaspora in shaping the early modern Atlantic world. Both Bushnell and Morgan stress, respectively, Indian and African agency in these developments. In chapter 9, Carla Rahn Phillips takes a selective approach to the complex problem of the impact of Atlantic expansion upon Europe, focusing particularly on the political and economic ramifications of that expansion and using the Iberian experience as illustrative.

Part III, "Competing and Complementary Perspectives," considers alternative frameworks for understanding those aspects of early modern development that Atlanticists have so far neglected. Using North America as a case study, Peter H. Wood, in chapter 10, explores the tensions between an Atlantic and a multicultural view of the North American past. Advocating a continental approach to the history of the Americas, he emphasizes the importance of a perspective deriving out of developments in the middle and western portions of the North American continent, most of which, by the close of the early modern period, still remained under indigenous control. In chapter 11, Jack P. Greene proposes an American hemispheric approach as the most promising avenue toward constructing an understanding of developments within the New Worlds of the Americas and as a device for promoting both an appreciation of the variations among and within those worlds and the comparative history of them. Nicholas Canny considers the merits of a global approach in chapter 12. Subjecting some of the more important recent work from that perspective to a critical analysis, he also makes a preliminary effort to classify the many varieties of Atlantic history that have emerged over recent decades. In chapter 13, Peter Coclanis explores the limits of the Atlantic approach, advocating a global perspective that emphasizes the extent to which developments in the early modern Atlantic both derived from and were connected to those in the Indian Ocean, China, and the Pacific. He puts particular stress on global circuits of trade and articulation of production models to build the case for what he calls a "*Conjuncto-Atlantic*" history." As comprehensive as this book is, the editors had hoped, if space had permitted, to include a chapter in this last part assessing the utility of the new imperial history (or the imperial turn) as an alternative framework for studying European overseas activities both in and beyond the Atlantic during the early modern era. To an important extent, however, the chapters in part I cover at least some of this ground.

Whatever its defects, the expanding subject of the Atlantic world represents a lively and exciting approach to the study of the changes that occurred on and around the Atlantic Ocean. If Atlantic history was initially designed as a perspective that would avoid the teleologies of United States and other national histories, it has already done far more. By raising historical discussions of the Atlantic world to a level that transcends both nations and empires, it has contributed to the development of analytical procedures for describing experiences and connections that were multiracial, multiethnic, multinational, and multi-imperial; it has provided students of small or marginalized groups and places with a broader context that offers the possibility of escaping from the parochialism formerly associated with such studies; and it has stimulated efforts to construct a coherent narrative. We have endeavored to present some of the rich variety of approaches and controversies that the Atlantic perspective has so far generated. No doubt, other avenues of analysis will emerge in the bold quest to comprehend the Atlantic world.

NOTES

1. John Elliott, "Afterword. Atlantic History: A Circumnavigation," in David Armitage and Michael J. Braddick, eds., *The British Atlantic World, 1500–1800* (New York: Palgrave, 2002), pp. 233–249, esp. 239.

2. Frank Tannenbaum, *Slave and Citizen: The Negro in the Americas* (New York: Knopf, 1947); Philip D. Curtin, *The Atlantic Slave Trade: A Census* (Madison: University of Wisconsin Press, 1969); Ian K. Steele, *The English Atlantic, 1675–1740: An Exploration of Communications and Community* (New York: Cambridge University Press, 1986); D. W. Meinig, *The Shaping of America: A Geographical Perspective on 500 Years of History*, vol. 1: *Atlantic America 1492–1800* (New Haven: Yale University Press, 1986).

3. Jacques Godechot, *Histoire de l'Atlantique* (Paris: Bordas, 1947); Leonard Outhwaite, *The Atlantic* (New York: Coward-McCann, 1957).

4. The early genealogy of an Atlantic perspective, which has political as well as scholarly origins, has been well traced by Bernard Bailyn, "The Idea of Atlantic History," *Itinerario* 20 (1996): 9–44, which in revised form can be found in his *Atlantic History: Concept and Contours* (Cambridge, Mass.: Harvard University Press, 2005), pp. 3–56. For a similar account, see William O'Reilly, "Genealogies of Atlantic History," *Atlantic Studies* 1, no. 1 (2004): 66–84.

5. For twenty years until 1990, when it evolved into the Global Center for the Study of Power, Culture, and History, the Johns Hopkins Program in Atlantic History and Culture engaged the attention not just of the historians and anthropologists who organized and presided over it, but also of a number of other social scientists, ranging from sociologists to economists, geographers, and social psychologists who were concerned with the histories of Europe, Africa, and the Americas, especially in the early modern era. The program, which always had a powerful tilt toward the South Atlantic, sponsored a heavy round of visiting scholars, seminars, and conferences; created a book series, *Studies in Atlantic History and Culture*, published by the Johns Hopkins University Press, that provided an outlet for some of the best work in the field (the first book in the series was issued in 1979); and helped to attract some outstanding doctoral students, three of whom are contributors to this volume. Between 1974 and 2000, 102 historians and 21 anthropologists associated with the Atlantic Program earned doctorates at Johns Hopkins. If the faculty involved in the program had to learn, as they constructed it, that they were Atlanticists and what that term implied, the large number of students who participated in it were Atlanticists from the start of their studies.

6. In 2000 the American Historical Association hosted a session at its Chicago meeting which explored "The Atlantic World: Emerging Themes in a New Teaching Field"; five years later, the subject was apparently mature enough to merit "A Critical Reassessment," the title of a panel discussion at the meeting in Seattle. In all, the Seattle meeting sponsored nine sessions featuring Atlantic history or the Atlantic world; in the most recent meeting (2007), the number of sessions had grown to eleven. Since 1998, the organization has also offered an annual prize for the best book in Atlantic history.

7. H-Atlantic has discussion logs, reviews, syllabi, bibliography, and links. The special issues or forums were *Itinerario* 23, no. 2 (1999): 48–173 ("Round Table: The Nature of Atlantic History"); *Dix-huitième Siècle* no. 33 (2001): 7–316 ("L'Atlantique"); *Historical Reflections/Réflexions Historiques* 29, no. 1 (2003): 1–188 ("Slavery and Citizenship in the Age of the Atlantic Revolutions"); and *William and Mary Quarterly* [hereafter, *WMQ*] 3rd ser., LVI, no. 2 (1999): 241–414 ("African and American Atlantic Worlds"); LVIII no. 1 (2001), pp. 3–251 ("New Perspectives on the Transatlantic Slave Trade"); LIX, no. 3 (2002): 551–696 ("Slaveries in the Atlantic World"); LXIII, no. 4 (2006): 675–742 ("Beyond the Atlantic"); and *American Historical Review* [hereafter, *AHR*] 111 (2006): 717–780 ("Oceans of History"). New book series include New World in the Atlantic World (Routledge); The Americas in the Early Modern Atlantic World (Palgrave); Atlantic Studies on Society in Change (Columbia University Press); The Atlantic World: Europe, Africa, and the Americas, 1500–1830 (Brill); Atlantic Cultural Studies (Lit Verlag); and The Carolina Low Country and the Atlantic World (University of South Carolina Press). The textbook is Douglas R. Egerton, Alison Games, Jane G. Landers, Kris Lane, and Donald R. Wright., *The Atlantic World: A History, 1400–1888* (Wheeling, Ill.: Harlan Davidson, 2007); and a new anthology is Alison Games and

Adam Rothman, eds., *Major Problems in Atlantic History: Documents and Essays* (Boston: Houghton Mifflin, 2008).

8. http://www.fas.harvard.edu/~atlantic has, among other things, a list of seminars and workshops, working paper abstracts, dissertation abstracts, and a bibliography. Bernard Bailyn established the Atlantic History Seminar at Harvard University, under the auspices of the Charles Warren Center for Studies in American History and with the support of the Andrew W. Mellon Foundation, which has committed funding at least through 2010. By my count, confirmed in helpful discussions with Pat Denault, the 12 international seminars (from 1996 to 2007) have discussed 320 papers; the anniversary conference of 2005, another 82; and the 18 workshops, 136 (although most of these were "talks")—for a grand total of about 540 papers or presentations.

9. These include New York University, which instituted its Atlantic World Workshop in 1997; the McNeill Center for the Study of Early America at the University of Pennsylvania, which offered its first Atlantic Seminar in 2004; and a joint University of Virginia and Oxford University video-conference-linked Atlantic World Colloquium, which began in 2005. To the best of our knowledge, at least six U.S. universities—Florida International University, Michigan State University, New York University, Rutgers University (graduate study in African-American history and the history of Atlantic cultures and the African diaspora), SUNY–Buffalo (North and South Atlantic history), and the University of Texas at Arlington—offer graduate degrees in Atlantic history, and others facilitate informal fields in Atlantic history. Both the University of Liverpool and the University of Essex in England offer MAs in Atlantic history. A French Atlantic history 1500–1830 group is active at McGill University and the University of Montreal in Canada. The scholarly organization the Forum on European Expansion and Global Interaction has also been active in promoting Atlantic history, even if, as its moniker suggests, it is devoted to a conception both more limited (privileging Europe) and more expansive (prioritizing the global) than the Atlantic basin alone. See www.feegi.org. See also the journal *Itinerario*, associated with FEEGI as its subtitle *European Journal of Overseas History* suggests, which has published important work in Atlantic history.

10. Pierre Chaunu and Huguette Chaunu, *Séville et l'Atlantique*, vol. 8 (part 1), p. xiii, as cited in Bailyn, *Atlantic History*, p. 31; Meinig, *Atlantic America*, p. 65; Peter A. Coclanis, "*Drang nach Osten*: Bernard Bailyn, The World-Island, and the Idea of Atlantic History," *Journal of World History* 13 (2002): 169–182 (quote on p. 170).

11. Fernand Braudel, *The Mediterranean and the Mediterranean World in the Age of Philip II*, trans. Siân Reynolds, 2 vols. (New York: Harper & Row, 1976), vol. 1, pp. 14, 17; Peregrine Horden and Nicholas Purcell, *The Corrupting Sea: A Study in Mediterranean History* (Oxford: Blackwell, 2000); and the same authors' "The Mediterranean and 'the New Thalassology,' " *AHR* 111, no 3 (2006): 722–740.

12. Elliott, "Afterword," in Armitage and Braddick, eds., *The British Atlantic World*, p. 234; "Round Table: The Nature of Atlantic History," *Itinerario* 23, no. 2

(1999): 48–173; Paul Gilroy, *The Black Atlantic: Modernity and Double Consciousness* (Cambridge, Mass.: Harvard University Press, 1993); Philip D. Curtin, *The Rise and Fall of the Plantation Complex: Essays in Atlantic History* (New York: Cambridge University Press, 1990).

13. William O'Reilly, "Genealogies of Atlantic history," *Atlantic Studies* 1, no. 1 (2004): 66–84; Jorge Cañizares-Esguerra, "Some Caveats about the 'Atlantic' Paradigm," *History Compass*, http://www.history-compass.com.

14. Paul W. Mapp, "Atlantic History from Imperial, Continental, and Pacific Perspectives," *WMQ* LXIII, no. 4 (2006): 713–724.

15. Elliott, "Afterword, in Armitage and Braddick, eds., *The British Atlantic World*, p. 237. For a useful set of essays on comparative history, see Deborah Cohen and Maura O'Connor, eds., *Comparison and History: Europe in Cross-National Perspective* (New York: Routledge, 2004).

16. David Eltis, "Atlantic History in Global Perspective," *Itinerario* 23, no. 2 (1999): 141; Meinig, *Atlantic America*, p. 64.

17. Martin W. Lewis, "Dividing the Ocean Sea," *Geographical Review* 89 (April 1999): 188–214.

18. William H. McNeill, "Transatlantic History in World Perspective," in Steven G. Reinhardt and Dennis Reinhartz, eds., *Transatlantic History* (College Station: Texas A&M University Press, 2006), pp. 3–18; Pier M. Larson, "African *Diasporas* and the Atlantic," in Jorge Cañizares-Esguerra and Erik R. Seeman, eds., *The Atlantic in Global History, 1500–1800* (Upper Saddle River, N.J.: Pearson Prentice Hall, 2007), pp. 129–148. Fitting the Atlantic into larger contexts is also the focus of the forum "Beyond the Atlantic," *WMQ* LXIII, no. 4 (2006): 675–742; C. A. Bayly, *The Birth of the Modern World, 1780–1914* (Oxford: Blackwell, 2004), pp. 42, 44–45.

19. Mapp, "Atlantic History from Imperial, Continental, and Pacific Perspectives," pp. 713–724.

20. Bailyn, *Atlantic History*, p. 60; Benjamin Schmidt, *Innocence Abroad: The Dutch Imagination and the New World 1570–1670* (New York: Cambridge University Press, 2001); T. M. Devine, *Scotland's Empire, 1600–1815* (London: Allen Lane, 2003); Tamar Herzog, *Defining Nations: Immigrants and Citizens in Early Modern Spain and Spanish America* (New Haven: Yale University Press, 2003). See also Henry Kamen, *Spain's Road to Empire: The Making of a World 1492–1763* (London: Allen Lane, 2002), in which the argument is that Castile did not create the Spanish Empire, but rather that the Empire made Spain.

21. J. H. Elliott, *Empires of the Atlantic World: Britain and Spain in America, 1492–1830* (New Haven: Yale University Press, 2006), pp. xvi, 247, 250. For another comparative study—only partly Atlantic in scope—see David Ormrod, *The Rise of Commercial Empires: England and the Netherlands in the Age of Mercantilism, 1650–1770* (Cambridge: Cambridge University Press, 2003). See also Bob Moore and Henk Van Nierop, eds., *Colonial Empires Compared: Britain and the Netherlands, 1750–1850* (Burlington, Vt.: Ashgate, 2003).

22. Alfred Crosby, *The Columbian Exchange: The Biological and Cultural Consequences of 1492* (Westport, Conn.: Greenwood, 1972); Sidney W. Mintz, *Sweetness and Power: The Place of Sugar in Modern History* (New York: Penguin, 1985); Mark Kurlansky, *Cod: A Biography of the Fish That Changed the World* (New York: Walker, 1997); Kurlansky, *Salt: A World History* (New York: Walker, 2002); Sophie D. Coe and Michael D. Coe, *The True History of Chocolate* (New York: Thames and Hudson, 1996); Cameron L. McNeil, ed., *Chocolate in Mesoamerica: A Cultural History of Cacao* (Gainesville: University Press of Florida, 2007); Jordan Goodman; *Tobacco in History: The Cultures of Dependence* (London: Routledge 1993); Tim Ecott, *Vanilla: Travels in Search of the Ice Cream Orchid* (New York: Grove, 2004); Amy Butler Greenfield, *A Perfect Red: Empire, Espionage, and the Quest for the Color of Desire* (New York: HarperCollins, 2005); Stuart B. Schwartz, ed., *Tropical Babylon: Sugar and the Making of the Atlantic World, 1450–1680* (Chapel Hill: University of North Carolina Press, 2004). For commodity studies that will become monographs, see Jennifer Anderson, "Nature's Currency: The Atlantic Mahogany Trade, 1725–1825" (Ph.D. dissertation, New York University, 2007); Michelle Craig McDonald, "From Cultivation to Cup: Caribbean Coffee and the North American Economy, 1765–1805" (Ph.D. dissertation, University of Michigan, 2005); Marcy Norton, *Sacred Gifts, Profane Pleasures: A History of Tobacco and Chocolate, 1492–1700* (Ithaca, N.Y: Cornell University Press, 2008); and Molly Warsh, "Adorning Empire: The History of the Pearl Trade, 1492–1688" (Ph.D. dissertation, Johns Hopkins University, 2009).

23. Matthew Mulcahy, *Hurricanes and Society in the British Greater Caribbean, 1624–1783* (Baltimore: Johns Hopkins University Press, 2006); the only other study of hurricanes is confined to one island and to a later century: Louis A. Pérez, Jr., *Winds of Change: Hurricanes and the Transformation of Nineteenth-Century Cuba* (Chapel Hill: University of North Carolina Press, 2001); Daviken Studnicki-Gizbert, *A Nation Upon the Ocean Sea: Portugal's Atlantic Diaspora and the Crisis of the Spanish Empire, 1492–1640* (New York: Oxford University Press, 2007), pp. 5, 65, 95. For other recent studies of diasporic, border-crossing communities, see Bertrand Van Ruymbeke and Randy Sparks, eds., *Memory and Identity: The Huguenots in France and the Atlantic Diaspora* (Columbia: University of South Carolina Press, 2003); Douglas Hamilton, *Scotland, the Caribbean, and the Atlantic World, 1750–1820* (Manchester, U.K.: Manchester University Press, 2005); Alexia Grosjean and Steve Murdoch, eds., *Scottish Communities Abroad in the Early Modern Period* (Leiden: Brill, 2005); and Van Ruymbeke, *From New Babylon to Eden: The Huguenots and Their Migration to Colonial South Carolina* (Columbia: University of South Carolina Press, 2006).

24. Nicholas Canny, "Atlantic History, 1492–1700: Scope, Sources, and Methods," in Horst Pietschmann, ed., *Atlantic History: History of the Atlantic System, 1580–1830* (Göttingen: Vandenhoeck & Ruprecht, 2002), pp. 55–64; April Lee Hatfield, *Atlantic Virginia: Intercolonial Relations in the Seventeenth Century* (Philadelphia: University of Pennsylvania Press, 2004). For further examples of

seeing Virginia in larger Atlantic and global contexts, see Robert Appelbaum and John Wood Sweet, eds., *Envisioning an English Empire: Jamestown and the Making of the North Atlantic World* (Philadelphia: University of Pennsylvania Press, 2005); Peter Mancall, ed., *The Atlantic World and Virginia, 1550–16241* (Chapel Hill: University of North Carolina Press, 2007); L. H. Roper, "Charles I, Virginia, and the Idea of Atlantic History," *Itinerario* 30, no. 2 (2006): 33–53; and Peter E. Pope, *Fish Into Wine: The Newfoundland Plantation in the Seventeenth Century* (Chapel Hill: University of North Carolina Press, 2004).

25. Peter Pope, "Comparisons: Atlantic Canada," in Daniel Vickers, ed., *A Companion to Colonial America* (Malden, Mass.: Blackwell, 2003), pp. 489–507; Michael Pearson, *The Indian Ocean* (London: Routledge, 2003); Daniel Vickers with Vince Walsh, *Young Men and the Sea: Yankee Seafarers in the Age of Sail* (New Haven: Yale University Press, 2005), pp. 60, 129 (quotes). For other portraits of life at sea, see Marcus Rediker, *Between the Devil and the Deep Blue Sea: Merchant Seamen, Pirates, and the Anglo-American Maritime World, 1700–1750* (Cambridge: Cambridge University Press, 1987); Pablo E. Pérez-Mallaína, *Spain's Men of the Sea: Daily Life on the Indies Fleet in the Sixteenth Century*, trans. Carla Rahn Philipps (Baltimore: Johns Hopkins University Press, 1998); Philip E. Steinberg, *The Social Construction of the Ocean* (Cambridge: Cambridge University Press, 2001); Paul A. Gilje, *Liberty on the Waterfront: American Maritime Culture in the Age of Revolution* (Philadelphia: University of Pennsylvania Press, 2004); Bernhardt Klein and Gesa Mackenthun, eds., *Sea Changes: Historicizing the Ocean* (New York, 2004); Daniel Finamore, ed., *Maritime History as World History* (Gainesville: University Press of Florida, 2004); Emma Christopher, *Slave Ship Sailors and Their Captive Cargoes, 1730–1807* (New York: Cambridge University Press, 2006); Jerry Bentley, Renate Bridenthal, and Kären Wigen, eds., *Seascapes: Maritime Histories, Littoral Cultures, and Transoceanic Exchanges* (Honolulu: University of Hawaii Press, 2007); Carla Rahn Phillips, *The Treasure of the San José: Death at Sea in the War of the Spanish Succession* (Baltimore: Johns Hopkins University Press, 2007).

26. David Hancock, *Oceans of Wine: Madeira and the Organization of the Atlantic Market, 1640–1815* (New Haven: Yale University Press, 2008); Michael Jarvis, *At the Crossroads of the Atlantic: Maritime Revolution and the Transformation of Bermuda, 1612–1815* (Chapel Hill: University of North Carolina Press, forthcoming); Philip D. Morgan, "The Caribbean Islands in Atlantic Context, circa 1500–1800," in Felicity A. Nussbaum, ed., *The Global Eighteenth Century* (Baltimore: Johns Hopkins University Press, 2003), pp. 52–64; John R. Gillis, *Islands of the Mind: How the Human Imagination Created the Atlantic World* (New York: Palgrave, 2004). See also Stephen A Royle, *A Geography of Islands: Small Island Insularity* (London: Routledge, 2001); Ileana Rodríguez, *Transatlantic Topographies: Islands, Highlands, Jungles* (Minneapolis: University of Minnesota Press, 2004); J. G. A. Pocock, *The Discovery of Islands: Essays in British History* (Cambridge: Cambridge University Press, 2005); and Lauren Benton, "Spatial

Histories of Empire," *Itinerario* 30, no. 3 (2006): 19–34. Most of the studies of Atlantic islands are somewhat old; there is much opportunity for new work here.

27. Richard White, *The Middle Ground: Indians, Empires, and Republic in the Great Lakes Region, 1650–1815* (New York: Cambridge University Press, 1991); Donna J. Guy and Thomas E. Sheridan, eds., *Contested Ground: Comparative Frontiers on the Northern and Southern Edges of the Spanish Empire* (Tucson: University of Arizona Press, 1998), p. 4; Jeremy Adelman and Stephen Aron, "From Borderlands to Borders: Empires, Nation-States, and the Peoples in Between in North American History," *AHR* 104, no. 3 (1999): 814–840; James F. Brooks, *Captives and Cousins: Slavery, Kinship, and Community in the Southwest Borderlands* (Chapel Hill: University of North Carolina Press, 2002); Jesús de la Teja and Frank Ross, eds., *Choice, Persuasion, and Coercion: Social Control on Spain's North American Frontiers* (Albuquerque: University of New Mexico Press, 2005); Kathleen DuVal, *The Native Ground: Indians and Colonists in the Heart of the Continent* (Philadelphia: University of Pennsylvania Press, 2006); Ned Blackhawk, *Violence Over the Land: Indians and Empires in the Early American West* (Cambridge, Mass.: Harvard University Press, 2006); Alan Taylor, *The Divided Ground: Indians, Settlers, and the Northern Borderland of the American Revolution* (New York: Knopf, 2006); Juliana Barr, *Peace Came in the Form of a Woman: Indians and Spaniards in the Texas Borderlands* (Chapel Hill: University of North Carolina Press, 2007); Claudio Saunt, " 'Our Indians': European Empires and the History of the Native American South," in Cañizares-Esguerra and Seeman, eds., *The Atlantic in Global History*, pp. 61–75 (quote on p. 61).

28. Allan Greer and Kenneth Mills, "A Catholic Atlantic," in Cañizares-Esguerra and Seeman, eds., *The Atlantic in Global History*, pp. 3–20; Dominique Deslandres, "Dans les Amériques," in Jean-Marie Mayeur et al., gen. eds., *Histoire du Christianisme dès origins à nos jours*, vol. 9: *L'Age de Raison (1620/30–1750)*, Marc Venard, ed. (Paris: Fayard, 1997), Troisième partie, "Le Christianisme dans le monde," ch. 1, pp. 616–736; and Deslandres, *Croire et faire croire: Les missions française au XVIIe siècle* (Paris: Fayard, 2003); John Thornton, "The Development of an African Catholic Church in the Kingdom of Kongo, 1491–1750," *Journal of African History* 25 (1984): 147–167; and John Thornton and Linda Heywood, *Central Africans, Atlantic Creoles, and the Foundation of the Americas, 1585–1660* (New York: Cambridge University Press, 2007). See also Nicholas Griffiths and Fernando Cervantes, eds., *Spiritual Encounters: Interactions Between Christianity and Native Religions in Colonial America* (Birmingham, U.K.: University of Birmingham Press, 1999); Allan Greer and Jodi Bilinkoff, eds., *Colonial Saints: Discovering the Holy in the Americas, 1500–1800* (New York: Routledge, 2003); Kenneth Mills and Anthony Grafton, eds., *Conversions: Old Worlds and New* (Rochester, N.Y.: University of Rochester Press, 2003); James Muldoon, ed., *The Spiritual Conversion of the Americas* (Gainesville: University Press of Florida, 2004); Daniel T. Reff, *Plagues, Priests, and Demons: Sacred Narratives and the Rise of Christianity in the Old World and the New* (Cambridge: Cambridge

University Press, 2004); Margaret Cormack, ed., *Saints and Their Cults in the Atlantic World* (Columbia: University of South Carolina Press, 2007). Unfortunately, Elaine G. Breslaw, ed., *Witches of the Atlantic World: A Historical Reader and Primary Sourcebook* (New York: New York University Press, 2000), is too New England-centered to be fully an Atlantic reader. For some recent work on Moravians, see Elizabeth W. Sommer, *Serving Two Masters: Moravian Brethren in Germany and North Carolina, 1727–1801* (Lexington: University Press of Kentucky, 2000); Jon F. Sensbach, *Rebecca's Revival: Creating Black Christianity in the Atlantic World* (Cambridge, Mass.: Harvard University Press, 2005); Aaron Fogleman, *Jesus Is Female: Moravians and Radical Religion in Early America* (Philadelphia: University of Pennsylvania Press, 2007); and Michelle Gillespie and Robert Beachy, eds., *Pious Pursuits: German Moravians in the Atlantic World* (New York: Berghahn Books, 2007).

29. Simon Schaffer, "Golden Means: Assay Instruments and the Geography of Precision in the Guinea Trade," in Marie-Noëlle Bourguet, Christian Licoppe, and H. Otto Sibum, eds., *Instruments, Travel and Science: Itineraries of Precision from the Seventeenth to the Twentieth Century* (London: Routledge, 2002), pp. 20–50; Londa Schiebinger, *Plants and Empire: Colonial Bioprospecting in the Atlantic World* (Cambridge, Mass.: Harvard University Press, 2004), 7; Richard Drayton, *Nature's Government: Science, Imperial Britain, and the 'Improvement' of the World* (New Haven. Yale University Press, 2000); Jorge Cañizares-Esguerra, *Nature, Empire, and Nation. Explorations of the History of Science in the Iberian World* (Stanford, Calif.: Stanford University Press, 2006); Susan Scott Parrish, *American Curiosity: Cultures of Natural History in the Colonial British Atlantic World* (Chapel Hill: University of North Carolina Press, 2006). See also Londa Schiebinger and Claudia Swan, eds., *Colonial Botany: Science, Commerce, and Politics in the Early Modern World* (Philadelphia: University of Pennsylvania Press, 2004); Chiyo Ishikawa, ed., *Spain in the Age of Exploration, 1492–1819* (Seattle: Seattle Art Museum, 2004), pp. 139–227; James Delbourgo, *A Most Amazing Scene of Wonders: Electricity and Enlightenment in Early America* (Cambridge, Mass.: Harvard University Press, 2006); Antonio Barrera-Osorio, *Experiencing Nature: The Spanish American Empire and the Early Scientific Revolution* (Austin: University of Texas Press, 2006); and James Delbourgo and Nicholas Dew, eds., *Science and Empire in the Atlantic World* (New York: Routledge, 2008).

30. Christopher Leslie Brown, *Moral Capital: Foundations of British Abolitionism* (Chapel Hill: University of North Carolina Press, 2006), p. 153. Brown mentions most of the previous relevant historiography. For another approach to the subject of antislavery, see Ian Baucom, *Specters of the Atlantic: Finance Capital, Slavery, and the Philosophy of History* (Durham: Duke University Press, 2005).

31. Emma Rothschild, "A Horrible Tragedy in the French Atlantic," *Past and Present* no. 192 (August 2006): 67–108; Laurent Dubois, "An Enslaved Enlightenment: Re-thinking the Intellectual History of the French Atlantic," *Social History* 31, no. 1 (2006): 1–14.

32. Anthony Pagden, *Lords of All the World: Ideologies of Empire in Spain, Britain, and France c.1500–c.1800* (New Haven: Yale University Press, 1995), pp. 78–79. More intensively, David Armitage, *The Ideological Origins of the British Empire* (Cambridge: Cambridge University Press, 2000), explores this subject for the British Empire within an explicitly Atlantic framework.

33. Lauren Benton, *Law and Colonial Cultures: Legal Regimes in World History, 1400–1900* (New York: Cambridge University Press, 2002). John Smolenski and Thomas J. Humphrey, eds., *New World Orders: Violence, Sanction, and Authority in the Colonial Americas* (Philadelphia: University of Pennsylvania Press, 2005), is an interesting collection of case studies of the ways officials and settlers used the provincial and local legal regimes they created to demarcate economic, social, political, and cultural boundaries and to reinforce their own claims to authority and status.

34. See, for instance, Mary Sarah Bilder, *The Transatlantic Constitution: Colonial Legal Culture and the Empire* (Cambridge, Mass.: Harvard University Press, 2004); Daniel J. Hulsebosch, *Constituting Empire: New York and the Transformation of Constitutionalism in the Atlantic World* (Chapel Hill: University of North Carolina Press, 2005); and Jack P. Greene, "The Cultural Dimensions of Political Transfers: An Aspect of the European Occupation of the Americas," *Early American Studies* 8 (2008): 1–26.

35. See, for instance, Elizabeth Mancke, "Negotiating an Empire: Britain and Its Oversea Peripheries, c. 1550–1780," in Christine Daniels and Michael J. Kennedy, eds., *Negotiated Empires: Centers and Peripheries in the Americas, 1500–1820* (New York: Routledge, 2002), pp. 235–265. The volume in which this essay appears contains chapters on all of the five most important early modern European empires in the Americas. See also Jack P. Greene, "Negotiated Authorities: The Problem of Governance in the Extended Polities of the Early Modern Atlantic World," in Greene, *Negotiated Authorities: Essays in Colonial and Political History* (Charlottesville: University Press of Virginia, 1994), pp. 1–24.

36. See Elizabeth Mancke, "Empire and State," in Armitage and Braddick, eds., *British Atlantic World*, pp.175–195 (quotations from pp. 176–177, 188); and Mancke, *Spatially Radical Empires: European Expansion and the Making of Modern Geopolitics* (forthcoming); Eliga H. Gould, "Zones of Law, Zones of Violence: The Legal Geography of the British Atlantic, Circa 1772," *WMQ* 3d ser., LX (2003): 471–510 (quotations from p. 509); Eliga H. Gould, "Entangled Histories, Entangled Worlds: The English-Speaking Atlantic as a Spanish Periphery," *AHR* 112 (2007): 764–786; and Gould, *Zones of Law, Zones of Violence: The American Revolution and the Legal Geography of the Atlantic World* (Cambridge, Mass.: Harvard University Press, forthcoming).

37. Jack P. Greene and J. R. Pole, eds., *Colonial British America: Essays in the New History of the Early Modern Era* (Baltimore: Johns Hopkins University Press, 1984); Alan L. Karras and J. R. McNeill, eds., *Atlantic American Societies: From Columbus Through Abolition, 1492 to 1888* (London: Routledge, 1992); Alison

Games, "Teaching Atlantic History," *Itinerario* 23 (1999): 162–173; Marvin Lunenfeld, ed., *1492, Discovery, Invasion, Encounter: Sources and Interpretation* (Lexington, Mass.: D.C. Heath, 1991); Bailyn, *Atlantic History*, p. 62.

38. Bailyn, *Atlantic History*, pp. 62–81 (quotes on pp. 68–69, 70); Elliott, *Empires of the Atlantic*, pp.1–114. Elliott later notes that Spanish immigrants were generally uninfected by egalitarian and communitarian ideals; for him, Protestant sectarians generated most of the utopian experiments of the New World (pp. 154–155).

39. Bailyn, *Atlantic History*, pp. 81–101; Elliott, *Empires of the Atlantic*, pp. 115–251, esp. pp. 223–224, 231. For a bracing argument against the notion of economic integration, see Pieter Emmer, "The Myth of Early Globalization: The Atlantic Economy, 1500–1800," *European Review* 11, no. 1 (2003): 37–47.

40. Bailyn, *Atlantic History*, pp. 101–111, esp. pp. 104–105; Elliott, *Empires of the Atlantic*, pp. 253–402, esp. pp. 319, 324, 329.

41. For a range of opinion, see Felipe Fernández-Armesto, "Atlantic Exploration Before Columbus," in G. R. Winius, ed., *Portugal the Pathfinder* (Madison: University of Wisconsin Press, 1995), pp. 41–70; R.W. Unger, "Portuguese Shipbuilding and the Early Voyages to the Guinea Coast," in Felipe Fernández-Armesto, ed., *The European Opportunity* (Aldershot, U.K.: Variorum, 1995), pp. 43–64; Karen Seaver, *The Frozen Echo: Greenland and the Exploration of North America, c. A.D. 1000–1500* (Stanford, Calif.: Stanford University Press, 1996); Felipe Fernández-Armesto, "Spanish Atlantic Voyages and Conquests Before Columbus," in J. B. Hattendorf, ed., *Maritime History*, vol. 1: *The Age of Discovery* (Malabar, Fla.: Krieger, 1996), pp. 137–147; Felipe Fernández-Armesto, "The Origins of the European Atlantic," *Itinerario* 24, no. 1 (2000): 111–128; Peter Russell, *Prince Henry"the Navigator": A Life* (New Haven: Yale University Press, 2000); Barry Cunliffe, *Facing the Ocean: The Atlantic and Its Peoples, 8000 BC-AD 1500* (Oxford: Oxford University Press, 2001).

42. David A. Lupher, *Romans in a New World: Classical Models in Sixteenth-Century Spanish America* (Ann Arbor: University of Michigan Press, 2003); Sabine MacCormack, *On the Wings of Time: Rome, the Incas, Spain, and Peru* (Princeton: Princeton University Press, 2006). For other such studies, see Benjamin Keen, *The Aztec Image in Western Thought* (New Brunswick, N.J.: Rutgers University Press, 1971), pp. 71–137; Michael T. Ryan, "Assimilating New Worlds in the Sixteenth and Seventeenth Centuries," *Comparative Studies in Society and History* 23 (1981): 519–538; Stuart Piggott, *Ancient Britons and the Antiquarian Imagination: Ideas from the Renaissance to the Regency* (London: Thames and Hudson 1989); John F. Moffitt and Santiago Sebastián, *O Brave New People: The European Invention of the American Indian* (Albuquerque: University of New Mexico Press, 1996), ch.5; Anthony Pagden, *The Fall of Natural Man: The American Indian and the Origins of Comparative Ethnology* (Cambridge: Cambridge University Press, 1982), ch. 6.

43. Donna Gabaccia, "A Long Atlantic in a Wider World," *Atlantic Studies* 1 (2004): 1–27.

1

THE ATLANTIC OCEAN AND ITS
CONTEMPORARY MEANINGS, 1492–1808

JOYCE E. CHAPLIN

Those who study Atlantic history are familiar with the criticism that their topic is an ex post facto concept, convenient for scholars today yet meaningless for people in the past. Critics of Atlantic history have also claimed that the field is little more than a new form of imperial history, a way to revive analysis of the top-down creation of modern empires in the Americas, a creation in which European-derived elites held pride of place. These criticisms are not without merit, but they themselves simplify the history of the Atlantic. In fact, the concept of "Atlantic" was a meaningful one for many of the people who lived around that ocean from the year 1492, when Columbus crossed the Atlantic, to 1808 and the abolition of the Atlantic slave trade in the United States and Britain. "Atlantic" was an actors' category, meaning one that historical actors themselves used to interpret the ocean as a specific, physical place. And it was not a top-down concept but a meaningful category even for the people at the lower levels of the societies that emerged in the post-Columbian world, especially for the sailors who had the strongest connection to the ocean.

Why have past views of the Atlantic Ocean received so little attention? For the most part, historians of the Atlantic have slighted ideas about the natural world, including its oceans. Alfred Crosby, and the handful of scholars who have followed his lead, are the exceptions. Yet the Columbian exchange that Crosby defined was to a large extent the unintended handiwork of Europeans, who transferred tobacco to the Old World and smallpox to the New World with little awareness of the consequences of their actions—they did not understand the natural world the way Crosby could understand it, long after the fact. That makes it different from a history that looks at how early modern people themselves comprehended the natural world, including the Atlantic Ocean. Moreover, the maritime historians who have examined sailors as economic, social, and political actors have not seriously considered the intellectual contribution that their subjects made to conceptions of the ocean. Scattered analyses—by historians of cartography, science, and the environment—nevertheless make clear that a history of the Atlantic Ocean's past meanings can and should be written.[1]

The history of the Atlantic's contemporary meanings occurred in three stages. In the first, Europeans thought of the Atlantic as a geographic space to *get across*, a rather belated idea that contradicted an ancient suspicion that the ocean was not a real space at all. In the second stage, the peoples in the post-Columbian countries that faced the Atlantic thought of that ocean as a space in which to *make or imagine physical connections*, both among different places and among different natural forces. In the last stage, people emphasized the Atlantic's value as a *route elsewhere*, especially when the Pacific became a new destination for them. These were not perfectly distinct ideas of the Atlantic Ocean. But different motives inspired each one and they fall, moreover, into a roughly chronological sequence, beginning with European ventures westward across the Atlantic, going through the creation of European empires that fostered a dense seascape of activity around the Atlantic, and then taking a new direction with Louis Antoine de Bougainville's and James Cook's voyages into the Pacific, which offered new opportunities to the residents of Europe as well as of the European colonies that had emerged around the Atlantic Ocean.

Europeans had had remarkably little interest in crossing the Atlantic for several millennia. Their earliest images of the ocean had represented it as a vast and mysterious barrier around the known world. Such representations followed the ancient Greek idea of the world as a circle on which a single ocean flowed around an Earth that lay at the center. Europeans and Arabs both adopted this Greek conception. For them, the Atlantic was the western part of the watery barrier that enclosed the world and led nowhere. It made perfect sense to them to think of the world this way. Ancient traders, migrants, and invaders had plenty of room for their activities within Europe, Africa, and Asia. Those places *were* the world, and smaller bodies of water, especially the Mediterranean, already connected most of that world.[2]

The western ocean was, in contrast, otherworldly, a place where the sun set, the gods dwelt, the dead retired. Consider two of the celebrated labors of Hercules. In one, he fetched the red cattle of Geryon, who lived far to the west, under the setting sun. On his way, Hercules set up twin pillars to mark the exit from the Mediterranean world. A second task required Hercules to fetch the golden apples of the Hesperides, nymphs whose enchanted garden lay far west in the realm of unearthly beings. Hercules appealed for help to the Titan Atlas, who had been condemned to hold the heavens up and away from the Earth, and who did so at the very western edge of the Mediterranean, close to the Hesperides. Hercules gamely held up the heavens while Atlas went and got him the golden apples, then tricked Atlas into shouldering the burden yet again. Doomed to his cosmic task at the very edge of the known world, Atlas was nevertheless honored when his name was bestowed on geographic features assumed to be near him: the Atlas Mountains, in northwest Africa, and the Atlantic Ocean, into which the Mediterranean ran—the Pillars of Hercules marked the transition between the two bodies of water. Altogether, these legends recorded an ancient fear that the Atlantic was not a real place, but an unearthly margin between the human realm and the nonhuman one.[3]

So otherworldly did the Atlantic seem that neither Europeans nor Arabs represented it as a full ocean. It appeared only as a narrow, external barrier on maps of the world down through the Middle Ages. It was certainly the case that Europeans, as well as people from North Africa and the Near East, were quite busy exploring Atlantic coastlines, but they paid attention only to the ribbon of water just alongside the land, which is all that they bothered to map, even though their maps might represent other bodies of water in considerable detail, including the Mediterranean, the North Sea, and (sometimes) the Indian Ocean. These features are apparent on a famous Latin version of Ptolemy's *Geographia*. That ancient Greek text had been known to Arab scholars but was not available in Europe until translated into Latin in 1406. The first printed edition with maps, of 1477, included a world map on which the main bodies of water are the Indian Ocean and the Mediterranean. The Atlantic Ocean appears as a strip of water off Africa, and its northern counterpart, the Western Ocean, is similarly indicated above it. (Even more tellingly, the Pacific is entirely absent.)[4]

It was impossible for Europeans to consider the Atlantic as a full ocean, so much so that those who made the first recorded crossing had a different idea about their accomplishment. When the Norse ventured out from Iceland and settled at L'Anse aux Meadows in what is now Canada, they believed themselves to be in Africa. They assumed they had traveled along the rim of the Atlantic, on an alternative route to part of the world they already knew. They could not conceive that they had actually crossed the dreaded barrier between their familiar world and the land of the setting sun. We cannot tell whether the English fishermen who followed the Norse had a different idea about their location. The English had begun fishing near

Iceland by the early 1400s and had, by the 1470s or 1480s, moved beyond Greenland toward Newfoundland. They were not eager to tell anyone what they were doing—the location of their activities was a trade secret of sorts. The information nevertheless seems to have slipped out to other maritime people, from whom Christopher Columbus got some intriguing information about sailing westward across the Atlantic and encountering land.[5]

Columbus would be the first person to transform the Atlantic from unknown barrier to physical entity although, significantly, he was not entirely aware that he had done so. He had underestimated the distance between Europe and Asia, and therefore had no conception of the extent of the ocean between those two continents, let alone any realization of the existence of a new continent at the western edge of the Atlantic. He continued to think of the places he explored on the opposite side of the Atlantic as parts of Asia; only later would subsequent explorers and cartographers grasp that the Atlantic led not to another part of the Old World but to a world entirely new to them. And even after Columbus's historic westward venture, Europeans continued to consider the Atlantic within the old mystical terms. Thus the Spanish used the mythical Pillars of Hercules to denote how their Atlantic empire connected two worlds. Other Europeans adopted the image, as well. One famous example is Francis Bacon's frontispiece to his *Great Instauration*, published in 1620, which indicated the frontiers of human knowledge with an image of a ship headed out into the Atlantic, beyond the Pillars of Hercules.[6]

The Spanish were also, however, quite busy demystifying the Atlantic. Shortly after Columbus's voyages, Spaniards began to produce sea charts and navigation manuals, some of which were printed and an increasing number of which would include information about getting to America: they cataloged prevailing currents, patterns of wind, useful landfalls, and dreaded obstacles. The first printed Spanish navigation guide, Martín Fernández de Enciso's *Suma de geographía* (1519), featured the earliest printed sailing directions for all parts of the world, including the West Indies. By 1540, Roger Barlow had translated the book into English, a translation that may have circulated in manuscript; by 1578 John Frampton had done another translation, of the sailing directions to America alone, and had it printed in London. Similarly, Martín Cortés's *Breve compendio de la sphera y del arte de navegar* (1551, 1554) ran through ten English editions by the year 1630, a significant measure of the importance of Spanish knowledge of the Atlantic for other Europeans.[7]

Thus the crossing of the Atlantic Ocean represented several shifts in the ways Europeans saw the physical world. They questioned a view of the western ocean as a barrier between the known and unknown worlds, with themselves at the center of the known world. Instead, they adopted a view of the Atlantic as the conduit to what was to them a new world, a globe with interconnected parts. These shifts are apparent in a map of the world that illustrated a 1508 edition of Ptolemy's *Geographia*, a contrast to the 1477 version with its tight focus on the Old World. This post-Columbian edition is remarkable for its new sense that the Atlantic Ocean led outward, around Africa to the Indian Ocean, and to the west, toward the newfound lands and then beyond, a new route to the Orient. Information about the Atlantic was becoming part of public knowledge within Europe, as well as in the Near East and, eventually, Asia.[8]

The publication of such knowledge was nevertheless often contested. Sailors were eager to keep some secrets to themselves—European monarchs may have commanded American soil, but the seas necessary to maintain that command remained under a remarkably plebeian control. Moreover, Europeans split into competing national groups in order to exploit the different parts of the Americas to which they sailed, and their rulers often regarded information about watering stations, fishing or whaling opportunities, trade winds, and ocean currents as proprietary. Separatist conceptions of the Atlantic survived into the eighteenth century. It was quite common, for example, for European maps to label parts of oceans in terms of their geographic location, rather than use single names for entire oceans, as we now do. Thus the English named what we could call the North Atlantic for its position relative either from them or from the European continent: Western Ocean or North Sea. As Ian Kenneth Steele has pointed out, the designation "North Sea" particularly undermined any sense of a greater Atlantic; the English considered what we call the South Atlantic an ocean unto itself, usually called the Ethiopian Sea.[9]

If Columbus threw a line across the Atlantic, thousands of his successors knit a web of permanent ties over and around the ocean and, in the process, made significant discoveries about the physical nature of the Earth and its seas. Those tasks mobilized people from every part of the Atlantic and at every social or political level. Eventually, Native Americans, ordinary sailors, fellows of Europe's learned societies, as well as political or military leaders, would all make contributions. If crossing the Atlantic had been an overwhelmingly European or even imperial story, conceiving of that ocean as a network of places and natural forces involved a far wider range of actors.

Europeans quickly realized that Native American advice on geography and navigation would be invaluable. When he arrived in the Caribbean,

Columbus asked the people he encountered for information about neighboring islands. That strategy continued in a variety of American locales; the Spanish used native pilots to explore the Gulf Coast, just as the English consulted New England's natives about the configuration of their coastline. And native men were so quickly integrated into European maritime culture that it is clear that Europeans and colonists found their expertise valuable. Such was the case with the native Indians of Nantucket, who were, as Daniel Vickers has pointed out, the first whale men on that island, and early workers in the whaling industry that American colonists established in the eighteenth century.[10]

The Europeans who gathered information from native people, as well as from their own repeated experience with travel on the Atlantic, rapidly publicized their discoveries. From the sixteenth through the eighteenth century, printed sets of sailing directions, designed to send navigators from port to port, appeared in every European language: as Italian *portolani*, German *Seebücher*, Spanish *derroteros*, Portuguese *roteiros*, and English or Dutch *rutters*. Such guides might be specialized, as when they focused on a section of Atlantic coastline, often that of a particular nation or of its colonies in the Americas. More ambitious guides might specify certain routes between an imperial power and its far-flung colonies. Dutch sea atlases, often called "waggoners," after the very successful pilot books of Lucas Janszoon Waghenaer, published comprehensive sea charts (which showed the way to a place) accompanied by coastal views (which signaled arrival at a place—preferably before running into it), which together made navigation safer. Other cartographers followed suit, often emphasizing the national identity of their publications, as with the many editions of *The English Pilot*, first published in 1671 and republished in more than 111 editions over the next 133 years.[11]

These many guides made possible something amazing: getting from one part of the Atlantic to another became an everyday occurrence. As time went on, more things and people moved around the ocean; raw commodities, manufactured goods, curiosities, scientific specimens, books, and correspondence would all proliferate, so that contact with something from a faraway place became an everyday experience. Even those who did not venture upon the ocean could, if they were literate, read about Atlantic experiences. Newspapers throughout the Atlantic world advertised the arrival of commodities produced elsewhere around the ocean and made news out of a colorful array of maritime incidents, from naval victories to shipwrecks. Novelists likewise used the Atlantic as a stage of action; both Daniel Defoe's *Robinson Crusoe* (1719) and Tobias Smollett's *The Adventures of Roderick*

Random (1748) feature heroes whose ill fortune culminates in their ill-fated adventures at sea.

Nothing makes the development of an everyday Atlantic clearer than the horrifying increase, over time, in the Atlantic slave trade. From scattered shipments of Africans in the sixteenth century, the trade gradually expanded over the seventeenth century and became an important economic mainstay of the plantation systems emerging in the different European colonies. Yet it was the eighteenth century that was the heyday of the slave trade. More captives were shipped out of Africa, and they were shipped to more places, including Europe and the colonies in temperate zones. The ease with which people and things could be sent around the Atlantic Ocean in the eighteenth century was apparent to anyone who was sold as a slave or who tasted sugar. The routine barbarities of Atlantic slavery form the pivot of Voltaire's satire *Candide* (1759), in which the protagonist's characteristic optimism is at last confounded after he crosses the Atlantic and encounters a black slave hideously maimed through labor at a sugar mill in Surinam.[12]

The tragic correlation between enslavement and the growth of an Atlantic world is only slightly offset by the fact that free black men entered the ranks of Atlantic mariners. Africans themselves had not ventured far out into the Atlantic, but did so once they were swept up into the slave trade. Their ironic presence as maritime workers on the very ocean that had delivered them or their ancestors into bondage is apparent in one of the best eighteenth-century sea paintings, John Singleton Copley's "Watson and the Shark" (1778). There, a sailor-laden boat and a swimming Brook Watson float in Havana Harbor. The swimmer and the boat's crew are English and are in Cuba (the year is 1749) because the British had recently regained the *asiento de negros*, the legal contract to supply the Spanish colonies with African slaves. The title characters of the painting have already met: the shark has taken two chunks out of Watson's right leg. As the beast returns for another nibble, the other men are poised to harpoon it and to haul Watson aboard. The incident really happened, and the real Watson lived to stump about on a prosthetic leg. But the picture only hints at his deliverance—so far, the impending attack is merely balanced, not canceled, by the dramatic efforts of the rescuers. Likewise, a sailor of African descent, who dominates the physical center of the painting, embodies the uncertain energies of the maritime Atlantic. Is he a free man? Or is he a slave? Either way, what might he have thought of the commercial opportunities that Cuba offered as the Atlantic slave trade expanded and became ever more routine?[13]

Who created this world of everyday Atlantic travel? The European states that controlled American empires were sometimes involved, though not always. Printers produced pilot books as independent, commercial ventures, though some European states often encouraged such productions, whether discreetly or overtly. The rulers of Spain and Portugal had, respectively, established the Casa de la Contratación in Seville and the Casa da India at Lisbon, each of which solicited or sponsored improvements in navigational techniques and routes. (There was not always agreement, let alone cooperation, between navigational theorists and actual sailors, however.) The Spanish and Portuguese lavished attention on the South Atlantic routes that held their empires together; these southerly routes were especially important for the silver fleets that conveyed New World treasure back to Spain, and for the traffic in African slaves and sugar. The North Atlantic remained comparatively less studied, for the simple reason that England (later Britain), the nation which sent the most colonists to North America, did not have the official agencies to gather and circulate information about navigation that Spain and Portugal did, a fact that Englishmen interested in colonization of the Americas steadily lamented.[14]

France's rulers did follow the Iberian model. They established a specialized Office of Hydrography that was fairly well integrated into the Académie Royale des Sciences. The French also sponsored voyages of exploration and cartographic projects. The French statesman Jean-Baptiste Colbert commissioned an atlas of charts to survey the European coast from Gibraltar up to Norway. The resulting *Le Neptune françois* of 1693, a gorgeously decorative sea atlas, reflected quite well Louis XIV's prodigious ambitions and set a new standard for hydrographical representations of the Atlantic as projects of national prestige.[15]

Other nations, including England and the Netherlands, did not have such an official sponsorship of maritime cartography. The Dutch nevertheless excelled in this area because they had a well-established community of commercial printers—the envy of other nations during the seventeenth century. Dutch cartographers published and reprinted navigational guides for other nations, as for the Spanish and French. Britain had a much weaker tradition of marine cartography—it would not establish an Office of Hydrography until 1795, when the Napoleonic Wars finally encouraged an official effort.[16] Hence, published information about the North Atlantic would not develop as quickly as that for the southern part of the ocean. Yet the most innovative interpretations of the Atlantic Ocean that would be done during the long eighteenth century were done by the British, who had seemed to be lagging behind other Europeans in their focused interest in that ocean.

The British may have trailed behind other European nations in empire building and cartography, but they were, by the late seventeenth century, creating unprecedented naval power and scientific prowess. One result was that both British sailors and men of science studied the sea. A long line of fellows of the Royal Society of London examined maritime matters. Isaac Newton and Robert Boyle addressed questions about marine phenomena; Robert Hooke and Stephen Hales designed instruments to sample the temperature and density of seawater at different depths. If official connections between the Royal Society of London and the Royal Navy and Admiralty were scarce, certain men nevertheless bridged the gap. Samuel Pepys, for instance, was both Secretary of the Navy and President of the Royal Society. That society solicited information from mariners as well as any travelers who had knowledge of sea voyages.[17]

Many sailors, even of low rank, responded to scientific interest in the sea. Whatever the growing prestige of naval service for highborn men in the eighteenth century, it was still the case that men who came up through the ranks, let alone self-made merchant mariners, garnered little social respect. But they were respected for what they knew about the sea. The *Philosophical Transactions of the Royal Society of London* are studded with communications from sea captains about tidal patterns, waterspouts, marine life, and so on. To a remarkable extent, one man had pioneered the way for all of these eager correspondents: William Dampier, the English sailor who combined intriguing careers as a buccaneer, a circumnavigator, and a maritime expert. In 1699, Dampier had published *A Discourse of Winds, Breezes, Storms, Tides, and Currents,* the earliest comprehensive study of the patterns of motion in and over the oceans. Dampier also provided a chart that indicated the winds over the Atlantic and Indian oceans, and another that did the same for the Pacific.[18]

Because of his work, Dampier became a protégé, though not a fellow, of the Royal Society of London. He also became one of the most widely cited hydrographic experts. And his work indicates something else about maritime knowledge: it seems to have been English sailors who used the term "Atlantic" routinely to describe the ocean we now recognize under that name. Dampier used the name regularly in his writings, and used it, moreover, for both the north and the south parts of the ocean. The eventual English use of the ocean name "Atlantic" may be an instance, therefore, of an idea that did not trickle from the top of a society downward, but instead rose from the bottom up.[19]

Other work on the Atlantic depended on the cooperation, however uneasy, between mariners and men of science. That was the case with investigation of magnetic variation, a considerable problem for navigators who depended on compass readings. Earth's magnetic field is not uniform, a fact that became ever more apparent as ships ventured over a greater extent of the globe. The first systematic attempt to map magnetic variation was done in the Atlantic, and by an Englishman, Edmond Halley, after whom the recurring comet is named. Yet Halley did his work without the strong state sponsorship that a contemporary French or earlier Spanish venture might have received. He had the support of the Admiralty, which gave him the use of a vessel, the *Paramore*, for his three Atlantic voyages, though he was not formally subject to the Admiralty's orders. And Halley was frustrated by his crew's unwillingness to be commanded by him, a landsman. After his first voyage, he had one of the mates of the *Paramore* court-martialed for his conduct and was careful on his next voyages to have undisputed command of his vessel. Using the data gathered from his three voyages, Halley produced history's first thematic map—which took as its focus, significantly, the Atlantic Ocean. (A thematic map emphasizes some feature that is not a visible physical phenomenon, such as differently shaded areas to indicate stocks of fish, or larger or smaller circles to show distribution of urban populations, and so on.)[20]

The well-known British quest for longitude was a similarly Atlantic story. In 1714 Parliament set up the Longitude Prize in the wake of Sir Cloudsley Shovell's devastating wreck in the Atlantic, on his return from action in Queen Anne's War. The competition would award £20,000 for any device or method, usable at sea, that determined longitude (east–west position) within thirty nautical miles of its true location; lower sums would be awarded to less accurate solutions to the problem. And it was tests on the Atlantic which demonstrated that John Harrison's chronometer was probably the winner of that prize, not without acrimony among the contending parties and resentment by the French, who had developed their own chronometer. In any case, the actual use of chronometers remained rare until well into the nineteenth century, because of their prohibitive expense.[21]

Harrison's and Halley's efforts were typical of a British style of engagement with the Atlantic: efforts to understand the ocean were encouraged but not commanded by the state. A voluntary and sometimes competing set of ambitions from a variety of English-speaking people was precisely what made the North Atlantic Ocean into a meaningful physical entity. It was a contrast to the Iberian situation. Spain continued to gather information about the Atlantic and other oceans but, in contrast to Britain, allowed less and less of it to be published during the eighteenth century, perhaps to prevent proprietary information from becoming public knowledge. Much accomplished work was returned to Spain, but only to be shelved in archives and forgotten.[22]

British colonists, too, made significant contributions to knowledge of the North Atlantic, contributions that demonstrated how definitions of the ocean went not just from center to periphery, but also traced the reverse pattern. The first chart of the Gulf Stream, for instance, was entirely the handiwork of two Americans. That chart was made because of a question put to Benjamin Franklin in 1768. Franklin was Deputy Postmaster General for the American colonies; the Board of Trade had asked him why on earth it took longer for mail to get from England to Boston than it did coming the other way. Franklin consulted one of his many Nantucket cousins, Timothy Folger, a ship's captain who knew the whalers who worked the waters between England and New England. Folger told Franklin that the Gulf Stream's eastwardly flowing waters slowed traffic trying to get west but speeded up the traffic going in the other direction. Franklin asked his cousin to mark the size and extent of the current on a chart of the ocean and then requested that the British Post Office have it engraved, the better to assist packet boat captains in charge of the mail service.[23]

Eventually, Britons and British Americans managed to convince themselves that the ocean at the center of their attention deserved a distinctive name. The keyword-searchable electronic compendium of early American newspapers shows this trend. Instances of the word "Atlantic," spelled with or without a terminal "k," rise from one occurrence in the 1720s to 760 in the 1790s. Within this upward trend, the key decade is the 1760s, which saw 126 uses, up from a mere seven instances in the preceding decade. The reason for this is obvious: the Seven Years' War, which consolidated British and American ambitions to control North America, the Caribbean, and the Atlantic Ocean that conveyed the trade of both places back to Britain.[24]

And back in Britain itself, maritime officials were at last organizing a great cartographic project to survey the Atlantic—under that name. The *Atlantic Neptune* drew upon decades of British surveying efforts. These had peaked during the Seven Years' War, when Britain dispatched maritime surveyors to map the coastlines of strategic areas. James Cook, later the Captain Cook of Pacific fame, was one of many young mariners who got his surveying experience in the Atlantic—in Cook's case, the coastline of New France. In 1774, the Admiralty ordered Colonel J. F. W. Des Barres of the British Engineers to compile an atlas of sea charts that the Royal Navy could use in American waters. Des Barres complied and, between 1777 and 1780, produced four volumes which included 247 charts and colored views of the coastline. *Atlantic Neptune* proved unexpectedly useful to the British during the American Revolution, though that conflict also delayed completion of the project and guaranteed that Britain's American and French enemies would consult and even pirate Des Barres's charts during the War for Independence.[25]

It was also important for the independent Americans to claim the Atlantic for themselves. Benjamin Franklin recycled his 1768 Gulf Stream chart twice, first as part of a plan to establish a Franco–American packet boat service around 1782, then as part of his long essay "Maritime Observations," published in the *Transactions of the American Philosophical Society* in 1786. Each subsequent chart was smaller; it focused more narrowly on the North Atlantic in the 1782 version and in the 1786 version, which also omitted many place-names on the continent. Subsequent American publications likewise zeroed in on the parts of the Atlantic important to them and, even if they were adapted from British charts, pointedly renamed them as American ones. The first set of sailing instructions to be printed in the United States, Lawrence Furlong's *American Coast Pilot* of 1796, thus guided American navigators up and down their nation's now independent coastline as well as toward the waters of the much-contested Mississippi River, which Americans were determined to control for themselves.[26]

With so much taking place in and around the Atlantic, it is hard to believe that people looked beyond it, but they did. They began to see their familiar ocean as a route to others, particularly the Pacific. To a certain extent, knowledge of Atlantic sea routes had been facilitating travel to other oceans all along; the shipping stations established on St. Helena, at the Cape of Good Hope (the "Tavern of Two Seas"), and around Cape Horn had shown the utility of the Atlantic to world travel. There had long been parallel European interest in the Indian Ocean, and Portuguese navigators had of course pioneered an Atlantic route around Africa and to India. And the Spanish had, since the sixteenth century, a Pacific foothold in the Philippines, giving Spain the only empire that passed through the Americas and included the two oceans on either side.

No wonder so many people yearned for a Northwest Passage. Whoever discovered that conduit would be able to connect the two oceans more easily than the Spanish could, because they could then avoid the tedious overland route through Panama or the dangerous sea passage around the tip of South America. Although plenty of tall tales and hoaxes mark the history of the Northwest Passage, the search for it was not in fact the pastime of cranks and nobodies—many sober and reasonable people scanned maps, pored over explorers' accounts, and even fitted out expeditions in order to find some passageway through the North American continent that might lead to

Asia via the South Sea, as the Pacific was commonly known. In 1745, the British Parliament offered a £20,000 reward—equivalent to the Longitude Prize—to anyone who could sail from Hudson's Bay to the South Sea.[27]

Although no such passage was possible until the twentieth century and the development of vessels with ice-breaking capability, attempts to find one were nevertheless productive in establishing a variety of other knowledge about the North Atlantic. Henry Ellis's 1748 account of his northward venture, *A Voyage to Hudson's Bay*, for instance, was widely read and respected. It won Ellis a fellowship in the Royal Society and advanced his naval career significantly. The same was true of Olaudah Equiano, the freed slave later famous for his antislavery memoirs and career, who made a similar voyage in 1773. In that year, Equiano served—along with a young Horatio Nelson—as part of a British attempt to find a passage from Europe to Asia through the North Pole. Though the venture failed to find anything of promise, Equiano's presence on the expedition again indicates how a variety of people, from all corners of the Atlantic world and every level of society, were attempting to expand knowledge of the world's oceans.[28]

If the search for the Northwest Passage indicated a desire to connect Atlantic to Pacific, subsequent interest in the latter ocean represented a desire to leave the Atlantic entirely. After France's devastating loss of New World territories in the Seven Years' War, the French shifted attention to the Pacific, sending out the famous Bougainville expedition of 1766–1769. The British countered by organizing three voyages led by James Cook. Each of these ambitious undertakings required tremendous investment of the French or British state. The first Cook expedition of 1769–1771, for example, was charged with charting as much of the Pacific and its landmasses as possible; with observing the transit of Venus over the sun (observations of which would help determine the distance from the Earth to the sun); with bringing back sketches, narrative descriptions, and specimens; and with generally scaring the French out of the Pacific and especially away from the rumored continent in the South Pacific, meaning Australia. Significantly, native people proved yet again essential to oceanic exploration. Cook relied on a Tahitian man, Tupaia, who volunteered to help him navigate through the South Pacific and generated a valuable map of the location of some of its islands.[29]

As Europeans took a new and serious interest in the Pacific, they systematically began to call that ocean the Pacific, instead of using its older name, the South Sea. They also began to produce maps that placed the Pacific, rather than the Atlantic, at the center of the world, as in the map that showed the track of Bougainville's passage. That shift continued the trend, which had begun after Columbus, no longer to see Europe at the center, but to envision it at the edge of a larger world, one that began with the Atlantic. After Bougainville and Cook, the world was even bigger and could most meaningfully be represented as centered on an ocean that lay half a world away from Europe. Cook was rewarded for having helped create this new world. The coat of arms granted him is unique in bearing a globe. Not just any globe—this one pointedly showcases the Pacific.[30]

If the Pacific was now the center of attention, it also represented an alternative to the Atlantic, especially that ocean's worst feature, the slave trade. European discovery of the Pacific and a growing antislavery movement occurred together in time and became misleadingly associated. The old belief that the Atlantic was the means by which commerce, Christianity, and civility might be expanded was now challenged by an argument that the slave trade left the waters of the Atlantic red with gore. Slaves had long known this, of course. But especially after the *Zong* affair of 1781, when the captain of a Liverpool slaver of that name dumped disease-stricken and malnourished slaves into the Atlantic Ocean in order to collect the insurance on their (now guaranteed) deaths, the white population of Europe and the colonies began to adopt a more critical view of the slave-dependent traffics that crossed their nearby ocean. Different nations began to renounce the slave trade; the United States and Great Britain independently decided to abolish their trades by 1808. The shadow that chattel slavery had cast over the Atlantic lingered past the abolition of the slave trade and even the emancipation of slaves. In 1840, the English artist Joseph Mallord William Turner painted his horrifying "Slave Ship," which showed human cargo being jettisoned into the water in order to lighten the craft before an oncoming hurricane.

The Pacific, some architects of empire vowed, would never be so polluted by the inhumanity of slave trafficking. It is true that extremely few slaves were carried to the antipodes, the new worlds of the Pacific that Britain was now colonizing. But British convicts were carried there, and the freed slaves who found their way to Australia did not enjoy a paradise of racial equality—the Atlantic world of sorrow and shackles was difficult to escape, even in a place that was supposed to resemble the peaceful name of the ocean around it.[31]

A Pacific unmarked by the inequalities of the Atlantic was probably impossible to attain. But the hope that such an ocean might somehow exist represented quite powerfully the new uncertainties over the nature of the worlds that had been, in the wake of Columbus, created around the Atlantic. That ocean had once, in ancient times, been the border of the meaningful world, the end of the truly possible. By the height of European colonization of the Americas and as modern European empires began to flourish elsewhere, the ocean itself contained many possibilities: violent, liberating, ironic, lucrative, exhilarating, routine, or sublime—or some salty brew of them all.

NOTES

1. Alfred W. Crosby, *The Columbian Exchange: Biological and Cultural Consequences of 1492* (Westport, Conn.: Greenwood Pub. Co., 1972). For the most important maritime contribution along these lines, see W. Jeffrey Bolster, "Putting the Ocean in Atlantic History: Maritime Communities and Marine Ecology in the Northwest Atlantic, 1500–1800," *American Historical Review*, 113 (2008), 19–47.

2. Denis Cosgrove, "Mapping the World," in James R. Akerman and Robert W. Karrow, Jr., eds., *Maps: Finding Our Place in the World* (Chicago: University of Chicago Press, 2007), pp. 78–88; Valerie I. J. Flint, *The Imaginative Landscape of Christopher Columbus* (Princeton: Princeton University Press, 1992), ch. 1.

3. Barry Cunliffe, *Facing the Ocean: The Atlantic and Its Peoples, 8000 BC–AD 1500* (New York: Oxford University Press, 2001), p. 2.

4. Cunliffe, *Facing the Ocean*, pp. 88–99; John B. Hattendorf, *"The Boundless Deep...": The European Conquest of the Oceans, 1450 to 1840* (Providence, R.I.: John Carter Brown Library, 2003), pp. 4–5.

5. Kirsten A. Seaver, *The Frozen Echo: Greenland and the Exploration of North America, ca. A.D. 1000–1500* (Stanford, Calif.: Stanford University Press, 1996), pp. 34–35, 179–182, 193–198, 214–229, 264–311; David Harris Sacks, *The Widening Gate: Bristol and the Atlantic Economy, 1450–1700* (Berkeley: University of California Press, 1991); Flint, *Imaginative Landscape of Christopher Columbus*, ch. 3.

6. Flint, *Imaginative Landscape of Christopher Columbus*, passim.

7. J. H. Parry, *The Spanish Seaborne Empire* (New York: Knopf, 1966), chs. 1, 6; Ricardo Cerezo Martínez, *La cartografía náutica española en los siglos XIV, XV, y XVI* (Madrid: C.S.I.C., 1994); Hattendorf, *"Boundless Deep,"* pp. 5, 20.

8. Johannes Ruysch world map, in Claudius Ptolemy, *Geographia*, ed. Marcus Beneventanus and Johannes Cota (Rome, 1508).

9. Martin W. Lewis, "Dividing the Ocean Sea," *Geographical Review* 89 (1999): 188–214; Ian K. Steele, *The English Atlantic, 1675–1740: An Exploration of Communication and Community* (New York: Oxford University Press, 1986), pp. 14–15.

10. Irving I. Leonard, "The Spanish Re-exploration of the Gulf Coast in 1686," *Mississippi Valley Historical Review* 22 (1936): 549; Joyce E. Chaplin, *Subject Matter: Technology, the Body, and Science on the Anglo-American Frontier, 1500–1676* (Cambridge, Mass.: Harvard University Press, 2001), p. 70; Daniel Vickers, "The

First Whalemen of Nantucket," *William and Mary Quarterly* 3rd ser., 40 (1983): 560–583.

11. Günter Schilder, "Lucas Janszoon Waghenaer's Nautical Atlases and Pilot Books," in John A. Wolter and Ronald E. Grim, eds., *Images of the World: The Atlas Through History* (Washington, D.C.: Library of Congress, 1997), pp. 135–160; Hattendorf, *"Boundless Deep,"* pp. 54, 56, 102.

12. See chapter 8 in this volume, Philip D. Morgan, "Africa and the Atlantic, c. 1450 to c. 1820."

13. John Thornton, *Africa and Africans in the Making of the Atlantic World, 1400–1680* (New York: Cambridge University Press, 1992), pp. 15–27; W. Jeffrey Bolster, *Black Jacks: African-American Seamen in the Age of Sail* (Cambridge, Mass.: Harvard University Press, 1997).

14. Alison Sandman, "Mirroring the World: Sea Charts, Navigation, and Territorial Claims in Sixteenth-Century Spain," in Pamela H. Smith and Paula Findlen, eds., *Merchants and Marvels: Commerce, Science, and Art in Early Modern Europe* (New York: Routledge, 2001), pp. 83–108.

15. Josef W. Konvitz, *Cartography in France, 1660–1848: Science, Engineering, and Statecraft* (Chicago: University of Chicago Press, 1987), chs. 1, 3; Hattendorf, *"Boundless Deep,"* pp. 93, 100–101.

16. C. R. Boxer, *The Dutch Seaborne Empire, 1500–1800* (New York: Knopf, 1965), pp. 164–168; Mary Blewitt, *Surveys of the Seas: A Brief History of British Hydrography* ([London]: Macgibbon & Kee, [1957]), p. 29.

17. Margaret Deacon, *Scientists and the Sea, 1500–1900: A Study of Marine Science* (London: Academic Press, 1971), chs. 4, 6, 8; Robert Latham and William Matthews, *The Diary of Samuel Pepys*, vol. 10: *Companion* (Berkeley: University of California Press, 1983), pp. 1–5, 282–299, 361–368, 381–393.

18. Matthew Mulcahy, *Hurricanes and Society in the British Greater Caribbean, 1624–1783* (Baltimore: Johns Hopkins University Press, 2006), ch. 2; Anna Neill, "Buccaneer Ethnography: Nature, Culture, and Nation in the Journals of William Dampier," *Eighteenth-Century Studies* 33 (2000): 165–180; Diana Preston and Michael Preston, *A Pirate of Exquisite Mind: Explorer, Naturalist, and Buccaneer—The Life of William Dampier* (New York: Walker, 2004).

19. William Dampier, *A Collection of Voyages in Four Volumes* (London, 1729), vol. 2, p. 3.

20. Norman J. W. Thrower, ed., *The Three Voyages of Edmond Halley in the Paramore, 1698–1701* (London: Hakluyt Society, 1981); Patricia Fara, *Sympathetic Attractions: Magnetic Practices, Beliefs, and Symbolism in Eighteenth-Century England* (Princeton: Princeton University Press, 1996), ch. 4; Alan Cook, *Edmond Halley: Charting the Heavens and the Seas* (Oxford: Clarendon Press, 1998), chs. 3, 10. Halley had also done a thematic chart of winds. See Arthur H. Robinson, *Early Thematic Mapping in the History of Cartography* (Chicago: University of Chicago Press, 1982), pp. 46–51; Michael Friendly and Gilles Palsky, "Visualizing Nature and Society," in Akerman and Karrow, eds., *Maps*, pp. 219–221.

21. Dava Sobel, *Longitude: The True Story of a Lone Genius Who Solved the Greatest Scientific Problem of His Time* (New York: Penguin, 1995); William J. H. Andrewes, ed., *The Quest for Longitude: The Proceedings of the Longitude Symposium* (Cambridge, Mass.: Harvard University Press, 1996).

22. Iris H. W. Engstrand, *Spanish Scientists in the New World: The Eighteenth-Century Expeditions* (Seattle: University of Washington Press, 1981), pp. 184–185.

23. Joyce E. Chaplin, *The First Scientific American: Benjamin Franklin and the Pursuit of Genius* (New York: Basic Books, 2006), pp. 195–200.

24. Readex Digital Collections, Archive of Americana, Early American Imprints Series I, Evans (1639–1800).

25. Victor Suthren, *To Go Upon Discovery: James Cook and Canada, from 1758 to 1779* (Toronto, Ont.: Dundurn Press, 2000); Hattendorf, *"Boundless Deep,"* pp. 106–107; J. B. Harley, Barbara Bartz Petchenik, and Lawrence W. Towner, *Mapping the American Revolutionary War* (Chicago: University of Chicago Press, 1978), pp. 87–91.

26. Ellen Cohn, "Benjamin Franklin, Georges-Louis Le Rouge and the Franklin/Folger Chart of the Gulf Stream," *Imago Mundi* 52 (2000): 124–142; Chaplin, *First Scientific American*, pp. 289–292, 317–325; Hattendorf, *"Boundless Deep,"* pp. 58, 59, 108.

27. Glyn Williams, *Voyages of Delusion: The Northwest Passage in the Age of Reason* (London: HarperCollins, 2002).

28. Williams, *Voyages of Delusion*, pp. 146, 191–194, 211–212; Vincent Carretta, *Equiano the African: Biography of a Self-Made Man* (Athens: University of Georgia Press, 2005), ch. 7.

29. P. J. Marshall and Glyndwr Williams, *The Great Map of Mankind: Perceptions of New Worlds in the Age of Enlightenment* (Cambridge, Mass.: Harvard University Press, 1982), pp. 258–265; David Mackay, *In the Wake of Cook: Exploration, Science, and Empire, 1780–1801* (London: Croom Helm, 1985).

30. Mark Peterson, "Naming the Pacific," *Common Place* 5 (January 2005) (www.common-place.org).

31. Cassandra Pybus, *Epic Journeys of Freedom: Runaway Slaves of the American Revolution and Their Global Quest for Liberty* (Boston: Beacon Press, 2006), chs. 6, 8, 10.

PART I

New Atlantic Worlds

2

THE SPANISH ATLANTIC SYSTEM

KENNETH J. ANDRIEN

The overseas enterprises of Spain expanded dramatically following the first voyage of Christopher Columbus in 1492.[1] Even before this historic Atlantic crossing, Spaniards had begun the conquest of the Canary Islands (between 1478 and 1493), which served as a base and proving ground for the invasion and conquest of Spanish America, known as the Indies. After 1492 Spain's possessions spread from a few isolated Caribbean outposts to include Mexico, as the army of Fernando Cortés and his Amerindian allies overthrew the Aztec (Mexica) Empire and later moved southward to annex the Maya domains in southern Mexico and Central America. Within a decade the equally spectacular victories of Francisco Pizarro and Diego de Almagro brought down the Inca Empire (Tawantinsuyu), giving the Spaniards control over extensive human and mineral resources in South America. Over the course of the sixteenth century the conquistadors, followed by Crown bureaucrats and Catholic clergymen, slowly but firmly consolidated control over the central regions of Mexico and Peru. These possessions collectively served as the foundation of the Spanish Atlantic system. By 1600 the Spaniards claimed control over a vast region extending from the current southwest of the United States to the southern tip of South America.[2] It was a massive domain that brought unimaginable wealth to the kingdoms of Spain for over 300 years.

The Spanish conquest created a "New World" that was not entirely European, Native American, or African. The Crown established a royal bureaucracy in the Indies to enforce directives from Madrid, while indigenous commercial exchanges gave way to an expanding nexus of regional markets connected to the wider Atlantic world. The importation of African slaves and intermarriage and casual sexual unions between Europeans and the indigenous peoples led to a racial, ethnic, and cultural mosaic. The conquest also altered social hierarchies, as Europeans replaced indigenous elites at the apex of society and politics. Furthermore, Spanish clergymen converted millions of indigenous people to Roman Catholicism. The Spanish Atlantic Empire encompassed small Caribbean settlements, remote frontier outposts, and densely populated central regions in North and South America, all with stark climatic and geographical differences. Moreover, changes over time in both the metropolis and the Indies affected the political, social, economic, and religious configuration of the whole Spanish Atlantic.[3] In short, the Spanish Atlantic system was ethnically, culturally, and geographically diverse, yet constituted a defined political, economic, and religious space that held together from the sixteenth to the nineteenth century.[4]

The Spanish Atlantic system represented the first great wave of European expansion across the Atlantic Ocean. The French, Dutch, and English would follow, but over 100 years later, and their overseas colonies were shaped by a set of European cultural values and customs that had changed markedly since the voyages of Columbus. The earlier Spanish invaders of the sixteenth century sought wealth esteemed in their homeland, and they found it in large deposits of precious metals (particularly silver), rich lands, and dense Amerindian populations.

Exploiting and profiting from these resources shaped the socioeconomic configuration of the Spanish Atlantic system. Silver was a valuable asset but easy to smuggle. Moreover, the Spaniards had to govern large, wealthy, and sedentary indigenous populations in the central regions who could not be ignored, pushed off their lands, or placed on reservations. As a result, the Crown set up the New World's largest professional bureaucracy to govern, to tax, and to control the people and wealth of the Indies. Crown officials also established strict mercantile regulations over the flow of commerce across the Atlantic. Finally, Spaniards imposed a rigid Roman Catholic orthodoxy, establishing the Holy Office of the Inquisition in their capitals, Lima and Mexico City. Clergymen accompanied the original conquistadors, and the Church launched a moral crusade to evangelize all indigenous inhabitants of the central regions and sent missionaries to convert Amerindians in the transitional or frontier zones. Collectively the political, economic, and religious policies of the Spaniards attempted to establish an Atlantic system that was more "closed" to outside influences than its later European counterparts.

I. Scholars and the Spanish Atlantic System

Although scholarly antecedents of Spanish Atlantic history go back many years, the historiography is modest, particularly compared to the recent outpouring of works on the British Atlantic world.[5] Since Herbert Eugene Bolton's call for a common history of the Americas in 1933, succeeding generations of scholars have advanced paradigms for studying the Spanish Atlantic, particularly after World War II, when the establishment of the North Atlantic Treaty Organization brought the notion of a common Atlantic heritage to wide public attention.[6] The massive compilation of Spain's transatlantic trade statistics by Annales historians Pierre and Huguette Chaunu (1955–1959) defined the Spanish Atlantic as commercial "space," and in 1966 J. H. Parry emphasized the maritime dimensions of the Spanish Empire in his classic *The Spanish Seaborne Empire*.[7] Historians of the transatlantic slave trade, as early as Philip Curtin's seminal study in 1969, examined the role of Africa and slavery in the Spanish Atlantic system.[8]

In the late 1960s, historical debate shifted to problems of colonialism, imperialism, and underdevelopment, with most of this literature influenced by the neo-Marxist dependency paradigm. Advocates of the dependency paradigm postulated that the expansion of capitalism from Europe (and later the United States) led to the economic subordination and underdevelopment of less-developed regions in the Atlantic trading system.[9] In their influential study in 1970, Stanley and Barbara Stein postulated that from as early as 1492, Spain was an economic dependency of northern Europe which incorporated its new possessions in the Spanish Indies into a preexisting web of economic subordination, domestic inequalities, and structural underdevelopment. The spread of capitalist commercial transactions over the course of the sixteenth century simply promoted the widespread underdevelopment and subordination of the Spanish Atlantic system to the economic core nations in northern Europe—the Netherlands, France, and finally England.[10] Despite its seductive explanatory power, linking Europe and the Indies in a single system, most historians are now quite critical of (or even ignore) the dependency paradigm. These critics focus on a central paradox of *dependencia*: it is not a theory to be proven but a paradigm that cannot be verified by the sort of empirical research that underpins most academic histories.[11] As a result, the long-term influence of *dependencia* on studies of the Spanish Atlantic has diminished markedly in recent decades.[12]

Since the late 1980s, scholarly works have begun to elaborate more coherent methodological perspectives that broaden and deepen an understanding of the Spanish Atlantic system. After years of research by scholars working on individual colonial empires, historians such as Anthony Pagden, John Robert McNeil, Peggy Liss, Patricia Seed, and Camilla Townsend have written bold comparative studies.[13] The most ambitious of these comparative works, however, is the magisterial synthesis by J. H. Elliott, *Empires*

of the Atlantic World: Britain and Spain in the Americas, 1492–1830.[14]
Studies of migration across the Atlantic and the spread of diseases also
have made substantial contributions.[15] Intellectual and cultural approaches
have appeared, most recently with Jorge Cañizares Esguerra's book *How
to Write a History of the New World: Histories, Epistemologies, and Identities in the Eighteenth-Century Atlantic World*.[16] Moreover, historians of
the Enlightenment, eighteenth-century Bourbon reforms, and independence
have placed these issues into a wider imperial or Atlantic context.[17] The
pioneering overview remains Horst Pietschmann's edited volume *Atlantic
History: History of the Atlantic System, 1580–1830*.[18] Nonetheless, much
remains to be done; since the decline of the dependency paradigm, scholars
of the Spanish Atlantic system are only now defining and giving greater
direction to the field.[19]

II. New World Beginnings to the Consolidation
of the Spanish Atlantic, 1492–1610

The Spanish invasion of the New World proceeded from the Caribbean
islands to Mexico and Central America and then to Peru, as expeditions
fanned out across North and South America to incorporate new lands
into the Crown's domain. The major expeditions of Cortés in Mexico and
Pizarro in Peru both benefited from having large numbers of Amerindian
allies, and their victories resulted from leading small, highly mobile, and
technologically superior Spanish forces, which headed indigenous uprisings against the unpopular, divided Aztec and Inca states. Under these
circumstances, the position of the conquistadors was hardly secure after the
overthrow of the major indigenous polities. As a result, Spanish invaders
consolidated their newly-acquired wealth, status, and power by making
strategic alliances with powerful indigenous ethnic groups, often marrying
or taking as concubines the daughters of local elites. In Peru, the Spaniards
even put a seemingly docile member of the Inca royal family, Manco Inca,
on the throne to legitimize their rule in the Andes.[20]

The Spanish conquistadors were drawn from the middle sectors of
Spanish society, and they ventured to the Indies in search of the wealth,
status, and power denied them in Europe.[21] Some had military experience
in Europe or the Indies, but they were hardly professional soldiers. In fact,
they were closer in background and temperament to the Puritans of New
England than to mercenaries fighting in the army of Flanders. They were
religious men with a hardheaded entrepreneurial spirit, filled with an innate

sense of their destiny to win new lands for the king and to enrich themselves. The conquistadors engaged in every type of economic activity—investing in mines, landed estates, and commerce. Those areas with dense indigenous populations, mines of silver and gold, and the potential to produce goods for local consumption or for export to Europe became the core regions of the Indies, while less lucrative zones became transitional or frontier zones (at least until Spanish settlers found new economic opportunities and came in greater numbers). These early conquistadors represented a true advance guard of European expansion, and they laid the foundation of the Spanish Atlantic system.

To divide the spoils and ensure their wealth and status, the conquistadors parceled out grants of *encomienda*, which allowed them to collect taxes and labor services from a designated group of indigenous towns in return for military protection and religious instruction. These grants gave the Spanish holder (called an *encomendero*) social status and economic wealth—a source of capital and labor to buy property, engage in mining, or pursue commercial opportunities. The *encomienda* allowed the conquistadors to drain surplus resources from the existing Amerindian economies and invest them in emerging colonial enterprises.

After encountering the diverse Amerindian societies of the Indies, intel lectuals in Spain debated both the humanity and the proper social role of indigenous peoples in the emerging Spanish Atlantic system. Intellectuals struggled with basic questions such as whether the Amerindians were "beasts" (mere brutes incapable of living in civilized society), "barbarians" (rude outsiders best kept apart from civilized people), or "brothers" (men and women capable of accepting Christianity and being "restored" to civility).[22] In 1512 King Ferdinand convoked a group of learned theologians and officials to debate the issue, and the resulting Laws of Burgos decisively declared Amerindians brothers—free and entitled to own property and receive wages for their labors, and suitable for instruction in the Catholic faith.[23] Over the ensuing decades, however, reports of abuses perpetrated by the *encomenderos* against the Native American peoples cast doubt on the Crown's claims to secure the protection and evangelization of these Amerindian brothers. Advocates of Amerindian rights, such as the Dominican Bartolomé de las Casas, urged the Crown to end the *encomienda* and grant the right to supervise the evangelization of Amerindians directly to the Church. Others, such as the king's chaplain, Juan Ginés de Sepúlveda, argued (on the basis of his reading of Aristotle) that the indigenous peoples were inferior and by nature slaves, not worthy or capable of becoming full citizens. This dispute reached a climax in 1550 when King Charles

I convened a meeting in Valladolid, with both Las Casas and Sepúlveda on hand to debate the issue of Amerindian rights. After hearing both sides, the Crown eventually sided with Las Casas and suppressed Sepúlveda's views.[24] After this landmark decision, the Crown viewed the Amerindians as "brothers," but with the legal status of children (neophytes)—free people who could be made into good citizens, evangelized, and governed, but who also owed the Crown taxes and labor. In this way, the Native American peoples occupied a subordinate position in an organic, hierarchically organized, multiracial society, governed by Crown-appointed bureaucrats and instructed by the Church in the Roman Catholic faith.

By the middle of the sixteenth century the Crown slowly phased out the *encomienda* in wealthy, densely populated central areas in Mexico and Peru, although it persisted for longer periods along the fringes of the empire. Squabbles among the fractious conquistadors led to disorder, particularly in Peru, and the onset of European epidemic diseases dramatically reduced the Amerindian population in the central zones of the Spanish Indies. In Mexico, for example, the indigenous population declined from 20–25 million before the European invasion in 1519 to under 1.5 million a century later.[25] Moreover, Crown authorities wished to limit the political and economic power of the independent-minded *encomenderos*, while churchmen wanted control over evangelizing the indigenous peoples. The rise of new colonial cities and the discovery of fabulously rich gold and (especially) silver mines—such as Zacatecas, Guanajuato, and Sombrete in current-day Mexico and Carabaya, Oruro, and Potosí in current-day Peru and Bolivia—attracted a new influx of migrants from Spain who resented the political, social, and economic dominance of those first conquistadors, who monopolized *encomiendas*.

As the power of the *encomenderos* waned, the Crown sent bureaucrats, churchmen, and other settlers to rule, convert, and populate the newly-acquired lands. In Spain, the Crown established the Board of Trade (1503) to control colonial commerce and the Council of the Indies (1524) to serve as a court of appeals in civil cases, a legislative body, and an executive authority to enforce laws for the Indies. In America, the Crown set up an extensive bureaucracy to rule the newly conquered lands, headed by a viceroy in each of the two major political units, the Viceroyalties of New Spain and Peru. New Spain encompassed all the lands in southern portions of what are now the United States, the Caribbean, Mexico, and Central America to the borders of current-day Panama. The Viceroyalty of Peru included all the territory from Panama to the southern tip of South America, except for Brazil, which fell under Portuguese control. Within these two massive territorial units, the metropolitan government founded a series of high courts, called *audiencias* (six in Peru and four in New Spain) to hear civil and criminal cases. These justices worked with the viceroys to enforce legislation sent from Spain and to issue any necessary laws dealing with local matters. To limit the regional power of the *encomenderos*, authorities in Spain created a network of rural magistrates (*corregidores de indios*) to regulate contact between Spaniards and Amerindians, to collect the head tax or tribute, and to assign forced (corvée) labor service for state projects. Magistrates (*corregidores de españoles*) served in municipalities to hear court cases and to regulate local affairs in conjunction with the city council (*cabildo*).

Roman Catholic clergymen took firm control of converting the Amerindians to Catholicism in the two viceroyalties. At first the religious orders—primarily the Franciscans, Dominicans, Augustinians, Mercedarians, and later the Jesuits—played a leading role in evangelizing the indigenous peoples.[26] Over time, members of the secular clergy established parishes under the overall supervision of bishops appointed by the Crown (seven in New Spain and eight in Peru).[27] The regular orders maintained a number of rural parishes, and they kept missions in the frontier zones of the empire. But over time, the Crown tended to favor the secular clergy, because the pope gave the king control over appointments to the high ranks of the secular clergy and a share of the tithes paid to the Church.[28] The orders, responsible only to the heads of their order and the pope, always remained more independent of royal authority.

As colonial trade grew, the Crown promulgated strict regulations on the flow of goods to and from the Indies. Commerce was funneled through Spain's inland port of Seville (and after 1717 Cádiz) and licensed ports in the Indies.[29] From 1561 all trade went in legally sanctioned annual convoys (*flotas y galeones*) dispatched from Seville to designated locations, where trade fairs (at Veracruz, Cartagena, and Portobelo) were held to exchange European wares for colonial products, particularly silver from the mines in New Spain and Peru.[30] Merchant guilds (*consulados*) in Seville, Mexico City, and Lima regulated commercial transactions in the transatlantic trade between Spain and the Indies. In short, by the first decade of the seventeenth century, the turbulent early years of the Spanish invasion and conquest of the New World gave way to a more stable colonial political, economic, and religious order.

From the early seventeenth century, commerce was organized around a series of internal regional markets connected to the emerging economy of the Atlantic world. The introduction of European-style market exchanges began slowly, but the discovery of gold and particularly of silver led to an accelerated expansion and integration of regional market economies by the late sixteenth century. The historian James Lockhart has used the railroad metaphor of "trunk lines and feeder lines" to describe this expanding network of colonial markets and their links to the wider world.[31] In railroads, the central transportation route is called the trunk line, with smaller, subsidiary feeder lines connected to it. In much the same way, in New Spain the principal avenue for market exchanges, or trunk line, extended through the port city of Veracruz to Puebla and Mexico City. It then moved northward to the major mining districts, particularly Zacatecas. Feeder lines proceeded southward to Oaxaca and Guatemala, east to the Yucatán, and west to Acapulco. In the Viceroyalty of Peru the trunk line was more abstract. It went from the viceregal capital of Lima, first by sea to Arica, and then inland through Arequipa and the populous indigenous zones of Bolivia to its terminus at the famous silver mines at the "red mountain" of Potosí. Feeder lines extended north to Quito, south to Chile, and east to Cusco. The produce of economic exchanges along the Peruvian trunk and feeder lines was then shipped by sea to Panama and carried by river and overland across the Isthmus to Portobelo on the Caribbean. In this way, the goods produced in the Pacific trading zone became a vital component in the Spanish Atlantic system.[32] It was an awkward series of trade routes that paid little attention to geographical realities or economic rationality, particularly the Peruvian trading system. Nonetheless, it made sense to mercantilists in Spain, seeking to control markets, to maximize wealth (particularly bullion) and to keep out their European rivals (the Dutch, French, and English). Any Spanish or indigenous communities located along the trunk line became progressively drawn into market exchanges, while those on the smaller, subsidiary feeder lines took longer to feel the influence of the new economic order.

III. The Mature Colonial Order, 1610–1740

After the turbulent conquest era, the Spanish Atlantic system underwent a long period of expansion and consolidation. By 1610 Spaniards had subjugated the major Amerindian populations, ended the disruptive civil wars among the conquistadors in South America, and imposed an extensive imperial bureaucracy to ensure their dominance. The era of epidemics that had decimated the indigenous peoples slowly passed, and by the 1650s most Amerindian populations had begun to recover. Immigration from Europe continued, and a stratified Spanish society was transplanted to the New World.[33] Ever larger numbers of African slaves were imported to work in the cities, in placer gold mining, and in burgeoning plantation economies. The expansion of a market economy continued apace, as the nexus of trunk and feeder lines grew steadily and became ever more complex. Silver mining still predominated in the central regions, but colonial economies became more diverse and self-sufficient. Intercolonial trade links in legal and contraband goods expanded throughout the Indies, extending even to Spanish holdings in the Philippines and from there to China. The primitive conquest economy based on the *encomienda* and mining gave way to a more stable, self-sufficient economic order in the Spanish Atlantic system.

While the mature period produced evolutionary changes in the Indies, it was a time of war, defeat, and decline in Europe for the metropolis. Following the assertive imperialism of Philip II (1556–1598), his son and successor, King Philip III (1598–1621), made few changes in the Spanish Atlantic system. During his reign there was peace and retrenchment in Europe, while tax remittances and commerce with the Indies remained substantial. With the accession of Philip IV (1621–1665), however, Spain pursued a more active, militant policy in Europe, leading to a series of expensive foreign wars. Given that silver remittances from the Indies had begun a century-long decline, the Crown was forced to finance its European wars by a ruinous set of policies—borrowing from foreign and domestic bankers, debasing royal currencies, and selling public offices throughout the empire. By 1640 Spain was on the verge of bankruptcy and collapse, particularly after Catalonia and Portugal revolted against Castilian domination.[34] Although the Portuguese ultimately prevailed and won their independence, the Catalans were forced to remain under Habsburg control. Nevertheless, Spain suffered defeat on sea and on land at the hands of its rivals, the Dutch and French. During the reign of the inept Charles II (1665–1700) the metropolis continued its overall decline. After Charles II died childless in 1700, the situation only worsened during the War of the Spanish Succession, when Austrian Habsburg and French Bourbon armies and their Spanish partisans fought to determine which claimant would replace the last of the Spanish Habsburg dynasty. Although the Bourbon candidate prevailed by 1713 and was crowned as Philip V (1700–1746), Spain remained politically divided and economically prostrate.[35]

The Crown bureaucracy in the Indies underwent significant changes amid this turmoil in the metropolis. The fiscally strapped Spanish Crown began systematically selling appointments for most key bureaucratic posts (treasury offices in 1633, *corregimientos* by 1678, *audiencia* judgeships in 1687, and even the viceregal thrones by 1700). This policy allowed creoles (people of European descent born in the Indies) to purchase key posts, even in their own cities and towns, thus giving locals the opportunity to gain unprecedented political clout.[36] Corruption, graft, and influence peddling abounded as the new venal officeholders enriched themselves and their allies at the expense of the embattled European metropolis. Nonetheless, empowering these creole elites did little to better the lot of the great mass of Amerindian, African, and mixed-blood peoples in the Indies, who occupied the lowest positions in the colonial socioeconomic order.

Colonial law came to reflect the rising influence of local power brokers in the Spanish Indies. After the conquest of the Americas, Castilian law formed the foundation of the colonial legal system, but by 1614 the Crown decreed that only legislation formulated specifically for the New World would have the force of law. Both Crown officials and local settlers played a role in the creation of this discrete body of law (*derecho indiano*). According to *derecho indiano*, public officials throughout the Indies had the prerogative (*arbitrio judicial*) to resist or delay the imposition of any controversial laws, whenever they felt that new legislation violated local customs or notions of justice and the common good. Colonial officials never administered justice by adhering mechanically to written laws, but constantly exercised their *arbitrio judicial* to forge compromises between royal objectives and local ideas about proper custom and communal fairness. As Crown power declined and venal officeholders took power, they could manipulate these provisions in the law to advance local or regional interests over the needs of the Crown. Indeed, by the eighteenth century, this tension between peninsular and colonial conceptions of justice had produced a colonial legal system that was often quite distinct from that of Castile.[37]

As racial and ethnic diversity in the empire advanced, Crown authorities and Spanish settlers tried to impose rigid social hierarchies with Europeans at the apex. Nonetheless, this hegemony was always imperfect, and the rising amount of racial mixing made for a diverse colonial social and cultural landscape. Europeans continued to emigrate to the Indies, African slaves were imported in larger numbers to supplement indigenous laborers, and the recovery of the Amerindian population from epidemic diseases all promoted great racial and ethnic diversity. European rule had not destroyed indigenous and African culture in the Indies; instead, they became "mutually entangled," producing a complex and constantly evolving mixture that varied over time and across geographical space. In the Caribbean and coastal regions of New Spain and Peru, African and European cultures intermingled, while in the central regions of both viceroyalties, European, indigenous, and mestizo (mixed European and Amerindian blood) influences remained strong.

The Roman Catholic Church had converted millions of Amerindians and African slaves and freedmen since the sixteenth century. As priests and friars introduced the rituals of their faith, indigenous and African converts eagerly embraced the elaborate rites of Roman Catholicism—veneration of the cross and other devotional objects, cults of saints, ornate churches, and the ritual use of music, dances, and prayer. African émigrés and indigenous converts also formed lay brotherhoods, which added social cohesion to their communities. Despite these successes, Catholic authorities found persistent signs of enduring pre-Christian religious practices. In response, some churchmen in the Andes initiated systematic efforts to uncover and extirpate all deviant religious practices among highland indigenous peoples during the seventeenth century.[38] Although clerical authorities experienced frustration over the incomplete "spiritual conquest" of the New World, they differed between those who considered all "pagan" beliefs an apostasy deserving harsh punishment, and those who saw the problem as "religious error," which could most effectively be countered by gentle persuasion and education. Nonetheless, the widespread acceptance of Church rituals and popular devotions (however unorthodox) demonstrated the inroads made by Roman Catholicism in the Indies. The Spanish Atlantic remained essentially a Roman Catholic world where religious toleration was considered a dangerous sign of social disorder.

During the years from 1610 to 1740, growing economic diversification in the Spanish Indies prompted a series of realignments in the simple network of trunk and feeder lines that had emerged during the sixteenth century. Silver mining remained the cornerstone of the Spanish Atlantic economy, but as production stabilized in New Spain and declined in South America (particularly at Potosí), investment capital increasingly flowed to other prosperous economic sectors, such as agriculture, grazing, manufacturing, and artisan production.[39] Population centers shifted and commercial exchanges became more widespread as feeder lines extended into regions that had been transitional or frontier zones a century earlier. Provinces such as Guanajuato and Guadalajara in New Spain emerged as prosperous market centers, and in South America economic growth in Chile to the south, Buenos Aires to the southeast, and Colombia and Venezuela to the north saw the extension of a more complex network of feeder lines into these regions, often only tangentially tied to the original trunk lines emanating from Mexico City and Lima. Although these regional economies experienced cycles of growth and contraction, the overall trend was toward greater self-sufficiency and diversification.

By the 1660s, the Spanish commercial system of *flotas y galeones* began to break down. The intervals between fleet sailings became longer as mining production slowed, Spain's economy faltered, local economies diversified, and trade in contraband goods expanded. Moreover, between the Treaty of Wesphalia in 1648 (ending the Thirty Years' War) and the Treaty of Utrecht in 1713 (ending the War of the Spanish Succession), Spain's European rivals forced her to accept a series of commercial concessions.[40] These treaties allowed the English, Dutch, and French to control more legal commerce in silver by providing trade goods and capital to Spanish merchants trading through Seville and later Cádiz. Indeed, these Spanish merchants became mere front men (*presta nombres*) for merchants based in England, the Netherlands, or France. The treaties also recognized Spain's enemies' right to hold strategic Caribbean bases, which became centers for contraband commerce to the Spanish Indies. The British gained the right to supply slaves to the Spanish Atlantic after Utrecht, which they used to flood the Caribbean with illicit trade goods, while French contrabandists plied the Pacific with impunity in the first thirty years of the eighteenth century. Meanwhile, colonial traders from throughout the Indies exchanged goods illegally, which further undermined the Spanish commercial system. The Madrid government made repeated attempts to rejuvenate the fleet system, but to no avail. In 1740 the Crown finally abandoned the system of *flotas y galeones* (except for New Spain), relying on individual sailings of legally registered ships from Cádiz to licensed ports in the Indies.[41] While the Crown tried to maintain a more "closed" commercial system, by the 1740s it was increasingly porous.

IV. Reform, Resistance, and the End of the Spanish Atlantic System, 1740–1825

When Philip V surveyed his war-torn patrimony at the end of the War of the Spanish Succession in 1713, the pressing need for reform was obvious. Under Philip and his son and successor, Ferdinand VI (1746–1759), Spanish reformers attempted to curb contraband commerce, regain control over transatlantic trade, modernize state finances, establish political control within the empire, end the sale of bureaucratic appointments, and fill the depleted royal coffers. The first great wave of reform under King Ferdinand's minister, the Marqués de la Ensenada, ended in 1754 when a combination of corrupt bureaucrats in Cádiz, the entrenched merchant community (centered in the Cádiz merchant guild), and their powerful foreign allies combined to halt the reforming impulse and topple Ensenada from power.

During the reign of King Charles III (1759–1788) the reforming impulse regained momentum, particularly after Havana fell to the English in 1762.

The loss of this major Caribbean stronghold forced King Charles and his advisers in Madrid to shore up defenses in the Indies. The expenses incurred with higher defense outlays prompted the Crown to tighten administrative controls and raise taxes throughout the empire. It also required more systematic efforts to curtail contraband commerce and the control exercised by foreign merchants over legal trade within the empire. In short, the Crown sponsored a major effort to rethink the nexus of political, economic, social, and religious relationships within the Spanish Atlantic system and to initiate policies aimed at enhancing royal authority.

These reforms were strongly influenced by intellectual currents in Europe associated with the Enlightenment, which began in northern Europe and spread throughout the Euro–Atlantic world. During the eighteenth century, Madrid was a cosmopolitan capital city where ideas from Europe and the Indies continuously intersected. In the Indies, Enlightenment ideas spread through the universities, the creation of new magazines and pamphlets, and the visits of educated foreign travelers to the empire.[42] In renovating the Spanish Atlantic system, reformers attempted to use "enlightened," scientific, rationalist thought to present specific proposals for the renewal of the empire.[43] At the same time, creoles, Crown bureaucrats, Spanish travelers to America, and elite indigenous intellectuals all developed their own proposals for renovating the Spanish Atlantic system. In 1749, for example, a mestizo member of the Franciscan order, Fray Calixto de San José Túpac Inka, wrote a memorial to the king complaining about abuses of the colonial order in Peru. As remedies, he called for the end of forced labor drafts (*mita*), and demanded that Andeans obtain appointments as *corregidores* and be eligible for the priesthood, receive access to schooling, and serve in a new tribunal (composed of Spanish, mestizo, and Andean leaders that would be independent of the viceroy and the *audiencias*) to set policy for the viceroyalty. Although the Crown decided not to act on these recommendations, later reformist politicians under Charles III, such as the Marqués de Esquilache, the Conde de Floridablanca, Pedro Rodríguez Campomanes, and José de Gálvez pulled together ideas from throughout Europe and also from the empire to fashion concrete proposals for making the Spanish Atlantic system more closed to outside economic influences and more firmly under metropolitan control.

Charles III and his ministers began the reform process by dispatching royal inspectors (*visitadores*) to various parts of the Indies to gain information and to initiate administrative, fiscal, military, and commercial changes. After ending the sale of appointments to all high-ranking colonial offices by 1750, for example, the Crown began replacing creole officeholders with younger, well-trained, peninsular-born bureaucrats loyal to the Crown. Officials in Madrid also created two new viceroyalties in formerly peripheral regions of South America which had evolved into centers of contraband trade. The Madrid government established the Viceroyalty of New Granada (present-day Ecuador, Colombia, and Venezuela) in 1739, even before Charles III had acceded to the throne, and in 1776 created the Viceroyalty of the Río de la Plata (current-day Argentina, Bolivia, Paraguay, and Uruguay). Both reforms enlarged the local bureaucracy, which effectively decreased the inflow of contraband goods and the illicit outflow of silver through the Caribbean and the South Atlantic. In many areas of the empire the Crown also sent out a series of intendants (an innovation modeled on the French Bourbons) who were responsible for administration, fiscal affairs, justice, and defense.[44] These new officials linked provincial officials with *audiencias* in the major cities. The government strengthened local defenses, enlarged the fleet, built up the regular army, and formed local disciplined militia regiments, composed largely of local colonial citizens. To pay for these costly reforms, royal officials raised new taxes, collected key levies more effectively, and created royal monopolies for the sale and distribution of important goods, such as tobacco. It was a time of sweeping imperial changes.

After ending the transatlantic fleet system (except for New Spain) in 1740, the sailings of individual registered ships increased the volume of trade across the Spanish Atlantic system, but contraband and foreign control over legal trade networks continued to trouble reformers. In 1765 the government of the Marqués de Esquilache freed up colonial trade by extending imperial free trade (*comercio libre*) for Spain's Caribbean islands. This policy galvanized the opponents of reform (particularly British and French merchants and their allies among the Cádiz merchant guild), who conspired to topple Esquilache after a popular uprising in Madrid in 1766.[45] Despite the fall of Esquilache, the debate over commercial reform continued, reaching its zenith with the extension of imperial free trade throughout the empire in 1778, except for New Spain (which received the privilege in 1789).

Among the earliest reforms in the eighteenth century were attempts to regulate the power of the Roman Catholic Church. The Crown was alarmed by the proliferation of monasteries and convents in colonial cities, and by 1717 had issued laws prohibiting the foundation of any new religious institutions or hospitals without approval from Madrid. The most serious attack on the Church, however, occurred in 1753, when the Crown ordered that all parishes administered by the religious orders be transferred to the secular clergy.[46] This deprived the regular clergy of lucrative parishes that they had administered, often since the conquest era, and it was a serious blow to their finances and prestige. The Crown followed this measure in 1767 by expelling the wealthy and independent-minded Society of Jesus from Spain and its possessions. The Jesuits had been favored by the Crown until the accession of Charles III, but the king's suspicions about the order were confirmed when the Society of Jesus was allegedly implicated in fomenting the popular riot in 1766, which had toppled the Marqués de Esquilache and forced King Charles to flee Madrid.[47] The Crown further limited the power of local clergymen by issuing the Royal Pragmatic on Marriages (1776 in Spain and 1778 in the Indies), which allowed fathers, not priests, to approve marriages when the partners were not deemed to be of equal social standing.[48] Finally, the Crown issued two economically devastating edicts in 1798 (in Spain) and in 1804 (in the Indies) ordering the sale of Church properties, with the proceeds going to the Crown in exchange for annuities paying three percent interest on the value of the expropriated properties. Although the Spanish Atlantic system remained Roman Catholic, the power of the institutional Church was slowly subordinated to the Bourbon state.

While the Bourbon reforms in the Spanish Atlantic world dramatically increased Crown revenues and enhanced colonial commerce, they also produced specific grievances in the Indies. Merchants in former monopoly centers, such as Cádiz, Mexico City, and Lima, saw their commercial primacy undercut by the establishment of imperial free trade between 1765 and 1789. Even elites in the new viceregal capitals of Santa Fé de Bogotá and Buenos Aires resented increased imperial controls over contraband trade and the influx of peninsular Spaniards, who dominated local politics and commerce. Petty merchants and indigenous groups also suffered as traditional trade routes were disrupted by the establishment of new political units, such as the Viceroyalty of the Río de la Plata, and more effective tax collection. Stopping the sale of bureaucratic appointments also ended a long era of creole political empowerment. In short, many lost power and prestige with the introduction of Bourbon innovations.

In some areas of South America this unrest exploded into violent and bloody upheavals. The Rebellion of the Barrios in Quito in 1765 and the Comunero Revolt in New Granada in 1781 resulted from anger over rising fiscal burdens following reforms of the sales tax and royal monopolies.[49] Even more serious were indigenous-led rebellions in South America by Tómas Katari (north of Potosí), Túpac Amaru (in the Cusco region), and Túpac Katari (around La Paz), which nearly ended Spanish authority in the Andean highlands between 1781 and 1783.[50] Among the common grievances in these rebellions were corruption and the abuses of local Spanish officials (frequently surrounding the forced distribution of European merchandise, called the *repartimiento de comercio*), local economic pressures associated with increased taxes, millennarian movements calling for a return of the Inca Empire, and jurisdictional disputes prompted by Bourbon innovations in the provinces. Although Spanish authorities put down these rebellions, colonial discontent appeared anew with the outbreak of European wars in the 1790s, which disrupted transatlantic trade and local economies throughout the Spanish Atlantic system.

Metropolitan authority within the Spanish Atlantic system, although shaken, endured until Napoleon Bonaparte's army invaded the Iberian Peninsula in 1807 to attack Portugal, a close ally of Great Britain, the French emperor's bitter foe. Napoleon forced the Spanish monarch, Charles IV, to abdicate on May 5, 1808, and his heir, Ferdinand, to renounce his rights to the throne. Both men were kept as captives in France, and Napoleon placed his elder brother, Joseph, on the Spanish throne. The invasion and the abdication of the king and his heir led to a massive popular uprising against the French usurper, which spread throughout the peninsula. This tumult in Spain promoted a serious constitutional crisis in the Indies, where many creoles believed that without a legitimate monarch, power reverted to the people. As a result, creole elites felt emboldened to establish provincial councils (*juntas*) in major cities of the Indies, usually to rule until a legitimate monarch or stable government was restored in Spain. Meanwhile, in the metropolis, Liberals favoring a constitutional monarchy rallied to form a provisional government in Cádiz, where they wrote and promulgated the Constitution of 1812. This document not only put constraints on Crown power, but also extended the vote and rights of citizenship to people in the Indies, including Amerindians.[51] Spanish armies crushed most local *juntas* in the Indies, and when Ferdinand VII returned to the throne in 1814, he suppressed the Liberal government in Cádiz and dispatched more royal armies in a futile attempt to finish off any local resistance in the Indies. This effort only intensified the bloody wars in the Indies between the royalists and creole nationalists, which culminated in the independence of Mexico and Central America by 1822 and of South America by 1825.

Independence destroyed the Spanish Atlantic system, but it did not lay the foundations for peace and prosperity. Spain was divided by conflicts between Liberals and Conservatives, and this political instability retarded economic development for decades. Things were even more dismal in the former Spanish Indies. As the political apparatus of colonialism slowly collapsed between 1808 and 1825, colonial market economies, ordered into a complicated series of trunk and feeder lines, unraveled. Regions united by market ties and the colonial state apparatus—whether oriented for export or for local and regional consumption—broke apart as political, economic, and social disorder in the various regions of the Indies impeded the formation of stable national states. Divisions among colonial elites further undermined national unity, and regional political warlords (called *caudillos*) became political arbiters among competing national, regional, and local interest groups. Regionalism, not nationalism, characterized much of the post-independence era in Latin American nations, leading to endemic strife and instability for much of the nineteenth century. During this period of unrest, independent Latin American nations were less well integrated into the Atlantic world until the second half of the nineteenth century, when commercial ties with Europe and later the United States drew these republics directly into a new, even stronger Atlantic commercial system.

V. Conclusion: Historians and the Spanish Atlantic System

From its foundation in the late fifteenth century until its dissolution in the 1820s, the Spanish Atlantic system was united by an imperial bureaucracy, ongoing commercial exchanges, and the movement and mixture of peoples from all four continents surrounding the Atlantic Ocean. It was an immensely varied agglomeration of landscapes, climates, disease environments, cultures, languages, and customs. The Spanish Atlantic was infinitely more diverse than the Mediterranean world that Fernand Braudel identified in his pathbreaking two-volume opus, yet it also had unifying networks of political, economic, and social cohesion.[52] After the first violent encounters between the Spanish invaders and the Amerindian peoples, a series of profound changes altered indigenous modes of production, technology, commerce, politics, social hierarchies, patterns of diet and disease, and religion. The forced migration of African slaves only added to ethnic and cultural complexity in the Spanish Atlantic system. At the same time, African and Amerindian peoples managed to incorporate these changes into their own political, social, and religious practices, producing a constantly evolving mixture that was neither Spanish, nor indigenous, nor African. Spanish notions of wealth, for example, led to intensive mining of precious metals, commercial agriculture, and the introduction of new foodstuffs and animals, which transformed the Indies in significant ways over three centuries. At the same time, indigenous food products (such as chocolate, potatoes, and tobacco) and cultural practices also reshaped creole and European life ways. In this sense, the Spanish Indies represented a New World, but one tied to Europe and the wider Atlantic basin.

Studying the Spanish Atlantic system allows historians of Spain and Latin America to emphasize the interconnections of global, regional, and local processes.[53] The Atlantic perspective allows historians to examine important historical changes without regard to modern political borders, and even encourages comparisons with the Portuguese, Dutch, French, and English empires. It also highlights the differences within the Spanish Atlantic system, between the densely populated central regions and the more sparsely settled frontier zones—where Spanish rule was more insecure as various indigenous groups challenged Spain's control, along with competing European powers. Studying these frontier zones, such as Florida, Louisiana, New Mexico, and Paraguay, also has led to renewed scholarly interchanges among specialists in Spanish, Portuguese, French, and English America. Moreover, an Atlantic perspective emphasizes the world of merchants and maritime commercial exchanges, including the marginal people—sailors, pirates, innkeepers, and prostitutes—who played a role in this trade, particularly in regions such as the Caribbean. Wars connected the Spanish Atlantic world, too; conflicts in Europe often spread to America and beyond, and the commerce in slaves sometimes prompted wars among African polities. An Atlantic perspective places renewed emphasis on movement, particularly migration back and forth across the ocean. In addition, it brings greater scholarly attention to the role of Africa in the Atlantic world, demonstrating the central role of the slave trade and the lives of enslaved and free Africans living in the Indies. In short, an Atlantic perspective encourages scholars of Spain and Latin America to explore a wide range of topics and relationships and to see old problems from different perspectives.

Despite these possibilities, historians of early modern Latin America have displayed a more limited interest in an Atlantic perspective than colleagues studying the British Atlantic.[54] Since the 1970s, scholars of colonial Latin America have emphasized local or regional studies of urban and rural groups (such as merchants, *encomenderos*, artisans, women, and, to a lesser extent, slaves), indigenous communities and their resistance to Spanish oppression, and agricultural holdings (particularly landed estates, called *haciendas*, and plantations). These studies eschew a Eurocentric approach to Latin American history, preferring to examine both elites and common people from a local or regional vantage point. Historians of early modern Latin America have devised innovative methods and examined an array of sources to study these groups, drawing inspiration from anthropology, cultural studies, art history, and philology. Nonetheless, this scholarship seldom attempts to connect local or regional communities to the wider Atlantic world. Likewise, scholars studying ordinary people—artisans, petty traders, innkeepers, small farmers, Amerindian miners, slaves, and poor Spaniards or mestizos eking out a living in urban areas—have found it difficult to link their everyday lived experiences to broader structural changes occurring in the Atlantic world.[55]

Studying the huge Spanish Atlantic system is a daunting task, made more complicated by the problem of perspective: the Atlantic world looks very different, for example, from large capital cities, such as Lima or Mexico City, than from frontier cities such as New Orleans or Asunción. Atlantic commercial connections are also very influential in the lives of some social groups, such as merchants or sailors, but less important in the lives of many ordinary people on the frontiers who seldom took part in long-range market exchanges. Nonetheless, it is inescapable that the Spanish invasion and conquest of the Indies introduced profound economic, political, and social changes. It displaced thousands of Amerindian corvée laborers each year from their home communities to work in silver mines, such as Potosí; uprooted generations of Africans to serve as slave laborers; and rearranged or established new market exchanges throughout the Indies, tying them to the wider Atlantic world. The incorporation of America, Africa, and Europe into a more integrated Spanish Atlantic system also led to the evangelization of millions of Amerindians and Africans by the Roman Catholic Church. In short, the Spanish Atlantic was a functional system of religious, cultural, political, social, and economic interchanges that continued for over 300 years.

Just as historians have used innovative methods and sources to examine the history of different socioeconomic groups in Spain and Latin America, so too they must devise new methodologies to examine the connections between the individuals, localities, and regions with the wider Atlantic world. The success or failure of such scholarly efforts in the next decade or two will determine how much historians of the Spanish Atlantic system will contribute to the wider field of Atlantic history.

NOTES

1. The expansion into the Indies was actually funded by Queen Isabel of Castile, and so these domains actually belonged to that kingdom. When Ferdinand and Isabel married in 1469 and consolidated their rule ten years later, the union was dynastic, and in most respects Castile and Aragon remained separate political entities until

the accession of the Bourbon king, Philip V, in 1713. As a result, most of the first conquistadors were from Castile, not Aragon. Nonetheless, for the sake of simplicity, I will use the term "Spaniard" to describe them. J. H. Elliott, *Imperial Spain, 1469–1716* (London: Penguin, 2002 [1963]), pp. 15–76; Henry Kamen, *Spain, 1469–1714: A Society of Conflict* (New York: Pearson-Longman, 2006), pp. 1–59.

2. This did not include Brazil, which by papal donation (later ratified by the Treaty of Tordesillas in 1496) was a Portuguese possession. Elliott, *Imperial Spain*, p. 63.

3. Control of the Indies also influenced the metropolis; the massive influx of American silver to fuel the imperial aspirations of the Crown in Europe provides only the most obvious example of this impact. Earl J. Hamilton, *American Treasure and the Price Revolution in Spain, 1501–1650* (Cambridge, Mass.: Harvard University Press, 1934), passim.

4. The term "Atlantic system" is drawn from Horst Pietschmann, "Introduction: Atlantic History—History Between European History and Global History," in his *Atlantic History: History of the Atlantic System, 1580–1830* (Göttingen: Vandenhoeck & Ruprecht, 2002), pp. 38–41.

5. For a survey of this literature and its contributions, see chapter 4 in this volume.

6. See Herbert Eugene Bolton, "The Epic of Greater America," *American Historical Review* 38(3) (April 1933): 448–474; Bernard Bailyn, *Atlantic History: Concepts and Contours* (Cambridge, Mass.: Harvard University Press, 2005), pp. 6–12.

7. John H. Parry, *The Spanish Seaborne Empire* (New York: Knopf, 1966); Huguette Chaunu and Pierre Chaunu, *Seville et l'Atlantique, 1504–1650*, 8 vols. (Paris: Colin, 1955–1959). A number of Spanish scholars have explored the commercial reach of the Spanish Atlantic system. A few of the most prominent examples are Antonio García Baquero González, *Cádiz y el Atlántico, 1717–1778. El comercio colonial español bajo el monopolio gaditano*, 2 vols. (Seville: Escuela de Estudios Hispano-Americanos, 1976); Enriqueta Vila Vilar, *Los Corzo y los Mañara: Tipos y arquetipos del mercader con América* (Seville: Escuela de Estudios Hispano-Americanos, 1991); Antonio-Miguel Bernal, *La financiación de la carrera de Indias (1492–1824). Dinero y crédito en el comercio colonial español con América* (Seville: Escuela de Estudios Hispano-Americanos, 1992); Lutgardo García Fuentes, *El comercio español con América, 1650–1700* (Seville: Diputación Provincial de Sevilla, 1980); Pablo Emilio Pérez-Mallaína Bueno, *Los hombres del océano. Vida cotidiana de los tripulantes de las flotas de India, siglo XVI* (Seville: Escuela de Estudios Hispano-Americanos, 1992).

8. Philip Curtin, *The Atlantic Slave Trade: A Census* (Madison: University of Wisconsin Press, 1969), is the seminal work, but the literature on the Atlantic slave trade is immense. The most recent overview is David Eltis, *The Rise of Atlantic Slavery in the Americas* (Cambridge: Cambridge University Press, 2000). See also Stuart Schwartz, ed., *Tropical Babylons: Sugar and the Making of the Atlantic World, 1450–1680* (Chapel Hill: University of North Carolina Press, 2004).

9. For a summary of the dependency literature and the closely related world-system's paradigm, see Kenneth J. Andrien, *The Kingdom of Quito, 1690–1830: The State and Regional Development* (Cambridge: Cambridge University Press, 1995), pp. 4–7.

10. Stanley J. Stein and Barbara H. Stein, *The Colonial Heritage of Latin America: Essays on Economic Dependence in Perspective* (Oxford: Oxford University Press, 1970), passim.

11. Andrien, *The Kingdom of Quito*, p. 6.

12. Two works by Stanley J. Stein and Barbara H. Stein provide obvious examples of empirical work directly influenced by the dependency paradigm. See Stanley J. Stein and Barbara H. Stein, *Silver, Trade, and War: Spain and America in the Making of Early Modern Europe* (Baltimore: Johns Hopkins University Press, 2000); and *Apogee of Empire: Spain and New Spain in the Age of Charles III, 1759–1789* (Baltimore: Johns Hopkins University Press, 2003).

13. Anthony Pagden, *Lords of All the World: Ideologies of Empire in Spain, Britain, and France c. 1500–c. 1800* (New Haven: Yale University Press, 1995); John Robert McNeil, *Atlantic Empires of France and Spain: Louisbourg and Havana, 1700–1763* (Baltimore: Johns Hopkins University Press, 1985); Peggy K. Liss, *Atlantic Empires: The Network of Trade and Revolution* (Baltimore: Johns Hopkins University Press, 1983); Camilla Townsend, *Tale of Two Cities: Race and Economic Culture in Early Republican North and South America Guayaquil, Ecuador, and Baltimore, Maryland* (Austin: University of Texas Press, 2000); Patricia Seed, *Ceremonies of Possession: Europe's Conquest of the New World* (Cambridge: Cambridge University Press, 1995); and *American Pentimento: The Invention of Indians and the Pursuit of Riches* (Minneapolis: University of Minnesota Press, 2001). Another broadly comparative book, focusing exclusively on the Spanish Empire, is David J. Weber, *Bárbaros: Spaniards and Their Savages in the Age of the Enlightenment* (New Haven: Yale University Press, 2005).

14. J. H. Elliott, *Empires of the Atlantic World: Britain and Spain in America, 1492–1830* (New Haven: Yale University Press).

15. Peter Boyd-Bowman, *Índice geobiográfico de cuarenta mil pobladores españoles de América en el siglo XVI*, 2 vols. (Bogotá: Instituto Caro y Cuervo, 1964); Ida Altman, *Transatlantic Ties in the Spanish Empire: Brihuega Spain and Puebla Mexico, 1560–1620* (Stanford: Stanford University Press, 2000), and *Emigrants and Society: Extremadura and America in the Sixteenth Century* (Berkeley and Los Angeles: University of California Press, 1989); Alfred Crosby, *Ecological Imperialism: The Biological Expansion of Europe, 900–1900* (Cambridge: Cambridge University Press, 1986); Noble David Cook, *Born to Die: Disease and the New World Conquest, 1492–1650* (Cambridge: Cambridge University Press, 1998).

16. Jorge Cañizares Esguerra, *How to Write a History of the New World: Histories, Epistemologies, and Identities in the New World* (Stanford: Stanford University Press, 2001); see also Cañizares Esguerra's provocative comparison

of Puritans and conquistadors: *Puritan Conquistador: Iberianizing the Atlantic, 1550–1700* (Stanford: Stanford University Press, 2006).

17. Some very important recent examples are Jeremy Adelman, *Sovereignty and Revolution in the Iberian Atlantic* (Princeton: Princeton University Press, 2006); Gabriel Paquette, *Enlightenment, Governance, and Reform in Spain and Its Empire, 1759–1808* (Houndsmills, U.K.: Palgrave/Macmillan Press, 2008); Jaime Rodríguez O., *The Independence of Spanish America* (Cambridge: Cambridge University Press, 1998), and *Mexico in the Age of Democratic Revolutions, 1750–1850* (Boulder, Colo.: Lynne Reinner, 1994); and Karen Racine, *Francisco de Miranda: A Transatlantic Life in the Age of Revolution* (Wilmington, Del.: Scholarly Resources, 2003).

18. Pietschmann, *Atlantic History: History of the Atlantic System, 1580–1830*.

19. Some very recent examples of work that is reshaping methodological perspectives in the history of the Spanish Atlantic system are Rafe Blaufarb, "The Western Question: The Geopolitics of Latin American Independence," *American Historical Review* 112(3) (June 2007): 742–763; Eliga H. Gould, "Entangled Worlds: The English-Speaking Atlantic as a Spanish Periphery," *American Historical Review* 112(3) (June 2007): 764–786; Jorge Cañizares-Esguerra, "Entangled Histories: Borderland Historiographies in New Clothes," *American Historical Review* 112(3) (June 2007): 787–799; Sanjay Subrahmanyam, "Holding the World in the Balance: The Connected Histories of the Iberian Overseas Empires, 1500–1640," *American Historical Review* 112(5) (December 2007): 1329–1358; Eliga H. Gould, "Entangled Atlantic Histories: A Response from the Anglo-American Periphery," *American Historical Review* 112(5) (December 2007): 1415–1422; Jorge Cañizares-Esguerra, "The Core and Peripheries of Our National Narratives: A Response from IH-35," *American Historical Review* 112(5) (December 2007): 1423–1433.

20. After suffering indignities at the hands of the Spaniards, Manco Inca led a rebellion in 1536 that nearly recaptured Cusco and drove the Spaniards from the highlands. When his army began to disintegrate later in the year, the Sapa Inca established a rival kingdom in the remote jungle region of Vilcabamba, and his successors remained there until the Spanish captured the fortress in 1572. See John Hemming, *The Conquest of the Incas* (New York: Harcourt, Brace, 1970), pp. 189–254.

21. James Lockhart, "Trunk Lines and Feeder Lines: The Spanish Reaction to American Resources," in Kenneth J. Andrien and Rolena Adorno, eds., *Transatlantic Encounters: Europeans and Andeans in the Sixteenth Century* (Berkeley and Los Angeles: University of California Press, 1991), pp. 90–120. Some more detailed works on the social composition of the Spanish conquistadors are Lockhart, *Men of Cajamarca: A Social and Biographical Study of the First Conquistadors of Peru* (Austin: University of Texas Press, 1972); Robert Himmerich y Valencia, *The Encomenderos of New Spain, 1521–1555* (Austin: University of Texas Press, 1991); José Ignacio Avellaneda, *The Conquerors of the New Kingdom of Granada* (Albuquerque: University of New Mexico Press, 1996).

22. Elliott, *Empires of the Atlantic World, p.* 66; the characterization of the debate over the nature of the Amerindians—whether to consider them "beasts,"

"barbarians," or "brothers"—was made by J. H. Elliott in a public lecture at The Ohio State University conference "Early European Encounters with the Americas," held October 9–11, 1986.

23. Elliott, *Empires of the Atlantic World*, p. 68. The pioneering work on this topic is Lewis Hanke, *The Spanish Struggle for Justice in the Conquest of America* (Philadelphia: University of Pennsylvania Press, 1949).

24. Elliott, *Empires of the Atlantic World*, pp. 76–77.

25. Woodrow Borah and Sherburne Cook, *The Aboriginal Population of Mexico on the Eve of the Spanish Conquest* (Berkeley and Los Angeles: University of California Press, 1963), passim.

26. The orders were called "regular clergy" because they lived according to the rules or *regula* established by the founder of the order. In Europe the religious orders most commonly lived communally in religious houses or monasteries. Charles Gibson, *Spain in America* (New York: Harper & Row, 1966), p. 77.

27. In contrast to the religious orders, the secular clergy ministered directly to the laity or sa*eculum*, and they were subject to the authority of the local bishop. The secular clergy were composed of the hierarchy of bishops, the cathedral chapters, and the parish clergy. The archbishoprics of Lima in Peru and Mexico City in New Spain were the central seats of clerical power in the New World. Gibson, *Spain in America*, p. 77.

28. The pope granted these privileges in two concessions, in 1501 and in 1503. See Clarence Haring, *The Spanish Empire in America* (New York: Harcourt, Brace, and World, 1952), pp. 167–170.

29. By the early eighteenth century the buildup of silt in the Guadalquivir River at Seville made it difficult for larger oceangoing vessels to reach the port, so the Crown gave Cádiz the right to monopolize Atlantic trade with the Indies. The merchant guild moved from Seville to Cádiz. Haring, *Spanish Empire in America*, p. 302.

30. The fleets seldom sailed annually, and by the early eighteenth century the intervals between fleets could be more than a decade. See Geoffrey Walker, *Spanish Politics and Imperial Trade, 1700–1789* (Bloomington: Indiana University Press, 1979).

31. Lockhart, "Trunk Lines and Feeder Lines," pp. 90–120.

32. The trade with the Far East through Manila was only tangentially related to the Atlantic trade, but one recent study of the volume of American silver passing to Asia indicates that it became increasingly important over time. See William Schell, Jr., "Silver Symbiosis: ReOrienting Mexican Economic History," *Hispanic American Historical Review* 81(1) (February 2001): 89–133.

33. James Lockhart, *Spanish Peru, 1532–1560: A Colonial Society* (Madison: University of Wisconsin Press, 1968).

34. Portugal was united with Spain in 1580 when the childless King Sebastian was killed in an ill-fated military crusade in Africa. The crown passed to Philip II of Spain, and Portugal remained part of a dynastic union with Spain until its revolt

in 1640. Elliott, *Imperial Spain*, pp. 266, 341–346; Kamen, *Spain, 1469–1714*, pp. 126, 241–243.

35. Henry Kamen has argued that Spain had begun a recovery during the reign of Charles II and that the War of the Spanish Succession did not produce as much economic dislocation as other historians have argued. Henry Kamen, *Spain in the Later Seventeenth Century* (London and New York: Longman Press, 1980), and *The War of the Succession in Spain, 1700–1715* (Bloomington: Indiana University Press, 1969).

36. Kenneth J. Andrien, *Crisis and Decline: The Viceroyalty of Peru in the Seventeenth Century* (Albuquerque: University of New Mexico Press, 1985), pp. 103–129; and Mark A. Burkholder and D. S. Chandler, *From Impotence to Authority: The Spanish Crown and the American Audiencias, 1687–1808* (Columbia: University of Missouri Press, 1977), passim.

37. Charles Cutter, *The Legal Culture of Northern New Spain, 1700–1810* (Albuquerque: University of New Mexico Press, 1995), pp. 30–36.

38. Kenneth Mills, *Idolatry and Its Enemies: Colonial Andean Religion and Extirpation, 1640–1750* (Princeton: Princeton University Press, 1997); Nicholas Griffiths, *The Cross and the Serpent: Religious Repression and Resurgence in Colonial Peru* (Norman: University of Oklahoma Press, 1996); Juan Carlos Estenssoro Fuchs, *Del paganismo a la santidad: La incorporación de los indios del Perú al Catolicismo, 1532–1750* (Lima: IFEA, 2003). An interesting discussion of an earlier controversy over evangelization in New Spain is Inga Clendinnen, *Ambivalent Conquests: Maya and Spaniard in the Yucatan, 1517–1570* (Cambridge: Cambridge University Press, 1987).

39. The figures for silver production have been dramatically revised by two historians relying on Dutch gazettes; they argue that silver production peaked at the end of the seventeenth century. See Michel Morineau, *Incroyables gazettes et fabuleux métaux: Les retours des trésors américains d'après les gazettes hollandaises (XVI–XVIII sièles)* (London and Paris: Cambridge University Press/Editions de la Maison des Sciences de l'Homme, 1985); and Kamen, *Spain in the Later Seventeenth Century*, pp. 113–152. These figures are much contested among scholars in the field.

40. Stein and Stein, *Silver, Trade, and War*, pp. 57–105.

41. Ibid, pp. 180–199.

42. John Tate Lanning, *Academic Culture in the Spanish Colonies* (Oxford: Oxford University Press, 1940).

43. Kenneth J. Andrien, "The *Noticias secretas de América* and the Construction of a Governing Ideology for the Spanish American Empire," *Colonial Latin American Review* 7(2) (1998): 175–192.

44. By 1714 the Crown began to bypass the Council of the Indies by setting up the Ministry of Marine and the Indies (*Secretaría de Marina e Indias*). By 1721 this ministry handled virtually all matters relating to political appointments, war, finance, commerce, and navigation. In 1787 King Charles III created a second ministerial portfolio with special responsibilities over justice and civil and judicial appointments (*gracia y justicia*). Both of these posts were abolished in 1790, however,

when the Crown reformed the ministerial portfolios once again, integrating their functions into five Spanish ministries that each exercised authority over the Indies within its jurisdiction. The Crown also began to establish intendancies in Spain by 1711. Haring, *Spanish Empire in America*, p. 107; John Lynch, *Bourbon Spain, 1700–1808* (Oxford: Blackwell, 1989), pp. 63–65.

45. Stein and Stein, *Apogee of Empire, pp. 82–115.*

46. The Crown began by ordering the secularization of parishes in the archdioceses of Lima, Santa Fé de Bogotá, and Mexico City in 1749, and in 1753 extended it throughout the empire. D. A. Brading, "Tridentine Catholicism and Enlightened Despotism in Bourbon Mexico," *Journal of Latin American Studies* 15(1) (May 1983): 9; William B. Taylor, *Magistrates of the Sacred: Priests and Parishioners in Eighteenth-Century Mexico* (Stanford: Stanford University Press, 1996), pp. 83–86, 506–510.

47. Lynch, *Bourbon Spain*, pp. 280–284.

48. Ann Twinam, *Public Lives, Private Secrets: Gender, Honor, Sexuality, and Illegitimacy in Colonial Spanish America* (Stanford: Stanford University Press), pp. 18–20.

49. See Anthony McFarlane, "The Rebellion of the Barrios: Urban insurrection in Bourbon Quito," *Hispanic American Historical Review* 49 (May 1989): 283–330; Kenneth J. Andrien, "Economic Crisis, Taxes, and the Quito Insurrection of 1765," *Past and Present* 129 (November 1990): 104–131; John Leddy Phelan, *The People and the King: The Comunero Rebellion in Colombia, 1781* (Madison: University of Wisconsin Press, 1978).

50. Sinclair Thomson, *We Alone Shall Rule: Native Andean Politics in the Age of Insurgency* (Madison: University of Wisconsin Press, 2002); Ward Stavig, *The World of Túpac Amaru: Conflict, Community, and Identity in Colonial Peru* (Lincoln: University of Nebraska Press, 1999); and Sergio Serulnikov, *Subverting Colonial Authority: Challenges to Spanish Colonial Rule in Eighteenth-Century Southern Andes* (Durham, N.C.: Duke University Press, 2003).

51. Rodríguez O., *Independence in Spanish America*, pp. 75–106.

52. Fernand Braudel, *The Mediterranean and the Mediterranean World in the Age of Philip II*, 2 vols., trans. Sian Reynolds (New York: Harper & Row), passim.

53. An important survey of Atlantic history is Alison Games, "Atlantic History: Definitions, Challenges, and Opportunities," *American Historical Review* 111(3) (June 2006): 741–756.

54. The one outstanding exception is the work of John Lynch, particularly his pioneering and highly influential study, *Spain Under the Habsburgs*, 2 vols. (Oxford: Basil Blackwell, 1968).

55. As Braudel indicates in his three-volume world history, the vast majority of people in the early modern world lived and died without being drawn into market exchanges of significance, let alone participating in vibrant long-distance trade across the Atlantic. See Fernand Braudel, *Civilization and Capitalism, 15th–18th Century, vol. 1: The Structures of Everyday Life: The Limits of the Possible*, trans. Sian Reynolds (New York: Harper & Row, 1981 ed.), passim.

3

THE PORTUGUESE ATLANTIC, 1415–1808

A. J. R. RUSSELL-WOOD

In 1415 Prince Henry, "The Navigator," participated in the capture of the Muslim city of Ceuta in Morocco, marking the beginning of a formal Portuguese presence outside continental Europe. In 1822 Brazil declared its independence from Portugal. In the intervening centuries, Portuguese navigators sailed as far north as the Arctic Circle and west of Greenland and the Labrador Sea, and pioneered southeast and southwest passages from the Atlantic to the Indian Ocean and the Pacific, respectively. The Portuguese Crown claimed sovereignty over Atlantic archipelagoes and the territories bordering the Atlantic in continental Africa and South America. Merchants created networks of trade as far north as the Baltic and as far south as Benguela and Río de la Plata. Portuguese settled islands and continents bordering the Atlantic and established towns, cities, and institutions. Portuguese became the most widely spoken European language in the Atlantic sphere. By exposing them to Christianity and slavery, Portuguese transformed the lives of millions of Amerindians and Africans.

Either of two perspectives might serve as a framework for this chapter. The first is the conventional imperial history approach, which emphasized the role, in the metropolis, of the Crown and advisory councils and legislative and regulatory institutions and, in the colonies, of Crown representatives, institutions modeled on those in the mother country, and colonial societies being analyzed in terms of their compliance with or deviation from metropolitan norms. With this approach, metropolitan interests predominated over colonial interests, colonies were essentially "milch cows" that provided raw materials for the benefit of the metropolis; colonial priorities were subordinated to metropolitan interests, loyalty to king and country and adherence to Catholic orthodoxy was the norm, and the Crown's preference for Portuguese-born over overseas-born in terms of appointments was justified.

By contrast, my approach operates over a broader conceptual canvas. Instead of focusing on communities and societies in terms of their Portugueseness, religious orthodoxy, social stratification, occupations, mores, and language, or on groups or institutions exerting social control, instead of emphasizing stability, continuity, and homogeneity, this approach views the Portuguese Atlantic from the perspective of what was occurring overseas in Africa and Brazil. While there was no Atlantic counterpart to the "shadow empire" that seems to have been present in Portuguese Asia, this extra-Portugal perspective shows that some characteristics associated with Portuguese Asia were also present in the Atlantic: complex, convoluted, and intercolonial commercial diasporas without a metropolitan component; multinational, multiethnic, and polyglot populations; a prominence of mixed-race individuals; ambiguity and ambivalence concerning color, race, social status, and individual and collective identity; and a religious life in which individuals could be concurrently devout Catholics and devout adherents to other belief systems and practices. This approach emphasizes the individual over the Crown, examining how individuals created their own spaces and led productive and prominent lives without dogged adherence to Crown or Church, or deferring to governors, magistrates, or bishops. Much occurred in the Portuguese Atlantic—commerce. movements of peoples, creation of pan-Atlantic families, settlements, economic production, and boundary crossings—despite the Crown. In this Portuguese overseas Atlantic, frontiers were blurred; perception and "quality of the person" replaced traditional metropolitan social criteria for assessing a person's standing; negotiation was more effective than mandates; charisma replaced delegated authority; lines between what was legal and illegal were blurred; and application of the letter of the law was negotiable. Transition, porosity, permeability, and elasticity characterized this other Portuguese Atlantic. The characteristics outlined above were themselves inconstant and transitory, and varied by region and period.

This historical overview of the Portuguese Atlantic spans time and space. Part 1 surveys Portuguese holdings, emphasizing activities in the archipelagoes and on the African mainland in the fifteenth and sixteenth centuries. Part 2 moves to Brazil and Angola in the seventeenth and eighteenth centuries. Part 3 has a maritime focus showing how the ocean facilitated interaction between discrete parts of the Portuguese Atlantic. Part 4 addresses what was distinctively Portuguese. Part 5 discusses the centrality of the Atlantic to continental Portugal and its overseas holdings, and how that centrality has been reflected in the historiography. It also examines the usefulness of the concept of Atlantic history for scholars of the Portuguese Atlantic and assesses what the Portuguese example can contribute to scholarship on other national Atlantics.

1. Portuguese Space in the Atlantic

In the fifteenth century, the Atlantic was a contested region. Treaties and papal bulls created a framework for Portuguese settlement in the Atlantic. The Treaty of Tordesillas (1494), fruit of binational negotiations and confirmed by the pope, divided the world along a pole-to-pole demarcation line 370 leagues west (between 48° W and 49° W) of the Cape Verde Islands. Castile could explore, trade, and conquer west of this line, and Portugal east of it. Other Europeans rejected the notion of an Iberian *mare clausum*. Like other nations and states, Portugal controlled access to ports, rivers, and estuaries in its territorial holdings in Europe and overseas, but the Atlantic remained open to all. Portuguese kings did not refer to an "Atlântico português," a term currently applied to a Portuguese presence on archipelagoes and continents whose shores are bathed by the ocean, where the Portuguese created social spaces and made an imprint on territories over which the Crown claimed sovereignty.[1]

Islands were integral to the formation and consolidation of the Portuguese in the Atlantic, playing pivotal roles in commerce and migration, becoming essential hubs in oceanic and interoceanic connections during the age of sail, and, to this day, remaining as enduring parts of a Portuguese-speaking Atlantic. To limit their importance to the "age of discoveries" is a gross misrepresentation. In the fifteenth century Portugal claimed sovereignty over four archipelagoes: the Madeiras, Azores, Cape Verdes, and São Tomé and Príncipe.[2] Portugal looked to these for agricultural products and commodities for consumption and sale in Portugal or for reexport to northern Europe, Spain, and Italy, in exchange for manufactured and other items in demand in Portugal or overseas. Strategic locations and comparative prosperity made archipelagoes targets of attacks and plunder by Europeans. All archipelagoes were also points of convergence and cultivation of plants native to the Americas, Europe, and Africa.

The Madeiras and Azores were oriented to Portugal and attractive to Portuguese emigrant couples and family groups.[3] Settlers were predominantly farmers or engaged in commerce. Madeira attracted migrants of higher social standing and with disposable income. As Madeira became overpopulated, some residents moved on to the Azores. European financiers, investors, and merchants showed great interest in these islands. An island in the Azores was known as "island of the Flemings" because of its settlers. Topography, climate, rainfall, and soil quality varied among these archipelagoes and within a single archipelago. Madeira and Porto Santo had resins, dyes from plants and trees ("dragon blood"), and woad, whose leaf gives a blue dye. Though sugar was its principal export, Madeira also produced timber, wheat, cereals, sweet grapes, and wines, and had stock farms. The Azores had similar exports: salt, grains, dyewoods, timber, cattle, sheep, and later cotton, but sugar cultivation never took off. Each archipelago and waters separating them from one another and from the African mainland were rich in fish, whales, and seals. These islands prospered in the sixteenth century as settlers created towns, populations grew, and dioceses came into being. Madeira counted a labor force made up of indigenes from the Canary Islands and individuals from the African mainland. A yardstick of the high levels of urbanization, material amenities, social and hospital services, churches, stable populations, social stratification, and financial standing was the presence in Madeira and the Azores of lay brotherhoods (of whites and blacks) and, by the 1580s, of some twenty Misericórdias.[4] On Madeira, sugar production increased until undermined by Brazilian competition in the second third of the seventeenth century. One ramification was a sharp decrease in imported slaves. Wine replaced sugar as the primary export. Funchal was a major port in Atlantic trade, but the rugged terrain and smallness of Madeira limited its growth potential. The Azores had more islands, more space for population growth, flatter terrain amenable to settlement, and soils conducive to cultivation. By the mid-sixteenth century, the archipelago boasted the cities of Angra dos Reis and Ponta Delgada and a dozen or so townships, but immigration plateaued and then declined. Azorean wheat and woad remained major contributors to the Portuguese economy, with primacy going to woad until it succumbed to American indigo. Whaling and fishing were central to settlers' lives. In the late sixteenth century wheat, wine, flax, and oranges were important exports, as was corn, indigenous to the Americas and brought to the Atlantic archipelagoes. The Azores also were the stage for technology developed specifically to overcome the by-blows of volcanic eruptions.

Five hundred kilometers off the coast of Senegal are the volcanic Cape Verde Islands (settled in the 1440s–1460s).[5] The islands were not attractive to European migrants, in part because of harsh natural conditions. The predominance of single males among immigrants created a marked gender imbalance among Europeans. Africans moved from the mainland to some of these islands, and became a majority. A mixed-race population soon came into being. African languages predominated and creole languages emerged. The archipelago was slow to develop, some islands remaining uninhabited because of aridity, prolonged droughts, torrential downpours, and soil erosion. Land, distributed in smallholdings under the terms of entailed properties inalienably associated with a family but without the potential for individual ownership, created a pattern of landholding that was a disincentive to immigration and population growth. Each island had its historical individuality, but the Crown introduced civil and ecclesiastical government in all of them, and a papal bull of 1533 authorized an episcopal see. The island of Santiago was predominant and included the major settlements of Ribeira Grande and Praia, each of which became a major urban center (Ribeira Grande was accorded the status of a city in 1533 and made a bishopric by papal bull), and were rivals as administrative capitals and ports of call until, in the eighteenth century, Ribeira Grande fell into decline and Praia grew in population and importance. Early exports included salt, grains, and orchil (a lichen producing a red dye), and indigo. Plants indigenous to Africa and America converged in the Azores with plants indigenous to Europe. Sugarcane prospered with slave labor from the mainland. A viable economy based on livestock (cattle and horses) developed, and there was self-sufficiency in foodstuffs such as meat and dairy products. Exports continued to include salt, corn, cotton, and dyes, with hides and cotton playing a major role. Whereas overall the archipelago failed as a settler colony, the island of Santiago was a success story with a vigorous economy, cottage industries, prosperous and socially prominent elites, and a *mestiço* population. But, overall, the archipelago declined economically and out-migration grew in the later seventeenth century. Its saving grace was the archipelago's location on multiple long- and short-distance oceanic routes involving networks of trade between the Iberian Peninsula, the African mainland (Upper and Lower Guinea and Angola), Brazil, and ports in the Caribbean and on the west coast of India, and as a launching point for commercial ventures and expeditions into the African interior.

In equatorial Africa, the archipelago of São Tomé and Príncipe (which included Ano Bom and Fernando Po; settled c. 1485) is in the Gulf of Guinea some 170 miles from the mainland.[6] São Tomé's first Portuguese settlers included some migrants who had left Portugal of their own volition, while the Crown dispatched others, such as children aged ten and below separated from their Jewish parents, criminals, and undesirables (Gypsies, vagabonds) whom the Crown saw as disposables. Slaves were transported from the African mainland. Miscegenation increased the island's population and created a creole *mestiço* elite. With dense forests and mountainous terrain, São Tomé offered a less disease-ridden environment than the mainland, but

Portuguese nevertheless died from diseases to which they had no immunity. By 1500 the archipelago's population may have reached 10,000. A tropical climate, two rainy seasons, fertile soil, and water to power sugar mills made São Tomé ideal for cultivation of sugarcane, especially in the northeast. Timber was a major resource. The island developed a diversified domestic economy around raising goats and cattle and growing wheat, millet, barley, figs, and olives, all brought initially from Portugal. Plants were introduced into the archipelago from the African mainland and, later, from Brazil. São Tomé was the world's largest sugar producer in the sixteenth century, then yielded to higher-quality Brazilian sugar in the first decade of the seventeenth century. A slave trade, both legal and clandestine, was largely in the hands of *mestiço* entrepreneurs, and was crucial to the islands' economies. São Tomé was a major assembly point for slaves from the Gulf of Guinea, and later from Angola, bound for the Americas. Crown permission to trade with São Jorge da Mina in the 1490s and, later, with Kongo encouraged shipbuilding.

São Tomé became the major city (1534), capital of the Crown captaincy of the same name, and residence of the governor. A papal bull of 1534 authorized an episcopal see with wide jurisdiction over the mainland from Lower Guinea southward. Seminary-educated indigenous black and mulatto clergy, as well as mission schools, made São Tomé highly influential.[7] Between the 1560s and the 1590s, French, English, and Dutch corsairs attacked São Tomé city. The population was predominantly mulatto, and women played a prominent role in the local society. Clashes between whites and mulattos and between islanders and mainlanders contributed to political and social mobility which was a constant in São Tomé's history and was exacerbated by slave revolts, *angolares* who refused to leave their fishing to work on plantations, powerful and defiant planters with their own slave militias, and constant turf battles between Crown appointees and local interests and between ecclesiastical and secular authorities. Disruption and insecurity, coupled with a declining market for São Tomense sugar, prompted some planters to migrate to Brazil. The islands of São Tomé, Príncipe, and Ano Bom reinvented themselves by provisioning slave vessels and collecting slaves along the coast from Lower Guinea to Angola, and also by stocking storehouses with ivory and ebony, commodities in high demand by merchants and traders, and saving ships' captains time in acquiring and loading cargoes. In the 1750s, Príncipe replaced São Tomé as the administrative center, residence of the governor, and major port city of the archipelago.

On the African continent, Ceuta did not become an anchor for Portuguese colonization. It was important as the place where, in economic terms,

Mediterranean Morocco met Atlantic Morocco. Portuguese kings built coastal forts and opted for garrisons peopled by soldiers and their dependents, and there developed a multicultural, multireligious, and polyglot population of artisans, merchants, and traders. Ceuta had a royal municipal charter and was an episcopal see. Portugal had minimal control of lands beyond the vicinity of forts. Whether a Portuguese presence was a waste of men and money was hotly debated. An expedition against Tangiers (1437) was a disaster, but King Afonso V (1438–1481) nonetheless advocated a continued presence. Portuguese Morocco depended on the Atlantic. Soldiers, munitions, food, beverages, and construction materials arrived by sea. Forts guaranteed access for vessels returning to Portugal with cargos of textiles, barley, wheat, honey, dates and grapes, gum arabic, wax, indigo, precious and base metals, and cattle. Portuguese merchants reexported Moroccan cereals and other commodities to northern Europe. Profit, as much as crusade, was part of the Crown agenda.

The arrival (1482/1483) of the navigator Diogo Cão at the River Zaire opened a new phase in Portuguese history. Their southward maritime trajectory had kept the Portuguese removed from centers of political power in Africa, but the kingdom of Kongo had a long coastline. The capital of the supreme ruler (*manikongo*) was accessible from the coast or river. Four Kongolese nobles visited Portugal, and Portuguese emissaries were present at the royal court. In a unique cross-cultural experiment, Portugal and Kongo exchanged embassies. Portugal dispatched missionaries, and the *manikongo*, his immediate family, and his courtiers were baptized and took Christian names. Kongolese elites adopted Portuguese dress. Intrigued by Portuguese administration and laws, the *manikongo* sent young men to Lisbon to be educated. Portugal dispatched tools and artisans, who rebuilt the capital in stone, naming it São Salvador. It was located on the central plain and renowned for its prosperity and agricultural production. Kongo also became a point of convergence of African, European, and, later, American foodstuffs.

Morocco and Kongo had points in common. In each, the Portuguese motivation for exchange was both religious and commercial. They saw in Morocco an extension to African soil of the crusade against "infidels." In Kongo, they envisioned a new mission field and the potential for coming closer to the land of the legendary Christian ruler Prester John in Ethiopia, thereby giving an Atlantic dimension to the Prester John story. They also anticipated access to precious metals and minerals. Portuguese kings supported, albeit inconsistently, such aspirations and ventures. Merchants were reluctant to follow the royal lead, and the royal exchequer largely met costs. Morocco and Kongo showed potential, but neither lived up to expectations.

Morocco contributed goods to Portuguese markets and for reexport to Europe and to West and Central Africa, thereby making African goods part of an Atlantic economy. Portuguese forts in Morocco exerted control over the Atlantic coast and a degree of regulation over the western Mediterranean. But Morocco became ever more dependent on imported wheat from Madeira and the Azores, and on military reinforcements. The Portuguese in Morocco turned their backs on the Atlantic and became preoccupied with military and political ambitions. The Treaty of Sintra (1509) resolved territorial disputes in North Africa between the Iberian nations, fort construction continued, and more local rulers accepted Portuguese suzerainty. Conquest of the kingdom of Fez opened the way to a greater Portuguese presence in the south and Atlantic southwest. The death of 4,000 Portuguese at Mamora (1515) was crucial in King João III's (1521–1557) decision to reduce a Portuguese military presence. The spirit of crusade died on the battlefield of Alcácer Quibir (1578) with the massacre of King Sebastião and much of his army. The declining importance of Morocco for Portugal had a maritime component. European nations horned in on sea routes; corsair activity increased; Ottoman Turkish fleets advanced from Egypt; and the caravan trade was undermined by Portuguese maritime commerce.[8]

In Kongo, Afonso I (*manikongo*, 1507–1543) and his successors embraced anything Portuguese. They hoped for technical and military assistance, commerce, and a political alliance. Portugal was still interested in evangelization. Misinformation about the breadth of Africa led the Portuguese to believe that they were in the vicinity of the Arabian Gulf. For them, Kongo was not only a potential partner in evangelizing Africa, repelling Ottoman Turks, and saving Christian Ethiopia, but also a way station to India. Mutual disillusionment crept in as it became apparent how different the agendas of the two rulers were, how great the behavioral and cultural abyss between the two peoples was, and how total the disconnect between Portuguese priorities and Kongolese expectations was. The Portuguese realized that Kongo had little to offer except slaves and ivory. Crucial to this realization was a Portuguese shift in priorities from evangelization to the slave trade. The slave trade between São Tomé and Ndongo, and Portuguese relations with its ruler, infuriated the *manikongo*, but the demand for slaves for Brazilian agriculture doomed reconciliation. Mpinda was the major port of the trade. Kongo may have been an early victim of the destabilizing force of the slave trade. Portuguese commitment to Kongo did not fully cease, however. In 1570–1571 a Portuguese force defeated the Jaga, who occupied São Salvador and restored it to the *manikongo*, but again abandoned it in 1678. São Salvador thrived as the place of royal residence, headquarters of the Portuguese, home to a dozen churches, and seat of the newly created (1596) diocese of Kongo and Angola. At the battle of Mbwila (1665) Portuguese troops defeated the Kongolese army and killed the king. Kongo became a sort of Portuguese protectorate. By the end of the century, São Salvador was in ruins and deserted, the victim of Dutch hostility to a Portuguese presence in Africa.[9]

As the Portuguese moved southward in the fifteenth century from Mauretania to Senegambia and Guinea, they had built forts and trading posts on the mainland or nearby islands. Prince Henry ordered missionaries to evangelize, and the Portuguese Crown claimed sovereignty over some regions. In 1486 King João II took the title of Lord of Guinea. For the Portuguese, Guinea was associated with gold dust. Hopes of reaching the source of this gold and the trans-Saharan caravan trade had encouraged kings to pursue a maritime route. When the Portuguese made the rare venture inland, they counted on the sufferance of local rulers. Small settlements and trading stations multiplied in the sixteenth and seventeenth centuries, but the number of Portuguese-born whites remained minimal. Commerce was largely in the hands of indigenous middlemen or entrepreneurs who might identify themselves as Portuguese and whose pigmentation permitted them to pass as white, though they were in fact of mixed race and better characterized as creoles. Only in the eighteenth century did skin color take on importance in terms of self-identification and identification by others.[10] São Jorge da Mina (1482) counted a nucleus of Portuguese and retained its importance until capture by the Dutch in 1637. Dutch occupation of São Tomé city (1641–1648), English attacks, and changing slave trade patterns in the Gulf of Guinea affected Lower Guinea. Despite a waning Portuguese presence, the Gulf of Guinea attracted other Europeans engaged in commerce and remained an active player in the slave trade to Brazil.

2. A Portuguese Empire in the South Atlantic

In the sixteenth century Brazil and Angola were the focus of Portuguese interests in the South Atlantic. Initial Crown reaction to Brazil was dismissive. Only in the early 1530s did the Crown allocate captaincies to twelve lords proprietor. Two succeeded, due to outstanding leadership and cultivation of sugarcane. Some donataries never came to Brazil; others lacked leadership and capital. Captaincies fell victim to Amerindian attacks and were torn by enmity between lords proprietor and settlers or by violent arguments among settlers. Barter with Amerindians gave way to slavery, few towns were established, and evangelization was minimal. Confronted by the prospect of a failed colony and, perhaps, moved by strategic considerations to establish a Crown presence in the Atlantic to counterbalance, but also to strengthen, its substantial investment and presence east of the Cape of Good Hope, the Crown in 1548 made a commitment to Portuguese America. King João III appointed a governor-general and, in 1549, established royal government in Brazil. This set in motion a process to build a capital, provide defenses, set up civil and ecclesiastical government, and promote migration, settlement, agriculture, evangelization, and "pacification" of Amerindians. The last half of the sixteenth century was decisive in grounding the new colony. Settlement occurred irregularly along the coast from the northeast to Santa Catarina in the south. São Paulo, the only inland town, owed its existence to Jesuit initiative. The Portuguese-born left exploration of the interior largely to *mestiços*, generally of European-Amerindian descent. In 1560, the Portuguese expelled the French from the Bay of Guanabara, and built ports on bays or estuaries; Salvador, Recife, and Rio de Janeiro became the "big three" ports. Cutting of timber eventually led to virtual annihilation of coastal forests, and sugar became the preferred export crop. Settlers introduced cattle, horses, and mules, and livestock took on economic importance. Papal bulls authorized episcopal sees. Jesuits established mission villages for Indians. On the whole, the secular clergy was ineffective. The first Inquisitional visitations occurred in the early 1590s, but the Holy Office was not formally established. Establishing Brazil as a viable colony took its toll in human lives. Ignoring indigenous sovereignty, during the 1570s settlers decimated Amerindians in the coastal northeast in brutal war, and others fell victim to European diseases to which they had no immunity. Enslavement of Amerindians was commonplace. A more intensive slave trade from Africa led to Amerindians and Africans working side by side on Bahian plantations in the latter part of the century.[11]

On the other side of the Atlantic, the second phase of Portuguese involvement on the African mainland focused on Ndongo in the south of the kingdom of Kongo.[12] The Portuguese name for the region—Angola—derived from *ngola* (ruler). In Africa, Portuguese were intruders into regions with established rulers and chiefs; social hierarchies; more homogeneous societies than in Upper and Lower Guinea; established patterns of trade and of weights and measures for exchange; and fearsome warriors. Initially, in the 1520s, the Portuguese strategy was low key, consisting of a trading factory, playing to the ruler's professed interest in Christianity and commercial relations, and an expedition to report on natural resources and metals. Further Portuguese initiatives failed. In 1560 the *ndongo* insulted, physically abused, and held hostage the Portuguese under Paulo Dias de Novais, outmatching his soldiers and killing Jesuits. In the meantime, the slave trade flourished. The royal decision to make Angola a Portuguese colony, by force if necessary, was crucial. In 1571 the Crown gave Paulo Dias a royal charter as hereditary proprietor and governor of Angola, and he brought in 400 settlers. This charter granted him lands and privileges to compensate him for the tasks at hand: raising a garrison, building forts, settling 100 European families, promoting agriculture, building churches, and supporting missionaries. In 1576 Dias established São Paulo de Luanda on the mainland, which Jesuits made the center of missionary efforts, only to be thwarted by high mortality. Expeditions probed the interior, but found no silver or other precious metals. Instead, the Portuguese aroused intense hostility. They suffered heavy mortality in warfare and from fever. When Dias died in 1589, he left no semblance of a balanced economy, systematic evangelization, regular colonization, or rule of law. His sole legacy was a line of fortified garrisons. In 1595, twelve white women accompanied the new governor to Angola and rapidly found spouses, but did little to alter the substantial gender imbalance among settlers. At the close of the century, Angola counted settlements in Luanda and Benguela-a-Velha on the coast and Massangano in the interior. Minimal territorial gains had been made even with the assistance of African allies. A papal bull of 1596 created the diocese of Angola and Kongo, but São Salvador, rather than Luanda, was its see. The Crown abolished the hereditary captaincy system and in 1592 appointed a governor-general of Angola.

The seventeenth and eighteenth centuries were decisive for Brazil and Central Africa.[13] Immigration to Brazil from Portugal, Madeira, and the Azores increased. A typical immigrant was male, aged seventeen to thirty-five, single, and with limited resources. Many were agricultural workers, and others were artisans. Few families came initially, but this pattern changed as Brazil gained a reputation as a land of opportunity. More families arrived, more migrants had monies to invest, and immigrant merchants married into local families. Gender balance among whites improved, albeit in 1722 a governor of Minas Gerais still bemoaned the dearth of white women of marriageable age. Crown-sponsored migration had a mixed record.

Settlement remained predominantly coastal and in pockets, rather than evenly distributed. Bands of frontiersmen (*bandeirantes*), often of Amerindian–European descent, probed the interior and far north, and were forerunners of migratory movements from the coast to the interior, to the far north and far south in the seventeenth century, and to the west in the eighteenth century. Disillusionment awaited the waves of humanity descending on Brazil in the seventeenth and eighteenth centuries, but artisans, especially those in building trades, tailors, shoemakers, and even hatters, were in constant demand. The makeup of the population—Amerindians, Portuguese, Africans and Afro-Brazilians, and persons of mixed race—varied greatly, depending on period, region, and prevailing economies in Brazil, events within Africa, and markets in Europe. Colony-wide assessments remain, at best, informed estimates. Brazil's Amerindian population in 1500 has been put at 2,431,000. Excluding Amerindians, Brazil's population was about 30,000 in 1600, 300,000 by 1700, 2 million in 1776, and about 3 million in 1808. At the end of the colonial period, over 90 percent of Indians still lived outside settled areas.

In the seventeenth and eighteenth centuries, settlers established towns and cities in greater numbers, including the larger ports of Belém do Pará and São Luis do Maranhão, and coastal and inland towns. Many settlements remained isolated. In the eighteenth century, mining encampments grew into towns, and the Crown created captaincies in Minas Gerais, São Paulo, Goiás, and Mato Grosso, each with its own governor, to bring law and order to the west. These centuries saw an influx of friars and the building of monasteries. The first convent dated from 1677. A papal bull of 1676 elevated the bishopric of Salvador to the standing of a metropolitanate, the only archbishopric in colonial Brazil. By 1808, Brazil counted one archbishopric and six bishoprics. The secular clergy were less committed and less educated than the regulars—Franciscans, Dominicans, Augustinians, Capuchins—but it was the Jesuits who predominated as missionaries, educators, and powerful influences in the social, political, economic, and spiritual life of the colony. An Inquisition was not formally established in Portuguese America, but Inquisitional inquiries reached their peak in the first half of the eighteenth century. The impact of Crown or ecclesiastical government was often limited to a region in the vicinity of a governor's residence or episcopal see. Blasphemers, bigamists, renegade clerics, deserters, and criminals simply left town when soldiers, circuit judges, fiscal officers, or Inquisitional visitors threatened their existence.

Crown incentives and sugar cultivation lured the ambitious and those with capital to Brazil. Stock farming developed away from the coast. Gold strikes in the 1690s and the first half of the eighteenth century inspired serial gold rushes, which siphoned off individuals from Portugal, Africa, and coastal and northern Brazil to the interior and to the west. Diamonds from northern Minas Gerais came on the market in the 1720s, and other discoveries followed in succeeding decades. Brazil had seemingly limitless land, but settlers were deterred by difficulty of access to potentially productive lands, inadequate capital to make those lands viable, and bureaucratic hurdles in getting claims measured and certified by a land grant or mining allotment. Grants of huge tracts to a powerful minority, and failure to monitor their use, decreased land available for cultivation. Other obstacles included fees for issuing documents, multiple taxes, bureaucratic inertia, and corruption.[14] Even in the early nineteenth century, much of Brazil was unknown to Europeans, and only small areas had been surveyed. Though export commodities—sugar, cattle hides, cotton, gold, and diamonds—and their contribution to the political and social formation of Brazil are well-known, smallholders and peasant producers contributed to thriving local economies. Tobacco was a smallholder crop whose rolled leaves were exported to Africa, Asia, and Europe.[15] Agricultural diversification was as much a reality as were plantations and large stock farms. Occupational distinctions became blurred, as miners farmed; planters bought town houses and engaged in commerce; merchants bought plantations; and former slaves owned houses, farms, and even mining allotments. Throughout the colonial period, diversity characterized the economy.

Angola in the seventeenth and eighteenth centuries had a checkered history.[16] The first half of the seventeenth century saw Portuguese military aggression, punitive expeditions, temporary alliances, and a policy of divide and rule. In this context of uncertainty and unpredictability, the Portuguese Crown attempted to put in place measures to achieve its objectives. A high priority was to explore the interior and south for copper and silver and to establish a town. To this end, in 1615 the king had appointed a governor of Benguela. But acrimonious relations between the governor-general in Luanda and his subordinate, spurred by this effort, only illustrated the inadequacy of Crown support for the southern region. Evangelization yielded meager returns, and the Catholic Church failed to improve its capacity to impose its authority as a regulatory, moral, or spiritual force. Climate, disease, and epidemics were hostile to Europeans, garrisons were chronically undermanned, and agricultural and commercial potential remained unfulfilled. Portuguese settlers were few and predominantly male, effectively ruling out a strong Portuguese imprint. Markers of a Portuguese identity—language, religion, family—were frail. Demands by American planters for labor exacerbated existing conflicting interests. Administrative inconsistency and physical insecurity were obstacles to imposing effective governance on Angola, and instability and constant warfare ravaged the region as Portuguese, local rulers, and African middlemen probed every way to fulfill the demand for slaves. The Portuguese moved from barter to raids to warfare that increasingly involved local rulers and African middlemen. The slaving frontier moved farther eastward. Though some kingdoms flourished, others declined. The slave trade created a culture of corruption and avarice in Africa from the poorest colonist to governors and bishops who abused their offices, and in Europe, where, during the union (1580–1640) of the two crowns, civil servants in Madrid and Lisbon bartered licenses to obtain slaves in return for payments to the Crown. Social and economic inequality in Angola grew, no more so than in Luanda, where exorbitant wealth accrued to a few who ostentatiously displayed silks, porcelain, and spices bought from captains and passengers on homeward-bound East Indiamen.

A balance sheet for the seventeenth century contains some accomplishments from a Portuguese perspective. Away from the coast, Portuguese made territorial gains on the lower Kwanza River: they established a handful of new garrisons, and from the 1620s regular public markets (*feiras*) grew in number. On the Atlantic, São Felipe de Benguela (1617) provided a southern port and opened new commercial networks and a direct slave trade to Bahia. Luanda grew, becoming in 1624 the site of a Jesuit college to educate what would become an African clergy, a fortress built in 1638, and a treasury board. Dutch conquest and occupation of Luanda (1641–1648) and Benguela briefly tarnished Portuguese standing in the region, but an expeditionary force from Brazil restored Portuguese control and reputation. The success of the Dutch constituted a warning of dangers posed by foreigners in ports in Kongo and Angola. The Portuguese failed to establish a transcontinental link between Angola and Mozambique, but expeditions provided invaluable information on terrain, river systems, crops, and polities. Conquests in the 1670s and 1680s by the brilliant soldier and strategist Luís Lopes Sequeira exterminated major opponents and brought an end to an extraordinarily violent phase in Angolan history. The Crown recognized Luanda's increasingly magnificent civic and religious buildings and private residences in 1698 by according it the status of a city, the only one in sub-Saharan Portuguese Africa.

The eighteenth century brought indicators that Angola might finally be on an upward curve. The first minister of Portugal, the marquis of Pombal, decreed freedom to trade by all Portuguese. This decree provided tacit acknowledgment of the end of Crown commercial monopolies but opened the gate to non-Portuguese. Pombal was also responsible for expelling the Jesuits from Angola and Brazil in 1759, thereby thwarting centuries of conversions and missionary effort.[17] Angola benefited from better leadership, notably under Governor Sousa Coutinho, exceptional for his enlightened attitude, reformist agenda, and vision. From 1764 to 1772, he encouraged agricultural production and regional commerce, identified indigenous commodities with export potential, promoted exploitation of mineral assets and production of saltpeter, built an iron foundry, and started a shipbuilding industry. He sought harmonious relations with chiefs and better living conditions for Africans, including payment for their labor, and strove to make Angola more attractive to whites. However, the slave trade and powerful vested interests were obstacles to change. Some of his successors were motivated to emulate him but could not prevent Angola from backsliding in the early nineteenth century.

Brazilian sugar and African slaves led Portuguese Africa and Brazil to experience a shared Atlantic history. The Dutch West India Company set its sights on sugar-producing northwestern Brazil, ravaging plantations in Bahia in the 1620s and occupying (1630–1654) captaincies from Pernambuco to the Maranhão. The Dutch turned to Africa for slaves to work their new Brazilian plantations, capturing São Jorge da Mina and Axim in Guinea, and São Tomé, Luanda, and Benguela. The canny and flamboyant Jinga, queen of the Jaga, illustrated the fluidity and complexity of the political and military challenge confronting the Portuguese and Dutch in Angola. A baptized Catholic, she signed a pact with the Portuguese governor, subsequently led her people to attack the Portuguese in the 1620s and 1630s, and then sided with the Dutch in the late 1640s against her erstwhile allies. So, too, in Brazil the Portuguese vied with the Dutch for the allegiance of Amerindian peoples and individuals of African birth or descent. Simultaneous Dutch predations in Brazil and Angola suggest interdependency and complementarity of trading commodities between Africa and Brazil, but that was not the case. The driving force came from Brazilian planters and miners who needed labor. Angola had no commodity to offer Brazil other than labor. Brazil offered no commodity which Africans could not have lived without. Items most in demand in Africa—cloth, manufactured objects of iron and copper, and firearms—were of European provenance, and traded by metropolitan Portuguese, or Portuguese residents in Rio de Janeiro, or as part of a triangular trade. Africans developed a taste for sugar and for tobacco to smoke, chew, and use as snuff. Brazilian rum and sugarcane brandy (*cachaça; geribita*) were much appreciated in Lower Guinea and Central Africa, and were preferred alternatives to local palm wine and beer or to Portuguese and Madeira wines and brandy. Contraband Spanish American silver was also in demand in Angola for barter.[18]

Brazil was the major destination for Africans transported to the Americas. What distinguished the slave trade to Brazil was its intensity, volume, and duration. Over a span of three centuries, chartered companies, merchant consortia, individuals, Portuguese and Brazilians, and illegal traders engaged in a trade carrying slaves variously from Upper Guinea to Pará and Maranhão, from Lower Guinea to ports between Belém and Rio de Janeiro, from Luanda and Benguela to Recife, Salvador, and Rio de Janeiro, and from Mozambique to Rio de Janeiro.[19] Africans coped with assimilation, accommodation, or rejection by Afro-Brazilians, and even by Africans who had preceded them to Brazil. In Brazil, as new regions were settled, more land came under cultivation, export crops grew, the agricultural sector diversified, and export and subsistence crops responded to new markets. Gold strikes spiked demand for slaves from Lower Guinea and Central Africa. Growing urban populations, flourishing commerce, and new networks of internal trade created demands for slave imports which an ever growing creole (Brazilian-born) slave population did not diminish.

Persons of African birth and descent, slave and free, were at their most numerous and most dense in regions associated with export agricultural production and extractive industries. Overall, whites in Brazil were a demographic minority, particularly in sugar and mining regions. African languages were more likely to be spoken than Portuguese, but Portuguese and African languages coexisted. Diet, food preparation, child rearing, household organization, and gender-related labor reflected an all-pervasive African presence. Africans had their own forms of dress, greetings, music and dances, burial ceremonies, healing practices, and religious beliefs. Walls between African and Portuguese cultures were porous. Syncretism occurred between different African peoples in Brazil, but there were brotherhoods whose statutes limited membership to persons of a specific ethnic or language group, or place of birth. Brazil was exceptional, vis-à-vis European colonies in the Americas, for the high rate of manumission and conditional freedom or conditional slavery.[20]

3. The Atlantic Ocean

Oceans were the sine qua non of imperial enterprise. Even kings did not have full control over the rhythm of empire. Winds and currents circulate in a clockwise direction in the North Atlantic and counterclockwise in the South Atlantic. Natural conditions determined preferred time frames for departures and arrivals of vessels. Delays could expose vessels to being becalmed in the equatorial zone or threatened by winter gales in the latitude of the Azores. The Portuguese were familiar with these patterns and specific currents. For them the Atlantic was an opportunity rather than an obstacle.

Portugal created networks within the North and South Atlantic and between the two hemispheres. Many combined long-haul routes, shorter routes, and coastal and riverine segments. These networks gave flexibility in adjusting to changing geopolitical and commercial conditions and markets. Early routes radiated out from Portugal to northern Europe, the Azores and Madeiras, Morocco, the Cape Verdes, West Africa, the Gulf of Guinea, and Central Africa, and there were interinsular routes between the Madeiras, the Azores, and the Cape Verdes. The Africa run from Portugal had ports in the Gulf of Guinea and Angola as final destinations. Vessels bound for Brazil traveled one route to ports on the north–south coast of Brazil, and another to the east–west coast of northern Brazil. A triangular trade developed among Portugal, Africa, and Brazil. Intercolony connections without a metropolitan component, as between Brazil and Africa, or Rio de Janeiro and the Spanish Río de la Plata, were rife with contraband as well as legal exchanges. Portuguese routes converged and intersected with routes plied by Spanish, Dutch, English, and French vessels. Dutch vessels often carried commodities from Portuguese Africa. Their southerly latitudes privileged Salvador, and especially Rio de Janeiro, as participants in legal and clandestine trade with Portuguese ports in India and Mozambique. Luanda was an irregular port of call for homeward-bound Indiamen, some of which continued on to Rio de Janeiro.

Geography favored continental Portugal and its overseas holdings to a degree unmatched by any other European power. Estuaries and bays capable of accommodating oceangoing vessels with ports capable of handling them were extensive in the Portuguese Atlantic. The Tagus River and estuary privileged Lisbon, as did the Sado privilege Setúbal. Some half a dozen major bays on the north–south axis of Brazil's coast provided secure anchorages. Large, and often navigable, rivers in Portugal, Africa, and Brazil facilitated penetration into the respective continents; permitted seamless transitions between oceanic, coastal, and riverine legs; and facilitated the distribution of imported goods and the assembling of commodities for transportation to ports for export. In Portugal, Oporto, Viana do Castelo, Setúbal, and Faro joined Lisbon as gateways to the Atlantic. In Africa there were few major ports. Luanda was alone in involvement in interoceanic trade, but numerous ports between Upper Guinea and Benguela, often associated with trading stations, played significant roles in Atlantic commerce and movement of peoples. In Brazil, some half a dozen ports from Belém to Santos participated in transoceanic trade. Portuguese archipelagoes each had at least one port suitable for long-haul vessels. The privileged position enjoyed by Portugal and its Atlantic holdings in terms of winds and currents, of estuaries and bays, and of large rivers was crucial to Portuguese preeminence in the North and South Atlantic. So, too, did shipbuilding under the aegis of the Crown, in royal arsenals and through private initiative, grow throughout the Portuguese Atlantic, to the degree that, before the end of the eighteenth century, Brazil was probably exceeding Portugal in numbers of vessels under construction.

4. Portuguese Distinctiveness

Portugal was the only European nation to have holdings in both the North and the South Atlantic before 1492 and was the first nation, from the sixteenth century, to exert sovereignty over vast territories on both sides of the subequatorial Atlantic; the only European power to have crown officials of the rank of governor concurrently in continental Africa and America before 1600; and the only European nation to have a full ecclesiastical structure in the North and South Atlantic before 1600. Portugal was blessed with archipelagoes which, already in the fifteenth century, possessed strategic importance for commerce, settlement, and defense. Ports on these islands were places of origin and destination and, with the development of the Cape route to India and the Brazil route, they became important as way stations for homeward- and outward-bound vessels. Brazil and Angola were unparalleled in size by the colony of any other European nation in the Atlantic, their major ports lay within a span of five degrees of latitude, and passage between Portuguese Africa and Portuguese America presented no major navigational challenges.

That ports were disproportionately represented among towns accorded the status of city underlines that ports were often synonymous with civil and ecclesiastical authority, wealth, and influence, and capitals of a colony or captaincy. Ports were listening posts for military, political, commercial, and social information. Sailors, soldiers, and passengers—missionaries, merchants, and Crown officials—circulated information throughout the Portuguese Atlantic. Information traveled beyond a Portuguese sphere of influence and informed colonists of events outside the Lusophone world. Contemporaries referred to one group which encapsulated the dissemination of information as the "Portuguese Nation," many of whom were of Jewish ancestry and had occupations linked to maritime commerce. Leaving Lisbon in the sixteenth and seventeenth centuries, they formed diasporic communities in Recife, Salvador, and Luanda, as well as in the Caribbean and cities of Spanish America and ports on the Pacific. An information network linked these locales, via Seville and Lisbon, to Venice and Livorno, Rouen and Paris, and London, Antwerp, Amsterdam, and Hamburg.[21]

Portugal took full advantage of the diversity and complementarity of its colonies. What set it apart from other participants in the "Columbian exchange" were the African and Asian components: African yams, bananas, date palms, and oil to Brazil; peanuts, cashews, sweet potatoes, manioc, and corn from Brazil to the Atlantic islands and Africa. American corn and sweet potatoes transformed Azorean economies and, along with manioc, were important additions to the diets of Africans. Brazilian tobacco, pineapples, sweet potatoes, corn, and chili peppers were exported to Asia. The Crown exhorted viceroys in Goa to send samples of pepper, cloves, and cinnamon to Brazil. Jesuits, fascinated by botany and plants with medicinal qualities, carried seeds, cuttings, and plants from colleges in Asia to Brazil, and had field stations to test plant adaptation.[22]

The monarch enjoyed absolute authority and ruled with councils and boards which came to be located in Lisbon. From 1642 an Overseas Council formulated all legislation for all Portuguese overseas holdings. Codified laws applied to all overseas holdings and, in the case of Brazil, the *Ordenações Filipinas* (1603) were still in force at the time of independence, but even within the Atlantic there were varying degrees of compliance with laws and "royal letters with the force of law." Crown officials, even governors, let alone municipal councilors, often did not open, let alone read, edicts from Lisbon. In terms of governance, donatarial captaincies became instruments of colonization throughout the Portuguese Atlantic, but not in Portuguese Asia. These were modeled after institutions set up by Italians and others in the Mediterranean, brought to Portugal, and modified to meet the specific situation in the Portuguese Atlantic. This form of governance was well suited to island groups; had a mixed record in Brazil, with conflicts between lords proprietor and Crown officials; and proved unsuitable for Angola. Portuguese kings spent two centuries trying to regain control over the territories in Brazil held by such lords proprietor and their descendants. This recovery effort was but one manifestation of Atlantic-wide Crown policies specifically geared to keeping the colonial-born in their place and to enforcing a policy of "purity of blood" which effectively eliminated persons of African birth or descent, and persons of Jewish blood or descent, from holding public office.

But here, as in so many instances of royal decrees or orders, local officials looked the other way. New Christians became Catholic priests. At least one person of African descent held the office of governor of Angola and of a captaincy in Brazil, and in Brazil and Angola persons of African descent served on municipal councils. The marquis of Pombal outlawed such constraints, and the distinction between Old and New Christians, in the 1770s, but there was no corresponding legislation for persons of African birth or descent. Crown officers promulgated protectionist policies to forbid industry and trading practices which challenged metropolitan commercial and economic interests. Colonial Brazil numbered individuals (some of them charlatans) who were innovative, creative, and inventive, especially as regards machinery, but whose inventiveness was squelched by the Crown. Cultural life and education found a restraining force in the person of kings who attempted to monitor the book trade, refused to countenance a printing press in Brazil, and consistently rejected requests by municipal councils to authorize establishment of a university in the colony. Portuguese Crown policy was here at variance with Spanish and English Crown policy for colonies in the Americas, and only with the arrival of the royal court in Brazil in 1808 was it changed. Against this background of royal control of colonial commerce, society, and culture, it comes as a surprise to learn that the Holy Office, so strong in Spanish America, was not formally established in Portuguese America or Portuguese Africa.[23] Furthermore, despite this distancing between Crown and colonies, the Portuguese empire was intensely consultative. Kings and their counselors were forever requesting information from overseas officials, clerics, town councilors, and individuals.

Two uniquely Portuguese institutions were present the length and breadth of the Portuguese Atlantic. One was the *senado da câmara*, or municipal council; the other, the *Santa Casa de Misericórdia*, a brotherhood of white laymen and laywomen dedicated to social philanthropy.[24] Each was modeled on predecessors in Portugal, and each enjoyed Crown protection and privileges. For municipal councils, the election process was indirect; electors, referred to as "good men of the republic," were selected from the local elite or from people who had served on the council. Sometimes a "people's judge" had a voice at the table. Election to a *senado* was the only opportunity for a colonist to participate in the political process. Councilors defended colonial or local interests as they saw them, challenging decrees by governors, negotiating with viceroys over implementing the royal will, and making representations directly to the king. *Misericórdias* were instruments of neither Crown nor Church. The more affluent had a church, hospital, pharmacy, and foundling wheel; provided legal counsel and food for prisoners; often had a monopoly on biers for burials; cared for foundlings; distributed alms; and provided dowries. Members included artisans, shopkeepers, priests, lawyers, physicians, planters, miners, and merchants. The governing board often included leading citizens, senior Crown officials, and prominent clerics. Brothers, individually and collectively, exerted great influence locally, speaking out on social and urban issues, and had the immediate ear of governors and viceroys.

This picture would be incomplete if it did not include divisive forces. Revolts, such as that led by the sugar planter Manuel Beckman in the Maranhão in 1684, which led to a short-lived provisional government, and that in 1720 in Vila Rica, were rapidly and harshly suppressed. The "War of the *Emboabas*" (1708–1709) in Minas Gerais and "War of the *Mascates*" (1710–1711) in Pernambuco were local and failed. Failure also was the fate of uprisings in Minas Gerais in 1788–1789 and in Bahia in 1798. These uprisings reflected social and economic inquietude, resentment against the regime, and colonial aspirations to equal access to offices and to privileges enjoyed by the Portuguese-born, and to free trade. Manifestos of the later eighteenth century echoed the language and rhetoric that preceded the American and French revolutions. The most serious slave revolt, led by Amador, came within a hairsbreadth of taking over the island of São Tomé in 1595. With the exception of Palmares in the seventeenth century, a federation of villages populated by runaways with a hierarchy of leadership and organization, no group of runaway slaves (*quilombos*) challenged Crown rule in colonial Brazil. A concept of "purity of blood," first apparent in Portugal in the context of Jews, was transplanted overseas and was most apparent in the distinction between "Old Christians" and "New Christians," which persisted into the eighteenth century. The concept also took on a racial distinction in the Portuguese Atlantic when applied to persons of African birth or descent. There were cleavages between individuals born in Portugal (*reinóis*)[b] and Portuguese born in Africa or Brazil. In Brazil there were distinctions within the African community between African-born and Brazilian-born, and between slaves, freeborn, and those freed by manumission. How much these latter groups shared in the sense of Portuguese identity is questionable, but there are many examples of Africans as exemplary citizens and devout Catholics, and who fought for the Crown and Portugal. Others voluntarily removed themselves from a Portuguese sphere of influence. Some migrants (voluntary and coerced) chose to live far removed from Portuguese settlements: in Angola and Brazil, convicts, deserters, and renegade clerics went native; runaway slaves formed *quilombos*; Muslim slaves in Bahia had a closely knit community; Gypsies guarded their identity, language, and way of life; Jews and New Christians discreetly formed discrete communities in Senegal and Brazil; and that community known as the "Portuguese Nation," so exaggeratedly diasporic as to be stateless or transnational, developed what Jonathan Israel calls "diasporas within a diaspora."

Transfer (1763) of the capital of Brazil from Salvador to Rio de Janeiro formally acknowledged that Rio de Janeiro had long since become the major city and port—commercially, strategically, and politically—of Brazil. Rio counted a well-established, dynamic, wealthy, and influential merchant community whose entrepreneurship and vision resonated throughout the Portuguese Atlantic and beyond. Rio de Janeiro's standing was enhanced when, fleeing before Napoleon's forces, in late November 1807 the prince-regent, royal family, and court embarked on the voyage to Salvador and on to Rio de Janeiro. The presence of a European court in an overseas colony bestowed exceptional importance on Brazil. It transformed the power dynamic in the Portuguese Atlantic, shifting the center of gravity from Lisbon to Rio, from Portugal to Brazil, and from northern to southern hemisphere. Portuguese colonies in Central Africa saw in this move confirmation of what, for them, had been the status quo. Already in the eighteenth century, viceroys in Brazil had taken an intensive, even intrusive, interest in political, economic, defensive, and religious events in the Gulf of Guinea and in Angola. And cultural, social, familial, and economic and commercial ties between the Bay of All Saints and the Bight of Benin and Angola were extraordinarily strong from the seventeenth century onward. For their part, archipelagoes in the North Atlantic still felt oriented toward Portugal. Crucial was the decision (1808) to open Brazilian ports to international trade with friendly nations.[25] The Portuguese Atlantic was preserved and even strengthened, but the time had come to think in terms of a Luso-Afro-Brazilian Atlantic.

5. The Atlantic in Portuguese Historiography and Portugal in Atlantic History

The Atlantic has been an essential part of the historiography and literature of Portugal since the fifteenth century, and of Brazil since the sixteenth century. Rare is the Portuguese settlement in the Atlantic whose history does not have an oceanic perspective. The sixteenth century saw a small Portuguese presence in Africa and the beginning of the transportation of Africans and migration of Portuguese to Brazil. Cultural, linguistic, and physical exchanges occurred between Portuguese and Africans and, to a substantially lesser degree, between these two groups and Amerindians. Multiculturalism was prominent in histories of Portuguese Africa and Brazil, and continues to be. Historiography on Portuguese colonies in Africa and adjacent islands is rich, but often regional rather than pan-Atlantic. The late nineteenth and twentieth centuries saw increasing interest by Brazilian scholars in Amerindians and persons of African descent: in their cultures, ethnicity, languages, customs, and religions. Growing awareness that a knowledge of Africa was crucial to an understanding of Brazil has been reflected in monographs on exchanges between Africa and Brazil and on African-born and Afro-Brazilians. These monographs were the forerunners of what we now call diasporic studies.[26] Throughout the Portuguese Atlantic, historiography was often region- and period-specific, but displayed a real consciousness of locating individual regions in an Atlantic context. This development preceded the current spike of scholarly interest in the North Atlantic. In Portugal, colloquia and publications often use the term Ibero-Atlântico or Iberian-American Atlantic (Atlântico Ibero-Americano) alongside Portuguese Atlantic. Such publications and symposia tend to be Iberocentric insofar as approaches and topics are Iberian and then projected onto an Atlantic canvas, rather than reflecting noncontinental topics, priorities, and approaches.

Recently, Brazilian historians have emerged onto the Atlantic stage, bringing a perspective which differs from that of their Portuguese colleagues. Unlike the Portuguese, who privilege Atlantic archipelagoes, Portuguese Africa, and Portuguese Asia over Brazil, Brazilian scholars have no such conflicts of interest. Some have added a Brazilian dimension to well-established subjects such as the ancien régime, elites during the Restoration (1580–1640), or the concept of nobility as applied to colonial Brazil; others have examined governors and governance throughout the Portuguese Atlantic; one scholar of witchcraft has turned to Europe for clarification on the blending of indigenous, African, and European beliefs in Brazil on magic, witchcraft, and healing; others have consulted previously unused or underused archives to probe the interstices of Brazilian history; still others have projected Brazil onto an Atlantic stage—for example, *carioca* merchants whose trading interests ranged from Mozambique to Gibraltar—or have considered the "formation of Brazil in the south Atlantic" and how different Brazilian history would have been without the contribution of Angola.[27]

The slave trade in general, and the Middle Passage in particular, has an extensive historiography in Portuguese but was not, until the 1960s, the object of that same intensive scholarly attention by Portuguese, Angolan, or Brazilian scholars as has been displayed by scholars of British colonies in mainland North America and the Caribbean. This divergence sounds a cautionary note. Topics, research methodologies, lines of questioning, positing of hypotheses, and priorities of consuming concern to any one group of historians—such as "Atlanticists" in the United States or Great Britain—may differ considerably from those of historians of other national Atlantics. The Portuguese Atlantic underlines the degree to which historians of national Atlantics are marching to different drummers. The lesson is that there is no single problematic or set of questions for historians studying the Atlantic. The individuality of each nation's Atlantic experience and historical agenda must be respected. This observation raises the issue of comparability. The Portuguese established an early presence in the Atlantic almost by default and the virtual absence of European challenges, rivalry with Castile having been largely resolved by 1494. Other than in Central Africa, the Portuguese encountered minimal sustained indigenous resistance, and in Brazil the issue of sovereignty was moot. The chronological asymmetry between Portugal and Castile, and the even greater asymmetry between the Iberian and northern European nations, must be taken into account in comparing colonization, governance, urbanization, commercial and economic development, and the importance each nation gave to the Atlantic endeavor when measured against priorities and *mentalités* within the metropolis. Topics and groups described in my opening comments about the approach taken in this chapter are more susceptible to an "Atlanticist" rather than an imperial approach. Atlantic history is a fascinating exercise in parallax and has the potential to decenter the historiography (African Atlantic, Creole Atlantic, Jesuit Atlantic) and create a historiography very different from that resulting from the appropriation of the Atlantic for national histories.

Portugal has been described as having a "seaborne empire." There was a time when it was the most far-flung of European empires, but over the *longue durée* the Atlantic was the center of gravity for Portuguese settlement, the area of greatest influence and commerce, the location of its major contiguous territorial holdings, and the place where its legacy is most evident today. The Atlantic looms large in the histories of Africa, Europe, America, and Asia. To see the ocean solely as a body of water downplays an impact which transcended shorelines and extended its influence to landlocked regions of Europe, Africa, and America. To see the Atlantic or any part of it in isolation not only underestimates its importance but also forfeits an opportunity to study the impact of the Atlantic on dry land and even in landlocked regions in Europe, Africa, and the Americas. The Portuguese, more than their contemporaries, engaged in interplay between north and south and east and west within the Atlantic and beyond. Routes, commodities, cultures, and peoples of the Portuguese Atlantic were essential components in the establishment of the global interconnectedness of commerce, migration, and cultural exchange, and between hemispheres, in the early modern period.

Acknowledgments

I thank Professor Pedro Cardim of the Universidade Nova de Lisboa and Teresa Batista Gaivota for information on recent publications and colloquia.

NOTES

1. The Portuguese Atlantic is discussed in global histories of Portugal overseas: C. R. Boxer, *The Portuguese Seaborne Empire, 1415–1825* (London: Hutchinson, 1969); Bailey W. Diffie and George D. Winius, *Foundations of the Portuguese Empire, 1415–1580* (Minneapolis: University of Minnesota Press, 1977); M. D. D. Newitt, *A History of Portuguese Overseas Expansion, 1400–1668* (London: Routledge, 2005). Frédéric Mauro, *Le Portugal et l'Atlantique au XVIIe siècle (1570–1670): Étude économique* (Paris: S.E.V.P.E.N, 1960), remains a valuable, if dated, resource. See also Vitorino Magalhães Godinho, *Os descobrimentos e a economia mundial*, 4 vols. (Lisbon: Editorial Arcadia, 1963); *História da expansão portuguesa*. Edited by Francisco Bethencourt and Kirti Chaudhuri. Círculo de Leitores (Navarra: Gráfica Estrella, 1998), volumes 1, 2, and 3; *Portuguese Overseas Expansion, 1400–1800*. Edited by Francisco Bethencourt and Diogo Ramada Curto (Cambridge: Cambridge University Press, 2007); and Telmo Gomes, *Portuguese Ships, 14th–19th Century* (Lisbon: Edições INAPA, 1995).

2. An introduction is Alberto Vieira, *Portugal y las islas del Atlántico* (Madrid: Editorial Mapfre, 1992). For the period prior to 1460, see Peter Russell, *Prince Henry "the Navigator": A Life* (New Haven: Yale University Press, 2000).

3. "Crossroads of the Atlantic," Bentley Duncan's phrase to refer to the Cape Verdes in the seventeenth century, is applicable to the Azores and Cape Verdes at an earlier date. T. Bentley Duncan, *Atlantic Islands: Madeira, the Azores and the Cape Verdes in Seventeenth Century Commerce and Navigation* (Chicago: University of Chicago Press, 1972). On sugar, see Philip D. Curtin, *The Rise and Fall of the Plantation Complex: Essays in Atlantic History* (Cambridge: Cambridge University Press, 1990), pp. 17–25.

4. Isabel dos Guimarães Sá, *Quando o rico se fez pobre: Misericórdias, caridade e poder no império português, 1500–1800* (Lisbon: CNCDP, 1997), pp. 117–145.

5. *História geral de Cabo Verde*, vol. 1, coordinated by Luís de Albuquerque and Maria Emília Madeira Santos (Lisbon and Praia: Instituto de Investigação Científica Tropical and Direcção Geral do Património Cultural de Cabo Verde, 1991). António Carreira, *The People of the Cape Verde Islands: Exploitation and Emigration*, trans. and ed. by Christopher Fyfe (London. C. Hurst; Hamden, Conn.: Archon Books, 1982), pp. 4–25; Duncan, *Atlantic Islands*, pp. 158–238. Superbly researched and

comprehensive is André Pinto de Sousa Dias Teixeira, *A ilha de São Nicolau de Cabo Verde nos séculos XV e XVIII* (Lisbon: Centro de História de Além-mar, Universidade Nova de Lisboa, 2004).

6. Robert Garfield, *A History of São Tomé Island, 1470–1655: The Key to Guinea* (San Francisco: Mellen Research University Press, 1992); Tony Hodges and Malyn Newitt, *São Tomé and Príncipe: From Plantation Colony to Microstate* (Boulder, Colo: Westview Press, 1988), pp. 1–26.

7. C. R. Boxer, *The Church Militant and Iberian Expansion, 1440–1770* (Baltimore: Johns Hopkins University Press, 1978), pp.5–7.

8. António Dias Farinha, *Portugal e Marrocos no século XV*, 2 vols. (Lisbon: Imprensa Nacional, 1977). The case for inclusion of Morocco in an emerging world economy is made by Vincent J. Cornell, "Socioeconomic Dimensions of Reconquista and Jihad in Morocco: Portuguese Dukkala and the Sa' Did Sus, 1450–1557," *International Journal of Middle East Studies* 22 (1990): 379–418.

9. John K. Thornton, "Early Kongo–Portuguese Relations, 1483–1575: A New Interpretation," *History in Africa* 8 (1981): 183–204, and *The Kingdom of Kongo: Civil War and Transition, 1641–1718* (Madison: University of Wisconsin Press, 1983); Kate Lowe, " 'Representing' Africa: Ambassadors and Princes from Christian Africa to Renaissance Italy and Portugal, 1402–1608," *Transactions of the Royal Historical Society* 17 (2007):101–128. Anne Hilton, *The Kingdom of Kongo* (Oxford: Clarendon Press, 1985), is excellent. Essential reading is John Thornton, *Africa and Africans in the Making of the Atlantic World, 1400–1800*, 2nd ed. (Cambridge: Cambridge University Press, 1998).

10. This is south of Cape Bojador, from Gambia to Sierra Leone. Peter Russell, *Portugal, Spain and the African Atlantic, 1343–1490* (Aldershot, U.K., and Brookfield, Vt.: Ashgate Publishing, 1995); Walter Rodney, *The History of the Upper Guinea Coast, 1545–1800* (Oxford: Clarendon Press, 1970). See Peter Mark, "The Evolution of 'Portuguese Identity': Luso-Africans on the Upper Guinea Coast from the Sixteenth to the Early Nineteenth Century," *Journal of African History* 40(2) (1999):173–191, and his *"Portuguese" Style and Luso-African Identity: Precolonial Senegambia, Sixteenth–Nineteenth Centuries* (Bloomington: Indiana University Press, 2002); and George E. Brooks, *Eurafricans in Western Africa: Commerce, Social Status, Gender, and Religious Observance from the Sixteenth to the Eighteenth Century* (Athens: Ohio University Press; Oxford: James Currey, 2003).

11. Francis Dutra, "Centralization vs. Donatorial Privilege: Pernambuco, 1602–1630," in Dauril Alden, ed., *Colonial Roots of Modern Brazil* (Berkeley and Los Angeles: University of California Press, 1973), pp. 19–60; H. B. Johnson, "Portuguese Settlement, 1500–1580," in Leslie Bethell, ed., *Colonial Brazil* (Cambridge: Cambridge University Press, 1987), pp. 1–38; John Hemming, *Red Gold: The Conquest of the Brazilian Indians, 1500–1760* (Cambridge, Mass.: Harvard University Press, 1978), pp. 1–182.

12. David Birmingham, *The Portuguese Conquest of Angola* (London: Oxford University Press, 1965), and *Trade and Conflict in Angola: The Mbundu and Their*

Neighbours Under the Influence of the Portuguese,1483–1790 (Oxford: Clarendon Press, 1966).

13. James Lockhart and Stuart B. Schwartz, *Early Latin America: A History of Colonial Spanish America and Brazil* (Cambridge: Cambridge University Press, 1983); Bethell, ed., *Colonial Brazil; O império luso-brasileiro, 1620–1750*, coordinated by Frédéric Mauro, vol. 7 of *Nova história* (1991); *O império luso-brasileiro, 1750–1822*, coordinated by Maria Beatriz Nizza da Silva, vol. 8 of *Nova história* (1986); and Carl Hanson, "The European 'Renovation' and the Luso-Atlantic Economy, 1560–1715," *Luso-Brazilian Review* 6(4) (1983): 475–530.

14. Hal Langfur, *The Forbidden Lands: Colonial Identity, Frontier Violence, and the Persistence of Brazil's Eastern Indians, 1750–1830* (Stanford: Stanford University Press, 2006), pp. 21–160.

15. C. R. Boxer, *The Golden Age of Brazil, 1695–1750* (Berkeley and Los Angeles: University of California Press, 1962/1969), pp.162–225; A. J. R. Russell-Wood, "The Gold Cycle, c. 1690–1750," in Bethell, ed., *Colonial Brazil*, pp.190–243; Stuart B. Schwartz, *Sugar Plantations in the Formation of Brazilian Society: Bahia, 1550–1835* (Cambridge: Cambridge University Press, 1985); Stuart B. Schwartz, ed., *Tropical Babylons: Sugar and the Making of the Atlantic World, 1450–1680* (Chapel Hill: University of North Carolina Press, 2004); B. J. Barickman, *A Bahian Counterpoint: Sugar, Tobacco, Cassava, and Slavery in the Recôncavo, 1780–1860* (Stanford: Stanford University Press, 1998).

16. António de Oliveira Cadornega, *História geral das guerras angolanas, 1680,* 3 vols., edited by José Matias Delgado (Lisbon: Agência Geral das Colônias, 1972); C. R. Boxer, *Salvador de Sá and the Struggle for Brazil and Angola, 1602–1686* (London: Athlone Press, 1952), pp. 240–272; José Carlos Venâncio, *A economia de Luanda e hinterland no século XVIII: Um estudo de sociologia histórica* (Lisbon: Editorial Estampa, 1996).

17. On Jesuits in the Atlantic, see Dauril Alden, *The Making of an Enterprise: The Society of Jesus in Portugal, Its Empire, and Beyond, 1540–1750* (Stanford: Stanford University Press, 1996), esp. pp. 71–78, 206–226, 474–501, 597–603.

18. C. R. Boxer, *The Dutch in Brazil, 1624–1654* (Oxford: Clarendon Press, 1957); João-Baptiste Nardi, *O fumo brasileiro no período colonial: Lavoura, comércio e administração* (São Paulo: Editora Brasiliense, 1996); José C. Curto, *Enslaving Spirits: The Portuguese-Brazilian Alcohol Trade at Luanda and Its Hinterland, c. 1550–1830* (Leiden and Boston: Brill, 2004).

19. Robert E. Conrad, *World of Sorrow: The African Slave Trade to Brazil* (Baton Rouge: Louisiana State University Press, 1986). On specific trades, see Pierre Verger, *Bahia and the West Coast Trade (1549–1851)* (Ibadan: Ibadan University Press, 1964); Herbert K. Klein, *The Middle Passage: Comparative Studies in the Atlantic Slave Trade* (Princeton: Princeton University Press, 1978), pp. 3–94; Joseph C. Miller, *Way of Death: Merchant Capitalism and the Angolan Slave Trade, 1730–1830* (Madison: University of Wisconsin Press, 1988).

20. Mary C. Karasch, *Slave Life in Rio de Janeiro, 1808–1850* (Princeton: Princeton University Press, 1987), esp. pp. 214–301; Katia M. de Queirós Mattoso, *To Be a Slave in Brazil, 1550–1888* (New Brunswick: Rutgers University Press, 1986); James H. Sweet, *Recreating Africa: Culture, Kinship, and Religion in the African–Portuguese World, 1441–1770* (Chapel Hill: University of North Carolina Press, 2003); A. J. R. Russell-Wood, "Atlantic Bridge and Atlantic Divide: Africans and Creoles in Late Colonial Brazil". In *Creole Societies in the Portuguese Colonial Empire*. Edited by Phillip Havik and Malyn Newitt (Bristol: University of Bristol, 2007), 171–218; Pierre Verger, *Trade Relations Between the Bight of Benin and Bahia, from the 17th to 19th Century*, trans. by Evelyn Crawford (Ibadan: Ibadan University Press, 1976).

21. Daviken Studnicki-Gizbert, *A Nation Upon the Ocean Sea: Portugal's Atlantic Diaspora and the Crisis of the Spanish Empire, 1492–1640* (Oxford: Oxford University Press, 2007); Paulo Bernardini and Norman Fiering, eds., *The Jews and the Expansion of Europe to the West, 1450 to 1800* (New York: Berghahn Books, 2001).

22. A. J. R. Russell-Wood, *The Portuguese Empire: 1415–1808. A World on the Move* (Baltimore: Johns Hopkins University Press, 1998), pp. 148–180.

23. On administration, see Laura de Mello e Souza, *O sol e a sombra: Política e administração na América portuguesa do século XVIII* (São Paulo: Companhia das Letras, 2006); and Dauril Alden, *Royal Government in Colonial Brazil. With Special Reference to the Administration of the Marquis of Lavradio, Viceroy, 1769–1779* (Berkeley and Los Angeles: University of California Press, 1968); James E. Wadsworth, *Agents of Orthodoxy: Honor, Status, and the Inquisition in Colonial Pernambuco, Brazil* (Lanham, Md.: Rowman and Littlefield, 2007); Jorge de Souza Araújo, *Perfil do leitor colonial* (Salvador and Ilhéus: Editus, 1999); E. Bradford Burns, "The Enlightenment in Two Brazilian Libraries," *Journal of the History of Ideas* 25(3) (July–September 1964): 430–438.

24. C. R. Boxer, *Portuguese Society in the Tropics: The Municipal Councils of Goa, Macao, Bahia, and Luanda, 1510–1800* (Madison and Milwaukee: University of Wisconsin Press, 1965); A. J. R. Russell-Wood, *Fidalgos and Philanthropists: The Santa Casa da Misericórdia of Bahia, 1550–1755* (Berkeley and Los Angeles: University of California Press, 1968).

25. Kenneth Maxwell, "The Atlantic in the Eighteenth Century: A Southern Perspective on the Need to Return to the 'Big Picture,' " *Transactions of the Royal Historical Society* 6th ser., 3 (1993): 209–236, and A. J. R. Russell-Wood, "A projeção da Bahia no império ultramarino português", *Anais do IV Congresso de História da Bahia* (Salvador: Instituto Geográfico e Histórico da Bahia and Fundação Gregório de Mattos, 2001), vol. 1, 81–122; Roderick J. Barman, *Brazil: The Forging of a Nation, 1798–1852* (Stanford: Stanford University Press, 1988), pp. 9–41.

26. Patrick Manning, "Africa and the African Diaspora: New Directions of Study," *Journal of African History* 44(3) (2003): 487–506; Kristin Mann and Edna G. Bay, eds., *Rethinking the African Diaspora: The Making of a Black Atlantic World*

in the Bight of Benin and Brazil (London: Frank Cass, 2001); Linda M. Heywood, ed., *Central Africans and Cultural Transformations in the American Diaspora* (Cambridge and New York: Cambridge University Press, 2002).

27. Nuno G. F. Monteiro, Pedro Cardim, and Mafalda Soares da Cunha, eds., *Optima Pars. Elites ibero-americanas do antigo regime* (Lisbon: ICS, 2005); João Fragoso, Maria Fernanda Bicalho, and Maria Fátima Gouvêa, eds., *O antigo regime nos trópicos: A dinâmica imperial portuguesa, séculos XVI–XVII* (Rio de Janeiro: Civilização Brasileira, 2001); Maria Beatriz Nizza da Silva, *Ser nobre na colônia* (São Paulo: Editora UNESP, 2005); Maria Fernanda Bicalho and Vera Lúcia Amaral Ferlini, eds., *Modos de governar: Idéias e práticas políticas no império português, séculos XVI a XIX* (São Paulo: Alameda, 2005); Laura de Mello e Souza, *The Devil and the Land of the Holy Cross: Witchcraft, Slavery and Popular Religion in Colonial Brazil*, trans. by Diane Grosklaus Whitty (Austin: University of Texas Press, 2003); Luiz Felipe de Alencastro, *O trato dos viventes: Formação do Brasil no Atlântico Sul* (São Paulo: Companhia das Letras, 2000).

4

THE BRITISH ATLANTIC

TREVOR BURNARD

That the Atlantic from the fifteenth century to the present has been more than just an ocean, that it has also been a particular zone of exchange and interchange, circulation and transmission, is not only true, in the sense that these exchanges and interchanges shaped life on four continents over a very long period of time. It is also a conceptual leap forward, allowing historians to make links among places, peoples, and periods that enrich our understanding about how societies were formed. The receptiveness of colonial British Americanists to Atlantic history can be seen in the titles of recent books, the enthusiasm for conferences incorporating an Atlantic theme, the reorientation of research institutes with an early British American focus toward Atlantic studies, and the proliferation of courses on aspects of Atlantic history.[1] But Atlantic history also has limitations. Those limitations, increasingly apparent, have the potential to limit the usefulness of the Atlantic perspective as an exciting historical frame of reference.

Britain as an Atlantic Nation

The British came late into the Atlantic Ocean, or at least late into the Americas. Moreover, a complex and fiercely contested internal colonization within the British archipelago itself, led mostly by England, accompanied expansion across the Atlantic. Technically, we cannot talk about a *British* Atlantic until the eighteenth century. Although a composite monarchy comprising the three kingdoms of England and Wales, Scotland, and Ireland had existed since the accession of James VI and I to the three crowns of Britain in 1603, Great Britain came into existence only with the union of Scotland with England and Wales in 1707. If, during the sixteenth century, the English showed considerable interest in overseas expansion, their attention was mostly confined to subduing and subjugating the nearby island of Ireland and to working out an accommodation with Scotland. The question of England's relations with the other nations of the British archipelago was far from resolved during this long era. Nor was England safe within a Europe from which it was increasingly estranged as a result of its adoption of militant Protestantism. Whereas by 1600 Spain had consolidated itself as a mighty Atlantic empire, England's interest in permanent colonization in the Atlantic outside Ireland was minimal. The English remained content with their lucrative but limited penetration of the Newfoundland fisheries and with privateering voyages designed to prick the Spanish Empire.[2] Scotland was hardly involved in overseas expansion until the disastrous Darien expedition to Panama in the last decade of the seventeenth century. Its interests lay overwhelmingly in continental Europe.[3]

Yet England and then Britain soon made up for its late start. By the middle of the eighteenth century its Atlantic possessions, including a relatively subdued Ireland, were second only to Spain's in size and importance. By 1760, the British Atlantic comprised twenty-three colonies with a total population of 1,972,608, of whom 1,326,306 were white and 646,305 were black.[4] In addition, large numbers of unsubjugated and unincorporated Native Americans lived in the American interior, and a proportion of them were allied to the British.[5] Moreover, as was the case in Britain itself, the economic and social trajectory was decidedly upward. The major characteristic of the British Atlantic in the eighteenth century was growth in almost all areas. Rapid population growth was accompanied by even more rapid economic development in the northern American colonies from North Carolina to New Hampshire. Though white population growth was not so pronounced in the lower southern and island colonies, the maturation of the slave plantation complex designed to produce tropical commodities for a British market made these regions among the most valuable parts of the British Empire. Britain's stirring victories, especially in the Seven Years' War (mainly from 1759 to 1762), the first global war and the first war in which control of territory in the wider Atlantic was crucial, confirmed the success of Britain's intrusions into the Atlantic. As a result of a massive acquisition of territories, especially in Canada and the American interior, in Florida, and in the West Indies, by the Treaty of Paris in 1763, Britain had established itself as the dominant power in the Atlantic.[6]

Indeed, the British Atlantic had by the mid-eighteenth century become so powerful and its advances seemingly so inexorable that farsighted thinkers speculated that before long Britain's American possessions would outstrip Britain itself in wealth, population, and influence. In a pioneering foray into political economy in 1751, Benjamin Franklin calculated that continental British America's population was doubling every twenty years as a result of the availability of land, widespread marriage, and a healthy environment. Even without further migration, he averred, the population of North America would "in another Century be more than the people of England and [that] the greatest Number of Englishmen" would "be on this Side of the Water." This eager imperialist was ecstatic about the prospects of this development: "What an Accession of Power to the British Empire by Sea as well as Land!"[7] But it was not to be. British imperial policy turned calamitous in the 1760s and 1770s, leading to the American Revolution and an irreversible rupture between the majority of Britain's white American subjects and the British Empire. Nevertheless, the British Atlantic did not end with the loss of thirteen colonies in 1783. As P. J. Marshall insists, Britain's eastern empire did not begin to outstrip its Atlantic empire in importance until well into the nineteenth century. Britain retained significant holdings in the Americas—the West Indies and Canada—for well over a century after the American Revolution. Indeed, it still has possessions in the Atlantic: the quintessentially Atlantic colony of Bermuda remains formally attached to Britain.[8] Moreover, the transition from British colonies to independent nation in what became the United States did not end the involvement of that area in the British Atlantic world. On the contrary, the United States continued to be an important trading partner with Britain while forms of settlement, colonization, and imperial aggrandizement worked out during the colonial era continued to characterize United States expansion across the continent throughout the nineteenth century.[9]

Exceptionalism, Euro-Skepticism, and Atlantic History

Britain took particular pride in its Atlantic empire, its success in the Americas being a crucial component of the creation of a British identity. That pride in British achievement in establishing an Atlantic empire continued even after the American Revolution.[10] Those Britons (mostly English) who were ambivalent about Europe continued to advocate participation in an Atlantic world. More so than the French and Germans, Britons were—and still are—reluctant Europeans, viewing the English Channel less as a highway than as a convenient barrier to European contamination. That ambivalence toward Europe, ambivalence shared by North Americans then and now, is reflected in the historiography and may be one reason for the greater popularity of

Atlantic approaches for scholars of the Anglophone world than for those of the Francophone and possibly the Hispanic worlds.

Exceptionalism has a long history in the Anglophone world.[11] So, too, has Euro-skepticism. As the Tudor historian David Starkey argues, "the English Channel is much wider than the Atlantic."[12] Consequently, the Atlantic has often been used by the British as a counterpoint to Europe because it enabled the British, especially the English, to convince themselves that their destiny was not linked with other Europeans. Britons liked to believe that their history should be viewed in an insular and maritime context. Colonial British Americans shared those prejudices, especially after British victories in the Seven Years' War broadened their horizons and sharpened their ambitions, and as subsequent British actions in the 1760s disabused them of all dreams of fulfilling those ambitions. The future of continental British America was American, not British. Franklin, for example, once a stalwart of British imperialism, by 1767 had begun to think of America's "manifest destiny" as being in continental America, which, he observed, was "an immense territory, favoured by nature with all the advantages of climate, soil, great navigable rivers, and lakes etc." He predicted that it "must become a great country, populous and mighty; and" would, "in less time than is generally conceived, be able to break off any shackles that may be imposed on her, and perhaps place them on the imposers."[13]

To mention Euro-skepticism or American exceptionalism is to admit that a British Atlantic perspective has always had a political dimension. In his account of the origins of interest in the history of the Atlantic world, Bernard Bailyn stresses the interaction between contemporary politics and historiographical developments. He sees its origins in the ambitions of international foreign policy realists after 1945 to protect America and western Europe through an organized Atlantic alliance.[14] When historians such as the nineteenth-century imperial historian John Robert Seeley declared that the history of England in the eighteenth century was "not in England but in America and Asia," and when Henrietta Marshall's highly influential 1905 history book for children was titled *Our Island Story*, the political point was plain: England was not part of Europe but was an independent, outward-looking polity perched in the Atlantic Ocean.[15]

Reality, of course, was quite different. Britain had been closely tied to Europe since at least the Norman Conquest. Even during the eighteenth century, when the British Atlantic became a significant concern for policymakers and politicians, Britain's German possessions in the Holy Roman Empire were more at the heart of Britain's foreign policy strategy than were its Atlantic colonies. Not everyone was interested in the Atlantic, and among those not interested were leading Britons, including the Royal Family. Few prominent Britons ever ventured to the Americas or showed much knowledge of what went on there. The leading Whig oligarchical families—the Cavendishes, Russells, Churchills, and Pelhams—were no more involved in the Atlantic world than were the Hanoverians. Moreover, the apparatus of the fiscal–military state, including the Royal Navy and the standing army, was designed primarily to sustain Britain's international role in Europe and was only tangentially related to developments in the Atlantic.[16]

The political imperatives involved in expanding the geographical scope of English history can be seen as much in the turn to "new" British history, as in Atlantic history. Indeed, two of the leading proponents of "new" or "greater" British history—J. G. A. Pocock and David Armitage—have also been primary movers in urging historians to look at how ideas brought the British Atlantic world together through state formation, imperialism, and a vibrant republican tradition.[17] Greater British and Atlantic history developed together at roughly the same time (the early 1970s) and at least partly for the same reasons, including a desire to move away from what was perceived as the increasingly narrow parochialism of studies of small British or American towns or parishes, and a concomitant insistence that British history had been distinct from European history because of the particular importance of imperial expansion in British history and in British self-definition. With greater British history, Britain itself became the central problematic: how to write about the interconnected histories of England, Wales, Scotland, and Ireland in a way that avoided the entrenched assumptions that "England" could be a synecdoche for "Britain," and how to focus on British involvement in, and then withdrawal from, empire is a dominant underlying organizing theme. Family resemblances exist between, on the one hand, Pocock's call for a greater British history incorporating the histories of each part of the British archipelago and the imperial extension of those histories into the Atlantic as well as other places and, on the other hand, Seeley's late-nineteenth-century argument for a conception of Britain and its empire as a "Greater Britain." As Armitage notes, the "long, withdrawing roar of empire could be heard behind this plea." Yet the worthy aims behind the "new" British history, especially the integration of British history and British American history, have not been fulfilled. Although colonial British American historians eagerly adopted Atlantic perspectives, British historians have been wary about approaches that join the seventeenth and eighteenth centuries into a single "early modern era."[18]

A Chronology of European Expansion

Indeed, one major difference between the "new" British history and both British Atlantic and colonial British American history is that the former is more sensitive than the latter to chronological order. The writing of British history continues to be governed by the reigns of kings and queens or by reference to major historical events. It organizes books by time rather than by theme. Few scholars attempt to canvass the seventeenth and eighteenth centuries as a single period, as is customary in surveys of colonial British America.[19] By contrast, colonial British American historians organize their books either thematically or, more commonly, by region. Even those historians who insist on the importance of chronology tend to focus on very long time spans and on broad patterns of social development in which later settled regions, such as Georgia, are linked with earlier settled regions, such as Virginia, on the basis of shared processes of social articulation over time.[20]

The reason for this regional fascination is partly the historical continuity of strong regional identities in the United States and partly historians' wanting to see whether other regions accorded to patterns characteristic of New England, the region that before the late 1960s was for most colonial British American historians as much a synecdoche for early America as was England for Britain among English historians. Of course, this regional fixation was also a response to the obvious fact that the several reasonably coherent regions that developed in British America were conspicuously different from one another in how they were founded, how they developed socioeconomically, and how subject they were to metropolitan efforts to make them conform to a common standard. Consequently, the differences between colonial British American places seem to be more compelling than the similarities. British Americans could imagine their colonies as they pleased and had considerable latitude to shape societies to fit that imagination. Diversity in socioeconomic structures, however, was accompanied by shared political and ideological assumptions, the most important of which was settler insistence that, as Britons, colonial settlers enjoyed the same rights and privileges as British subjects resident in Britain. This insistence on the integrity of settler rights, together with settler defenses of a libertarian political culture, powerfully informed colonial resistance to metropolitan authority in the 1760s and 1770s, and such concerns remained important for white settlers in the British Caribbean and the white settler colonies of Canada, Australia, South Africa, and New Zealand long after the creation of an independent United States.[21]

The key event that allowed the white residents of the British Atlantic to articulate the nature of the establishments they had settled was the English Civil War. The tumults of the mid-seventeenth century in the British archipelago were analogous in their effects on colonial politics in British America to the collapse of central authority in Iberia after the French invasion in 1808. In both cases the colonies were left to fend for themselves as the imperial center imploded. As Carla Pestana claims, the importance of the English Civil War to early American history is that "no American colony of any other European state experienced a comparable breakdown at the imperial center until the French revolution." A major difference between events in British America and those in French and Spanish America, however, was that in British America the breakdown of authority came early in the settlement process, even before that authority had been fully established. It also gave emerging settler leaders enhanced confidence in their ability to manage their own affairs, a confidence seemingly justified by their consolidation of local power in the 1640s and 1650s at the expense of proprietors and the Crown. Although Charles II endeavored to assert his authority over the colonies after regaining his crown, British American colonies never lost the extensive autonomy they had gained during the English Civil War. Britain's Atlantic possessions after 1660 would be commercial and diverse, wedded to slave labor on the model developed in Barbados in the 1640s, and committed to the rights of local landowners.[22]

Pestana's concentration on the whole of the English Atlantic over a brief period of tumultuous change demonstrates the advantages that a chronological orientation can bring to British Atlantic history, and recent scholarship has clarified the chronological divisions in British Atlantic history. The first distinct period involved the imagining and then the realizing of late-sixteenth-century colonizing projects urged on the English Crown and on English merchants by propagandists such as Richard Hakluyt. That period lasted from roughly 1580 to the mid-1620s, covering Raleigh's early Roanoke Island ventures in the 1580s, the settlement of Virginia and Bermuda in 1607 and 1609, and the start of settlement in the West Indies and New England in the 1620s. In this early phase, English colonial enterprise in America emerged from a heady combination of national ambition, Protestant mission, economic pragmatism, and thirst for individual and collective greatness that, fermenting through the late Elizabethan period, coalesced during the reign of James VI and I. Shaped by competition in Europe with Spain, a desire to counter the Catholicization of the Americas with aggressive Protestantism, and a utopian urge to end English poverty through the exploitation of Atlantic resources, English entry into the Americas was, in one sense, a last act of the Renaissance. Yet, it failed to realize any of its initial expectations. Up to the mid-1620s, English colonies in America were straggling, unhappy places that met none of the English objectives for Atlantic expansion. The major achievement was negative: a prolonged assault on the vibrant yet vulnerable indigenes through the occupation of Native American lands and the deterioration of English–Indian relations, as initially positive views of the indigenes degenerated into violent conflict and racial denigration within a decade of permanent settlement.[23]

Failure was followed by success in a second stage marked by a great surge of English expansion across the Atlantic from the mid-1620s to the mid-1680s. By 1682, with the founding of Pennsylvania, England had established flourishing colonies along the Atlantic coast from New England to South Carolina and had acquired New York from the Dutch. In addition, the English had established settlements in Barbados and the Leeward Islands in the eastern Caribbean, and in 1655 had conquered Jamaica from the Spanish. Extraordinary numbers of Englishmen and a few Englishwomen left for these colonies and for Ireland—nearly 300,000 before 1660. Within a generation of settlement, English settlers in most colonies had established viable political and social structures, had developed economies that sustained themselves and pointed to future wealth, and had, largely independent from English control, started to articulate visions of what they wanted their embryonic societies to become. Most important, starting with Barbados and then in the Chesapeake and the lower South, Englishmen introduced African chattel slavery and began to transform their societies into slave societies producing tropical goods for European markets. These regions became sharply differentiated in socioeconomic and political character from northern farm colonies, where slaveholding was small-scale. These successes came at a cost, borne especially by indigenous peoples, many of whom died and some of whom were enslaved, and by Africans. Moreover, conflict was endemic between embryonic elites with few pretensions to civility and little inherited authority, and poorer whites, resentful that they were being excluded from political power. Thus, the successes of English colonization in the seventeenth century seemed to observers to be less than impressive, given the low standard of living enjoyed by most colonists and the combustible state of social and political life.

The British Atlantic became consolidated, in the sense of developing real and meaningful links among Europe, British America, and Africa, only in a third stage covering the first half of the eighteenth century. Until the late seventeenth century we cannot talk of an integrated British Atlantic community. Links with Britain were patchy, the African slave trade was flourishing but not yet fully developed, and connections among separate British American colonies were quite limited. But in the early eighteenth century, the integration of the British Atlantic world became sufficient to constitute a genuine Atlantic community. The emergence of this community was partly due to developments in Britain, especially in finance (the growth of the stock market and the creation of a national banking system) and commerce (massive growth around 1700 in the number of merchants trading with the Americas). Partial limitations on the Royal African Company's monopoly in 1698 and its abolition in 1712 were crucial in opening up the slave trade and making it more dynamic, and in expanding the numbers of Britons connected to Atlantic commerce. The frequent wars in which Britain engaged with Spain and France from the late 1690s through the end of the Seven Years' War in 1763 also facilitated rapid Atlantic integration. King Philip's War in 1675–1676 was the last war in the Americas that did not involve serious conflict with European powers or their American colonies. Even in settler conflicts with Native Americans, such as the Yamasee War in the Carolinas in 1715, war took place within a context in which American and European power politics were inextricably linked. The culmination was the Seven Years' War, in which Britain obtained European mastery through dominance in the North American interior.[24]

Throughout most of this period, the imperial touch was light. Britain largely left the colonies alone, abandoning in practice but not in theory, as Bernard Bailyn has pointed out, late Stuart attempts to bring the colonies under firmer centralized control. Despite considerable and growing ethnic and religious diversity, especially in the Middle Colonies of New York, New Jersey, and Pennsylvania, and a degree of factional politics, politics and social life were remarkably stable. Powerful local creole elites established and dominated strong representative institutions in which they proclaimed their adherence to the liberties they believed were their inheritance and that had been confirmed in Britain by the constitutional settlement of the Glorious Revolution. Simultaneously and fervently, they also expressed their allegiance to the Hanoverian monarchy. Divisions existed in North American and West Indian societies between rich and poor, between evangelicals of several denominations inspired by revivalist preaching in the Great Awakening of the 1730s and 1740s and conventional Anglicans, between tidewater and backcountry, among different ethnic groups, and above all between blacks and whites. But what impresses most about this period of remarkable and sustained growth in all areas is the degree to which these diverse societies developed along similar lines and converged culturally. One means by which this convergence was achieved was through the expansion of the world of goods and the development of a commercial culture based on the extensive importation of consumer goods from Britain that gave a stylistic uniformity to British American culture. Just as important was the rise to authority in every colony of creole elites who by midcentury not only dominated politics but also functioned as the arbiters of social style. Anxious to show their credentials as English gentlemen, these colonial elites shared devotion to gentility, improvement, and Anglicization that not only linked them culturally to elites in the British homeland but also made them culturally, socially, and politically similar to one another.[25]

The dark undercurrent to British American stability and prosperity was slavery. For British American slaves, most of whom were unwilling migrants from West Africa, the first half of the eighteenth century was the period of their greatest degradation. The wealth of plantation British America and the gentility that resulted from planters' rising wealth were derived from the increasingly efficient and brutal exploitation of slave labor. Whites and blacks may have been intimately connected in relationships that were both close and negotiated, but those negotiations were unbalanced, allowing a savage master to exploit and traumatize, culturally and physically, vulnerable, isolated, and malnourished Africans. Planters achieved great success in their creation of a vicious plantation regime—slave revolts were few and ruthlessly quashed. But the threat of slave violence was a constant undertone in eighteenth-century British American life, and the climate of fear that governed relations between masters and slaves permeated all social interactions. White reliance on slavery rendered colonial claims of improvement and gentility extremely problematic.[26]

The most difficult period to treat within the rubric of British Atlantic history is the fourth: the late eighteenth and early nineteenth centuries. These were years of epochal change and crisis that heralded both the completion of an integrated British Atlantic world and its partial destruction.[27] On the one hand, the imperial mistakes that led to the American Revolution, the underlying ideological causes of that conflict, and the reverberations of the conflict and its resolution indicate the extent to which Britain and its colonies were enmeshed in a common Atlantic world with a common political vocabulary. To take just one example of the Atlantic dimensions of the American Revolution: Christopher Brown argues that the radical commitment to egalitarianism espoused by the founders of the American republic (many of whom, of course, were slaveholders themselves) led to a re-envisioning of empire as based upon subjecthood without slavery rather than upon settler rights with slavery, a re-envisioning that informed the growing clamor during the 1780s for the abolition of the slave trade.[28]

On the other hand, the formation of an independent United States left the British Atlantic truncated and reduced in power. The remaining communities of white Britons in the British Atlantic were small, isolated minorities, especially in the West Indies. They had diminishing influence within an empire where the vast majority of subjects were now brown or black. Whether the abolition of the slave trade and slavery would have occurred as soon as it did in the British Empire had the slaveholding colonies of North America remained attached to Britain is doubtful. Of course, independence did not end United States involvement with the Atlantic, as evidenced by continuing trade between Britain and its former colonies and by the origins of the War of 1812. But the resolution of that war and United States' acquisition of vast new territories with the Louisiana Purchase of 1803 (itself a consequence of French defeat in the Atlantic, in Haiti) allowed the United States to turn inward, toward continental expansion. Moreover, the advent of the industrial revolution in Britain and in the northeastern United States, the transition from a world of empires to a world of nation-states, and, within the United States, the increasing urgency of internal disputes between southern and northern states all helped to diminish the importance of Atlantic concerns in the United States in the nineteenth century.[29]

The Advantages of British Atlantic History

If this chronology largely predates the rise of Atlantic history after 1970, an Atlantic perspective has produced some other significant advances. Perhaps the single most important advance attributable to the Atlantic perspective has been its encouragement of the incorporation of Africans and Native Americans into the making of colonial British America. The British Atlantic world was mostly a black Atlantic world. British Atlantic historians have demonstrated that Africans comprised the large majority of migrants to British America—2.3 million Africans came between 1600 and 1800, compared to 1 million Europeans.[30] What they did when they came to British America was even more important than their numbers. Africans and people of African descent were the principal workers in British America. Their labor produced the goods—tobacco, rice, cotton, and, above all, sugar—that made British America prosperous and valuable to Britain. As Barbara Solow comments, "What moved in the Atlantic was predominantly slaves, the output of slaves, the inputs of slave societies, and the goods and services produced with the earnings on slave products."[31] Africans were also important culturally and socially. As slaves, they did not have the power to articulate the values and imperatives of colonial society in the way that culturally dominant British elites were able to do, but their influence on colonial sociocultural development was powerful nonetheless. In the Caribbean, particularly, their presence was so strong that African values permeated every aspect of society.

Recognition of the importance of Africans within British American history has encouraged British American historians to take Africa seriously as a region. What has become clear is the extent to which Africa was not a place that was acted upon by Europeans as much as a part of the world where European control was weak. Africans, not Europeans, controlled the tempo of the slave trade, and Africans, not Europeans, determined patterns of African–European interaction in West Africa.[32] Yet if Africa can no longer be discounted as an originary region of American culture, its importance is still understated. Much of what we know about Africa in the Americas has been provided by historians of Africa who extrapolate from Africa to the Americas, rather than by historians of British America with a thorough understanding of African cultures. Even the best studies of slavery, for example, by Philip Morgan and Ira Berlin, talk little about the African origins of American slaves. Africa remains to be fully incorporated into British Atlantic history.[33]

Native Americans are also not well integrated into Atlantic history, even though the work done on Native American history has increased exponentially in recent decades. The problem is related to chronology. In the seventeenth century, Native Americans were vital to Atlantic history, because they were the people whom Europeans first encountered when they crossed the Atlantic. Their differences from and similarities to Europeans forced Europeans to re-evaluate who they were, what type of society they came from, and what kind of world they wanted to create in the Americas. Britons' encounters with Native Americans in Virginia and New England helped shape attitudes to race and the environment that influenced all areas of early settlement.[34] Yet by the end of the seventeenth century, Native Americans in the colonies north of Virginia had been largely removed from the Atlantic coastline, to areas beyond the bounds of British settlement and into areas long occupied by other Native Americans. Historians have paid much attention to how Europeans and Indians interacted on what Richard White has called the Middle Ground, an arena of conflict marked by neither complete assimilation nor outright antagonism, but by an uneasy mixture of both. Little attempt, however, has been made to link what was happening in the interior to what was happening in the Atlantic. That linkage needs to be investigated more thoroughly, because mobility, fluidity, and instability marked the interior of North America as much as these features marked the British Atlantic.[35]

A second advantage of an Atlantic perspective has been a shift in geographical focus away from New England, especially, and from the mainland British colonies, generally. Two areas in particular have benefited from this shift toward seeing the Atlantic as an integrated region. We now pay much more attention than formerly to the sea and to the people who made their livings upon the sea. Pirates, sailors, and, above all, merchants play a prominent part in the British Atlantic world. As Alison Games argues, this world "depended not on the coherent vision imposed by a monarch or Board of Trade but instead on the experiences of men who lived around the globe in a series of overseas experiments."[36] The emphasis is on networks created not in the metropolis but in the peripheries, especially in the interstices between centers and peripheries. Particular attention is paid to the people who moved between different places in the Atlantic world, their peripatetic careers helping to cement linkages between people in a variety of loosely connected areas in ways that made the Atlantic world surprisingly integrated.[37] An excellent example of how networks operated in practice is David Hancock's study of a group of powerful and interconnected London merchants, whom he describes as "marginal, opportunistic, global, improving, and integrative." These merchants dwelt in both the metropolis and the provinces of Britain and America in the middle decades of the eighteenth century. In their search for wealth, they devised strategies that linked different parts of the Atlantic world, helping to "integrate the empire as they integrated their own business operations."[38] Another example of linkages, from a period somewhat later than is usually associated with Atlantic history, is Catherine Hall's illuminating study of the contested notions of race, class, and gender that connected Jamaica and Birmingham in the first half of the nineteenth century.[39]

As Hall's work suggests, Atlantic history has also been instrumental in restoring the British West Indies to its rightful position as the most dynamic part of British America. In this respect, Atlantic history is a very welcome development, rescuing colonial British history from anachronistic assumptions that the regions of North America that became culturally and economically important as a result of the formation of the United States were the most vital parts of British America in the seventeenth and eighteenth centuries. The West Indies may have been charnel grounds, eating up whites and blacks in such numbers that enormous immigration led to relatively small populations, but the wealth they produced, mostly from sugar, was enormous, making the white residents of these islands not only the wealthiest

people in the empire but influential beyond their numbers in imperial calculations. The West Indies were so valuable to Britain that Britain hastened
the loss of her North American colonies by withdrawing the navy from
Yorktown in order to prevent the French from conquering Jamaica.[40] They
were also the forging ground for that characteristic Atlantic institution,
slavery, with all British slaveholding regions following in the footsteps of
mid-seventeenth-century Barbados.[41]

By acknowledging the central role of the West Indian colonies in the
British Atlantic and by emphasizing that the wealthiest, most dynamic, and
most diplomatically important areas of British America were the slaveholding areas, scholarship is returning to the perspective that early modern Britons themselves held about the relative importance of the regions
of British America. The Duke of Newcastle, for example, a leading British
politician of the mid-eighteenth century, thought of West Indians when he
employed the term "American." He and other British leaders considered
the West Indies the most valuable part of the empire, because it produced
wealth and attracted significant amounts of British mercantile and maritime
capital. They derided as unimportant and troublesome the martial peoples of
New England. To understand how the British got American opinion about
imperial actions so wrong following 1763 is difficult without appreciating
that Britons, continental Americans, and West Indians all thought of New
England as the most distinctive, least integrated, and most troublesome
region of British America. Lord North's fatal mistake was in supposing
that this near universal opinion of the distinctiveness and isolation of New
England would allow Britain to punish the region without outraging colonial opinion elsewhere.[42]

A third advantage of doing British Atlantic history is that it redresses
American and British exceptionalism. To study the British Atlantic without
recognizing that British actions were shaped and constrained by the actions
of other imperial polities, notably the Spanish and French empires, is no longer intellectually sustainable. Comparing the British Atlantic to the Spanish
and French Atlantics is important in two ways. First, comparisons show
that British settlement in the Americas would not have occurred in the way
that it did without the examples of other imperial polities. As John Elliott
insists, contemporary comparisons between the Spanish and British empires
were "not between two self-contained cultural worlds, but between cultural
worlds that were well aware of each other's presence."[43] The first settlers at
Jamestown in 1607 had the Spanish example before them when envisioning
their new dominions. They imagined that they would emulate the Spanish in
finding gold and silver and in turning the Indians among whom they settled

into tributaries on the Spanish model, who would work to produce food and export items for them in return for European goods.[44] As settlement proceeded, comparisons continued to be made, mostly to the disadvantage of Spain and its empire. From the late sixteenth century, the "Black Legend" of Spanish cruelty and incivility was always a powerful force justifying British colonization, and it became the cornerstone of British discourse about British moral superiority as, in the eighteenth century, Spanish power declined. Spain became emblematic of backwardness, cruelty, and superstition. J. Hector St John de Crèvecoeur summed up British condescension in his comparison of the "gaudy" merchants of Lima, stuck in religious error and moral torpor, with the independent citizens of North America, whose upright behavior, tolerance of religious difference, and intensive pursuit of commerce and learning was an example that Spanish Americans needed to emulate. The boot was now on the other foot: the Spanish had to copy the British who had once copied them.[45]

The example of the French in America, however, was less easy for the British to dismiss. By the first third of the eighteenth century, France seemed on the verge of displacing the British as the fastest-growing and most successful empire in the Americas. For half a century France and Britain competed for domination of both North America and the Caribbean, with the interior region of the Ohio country becoming a principal arena of contention in the mid-eighteenth century. For most of that period the French looked as if they were going to outstrip the British in power and influence. In the Ohio country and in the lower Mississippi Valley, the French established more cordial relations with Native Americans than the British, in part because there were fewer French settlers to intrude on indigenous life. In the Caribbean, Saint Domingue was the wonder of the age, an economic powerhouse producing nearly 40 percent of overseas exports to France by the 1770s and surpassing even Jamaica as the leading sugar producer in the Greater Antilles.[46] Moreover, the British could not deride France as a backward nation in the way that they increasingly did Spain, even if French absolutism and French Catholicism offended them. One of the advantages of seeing Britain and British America in an Atlantic context is that it makes the challenge of France to British power in the Atlantic apparent and demonstrates as well the growing importance of events in the peripheries of the Americas to European affairs. It also suggests the importance of the Seven Years' War—the first global war with an important theater in North America—in the history of both Britain and America. With the French threat largely removed, British North Americans were able to define themselves differently from how metropolitans saw them.[47]

Placing British America in an Atlantic context produces yet a fourth advantage by encouraging historians to see what was distinctive about it. The distinctive features of early British American social development are most evident when counterposed to developments in Spanish America. Whereas Spanish American colonies tended to be amazingly polyglot societies that were internally heterogeneous but very similar in social and political organization at the macro level, and were subject to steadier efforts of control from a more authoritarian and intrusive center, British American colonies were internally homogenous, with powerful mechanisms that excluded outsiders from social and political membership except, in the cases of African-Americans and incorporated Native Americans, as legal outsiders without a political presence. Conversely, their internal homogeneity made them, by Spanish American standards, heterogeneous as polities. That heterogeneity was enhanced by the relatively ineffectual interference that the British government exerted over their social and political direction. British colonies had more autonomy and more latitude to make their own way in the world, a way usually determined by the twin factors of the nature of their individual origins and their experience in fashioning workable societies.[48]

A fifth advantage of Atlantic history is that it has encouraged historians of colonial British America to study the connections and collisions of different cultural worlds and the identities formed as a result of them. The most obvious collisions were among Europeans, Africans, and Native Americans, making race and hybridity a particular focus in Atlantic history. But Atlantic historians have also been interested in how different groups of Europeans adjusted to new environments and new peoples in British America. Migration has been a particular interest among those historians specifically concerned to trace the formation of American identities, constructed out of the mix between inheritance and experience.[49] Those identities were also linked to both production and consumption; and commerce, especially in staples and slaves, the most dynamic areas of Atlantic commerce, has been much studied.

Merchants were the group who most symbolized British transatlantic connections, their trading relationships knitting together people on three continents[50] as they moved goods across the Atlantic. But the Atlantic was also a venue for the movement of ideas, including the republican ideology that linked British Americans with radical opposition in Britain and paved the way for the ideological split between the mother country and its American colonies in the 1760s and 1770s.[51] More recently, scholars have turned their attention to how common ideas of science and natural history also connected Americans with Europeans in a shared Atlantic culture of enlightened cosmopolitanism. They have shown how Europeans used their understanding of American knowledge systems to advance Enlightenment thought in Europe, while Americans advanced claims to equality with Europeans through their investigations into American natural phenomena.[52]

But the Atlantic world was also knit together in less pleasant ways. The British Atlantic world was a remarkably underinstitutionalized world full of unassimilated populations who had little to unite them except mutual fear and cultural misunderstanding. The threat and application of force and the acceptance of a level of violence in relations with the enslaved and with indigenous peoples marked the peripheries of empire as savage and outside the normal experience of Europeans, themselves not unused to brutality. The colonial world was one riven by wars.[53] In the seventeenth century, these wars were especially brutal, both in Ireland and Scotland during the Civil War and in British America throughout the seventeenth century, from the Indian massacre in the early 1620s in Virginia to the savagery of Bacon's Rebellion and King Philip's War in the mid-1670s. Unlike wars in continental Europe, the objectives of these Atlantic conflicts with the indigenes were not just to defeat an enemy but also to destroy by any means, including torture and genocide, the civilizations of people characterized as "others." The violence left great scars, not only on the victims but also on the perpetrators. The ferocity of King Philip's War, which laid waste the New England countryside, confirmed for many observers not only that New England was declining from its high-minded ideals but also that America had turned even Europeans savage.[54] In the eighteenth century, outright savagery in warfare receded to the frontier, which remained as lawless and barbaric as in the seventeenth century. Violence, however, remained a constant part of British Atlantic life, even in settled and improved areas, because of the expansion of slavery, which became notably more vicious with the expansion of the plantation system in southern North America and the West Indies.[55]

The Limits of British Atlantic History

Without question, an Atlantic perspective has reinvigorated colonial British American history, a field that was flourishing but was perhaps in danger of becoming too specialized and fragmented. It is a perspective, moreover, that in its emphasis on global connections and multicultural diversity speaks to contemporary concerns in the English-speaking world, especially in a United States undergoing significant Hispanicization. Yet it also has some distinct limitations. British Atlantic historians display strong assimilationist and homogenizing tendencies in their relentless search for connections to link disparate parts of the Atlantic world. An important weakness is blindness to the fact that networks, transatlantic connections, cosmopolitan attitudes, and flux and mobility can be as destructive as they are creative. If Atlantic networks allowed previously unconnected activities and lives to be brought together, they also permitted previously connected ones to be wrenched apart, as in the Atlantic slave trade. Notably, historians of African-American migration focus less on how the Atlantic experience transformed Africans than on how aspects of African culture managed to survive. One way of avoiding the conclusion that the Atlantic experiences destroyed their sense of selfhood and community is to insist on continuity between specific African cultural practices from geographically defined African regions and African–American cultural development in the New World.[56]

The excitement generated among British American colonial historians about the merits of Atlantic history, moreover, has not been shared by historians of either Britain or the United States. Atlantic historians pride themselves on escaping the straitjacket of nation-state history; United States histories remain implanted within a nation-state framework riven by the old assumptions that (1) United States history is exceptional and (2) that the audience for United States history consists mostly of Americans uninterested in how the United States interacts with the rest of the world. The number of studies using an Atlantic focus diminishes quickly after 1789 and comprises but a small proportion of the avalanche of scholarship produced by United States historians of the national era. Even Revolutionary and early republic scholars tend, in the main, to link their work with later periods, and are concerned mostly with illuminating themes in American national development rather than with the key findings on the colonial period. Colonial scholars are far more anxious than Revolutionary historians to avoid the teleology implicit in studying only those colonies that would later become part of the United States.[57]

The possibility of escaping nation-state boundaries is exciting for historians but is fraught with problems, in part because other groups of historians continue to find comfort in the nation-state as an organizing device. Colonial history, with its predilection for regional organization and expansive interest in the larger British imperial world, has always resisted integration into the history of the United States. The movement to Atlantic history, where discontinuities are welcomed, multiplicities of places and perspectives are normative, and chronology does not always revolve around traditionally important political events, has only highlighted this lack of integration.[58] No doubt, as Michael Zuckerman insists, floating free of the nation-state has costs, most notably in disconnecting the colonial history of British North America from its traditional role as a source for understanding the character of the United States.[59] To the extent that Atlantic historians have been reluctant to participate in this particular project, they have tended to distance themselves from the concerns of British and United States historians: chronological markers, national identities, and national institutions and development. One way of lessening this distance is to recognize that the colonial process did not end in North America with the creation of the United States.[60]

Whether an Atlantic history framework is the best device for examining the continuities between either colonial and metropolitan spheres in the early modern British world or colonial and national eras in North America is unclear. The period since the late 1980s has witnessed a growing interest in the study of the phenomenon of empire, a subject that almost an entire generation had abandoned as a reminder of a shameful past. If this resurgence of imperial studies, referred to by some scholars as the imperial turn, has to date focused more on nineteenth- and twentieth-century empires, it also suggests that an imperial perspective might in many respects be preferable to an Atlantic perspective in the illumination of the early modern British overseas world.[61] We do not have to discount the interconnections that existed among early modern American empires to appreciate the fact that competing national empires dominated the early modern Atlantic world, with the significant exceptions of West Africa and vast sections of the interiors of the two Americas. Organized into national entities, these empires represented dramatic expansions, if also significant reformulations, of emerging national European cultures that differed from one another in language, law, institutions, traditions, economic orientation, and religion. An imperial framework proceeds from recognition of the realities of power relations within the empire, realities that have been obscured by British Atlantic historians' emphasis on fluidity, connections, and transnational exchange.[62]

Yet Atlantic historians, perhaps especially in the United States, a nation traditionally ambivalent about the virtues of empire, seem to be resistant to making the imperial turn, perhaps fearing that such a project would subordinate the interests of the peripheries to those of the center, and would overstate the extent to which the center was able to dictate how peripheries evolved.[63] Ironically, however, some British Atlantic historians, while avowedly antiimperialist in orientation and methodology, have decidedly imperialist ambitions, arguing that the best way to see British Atlantic distinctiveness is within a global context.[64] Making Atlantic history a subsection of world history, however, is likely to blur rather than weaken anti-imperialist assumptions. For one thing, it might accentuate two of the most glaring weaknesses in Atlantic history: its inattention to the interior life of individuals, especially ordinary individuals, whose connections to the larger themes of the Atlantic world were tenuous; and its fixation on extraordinary individuals, whose very extraordinariness raises questions about typicality. Two excellent recent books illustrate this last weakness. Randy Sparks relates the tale of highborn African slave traders hijacked into the Atlantic slave trade, who, through their considerable linguistic and interpersonal skills and their advantage of being "princes," managed to return to being slave traders in Calabar. Jon Sensbach tells us about the remarkable life of Rebecca Protten, a converted Christian who proselytized in both the Caribbean and Africa. But such lives were wildly atypical for Africans and African-Americans condemned to a short and brutish life on sugar, rice, or tobacco plantations, and thus hide the normative experiences of most slaves. Clearly, we need to pay attention to people at both ends of the continuum.[65]

The real test for history done in a British Atlantic way is what happens next. Clearly, the interest in Atlantic history by early modern British American historians is not a fad. The British Atlantic is not a figment of the historical imagination. Its existence is undeniable, and the transmission of people, ideas, and goods across the Atlantic and among different regions led to important and lasting connections that shaped early American, British, and West African life. We need to study those connections and try to make sense of what the constant motion of the Atlantic world meant for power relations and quotidian existence. But the limitations of such an approach are real, and what we have gained from an Atlantic perspective is almost matched by what we have lost by abandoning other ways of doing history. Indeed, if we compare what has been achieved by Atlantic historians to the advances in our understanding of New England, the Chesapeake, and English society in the heyday of the "new" social history of the 1970s, Atlantic history scarcely comes out as superior. Moreover, the natural tendency of an approach in history is to expand until it reaches unworkable limits. With calls to expand the Atlantic world into Asia, the Pacific, and the world generally, and with increasing pressure for British Atlantic historians to master the languages and histories of other European nations and of West Africa, instead of concentrating on linking their work with the history of the United States and Britain, and with work done in disciplines other than history, we may be reaching a point at which the limitations of this rapidly expanding subject are beginning to become apparent.

NOTES

1. For a recent discussion, see "Forum: Beyond Atlantic History," *William and Mary Quarterly* 3rd ser., LXIII (2006): 675–742.

2. Peter E. Pope, *Fish into Wine: The Newfoundland Plantation in the Seventeenth Century* (Chapel Hill: University of North Carolina Press, 2004); Kenneth R. Andrews, *Trade, Plunder and Settlement: Maritime Enterprise and the British Empire 1480–1650* (Liverpool: Liverpool University Press, 1978).

3. For the relationship between British Atlantic history and "new" British history, see David Armitage, "Greater Britain: A Useful Category of Historical Analysis?," *American Historical Review* 104 (1999): 427–445, and *The Ideological Origins of the British Empire* (Cambridge: Cambridge University Press, 2000). For the European context, see Jonathan Scott, *England's Troubles: Seventeenth-Century English Political Instability in European Context* (Cambridge: Cambridge University Press, 2000). For Ireland, see Nicholas Canny, *Making Ireland British 1580–1650* (Oxford: Oxford University Press, 2001). For Scotland, see T. M Devine, *Scotland's Empire 1600–1815* (London: Allen Lane, 2003).

4. Jack P. Greene, *Pursuits of Happiness: The Social Development of Early Modern British Colonies and the Formation of American Culture* (Chapel Hill: University of North Carolina Press, 1988), p. 179.

5. See, inter alia, Jane T. Merritt, *At the Crossroads: Indians and Empires on a Mid-Atlantic Frontier, 1700–1763* (Chapel Hill: University of North Carolina Press, 2003); Daniel Richter, *Facing East from Indian Country* (Cambridge, Mass.: Harvard University Press, 2003); and Eric Hinderaker, *Elusive Empires: Constructing Colonialism in the Ohio Valley, 1673–1800* (Cambridge: Cambridge University Press, 1997).

6. Fred Anderson, *Crucible of War: The Seven Years' War and the Fate of Empire in British North America, 1754–1766* (New York: Alfred A. Knopf, 2000); Colin G. Calloway, *The Scratch of a Pen: 1763 and the Transformation of North America* (Oxford: Oxford University Press, 2006).

7. Benjamin Franklin, "Observations Concerning the Increase of Mankind," in Leonard W. Labaree et al., eds., *The Papers of Benjamin Franklin* (New Haven: Yale University Press, 1959), vol.4, pp. 233–234.

8. P. J. Marshall, "Britain Without Empire—A Second Empire?," in Marshall's *The Oxford History of the British Empire: The Eighteenth Century* (Oxford: Oxford University Press), p. 579. For Bermuda in the Atlantic world, see Michael Jarvis, *Bermuda and Bermudians in the Maritime Atlantic World, 1680–1800* (Chapel Hill: University of North Carolina Press, 2009).

9. Jack P. Greene, "Colonial and National History: Reflections on a Continuing Problem," *William and Mary Quarterly* 3rd ser., LXIV (2007): 235–250.

10. Linda Colley, *Britons: Forging the Nation, 1707–1837* (London: Verso, 1992); Eliga Gould, *The Persistence of Empire: British Political Culture in the Age of the American Revolution* (Chapel Hill: University of North Carolina Press, 2000).

11. Joyce E. Chaplin, "Expansion and Exceptionalism in Early American History," *Journal of American History* 89 (2003): 1431–1455; Jack P. Greene, *The Intellectual Construction of America: Exceptionalism and Identity from 1492 to 1800* (Chapel Hill: University of North Carolina Press, 1993).

12. David Starkey, "Little Englanders Have History on Their Side," *Sunday Times*, October 17, 2004.

13. Cited in G. S. Stourzh, *Benjamin Franklin and American Foreign Policy* (Chicago: University of Chicago Press, 1969), p. 98.

14. Bernard Bailyn, *Atlantic History: Concept and Contours* (Cambridge, Mass.: Harvard University Press, 2005), p. 9.

15. J. R. Seeley, *The Expansion of England: Two Courses of Lectures* (London: Macmillan, 1894), p. 9; H. E. Marshall, *Our Island Story: a child's history of England* (London: T.C. and E.C. Jack 1905).

16. For a vigorous exposition, see Brendan Simms, *Three Victories and a Defeat: The Rise and Fall of the First British Empire, 1714–1783* (London: Allen Lane, 2007). See also Jeremy Black, *America or Europe? British Foreign Policy, 1739–1763* (London: UCL Press, 1997); and Marie Peters, "The Myth of William Pitt, Earl of Chatham, Great Imperialist: I. Pitt and Imperial Expansion, 1738–1763," *Journal of Imperial and Commonwealth History* 21 (2003): 31–74.

17. David Armitage, *The Declaration of Independence: A Global History* (Cambridge, Mass.: Harvard University Press, 2006); J. G. A. Pocock, *Virtue, Commerce and History* (Cambridge: Cambridge University Press, 1985).

18. Armitage, "Greater Britain," pp. 434–446. See also J. G. A. Pocock, *The Discovery of Islands: Essays in British History* (Cambridge: Cambridge University Press, 2005), pp. 3–46. An extremely influential survey of colonial British America that provided a vital link between the "new" social history of the 1970s and British Atlantic history expressly insists in its subtitle that all of colonial British American history belongs to the early modern period. Jack P. Greene and J. R. Pole, eds., *Colonial British America: Essays in the New History of the Early Modern Era* (Baltimore: Johns Hopkins University Press, 1984).

19. A significant exception is J. C. D. Clark, *The Language of Liberty, 1660–1832: Political Discourse and Social Dynamics in the Anglo–American World* (Cambridge: Cambridge University Press, 1994), in which Clark sees England in terms of ancien régime during a very long eighteenth century.

20. See, for example, Greene, *Pursuits of Happiness*; Ira Berlin, *Many Thousands Gone: The First Two Centuries of Slavery in North America* (Cambridge, Mass.: Harvard University Press, 1998); and D. W. Meinig, *The Shaping of America*, vol 1: *Atlantic America, 1492–1800* (New Haven: Yale University Press, 1986).

21. David Lambert, *White Creole Culture: Politics and Identity During the Age of Abolition* (Cambridge: Cambridge University Press, 2005); Alan Lester, "British Settler Discourse and the Circuits of Empire," *History Workshop Journal* 54 (2002): 27–50. For indigenous opposition to settler assumptions, see Daiva Stasiulis and

Nira Yuval-Davis, eds., *Unsettling Settler Societies: Articulations of Gender, Race, Ethnicity and Class* (London: Sage, 1995).

22. Carla Gardner Pestana, *The English Atlantic in an Age of Revolution 1640–1661* (Cambridge, Mass.: Harvard University Press, 2004), pp. 9, 226; Russell R. Menard, *Sweet Negotiations: Sugar, Slavery, and Plantation Agriculture in Early Barbados* (Charlottesville: University Press of Virginia, 2006).

23. For representative works, see Karen Kupperman, *The Jamestown Project* (Cambridge, Mass.: Belknap Press of Harvard University Press, 2007); Peter Mancall, *Hakluyt's Promise: An Elizabethan's Obsession for an English America* (New Haven: Yale University Press, 2007); James Horn, *A Land as God Made It: Jamestown and the Birth of America* (New York: Basic Books, 2005); Jorge Cañizares Esguerra, *Puritan Conquistadors: Iberianizing the Atlantic, 1550–1700* (Stanford: Stanford University Press, 2006).

24. William A. Pettigrew, "Free to Enslave: Politics and the Escalation of Britain's Transatlantic Slave Trade, 1688–1714," *William and Mary Quarterly* 3rd ser., LXIV (2007): 3–38; Wayne E. Lee, "Early American Warfare: A New Reconnaissance," *Historical Journal* 44 (2001): 269–289; Ian K. Steele, *The English Atlantic, 1675–1740* (Oxford: Oxford University Press, 1986); Simms, *Three Victories and a Defeat*; and Anderson, *Crucible of War*.

25. Bernard Bailyn, *The Origin of American Politics* (New York: Alfred A. Knopf, 1968); Brendan McConville, *The King's Three Faces: The Rise and Fall of Royal America 1688–1776* (Chapel Hill: University of North Carolina Press, 2006); Alan Tully, *Forming American Politics: Ideals, Interests and Institutions in Colonial New York and Pennsylvania* (Baltimore: Johns Hopkins University Press, 1994); Cary Carson et al., eds., *Of Consuming Interest: The Style of Life in the Eighteenth Century* (Charlottesville: University Press of Virginia, 1994); Patricia U. Bonomi, *Under the Cope of Heaven: Religion, Society and Politics in Colonial America* (New York: Oxford University Press, 1986), pp. 161–186; and Michael Rozbicki, *The Complete Colonial Gentleman: Cultural Legitimacy in Plantation America* (Charlottesville: University Press of Virginia, 1998).

26. For the development of the mature plantation complex, see Anthony S. Parent, Jr., *Foul Means: The Formation of a Slave Society in Virginia, 1660–1740* (Chapel Hill: University of North Carolina Press, 2003); and Morgan, *Slave Counterpoint*. For close-grained studies of master–slave interactions, see Rhys Isaac, *Landon Carter's Uneasy Kingdom: Revolution and Rebellion on a Virginia Slave Plantation* (New York: Oxford University Press, 2004); and Trevor Burnard, *Mastery, Tyranny, and Desire: Thomas Thistlewood and His Slaves in the Anglo–Jamaican World* (Chapel Hill: University of North Carolina Press, 2004). For slave revolts, see David Barry Gaspar, *Bondmen and Rebels: A Study of Master–Slave Relations in Antigua with Implications for Colonial British America* (Baltimore: Johns Hopkins University Press, 1985).

27. For global crisis, see C. A. Bayly, *The Birth of the Modern World 1780–1914* (Oxford: Blackwell, 2004), pp. 86–120.

28. Christopher Leslie Brown, *Moral Capital: Foundations of British Abolitionism* (Chapel Hill: University of North Carolina Press, 2006), pp. 209–258, 333–390.

29. Armitage, *Declaration of Independence*; D. W. Meinig, *Continental America: 1800–1867*, vol. 2: *The Shaping of America: A Geographical Perspective on 500 Years of History* (New Haven: Yale University Press, 1993); Chaplin, "Expansion and Exceptionalism," pp. 1440–1441; and Adam Rothman, *Slave Country: American Expansion and the Origins of the Deep South* (Cambridge, Mass.: Harvard University Press, 2005).

30. Philip D. Curtin, *The Atlantic Slave Trade: A Census* (Madison: University of Wisconsin Press, 1969); James Horn and Philip D. Morgan, "Settlers and Slaves: European and African Migrations to Early Modern British America," in Carole Shammas and Elizabeth Mancke, eds., *The Creation of the British Atlantic World* (Baltimore: Johns Hopkins University Press, 2005), pp. 32–74.

31. Barbara L. Solow, ed., *Slavery and the Rise of the Atlantic System* (Cambridge: Cambridge University Press, 1991), p. 1.

32. David Richardson, "Shipboard Revolts, African Authority, and the Atlantic Slave Trade," *William and Mary Quarterly* 3rd ser., LVIII (2001): 69–70.

33. Berlin, *Many Thousands Came*; Philip D. Morgan, *Slave Counterpoint: Black Culture in the Eighteenth-Century Chesapeake & Lowcountry* (Chapel Hill: University of North Carolina Press, 1998).

34. See, inter alia, Joyce E. Chaplin, *Subject Matter: Technology, the Body, and Science on the Anglo-American Frontier, 1500–1676* (Cambridge, Mass.: Harvard University Press, 2001).

35. See the inattention to Atlantic history in "Forum: The Middle Ground Revisited," *William and Mary Quarterly* 3rd ser., LXIII (2006): 1–96.

36. Games, "Beyond the Atlantic," p. 692.

37. David Lambert and Alan Lester, eds., *Colonial Lives Across the British Empire* (Cambridge: Cambridge University Press, 2006), p. 13.

38. David Hancock, *Citizens of the World: London Merchants and the Integration of the British Atlantic Community, 1735–1785* (Cambridge: Cambridge University Press, 1995), pp. 3, 14.

39. Catherine Hall, *Civilising Subjects: Metropole and Colony in the British Imagination* (Cambridge: Polity Press, 2003).

40. Andrew Jackson O'Shaughnessy, *The Empire Divided: The American Revolution and the British Caribbean* (Philadelphia: University of Pennsylvania Press, 2000), pp. 231–233. For the wealth of the British West Indies, see Richard B. Sheridan, *Sugar and Slavery: An Economic History of the British West Indies, 1623–1775* (Bridgetown, Barbados: University of the West Indies Press, 1974).

41. Menard, *Sweet Negotiations*.

42. Julie Flavell, "British Perceptions of New England and the Decision for a Coercive Colonial Policy, 1774–1775," in Flavell and Stephen Conway, eds., *Britain and America Go to War: The Impact of War and Warfare in Anglo-America, 1754–1815* (Gainesville: University of Florida Press, 2004), pp. 95–115.

43. J. H. Elliott, *Empires of the Atlantic World: Britain and Spain in America 1492–1830* (New Haven: Yale University Press, 2006), p. xvii.

44. Horn, *A Land as God Made It*.

45. Crèvecoeur, "Sketch of a Contrast Between the Spanish and the English Colonies," in Dennis D. Moore, ed., *More Letters from the American Farmer* (Athens: University of Georgia Press, 1995); Charles Gibson, *The Black Legend: Anti-Spanish Attitudes in the Old World and the New* (New York: Alfred A. Knopf, 1971), pp. 82–89.

46. Laurent Dubois, *Avengers of the New World: The Story of the Haitian Revolution* (Cambridge, Mass.: Harvard University Press, 2004), pp. 20–21.

47. Colley, *Britons*; Anderson, *Crucible of War*, pp. 641–746.

48. Elliott, *Atlantic Empires*, pp. 409–411.

49. Bernard Bailyn, *Voyagers to the West: A Passage in the Peopling of America on the Eve of Revolution* (New York: Alfred A. Knopf, 1986); Alison F. Games, *Migration and the Origins of the Atlantic World* (Cambridge, Mass.: Harvard University Press, 1999); Aaron S. Fogleman, *Hopeful Journeys: German Immigration, Settlement, and Political Culture in Colonial America, 1717–1775* (Philadelphia: University of Pennsylvania Press, 1996).

50. John J. McCusker and Kenneth Morgan, eds., *The Early Modern Atlantic Economy* (Cambridge: Cambridge University Press, 2001); Sheryllynne Haggerty, *The British Atlantic Trading Community 1760–1810: Men, Women, and the Distribution of Goods* (Leiden: Brill, 2006).

51. The classic work is J. G. A. Pocock, *The Machiavellian Moment: Florentine Political Thought and the Atlantic Republican Tradition* (Princeton: Princeton University Press, 1975). For the ideological impact of the Revolution, see Gordon S. Wood, *The Radicalism of the American Revolution* (New York: Alfred A. Knopf, 1991).

52. Susan Scott Parrish, *American Curiosity: Cultures of Natural History in the Colonial British Atlantic World* (Chapel Hill: University of North Carolina Press, 2006); Londa Schiebinger, *Plants and Empire:Colonial Bioprospecting in the Atlantic World* (Cambridge, Mass.: Harvard University Press, 2005); Joyce E. Chaplin, *The First Scientific American: Benjamin Franklin and the Pursuit of Genius* (New York: Basic Books, 2006).

53. Bruce P. Lenman, *Britain's Colonial Wars, 1688–1783* (Harlow, U.K.: Longman, 2000).

54. Bailyn, *Atlantic History*, pp. 62–68; Canny, *Making Ireland British*, pp. 461–550; Chaplin, *Subject Matter*, pp. 264–270; Jill Lepore, *The Name of War: King Philip's War and the Origins of American Identity* (New York: Alfred A. Knopf, 1999).

55. James H. Merrell, *Into the American Woods: Negotiators on the Pennsylvania Frontier* (New York: W. W. Norton, 1999), pp. 285–288; Berlin, *Many Thousands Came*, pp. 98–116; Burnard, *Mastery, Tyranny, and Desire*, pp. 137–174.

56. Michael A. Gomez, *Exchanging Our Country Marks: The Transformation of African Identities in the Colonial and Antebellum South* (Chapel Hill: University

of North Carolina Press, 1998); Gwendolyn Midlo Hall, *Slavery and Ethnicities in the Americas: Restoring the Links* (Chapel Hill: University of North Carolina Press, 2005).

57. Chaplin, "Expansion and Exceptionalism."

58. Few scholars treat the Atlantic world as continuing into the nineteenth and twentieth centuries, but see Donna Gabaccia, "A Long Atlantic in a Wider World," *Atlantic Studies* 1 (2004): 1–27.

59. Michael Zuckerman, "Regionalism," in Daniel Vickers, ed., *A Companion to Colonial America* (Oxford: Blackwell, 2003), pp. 319, 329.

60. See Greene, "Colonial History and National History."

61. See essays by Christopher Schmidt-Nowara, Susan Pennybacker, Robert Gregg, and Tony Ballantyne, in Antoinette Burton, ed., *After the Imperial Turn: Thinking with and Through the Nation* (Durham, N.C.: Duke University Press, 2003).

62. A useful corrective is P. J. Marshall, *The Making and Unmaking of Empires: Britain, India, and America c. 1750–1783* (Oxford: Oxford University Press, 2005).

63. Bailyn, *Atlantic History*, p. 5; Jack P. Greene, *Peripheries and Centers: Constitutional Development in the Extended Polities of the British Empire and the United States 1607–1788* (Athens: University of Georgia Press, 1986), pp. 7–12.

64. Peter A. Coclanis, "Atlantic World or Atlantic/World?" *William and Mary Quarterly* 3rd ser., LXIII (2006): 725–742.

65. Randy J. Sparks, *The Two Princes of Calabar: An Eighteenth-Century Atlantic Odyssey* (Cambridge, Mass.: Harvard University Press, 2004); and Jon F. Sensbach, *Rebecca's Revival: Creating Black Christianity in the Atlantic World* (Cambridge, Mass.: Harvard University Press, 2005).

5

THE FRENCH ATLANTIC

LAURENT DUBOIS

In July 1967, French President Charles de Gaulle boarded the *Colbert* and set out across the Atlantic to Canada. In Montreal, he was greeted by crowds of well-wishers who occasionally sang the *Marseillaise*, and in a public speech he shouted, "Vive le Québec Libre!"—"Long live Free Québec!" After a brief moment of stunned silence, the crowd, 15,000 strong, exploded into applause: De Gaulle had just shouted the slogan of the movement for Québecois sovereignty. The Canadian government was furious, but one of De Gaulle's advisers complimented him by saying, "My general, you have paid the debt owed by Louis XV." In embracing the aspirations of the Québecois, according to this interpretation, De Gaulle had made up for the abandonment of their ancestors two centuries earlier. Quebec nationalists have, since then, used their history of participation in the French Empire as the foundation for their contemporary demands for cultural and political autonomy, notably by changing the province's slogan to "Je me souviens"—"I remember."[1]

Several decades later, in 2004, France was placed face to face with another, far less gratifying debt. Haitian President Jean-Bertrand Aristide, politically besieged—and soon to be forced out of power—used the occasion of the bicentennial of Haitian independence in 1804 to demand repayment of the large indemnity the French government had required Haiti to pay in 1825 in return for recognition of the former colony's independence. The indemnity was symbolically odious: it forced a nation created out slave revolution to reimburse its former masters. It also placed a heavy burden on the Haitian state well into the twentieth century; Aristide claimed that his nation's, poverty was "The result of a 200-year-old plot." The French government refused Aristide's demand, and soon French troops were actually back in Haiti, for the first time since 1804, as part of a United Nations mission to oversee new elections in the country.[2]

The story of these two debts, one paid symbolically, the other refused, highlight and frame the complex history and ongoing legacies of the history of the French Atlantic. The French imperial system in the Americas governed, or sought to govern, a diverse range of territories and populations from Canada to Louisiana, and throughout the Caribbean and the northern coast of South America. Through war and revolution, between the mid-eighteenth century and 1804, France lost most of its colonial holdings—to the British, to the United States, and to the revolutionaries who founded Haiti—though it maintained, as it still does, control of Guadeloupe, Martinique, and French Guiana. But the French-speaking populations left behind in North America, and their descendants, continued to define themselves culturally, and sometimes politically, as part of the French Atlantic.

This chapter begins by tracing the contours of the French Atlantic, identifying some of the structures and systems that held it together while also emphasizing the profound diversity of its populations and the historical trajectories within it. It then explores how the use of Atlantic approaches has contributed to our understanding of this history, and how it might continue to do so in future scholarship.

The French Atlantic was, as the historian Kenneth Banks has written, a region of startling geographic diversity, "ranging from ice floes to equatorial rain forests, from rocky islets to humid swamps and tundra, across two major oceanic wind and current systems and another half-dozen major regional subsystems." It encompassed a wide range of levels of control, involving claims—though sometimes difficult to justify—over "a wide swath of territory under direct or indirect French rule." The area as he defines it included:

> [T]he ports and their hinterlands of France's Atlantic littoral (called the Ponant), Marseille in the Mediterranean, and the center of administration at Paris/Versailles; the French slaving posts of West Africa, from the Senegambia to the Bight of Benin but centered at Fort Saint Louis and later Gorée; North America, with three affiliated settlement colonies of New France (Canada, Louisiana, and Ile Royale), plus "British-occupied" Acadia and the crucial fisheries of Terre-Neuve (Newfoundland); the Caribbean, centered on Saint-Domingue (Haiti after 1804) in the west and Martinique, Guadeloupe, and their dependent islands in the eastern arc of the Lesser Antilles; and the anemic colony of Cayenne on the South American mainland.[3]

Within this system, the size of territories was, interestingly, inversely proportionate to their ultimate economic and political importance. For it was the colonies of the Caribbean, first those of Martinique and Guadeloupe but later the "pearl" of the French Empire, Saint-Domingue, that were by far the most productive and economically successful colonies. Though the French government focused much energy on the colonization of Canada, over the long term, especially when war with England forced it to make choices, it centered its military and political attention on the Caribbean.

The French colonies in North America, in contrast to the British colonies, attracted comparatively small numbers of settlers. A maximum of 70,000 settlers departed for French Canada, and another 7,000 to French colonies in Acadia, Île Royale, and Terre Neuve. Louisiana, meanwhile, received no more than 7,000 settlers during its time as a French colony, with about 6,000 slaves arriving during the same period. Many more French settlers, meanwhile, went to the French Caribbean, though no historian has established a precise figure for this migration. Some have estimated as many as 300,000 over the course of the seventeenth and eighteenth centuries, although that number is probably too high, and the total may have been as low as 100,000.[4]

By far the largest group of arrivals in the French Americas were African slaves. According to the most recent calculations, a total of approximately 1,118,000 enslaved Africans were imported into the French Caribbean between the seventeenth and the nineteenth century. The vast majority of these—just under 800,000—arrived in Saint-Domingue, and just over 200,000 arrived in Martinique. Guadeloupe, which received most of its slaves via transshipment from Martinique, nevertheless received over 37,000 from the French slave trade, and at least another 30,000 from the British slave trade during periods of occupation. French Guiana received 26,000, with several thousand of those brought by the British. Even if French migration is estimated generously and slave imports are estimated very conservatively, enslaved Africans made up at least two-thirds of the population that came into the French Americas. This parallels the larger demographic patterns in the Atlantic world.[5]

Why did comparatively few voluntary migrants leave France for North America? The French colonies in the Americas got quite a bit of bad press, much of it exaggerated but some of it probably deserved. In the case of Louisiana, the combination of a sluggish economy and, most important, a devastating epidemiological environment—in which up to 60 percent of European arrivals died—explains why few people, even prisoners offered an alternative to their sentences there, wanted to go there. Settlers braved similar dangers from disease in the French Caribbean largely because they imagined, with relatively good reasons, at least during the first half of the

eighteenth century, that if they survived, they would have significant opportunities for social mobility. In Canada conditions, though often harsh, were
a little more inviting than in Louisiana, but still the economic prospects
were generally more limited than in the Caribbean.

There were very small numbers of settlers who went to French colonies to escape religious persecution, largely because the French Crown
generally excluded non-Catholics from their colonies. French Huguenots
did, however, migrate in significant numbers to non-French colonies in the
Americas, notably New York, and even to Dutch South Africa, thus creating crossings and connections between France and other Atlantic empires.
Migration to French Canada, meanwhile, was primarily an extension of patterns of movement taking place *within* France itself, drawing mainly from
the populations of the Atlantic coast of France, many of them more mobile
and better off—in part because of the expanding economy tied to colonial
expansion—than the population elsewhere in France. Canada, then, was a
destination for the more adventurous or determined migrants from a certain
region of France, driven less by misery than by a desire to continue to go
beyond the opportunities available to them within France. The transatlantic
crossing was often envisioned as the beginning of a short-term sojourn, and
many settlers did indeed return to Europe. Many of the migrants were soldiers, and they were overwhelmingly male. The French Crown repeatedly
did, however, send orphaned girls, granted a royal dowry to facilitate their
marriage, to Canada, in order to help create white settler families in the New
World.[6]

Canadian settlers had fertility rates that were higher, and death rates that
were lower, than populations in France. A few hundred French settlers in
Acadia had created, in part through intermarriage with indigenous communities, a population of about 15,000 by 1755, when the British carried out
the deportation of many of them, and the population of Quebec at the time
of the conquest in 1763 was 75,000. This relatively small pool of migrants
made up the ancestors of the approximately 6 million French Canadians
living today.[7]

The reverse was true in the Caribbean, where the largest group of arrivals,
African slaves, found themselves decimated by the harsh work regime. There,
deaths always outpaced births on the plantations, leaving the population of
Haiti at the time of independence at well under half a million, despite the
arrival of perhaps as many as twice that many people in the previous century.
The Haitian Revolution further decimated this population, partly through the
flight of whites but much more importantly through the death of people of
African descent as a result of warfare. After independence, however, with

the majority of the population better fed and of course more autonomous than during the period of slavery, the population of Haiti quickly grew, like the population of French descent in Canada.

The movement of people, both from France to America and from Africa to America, was largely governed by the policies of the French Crown. The French Empire was governed through a highly centralized system. This system always struggled with various differentiating, even centrifugal, forces within the empire. Nevertheless, there were dimensions that gave the larger imperial structure what Kenneth Banks calls a "coherency." All the colonies were overseen by a single state agency, the Marine, which connected the royal government to the colonies, oversaw the navy, and infused much of the governance of the colonies with a military ethos. The French government sought to establish a "standard language" for colonial governance, and "colonial administrators were drawn from across France and trained in different regions in order to enhance priorities based on the national vision set by the court," while "French settlers from distinct regions merged their inherited traditions within an increasingly 'creole' or 'habitant' one." All of the regions in the French Atlantic, meanwhile, were tied together by "a largely mercantilist set of policies" that linked their ports and shaped their governance while also producing tensions and sustained, often successful attempts at subversion. They were also, in principle, governed by a connected set of legal codes that included two versions (one from 1685 and another, specifically for Louisiana, from 1724) of the Code Noir "policing the conduct of slaves," a network of admiralty courts, and a set of legal traditions called the Coutume de Paris that was applied in the colonies. Finally, and perhaps in part because of its centralized character, "the French state consciously pursued policies of close diplomatic ties with independent Native nations in North America to enhance trade and security." The governance of this French Atlantic, Banks emphasizes, depended "on the collection, processing, analyzing, and selective redistribution" of information, and in this sense it was linked to the broader bureaucratization of the early modern French state.[8]

But there were significant limits on the actual control and comprehension exercised by this imperial system. The French Empire in North America was a vast crescent crossing present-day Canada to the Great Lakes and descending the Mississippi Valley to "Upper" and "Lower" Louisiana. But the vast majority of this territory was only *claimed* by France, and only nominally under its control. Within it the largest group of people, by far, were Native Americans. Their experiences of and contact with the French varied. The arrival of French settlers in Canada triggered a massive decline in the indigenous population through disease and war, with some communities experiencing a loss of 95 percent of their population within a few decades.[9] Nevertheless many groups—notably the Iroquois and the Huron—remained populous, strong, and autonomous throughout the period of French colonization in the North. Colonization in North America, as Gilles Havard and Cécile Vidal have argued, in fact primarily took the form of an "intercultural alliance" between French and Native Americans, who were "placed in a situation of interdependence."[10]

Outside of a few centers of French settlement, the main contact between Europeans and Native Americans took place through missionaries and fur traders. Missionaries, particularly Jesuits, played a remarkable and important role in French Atlantic history, both in North America and in the Caribbean. Although they often operated alone or in small groups, they nevertheless created significant mission communities among the Iroquois and other Native American groups. The experiences of Jesuit missionaries were communicated in a series of remarkably detailed accounts that were first produced for the order itself, but soon became widely read works of literature in France. Besides being an enormous resource for historians, notably those interested in Native American history, these "Jesuit Relations," as they came to be known, played a preponderant role in shaping European views of Native Americans, and indeed of the New World more broadly, as well as helping to recruit new generations of missionaries through tales of conversion and martyrdom in the Americas. By providing extensive descriptions of Native American societies, they became an important part of Enlightenment debates about human diversity, comparative history, and natural rights during the seventeenth and eighteenth centuries, serving as a conduit through which the experiences of the New World came to shape the political philosophy of Europe.[11] In North America, meanwhile, missionaries helped to create new communities. The Catholic practice that emerged within them, one often deeply shaped by the religious activities of women, brought together Native American and European cosmology and theology in complex ways.[12]

The other major representatives of French colonization in much of Canada were fur traders. They were essentially integrated into Native American communities and networks, and very often directly into family groups through marriage, bringing about change primarily as conduits to the fur economy in Europe rather than as settlers empowered to reorganize or control the societies in which they operated. The fur trade was, nevertheless, quite significant for Native American communities, one piece of a larger change in material culture. Indeed, European goods circulated among

Native American groups far in advance of settlers. Interest in, and competition for, such goods contributed to conflicts among groups, notably between Huron and Iroquois, conflicts that were deepened by the larger devastation wrought by disease and the population movements it caused. The larger imperial competition between France and Britain in the Great Lakes region and elsewhere both constrained and provided certain opportunities for Native American groups, who created and sustained what Richard White dubbed a "middle ground" that enabled them to preserve a certain degree of autonomy, one that was deeply undermined once Britain defeated France in Canada.[13] This was also true in the Caribbean, where, as Philip Boucher has shown, Caribs were able to take advantage of Franco–British conflict to carve out spaces of autonomy for themselves.[14]

The battlegrounds of the Seven Years' War stretched from the Caribbean to Canada, and the end of the war forced the French to consider the relative merits of their different colonies. The result of the Franco–British negotiations was that France regained control of Guadeloupe and Martinique, which had been occupied by the British, but gave up Canada and Louisiana. This dramatic imperial transformation effectively ended the history of the French Empire in North America, leaving nearly all of its remaining colonies (with the exception of a few holdings in coastal Canada) in the Caribbean.

The colonies of the Caribbean had, by the eighteenth century, developed into flourishing, and indeed industrialized, centers for the production of sugar and coffee for export. The obsessive focus on plantation production left little space for the production of provisions, and—though slaves working their garden plots produced food for local consumption—the colonies required a steady supply of food, lumber, and other goods from outside the Caribbean. In the seventeenth century Jean-Baptiste Colbert, Louis XIV's minister of finance, sought to link the Caribbean and Canada, in particular to bring supplies of food from Canada to the Caribbean colonies, but royal initiatives in this direction never really got off the ground.[15] There were attempts to create colonies in French Guiana, meant in part to help sustain development in Guadeloupe, Martinique, and especially Saint-Domingue. After the spectacular and devastating failure of the Kourou expedition in 1763, when several thousand French settlers died, the settlement of French Guiana progressed very slowly. The colony became best known for its deadly prison camps, which welcomed victims of the political purges of the French Revolution and, a century later, Alfred Dreyfus.[16] Instead, it was the North American colonies of Britain that came to supply, mostly illegally, provisions and lumber to the French Caribbean, shipping molasses back north in return. The economic result was crucial for both regions, helping to spur the economy of New England and allowing for the obsessive focus on the production of plantation commodities in Saint-Domingue. In the second half of the eighteenth century, the French administration realized that this trade was unstoppable, and made some concessions to colonists by declaring select Caribbean ports open to foreign commerce, though this never stopped the extensive contraband trade. Later, when Napoleon Bonaparte sought to reconstruct the French Empire in the Americas through the acquisition of Louisiana, his project was to integrate Louisiana and the Caribbean into a well-functioning imperial sphere, in which Louisiana would replace North America as a source of provisions for Saint-Domingue.

Of all of the French colonies, and indeed of the colonies of the eighteenth-century Atlantic, the most profitable and flourishing was Saint-Domingue, for a complex mix of environmental, political, and economic reasons. For one thing, the colony was particularly well-endowed with a series of plains ideal for sugar cultivation, along with good supplies of water necessary to sustain these plantations. The centralized nature of the French government helped to take advantage of these environmental advantages, funding and overseeing extensive irrigation projects, particularly in the western plain of Saint-Domingue, which made it nearly as productive as the rich northern plain over the course of the eighteenth century.[17] When there was no more land available for sugar cultivation, planters in Saint-Domingue, many of them free people of color, developed coffee plantations in the mountains, turning these into producers of a booming cash crop. Although the large population of free people of color would eventually pose profound political challenges to French authority during the Revolution, in the eighteenth century this community contributed in crucial ways to the wealth of the colony, both as merchants and planters who owned many plantations, notably in the indigo and coffee sectors, and also as soldiers and militia members who provided the security necessary to maintain the plantation society. The rich sugar production in Saint-Domingue, supplemented by that in Martinique and Guadeloupe, helped make France the leading re-exporter of sugar in the eighteenth century, so that the French port towns made enormous profits both from the slave trade and from the plantation commodities it helped to produce. Though it expanded and boomed, and despite the regular complaints of planters who railed against the monopoly regulations that forced them to sell their products only in France, the system was extremely profitable and effective while it lasted.[18]

In the last decade of the eighteenth century, however, the Haitian Revolution overturned the thriving slave system in the colony. It was the most radical revolution of the Age of Revolution, transforming a slave colony into an independent black state in just over a decade. And its central protagonists were slave revolutionaries who confronted, reformulated, and ultimately expelled empire.[19] The creation of Haiti had multiple, and in some ways contradictory, effects on the long-term history of the French Empire. What from one perspective registers as a defeat of imperial designs can also be seen as an impressive feature of the history of the French Atlantic. The French empire in the American created the conditions for a successful slave revolution, and—for a time at least—a revolutionary French State actually embraced that revolution.

The history of emancipation in the French Atlantic involves a remarkable series of advances and reversals that makes it rather unusual within the broader Atlantic context. As a direct result of slave revolution, a declaration of universal and immediate emancipation was issued by French representatives in Saint-Domingue in 1793. This decision was ratified the next year in Paris, and thus applied to all of the French Empire. The decision was never applied in Martinique, under British control throughout the 1790s, but was in Guadeloupe and Guiana. Emancipation was reversed in the early 1800s, leading to Haitian independence in 1804 but to re-enslavement in Guadeloupe and Guiana, and the maintenance of slavery in Martinique. The next decades saw a halting progression toward abolition, which was decreed only in 1848, after a revolution in Paris brought political leaders close to the abolitionist Victor Schoelcher to power. Even within 1848, however, there were many complications, since the decree of abolition, when it arrived in the Caribbean, turned out to be too late: slaves, having heard that emancipation was coming, had forced local governors to decree it earlier.

These transformations had multiple effects far beyond the reaches of the French Empire itself, helping to pave the way for the emergence of Cuba as the great sugar colony of the nineteenth century, and also directly causing the sale of Louisiana to the United States after its reacquisition by Napoleon Bonaparte. The French emperor's plans for Louisiana were thwarted when the resistance accelerated in Haiti in late 1802 and early 1803, inciting him to offer the territory to U.S. envoys. The French Caribbean would shape the history of Louisiana in other ways as well, bringing a wave of refugees from Saint-Domingue in the early nineteenth century. Many of these had first settled in Cuba, from which they were expelled in 1809. They arrived in such large numbers in Louisiana in that year that they doubled the size of New Orleans. Among these arrivals were a large number of free people of color, who profoundly shaped the political and legal history of Louisiana, carrying on many of the political projects and ideas that had shaped the revolutionary period in Haiti. Their political and cultural presence would help define the particular challenges issued from Louisiana to the order of racial discrimination and racial segregation throughout the nineteenth century. Through Louisiana, the political culture of the French Caribbean revolutions of the late eighteenth century became part of the terrain of struggle over slavery and emancipation in the United States.[20] During this period, then, different regions that were comparatively isolated within the French Empire actually found themselves connected, and integrated, in important ways through processes driven by the demise of that empire.

When comparisons are hazarded between the French and British empires in North America—as they were in Francis Parkman's classic work on the subject—they often dwell on the failure of the French to create settler colonies as populous as those of the British Atlantic.[21] Of course France's loss of its colonies, though it took place early, is just a part of the larger story of imperial "failure" in the Americas. And it is also just one case among others in which the end of imperial governance has not meant the end of the long-term effects of imperial processes. Still, the analysis of this difference between the French Atlantic and other imperial systems—whether we think of it as a failure or not—is certainly an intriguing one. But to answer it we need to explore further a range of questions about strategies of imperial governance, the relative merits of centralized versus decentralized methods of control, the cultural and social causes and effects of forms of alliance and trade, and the history of military tactics and systems. And in doing that, using a broad Atlantic approach has important advantages.

Traditionally, much of the scholarship on the French Atlantic has focused on a regional approach rather than an Atlantic one. Indeed, the approach of Atlantic history still has comparatively little traction within French academic institutions. Though there are centers devoted to the study of "la France Atlantique," their focus is on the towns and regions of the Atlantic coast of metropolitan France.[22] In part because the French Empire in North America ended before the French Revolution, still seen as the "foundational" event in terms of the history and identity of the French nation, the experiences in Canada and Louisiana have remained on the edges of public memory and historical writing in France. In Quebec, where a great deal of excellent historical work has been produced about French Canada, this history has been focused primarily on exploring the distinct regional history of this area within North America.[23]

The history of the French Atlantic has been, and still is, largely understood in ways determined by the institutional and political structures, both regional and national, that have emerged from it. As a result, much of the historical writing about the French Empire remains comparatively fragmented, told as a series of different stories with quite different plots. And both because of a lack of broader syntheses and integration and because of a lack of institutional sites for collaboration and exchange, there remain both striking dissonances and regrettable lacunae within study of the French Atlantic. Even as interest in the history of colonialism has accelerated in France, comparatively more attention has been paid to nineteenth- and twentieth-century empire in Africa and Asia, notably to the history of Algeria, than to the earlier experiences in the Americas.[24]

It is now broadly accepted, even canonical, that one of the advantages of an Atlantic approach is that it allows us to expand our approaches beyond those of national or regional history, and therefore generates new questions, new connections, and points us to hitherto neglected bodies of historical evidence. The Atlantic approach can help us understand historical links between regions, as well as to broaden our analytical and methodological imagination by encouraging us to think comparatively across regions. Such an approach is particularly crucial and useful for the study of the French Atlantic, for it can help us to overcome some of the fragmentation of this field. And there are numerous studies of the French Atlantic that provide examples and inspiration for how this can be done.

C. L. R. James's book *The Black Jacobins* is, among other things, a brilliant illumination of the world of the French Atlantic, and indeed can be considered one of the foundational texts of the field as a whole. Subsequent scholars working on the French Atlantic, such as R. R. Palmer and Paul Butel, have also played a central role in the development of the ideas and approaches of Atlantic history.[25]

In recent years, several studies have explored the ways in which the broader Atlantic context shaped economic, political, and legal life in metropolitan France. Studies of French port towns have raised important questions about the place of the slave trade in the economic history of France, although this topic has garnered comparatively less interest in France than it has in the Anglophone context. The historian Sue Peabody pioneered the study of the experiences of enslaved people in metropolitan France, and the court cases they undertook, often successfully, to win freedom there, as history that has interesting parallels with the British case. Such works have shown how much can be gained from studies of the cultural, political, and economic impact of the broader French Atlantic on the history of metropolitan France. This is an area which deserves much more scholarly attention.[26]

Other historians have taken the French Atlantic imperial system itself as an object of study. In the work by Kenneth Banks, for instance, an examination of communication within the French imperial bureaucracy illuminates a system of governance and knowledge production that improves our understanding not only of the empire but also and more broadly of the early modern French state as an institution.[27] Banks's study shows how the Atlantic approach can give us fresh perspectives on the history of certain of the core institutions that historians of early modern France have long expertly studied, particularly the monarchy and the Counter-Reformation Church. Both of these institutions were deeply shaped by the questions and problems raised by governance and conversion within the French Atlantic Empire. Looking at these institutions from the Atlantic can help us to understand the ideological and institutional changes that have fascinated generations of historians in new and fresh ways, and in the process have contributed to a revitalization and transformation of the rich traditions of French historiography in these areas.

Historians interested in the French Atlantic have also brought together approaches which traditionally have operated in parallel rather than in combination. In their history of French North America, Havard and Vidal have emphasized the need to "reconcile the two major axes of colonial history," bringing together the "diplomatic, military and economic history, traditionally presented from the European point of view" and the "sociocultural history" of the peoples—Native American, European, African—who created the societies of the New World. They sought to write a history including "all of the actors on the colonial scene: the State, the Church, the Companies, the European colonists, as well as the Native Americans and Africans, free and enslaved." [28]

A focus on social and cultural history also allows us to analyze the French Atlantic in its longer-term impacts and iterations, to escape from the strictures of the French Empire into the broader story of how peoples who were once a part of it continued to shape their worlds. This is well illustrated in the history of Louisiana, where weak and often ineffective attempts at imperial construction and control nevertheless produced a long-lasting cultural and social impact.

As Bradley Bonds has written, the history of Louisiana poses as one of its challenges understanding how "Native Americans, Africans, Canadians, French men and women, and Caribbean Islanders" managed to create "polyglot and fluid societies that ultimately prevailed longer than the French colony."[29] Recent studies have successfully explored such histories by bringing together a variety of methodologies—for instance, archaeology and social history, or focusing on religious institutions as the sites for cultural encounter and exchange.[30] Such studies provide examples of how interdisciplinary approaches could help us better understand many other domains: the history of music and dance, the history of religious practice, of literary production, and of architecture.[31]

In Louisiana, as in the Caribbean, the approaches of Atlantic history are central to the understanding of the roles and history of African individuals and communities. Gwendolyn Midlo Hall, who pioneered the study of Africans in Louisiana, has recently argued that the study of the French Atlantic can in fact help us rethink our broader understanding of Africans in the Atlantic. The archival resources produced by the French Atlantic, notably notarial records, she suggests, provide a vantage point from which to revise understandings of the place of African "ethnicity" in the Americas that have been dominated by an Anglo-Atlantic perspective.[32]

To make sense of evolution and reconfiguration of African ethnicities, historians necessarily need to comprehend historical developments on both sides of the Atlantic. The French Atlantic included a series of outposts in West Africa, which were connected to the interior of Senegambia; and these outposts, notably that at St. Louis, created their own new cultures born out of the interaction of Africans and Europeans.[33] But the study of Africa in the French Atlantic obviously includes not only the regions close to actual French outposts but also the region from which the largest number of slaves came to Saint-Domingue, the Kongo. John Thornton's work has powerfully suggested the ways in which a sustained study of African military and ideological influences on the Haitian Revolution can help us reorient our understanding of that event, an insight that could be much broadened and further explored in other domains, regions, and periods.[34]

An Atlantic approach can help us, in all of these ways, to draw a more connected map of the French imperial world. But it can also encourage historians to look for methodological and analytical inspiration in new places. The histories of European-African and European-Native American interactions, for instance, present interestingly parallel questions and problems that are well-framed within the French Atlantic. In both cases, actual European control was often extremely limited and constrained, and the Atlantic reshaped communities and economies largely through the movement of goods as well as, at times, of ideas and practices, that outpaced the movement of Europeans themselves. The history of the missions in Central Africa—which had important effects on the cultural worlds of the African slaves who came to dominate Saint-Domingue, for instance—has interesting parallels to the history of missions in Canada. While the cultural contexts are, of course, extremely different, certain processes and institutional developments might fruitfully be thought of in relation to one another. In both cases there is plenty of room to debate precisely to what extent different places and communities were "Atlantic" at different times, and what categories and distinctions are most fruitful in answering this question. The debate in both contexts, however, could probably profit from the insights, doubts, and methods applied in the other.

The historiography of the French Caribbean has long been deeply shaped by Atlantic approaches. The work of Gabriel Debien, which ranged widely across the Caribbean, metropolitan French ports, and West Africa, is a model in this regard.[35] Studies of the revolutionary period in the French Atlantic have also been consistently framed by an Atlantic perspective. The events of this period in many ways require such an approach, since people, news, and ideas crossed the Atlantic with a rapidity and intensity that profoundly shaped events in both Europe and the Caribbean. The comparative history of revolution in France and the Caribbean, furthermore, can help us better perceive both the relationship and the comparative evolution of the two.

In some ways, though, the history of the period of revolution that transformed the French Atlantic remains compartmentalized into two national histories, of France and of Haiti. There is an extremely rich historiography of the Haitian Revolution produced in Haiti itself, stretching back to the nineteenth century, which is relatively little known outside of the specialists of the Haitian Revolution, despite the fact that it is of great relevance to the broader understanding of the history of the French Atlantic, and to the broad study and theorization of race, politics, and slavery in the Atlantic world.[36]

The fact that the history of eighteenth-century Saint-Domingue and its revolution led to the creation of a new nation largely dominates not only the writing of history but also its reception. That national history is, perhaps inevitably, haunted by the image and place of Haiti in the nineteenth and twentieth centuries. And it also means that the multiple interlocking stories that connect Haiti to the history of the French Atlantic both before and after the birth of Haiti have tended to receive less attention. Despite a now wide acceptance of its crucial importance, the historiography of the Haitian Revolution continues to suffer from the fact that the event remains relatively overlooked in France and, largely because of language barriers but for other reasons as well, is not currently being renewed and invigorated by younger scholars in the United States to the extent one might hope, while scholars in Haiti struggle against many obstacles in their research and publication. Even in much of the historiography focused on the French Caribbean itself, Martinique, Guadeloupe, and Guiana often receive treatment both distinct from one another and distinct from Saint-Domingue/Haiti.[37]

In fact, much can be, and has been, gained by scholars who have allowed the histories of the two revolutions, and of different regions swept up in the revolutionary process, to cross-pollinate. There has been excellent work done on the history of debates about slavery in metropolitan France.[38] And the study of the responses to the Haitian Revolution in the United States, Cuba, and metropolitan France has expanded enormously in recent years.[39] Interestingly, there has been comparatively less focus, in terms of new, archivally grounded research, on the details of the political, social, and cultural histories of the revolution in Saint-Domingue itself as both a locally generated and a highly connected and international series of events, despite extensive and pertinent sources in the French national archives, in collections in the United States, and in a few collections in Haiti itself.[40] The materials generated by the Haitian Revolution are remarkable for their breadth and complexity, and promise to amply reward scholars who take the time to explore them with new perspectives and insights into political, social, and cultural history.[41]

Even if we retain and acknowledge the ways in which the histories of the French and Haitian revolutions were, and remain, national histories, an Atlantic approach can help us layer that story with others. It can help us to understand better the multiple and often divided perspectives and experiences of planters and merchants on both sides of the Atlantic who profited from and sustained the colonial system, but also debated its form and contested its governance in many ways. It can help us to understand more fully the links and influences between cultural and economic developments taking place in West Africa and in the Caribbean over the course of the eighteenth century, in order to illuminate the history of communities in both places over time. And it can help to highlight the stakes of imperial governance, particularly in its engagement with the question of slavery, within and between Atlantic empires both in conflict and in cooperation.

Part of what an Atlantic approach can help us to do is also to begin to bring together the histories of different French colonies *within* the Caribbean itself. Even here, historiographies—national in the case of Haiti, and sometimes *nationalist* in the case of Guadeloupe and Martinique—have not emphasized the interlocking histories of different colonial contexts. As a result interesting questions—about the formation of the Code Noir, driven by experiences in the eastern Caribbean, and its broader impact in Saint-Domingue and Louisiana, for instance—have remained relatively unexplored. Though each colony had its own particularities, the interplay between them was crucial at various key moments, such as during the Seven Years' War and the revolutionary period. Families and economies stretched between and tied together these different colonies as well, as they were tied to much broader networks in the Atlantic world.

A study by Christopher Hodson of the history of the Acadians, which follows them from coastal Canada to metropolitan France, Guiana, and Louisiana, provides a sweeping and richly human story of a remarkable series of Atlantic trajectories and provides a wonderful example of how such trajectories can be explored and pursued.[42] Similarly, Afua Cooper's study of the life and death of Marie-Joseph Angélique, a Portuguese-born slave blamed for starting a fire in Montreal in 1734, highlights the often overlooked place of slavery, and of people of African descent, in the history of French Canada.[43] And John Garrigus' study of free people of color in Saint-Domingue breaks down both regional and chronological boundaries, following figures such as the writer of the Haitian declaration of independence, Louis Boisrond-Tonnerre, back and forth across the Atlantic, and also tracing the history of families of color from prerevolutionary Saint-Domingue, through the period of the revolution and into postindependence Haiti.[44]

Despite much important work done recently, particularly on free people of color, the history of prerevolutionary Saint-Domingue remains curiously understudied. As the most successful colony in the Atlantic world, and one marked by an extremely rich cultural, economic, social, political, and legal history, Saint-Domingue provides historians with enormous opportunities to study many of the central questions about the construction of slave societies, the transformation of identities in the New World, and the intersection of a wide range of European and African cultures.[45] Representations of the colonies as spaces of "libertinage" had a profound cultural impact on both sides of the Atlantic, as Doris Garraway has shown.[46] Still, historians have yet to really fully address, in a rigorous and comparative context, the basic question of what made Saint-Domingue so successful as a plantation society. If the Haitian Revolution has sometimes been marginalized in part because of the woes of postindependence Haiti, Saint-Domingue's rich prerevolutionary history has in many ways also been overshadowed by the remarkable conflagration in which it ended.

Deepening our knowledge of both prerevolutionary and revolutionary Saint-Domingue, and highlighting the circuits of ideas and culture that connected the colony to other parts of the Atlantic, can encourage us to think differently about the history of ideas by changing our sense of where the sites of theorization and philosophizing actually were during the eighteenth century. Studies that connect developments on both sides of the Atlantic can help us understand the ways in which late eighteenth-century political culture was forged in multiple sites, with complicated repercussions and reactions that brought together actors as varied as *philosophes* and enslaved insurgents, in a web of influence and counterinfluence that was always multidirectional.[47]

This continued to be the case after Haitian independence. Throughout the nineteenth and early twentieth centuries, Haiti's intellectuals wrote in French, often in direct dialogue with French theorists. One classic example of this dialogue is Antenor Firmin's 1885 *De l'Égalite des races humaines*, a response to Gobineau's *De l'Inégalité des races humaines*.[48] In the 1920s, in the context of the U.S. occupation of Haiti, Jean Price-Mars and other intellectuals began writing about and revitalizing aspects of Haitian culture, particularly Vodou, to which elites had previously given little intellectual attention. Such writings had an impact far beyond Haiti, notably in the French Caribbean islands of Martinique and Guadeloupe, as well as French Guiana, and became part of the larger Atlantic circulation of ideas often collapsed into the term "Negritude," though there were enormous variations and fissures between thinkers in terms of their approaches to culture and politics. This movement, among other things, helped to generate some of the classic historiography of the French Atlantic itself, such as the work of C. L. R. James and Aimé Césaire.[49]

When does the period approached by "Atlantic history" appropriately end? This is obviously a difficult question, and one open to ongoing debate, but it takes an interesting and peculiar form in the case of the French Atlantic. If the period from the late eighteenth through the mid-nineteenth century signaled the gradual dismantling of the French Empire in the Americas with the loss of Canada and then Louisiana and Haiti, as well as the decline of the plantation economy in the remaining French possessions, the political and cultural effects of the formative period in the French Atlantic continued powerfully into the twentieth century, and continue today.

In North America, these effects took various forms. In Canada the presence of a French-language community continued to be an important political and legal issue throughout the nineteenth and twentieth centuries, notably in the past decades when mobilization around the idea of French culture and Quebécois identity have led to the revitalization of French-language instruction and broadcasting. Other parts of the French Atlantic have come to Montreal's assistance as a Francophone city and have therefore shaped patterns of migration to some extent, with French-speaking Haitians, as well as West Africans, becoming an important part of the city and contributing to the strength of its public Francophone policies. (Today, interestingly, Haitians may generally find themselves better welcomed in Montreal than, for instance, in Guadeloupe, where their presence has generated anti-immigration movements in recent years.) All of this has shaped developments in history, anthropology, and literature, with Montreal functioning as an important center for the study not only of French Canada but also of the French Caribbean.

Another part of French Canadian history ultimately found itself rooted in the history of Louisiana, where many of the deported Acadians arrived in the eighteenth century, and helped to found communities now often called "Cajun," a term derived from "Acadien." In recent years, a revival of French language and Cajun music has gathered steam, and as in Quebec the connection with the French Empire, and support from the contemporary French government, have played an important role in the evolution of local institutional and cultural history, as well as tourism.[50]

The French colonies of Martinique, Guadeloupe, and Guiana, meanwhile, were until 1946 governed directly by France as colonies. The French Empire was reoriented, starting with the 1830 occupation of Algeria, increasingly toward West and Central Africa, Madagascar, and South and Southeast Asia. In this process the Antilles played multiple roles. The history of plantation slavery, emancipation, and the development of what I have called "Republican racism" in the French Antilles served as a foundation for the complicated politics of inclusion and exclusion that shaped French colonial policies in the new colonies.[51] At the same time, Antilleans played important roles as members of the colonial administration, especially in Africa.[52]

Through all these interlocking histories, then, the particular cultural and political formations generated within the French Atlantic have continued to shape histories on both sides of the Atlantic, both inside and outside of the framework of the French Empire. This has helped to maintain and propel the history written about these regions, but at the same time it has defined the categories and barriers through which this history has been explored. An Atlantic approach cannot replace the regional and national political contexts that necessarily give meaning, and inspiration, to the writing of history. But it can and will sustain our ability to see, and imagine, new layers within and paths between these different regions.

NOTES

1. Gilles Havard and Cécile Vidal, *Histoire de l'Amérique française* (Paris: Flammarion, 2003), pp. 479–480.

2. Sharifa Rhodes-Pitts, "Reparation Day: A Call for $21 Billion from France Aims to Lift Haiti's Bicentennial Blues," *Boston Globe*, January 4, 2004. The

Debray Commission report is at http://www.ladocumentationfrancaise.fr/rapports-publics/044000056/index.shtml.

3. Kenneth Banks, *Chasing Empire Across the Seas: Communication and the State in the French Atlantic* (Montreal and Kingston: McGill-Queens University Press, 2002), p. 8.

4. On French emigration to Canada, see Leslie Choquette, *Frenchmen into Peasants: Modernity and Tradition in the Peopling of French Canada* (Cambridge, Mass.: Harvard University Press, 1997), p. 279; and Havard and Vidal, *L'Amérique française*, pp. 139, 164. My thanks to Philippe Boucher for sharing his thoughts about the migration from France to the Caribbean with me. On the early history of the French Caribbean, see his *France in the American Tropics to 1700* (Baltimore: Johns Hopkins University Press, 2008).

5. These numbers are calculated from the updated version of the DuBois Slave Trade Database, which will soon be placed online. My thanks to David Eltis for sharing these figures with me in advance.

6. Havard and Vidal, *L'Amérique française*, pp. 138–157; Choquette, *Frenchmen into Peasants*.

7. Havard and Vidal, *L'Amérique française*, p. 159.

8. Banks, *Chasing Empire*, pp. 9–10.

9. Havard and Vidal, *L'Amérique française*, pp. 131–138.

10. Havard and Vidal, *L'Amérique française*, p. 12.

11. On the Jesuits' Relations see Gilbert Chinard's classic *L'Amérique et le rêve exotique dans la littérature française au XVIIe et au XVIIIe siècle* (Paris: Hachette, 1913); and Marie-Christine Pioffet, *La Tentation de l'épopée dans les Relations des Jésuites* (Sillery: Septentrion, 1997). One famous example of the Jesuits as early pioneers of a kind of comparative ethnography is Joseph-François Lafitau's eighteenth-century *Customs of the American Indians Compared with the Customs of Primitive Times*, trans.William N. Fenton and Elizabeth L. Moore (Toronto: Champlain Society, 1974–1977).

12. See John Steckley, "The Warrior and the Lineage: Jesuits' Use of Iroquoian Images to Communicate Christianity," *Ethnohistory* 39 (1992): 478–509; James Axtell, *The Invasion Within: The Contest of Cultures in Colonial North America* (New York: Oxford University Press, 1995); John Demos, *The Unredeemed Captive: A Family Story from Early America* (New York: Knopf, 1994); Allan Greer, *Mohawk Saint: Catherine Tekakwitha and the Jesuits* (New York: Oxford University Press, 2005).

13. Bruce Trigger, *The Children of Aataentsic: A History of the Huron People to 1660* (Montreal: McGill-Queen's University Press, 1976); Richard White, *The Middle Ground: Indians, Empires, and Republics in the Great Lakes Region, 1650–1815* (Cambridge: Cambridge University Press, 1991); Daniel Richter, *The Ordeal of the Longhouse: The Peoples of the Iroquois League in the Era of European Colonization* (Chapel Hill: University of North Carolina Press, 1992); Demos, *The Unredeemed Captive*; Susan Sleeper-Smith, *Indian Women and French Men:Rethinking Cultural*

Encounter in the Western Great Lakes (Amherst: University of Massachusetts Press, 2001). Two recent and important contributions to the study of French Canada are Brett Rushforth, "'Little Flesh We Offer You': The Origins of Indian Slavery in New France," *William and Mary Quarterly* LX(4) (October 2003): 777–808; and Saliha Belmessous, "Assimilation and Racialism in Seventeenth- and Eighteenth-Century French Colonial Policy," *American Historical Review* 110(2) (April 2005): 322–349.

14. See Philip Boucher, *Cannibal Encounters: Europeans and Island Caribs, 1492–1763* (Baltimore: Johns Hopkins University Press, 1992).

15. See W. J. Eccles, *France in America* (East Lansing: Michigan State University Press, 1990), ch. 3.

16. See Emma Rotschild, "A Horrible Tragedy in the French Atlantic," *Past and Present* 192 (August 2006): 67–108; and Miranda Spieler, "Empire and Underworld: Guiana in the French Legal Imagination, 1789–1870" (Ph.D. dissertation, Columbia University, 2005).

17. The best comparative analysis of the economies of the French and British Caribbean is provided by Robin Blackburn in *The Making of New World Slavery: From the Baroque to the Modern* (London: Verso, 1997).

18. A good study of prerevolutionary Saint-Domingue is provided in three studies of free people of color: John Garrigus, *Before Haiti: Race and Citizenship in French Saint-Domingue* (New York: Palgrave Macmillan, 2006); Stewart King, *Blue Coat or Powdered Wig: Free People of Color in Pre-Revolutionary Saint-Domingue* (Athens: University of Georgia Press, 2001); Dominique Rogers, "Les Libres de couleur dans les capitales de Saint-Domingue: Fortune, mentalités et intégration à la fin de l'Ancien Régime (1776–1789)" (doctoral thesis, Université Michel de Montaigne, Bordeaux III, 1999).

19. The historiography on the Haitian Revolution is extremely rich, and includes the classic study by C. L. R. James, *The Black Jacobins* (New York: Vintage, 1963), as well as more recent studies by Carolyn Fick, *The Making of Haiti: The Saint-Domingue Revolution from Below* (Knoxville: University of Tennessee Press, 1990); and the foundational corpus produced by David Geggus, some of it collected in *Haitian Revolutionary Studies* (Bloomington: Indiana University Press, 2002). I present a narrative history of the Haitian Revolution in *Avengers of the New World: The Story of the Haitian Revolution* (Cambridge, Mass.: Harvard University Press, 2004).

20. On the arrival of these immigrants, see Paul Lachance, "Repercussions of the Haitian Revolution in Louisiana," in David Geggus, ed., *The Impact of the Haitian Revolution in the Atlantic World* (Columbia: University of South Carolina Press, 2001), pp. 209–230; on the broader history of Caribbean–Louisiana connections, Caryn Cossé Bell, *Revolution, Romanticism, and the Afro-Creole Protest Tradition in Louisiana, 1718–1868* (Baton Rouge: Louisiana State University Press, 1997); Rebecca Scott, *Degrees of Freedom: Louisiana and Cuba After Slavery* (Cambridge, Mass.: Harvard University Press, 2005); and Priscilla Lawrence and Alfred Lemmon, eds., *Common Routes: St. Domingue–Louisiana* (New Orleans: Somology, 2006).

21. Francis Parkman, *France and England in North America* (New York: Library of America, 1983 [1865–1892]).

22. See Cécile Vidal, "The Reluctance of French Historians to Address Atlantic History," *Southern Quarterly* (Summer 2006): 153–189.

23. An excellent review of the literature on New France is Allen Greer, "Comparisons: New France," in Daniel Vicker, ed., *A Companion to Colonial America* (Malden, Mass.: Blackwell, 2003), pp. 469–488. This literature includes the important work of Alan Greer, *The People of New France* (Toronto: University of Toronto Press, 1997), a translation of a French work originally published in Montreal, and Marcel Trudel's multivolume *Histoire de la Nouvelle-France*, also published in Montreal. Even French Canadian history, however, has often, as Havard and Vidal note, "confined itself to contemporary borders," focusing on events in the region that is today the province of Quebec; Havard and Vidal, *L'Amérique française*, pp. 9, 16. Historians have also found it difficult to bring together histories of French North America and the French Caribbean in a sustained way. In his synthesis *France in the Americas*, originally published in 1972 with a revised edition in 1990, for instance, the specialist in French Canadian history W. J. Eccles focuses primarily on the history of Canada. He argues that this is justified, given that Canada "played a much greater role in the history of the Americas than did any other of the French colonies," with the result that the Caribbean colonies play a very minor role in his tale; Eccles, *France in America*, p. v.

24. Christopher Hodson and Brett Rushforth are now preparing an overview of the history of the French Atlantic titled *Discovering Empire: France and the Atlantic World to 1804*, which promises to finally bring together all of the disparate regions into one narrative. In the meantime, two useful overviews of French imperial history are Jean Meyer et al., *Histoire de la France coloniale, dès origines à 1914* (Paris: Armand Colin, 1991); and Pierre Pluchon, *Histoire de la colonisation française* (Paris: Fayard, 1991).

25. James, *Black Jacobins*; R. R. Palmer, *The Age of Democratic Revolution: A Political History of Europe and America, 1760–1800* (Princeton: Princeton University Press, 1959–1964); Paul Butel, *Histoire de l'Atlantique:De l'Antiquité à nos jours* (Paris: Perrin, 1997). For a discussion of Butel and other French work on the Atlantic, see Bernard Bailyn, *Atlantic History: Concepts and Contours* (Cambridge, Mass.: Harvard University Press, 2005).

26. On the slave trade and the French ports see, for instance, Olivier Pétré Grenoulleau's examination of the impact of the money from the slave trade in Nantes, *L'Argent de la traite: Milieu négrier, capitalisme, développement. Un Modèle* (Paris: Aubier, 1996); and Erick Noël, *Les Beauharnais, une fortune antillaise, 1756–1796* (Geneva: Droz, 2003). On slaves in France, see Sue Peabody, *"There Are No Slaves in France": The Political Culture of Race and Slavery in the Ancien Régime* (Oxford: Oxford University Press, 1996); and Erick Noël, *Être noir en France au XVIIIe siècle* (Paris: Tallandier, 2006).

27. Banks, *Chasing Empire*.

28. Havard and Vidal, *L'Amérique française*, p. 11.

29. Bradley Bonds, "Introduction," in Bond, ed., *French Colonial Louisiana and the Atlantic World* (Baton Rouge: Louisiana State University Press, 2005), pp. ix, xx. Bonds notes that though Louisiana occupies the geographical center of North America, it has nevertheless often ended up "on the edge of scholarly and popular consciousness." This is in part because it occupied a "middle ground" between "Spanish and British colonies in North America and between France's Canada in the north and its Caribbean colonies in the south," and between "woodland Indians in the east and central plains Indians in the west."

30. See Shannon Lee Dawdy, "La Ville Sauvage: 'Enlightened' Colonialism and Creole Improvisation in New Orleans, 1699–1769" (Ph.D. dissertation, University of Michigan, 2003); Emily Clark, *Masterless Mistresses: The New Orleans Ursulines and the Development of a New World Society, 1727–1834* (Chapel Hill: Published for the Omohundro Institute of Early History and Culture by University of North Carolina Press, 2007).

31. A recent work that brings together all of the histories—European, Africa, Caribbean, North American—that shaped the culture of early New Orleans is Ned Sublette, *The World That Made New Orleans: From Spanish Silver to Congo Square* (Chicago: Lawrence Hill Books, 2007).

32. See Gwendolyn Midlo Hall, *Africans in Colonial Louisiana: The Development of Afro–Creole Culture in the Eighteenth Century* (Baton Rouge: Louisiana State University Press, 1992), and *Slavery and African Ethnicities in the Americas: Restoring the Links* (Chapel Hill: University of North Carolina Press, 2005). See, for instance, Ibrahima Seck, "The Relationship of St. Louis of Senegal, Its Hinterlands and Colonial Louisiana," in Bonds, ed., *French Colonial Louisiana*, pp. 265–290.

33. For an Atlantic approach to this region of Africa, see Boubacar Barry, *Senegambia and the Atlantic Slave Trade* (Cambridge: Cambridge University Press, 1998); see also Ibrahima Seck, "The Relationship of St. Louis of Senegal, Its Hinterlands and Colonial Louisiana." For a study of the communities that emerged from the French outpost at St. Louis, see Hilary Jones, "Citizens and Subjects: Métis Society, Identity and the Struggle over Colonial Politics in Saint Louis, Senegal, 1870–1920" (Ph.D. dissertation, Michigan State University, 2003).

34. John Thornton, "African Soldiers in the Haitian Revolution," *Journal of Caribbean History* 25(1 and 2) (1991): 58–80, and "I Am the Subject of the King of Congo: African Political Ideology and the Haitian Revolution," *Journal of World History* 4 (Fall 1993): 181–214. See also Gérard Barthélemy, *Creoles, Bossales: Conflit en Haïti* (Petit-Bourg, Guadeloupe: Ibis Rouge, 2000).

35. Debiens's best-known book is the work that remains the best synthesis on the history of slavery and slaves in the French Caribbean, *Les Esclaves aux Antilles françaises (XVII–XVIIIe siècles)* (Basse-Terre: Société d'Histoire de la Guadeloupe, 1974). Other examples include Jean Tarrade, *Le Commerce colonial de la France à la fin de l'Ancien Régime*, 2 vols. (Paris: Presses Universitaires de France, 1972); and Françoise Thésée, *Négociants bordelais et colons de Saint-Domingue* (Paris: Société Française d'Histoire d'Outre-mer, 1972).

36. The two greatest nineteenth-century historians of Haiti are Thomas Madiou, *Histoire d'Haïti*, 5 vols. (1847–1848; reprinted Port-au-Prince: Éditions Henri Deschamps, 1989). Beaubrun Ardouin, *Études sur l'histoire d'Haïti*, 11 vols. (Port-au-Prince: Dalencour, 1958 [1853–1865]). Though Madiou's work has been republished in Haiti, Ardouin's work has not been reissued in several decades and is comparatively difficult to find even in the well-stocked libraries of North America. Among more recent histories, Claude B. Auguste and Marcel B. Auguste, *L'Expédition Leclerc, 1801–1803* (Port-au-Prince: Éditions Henri Deschamps, 1985), remains, despite its modest title, the finest, and essentially the only, detailed study of the military and political history of the Haitian war of independence. The Augustes also produced a study of deportees from Saint-Domingue, *Les Déportés de Saint-Domingue: Contribution à l'histoire de l'expédition française de Saint-Domingue, 1802–1803* (Quebec: Éditions Naaman, 1979), and a study of the place of the Leclerc expedition in European diplomatic and political relations of the time, *La Participation étrangère à l'expédition française de Saint-Domingue* (Quebec, 1980). All these works, however, were published in small print runs and are now out of print and extremely difficult to find.

37. A good overview of French Caribbean historiography is Anne Pérotin-Dumon and Serge Mam-Lam-Fouck, "Historiography of the French Antilles and French Guyana," in B. W. Higman, ed., *General History of the Caribbean*, vol.6: *Methodology and Historiography of the Caribbean* (Paris: UNESCO, 1999), pp. 631–664. In the case of the French Caribbean, recent studies by Anne Pérotin-Dumon, *La Ville aux îles, la ville dans l'île: Basse-Terre et Pointe-à-Pitre, Guadeloupe, 1650–1820* (Paris: Kharthala 2000); and Fréderic Régent, *Esclavage, métissage, liberté: La Révolution française en Guadeloupe 1789–1802* (Paris: Grasset, 2004), represent an important expansion of the literature on Guadeloupe. Dale Tomich's *Slavery in the Circuit of Sugar: Martinique and the World Economy, 1830–1848* (Baltimore: Johns Hopkins University Press, 1990) remains an important touchstone on Martinique.

38. See, for instance, Yves Benot, *La Révolution Française et la fin des colonies* (Paris: Éditions de la Découverte, 1989), and *La Démence coloniale sous Napoléon* (Paris: Éditions de la Découverte, 1991); and, more recently, Alyssa Sepinwall, *The Abbé Grégoire and the French Revolution: The Making of Modern Universalism* (Berkeley: University of California Press, 2005).

39. See David Geggus, ed., *The Impact of the Haitian Revolution in the Atlantic World* (Columbia: University of South Carolina Press, 2001), for a range of approaches to this question. Three dissertations have considerably expanded our understanding of the impact of the Haitian Revolution in the United States and metropolitan France: Darrell Meadows, "The Planters of Saint-Domingue, 1750–1804: Migration and Exile in the French Revolutionary Atlantic" (Ph.D. dissertation, Carnegie Mellon University, 2004); Jennifer Pierce, "Discourses of the Dispossessed: Saint-Domingue Colonists on Race, Revolution and Empire, 1789–1825" (Ph.D. dissertation, SUNY Binghamton, 2005); and Ashli White, "'A Flood of Impure Lava': Saint Dominguan Refugees in the United States, 1791–1820" (Ph.D. dissertation,

Columbia University, 2003). See also the collection edited by Doris Garraway, *The Tree of Liberty: Cultural Legacies of the Haitian Revolution in the Atlantic World* (Charlottesville: University Press of Virginia, 2008).

40. One of example of this from France is the chronological bracketing chosen for a recent national examination for history teachers. Though the topic, promisingly enough, was "Revolutions in the Atlantic World," the dates chosen were surprising: 1776 to 1802. This meant that the end of the Haitian Revolution actually was placed outside of the period in question, with the end point defined by the shift in colonial policies of the metropole rather than by the victory of the former slaves of the Caribbean. Within the various guides for the examination produced in France, there was overall surprisingly little sustained attention to the French Caribbean. See Alyssa Goldstein Sepinwall, "Atlantic Amnesia: Memory and the Haitian Revolution in the United States and France," presented at "Atlantic History: Soundings" (Harvard University, August 11, 2005).

41. Work on gender and the political culture of the Haitian Revolution by Elizabeth Colwill, and on first-person accounts of the revolution by Jeremy Popkin, demonstrate the remarkable richness of this field. See Elizabeth Colwill, "Fêtes de l'hymen, fêtes de la liberté: Matrimony, Emancipation, and the Creation of 'New Men,'" paper presented at "The Haitian Revolution After 200 Years" (Brown University, June 17–20, 2004); and Jeremy Popkin, *Facing Racial Revolution: Eyewitness Accounts of the Haitian Insurrection* (Chicago: University of Chicago Press, 2007).

42. Christopher Hodson, "Refugees: Acadians and the Social History of Empire, 1755–1785 (Nova Scotia)" (Ph.D. dissertation, Northwestern University, 2004); see also Hodson, "A Bondage So Harsh": Acadian Labor in the French Caribbean, 1763–1766," *Early American Studies* 5(1) (Spring 2007): 95–131.

43. Afua Cooper, *The Hanging of Angélique: The Untold Story of Canadian Slavery and the Burning of Old Montreal* (Athens: University of Georgia Press, 2007).

44. Garrigus, *Before Haiti*.

45. Three excellent recent works have both expanded our understanding of Saint-Domingue and shown how much there is still to be learned about it: an important account of the legal history of Saint-Domingue, Malick Walid Ghachem, "Sovereignty and Slavery in the Age of Revolution: Haitian Variations on a Metropolitan Theme" (Ph.D. dissertation, Stanford University, 2001); an extensive exploration of music in Saint-Domingue, Bernard Camier, *Musique coloniale et société à Saint-Domingue à la fin du XVIIIème siècle* (doctoral thesis, Université des Antilles-Guyane, 2004); and an account of medicine and healing in the colony, Karol Weaver, *Medical Revolutionaries: The Enslaved Healers of Eighteenth-Century Saint-Domingue* (Urbana: University of Illinois Press, 2006).

46. Doris Garraway, *The Libertine Colony: Creolization in the Early French Caribbean* (Durham: Duke University Press, 2005).

47. An early and classic analysis of the intellectual currents in the French Atlantic is Michèle Duchet, *Anthropologie et histoire au siècle des Lumières* (Paris: Maspero,

1971). Building on Duchet, I have argued for the need to expand our understanding of the Enlightenment by including an "intellectual history of the enslaved" within it in "An Enslaved Enlightenment: Re-Thinking the Intellectual History of the French Atlantic," *Social History* 31(1) (February 2006): 1–14.

48. See the translation, with an introduction by Carolyn Fluehr-Lobban: Joseph-Anténor Firmin, *The Equality of the Human Races*, trans. Asselin Charles (Urbana: University of Illinois Press, 2002).

49. Aimé Césaire, *Toussaint-Louverture: La Révolution et le problème colonial* (Paris: Présence Africaine, 1981 [1961]) was an important analysis of the political and philosophical issues raised by the Haitian Revolution.

50. See Sara Le Menestral, *La Voie des Cadiens: Tourisme et identité en Louisiane* (Paris: Bellin, 1999).

51. I present this argument in *A Colony of Citizens: Revolution and Slave Emancipation in the French Caribbean* (Chapel Hill: University of North Carolina Press, 2004).

52. On Antilleans as colonial civil servants in Africa, see Véronique Hélenon, "Races, statut juridique et colonisation: Antillais et africains dans les cadres administratifs des colonies françaises d'Afrique," in Patrick Weil and Stéphane Dufoix, eds., *L'Esclavage, la colonization, et après ... France, États-Unis, Grande-Bretagne* (Paris: Presses Universitaires de France, 2005); and, for a study of the political history of Guadeloupe, see Jean-Pierre Sainton, *Les Nègres en politique: Couleur, identités et stratégies de pouvoir en Guadeloupe au tournant du siècle* (Villeneuve d'Ascq: Presses Universitaires du Septentrion, 2000). For an analysis of the roles of Antillean thinkers in the early twentieth-century French Empire, see Gary Wilder, *The French Imperial Nation-State: Negritude and Colonial Humanism Between the Two World Wars* (Chicago: University of Chicago Press, 2005).

6

THE DUTCH ATLANTIC:
FROM PROVINCIALISM TO GLOBALISM

BENJAMIN SCHMIDT

There was no such thing as a Dutch Atlantic, and this is an essay about it.[1] This is also an essay about the conceptualization of space, both in the early modern period and in modern historiography, especially scholarship since the 1980s, when the idea of Atlantic history and of an increasingly cohesive early modern Atlantic gained popularity. It is an essay, furthermore, on the relationship between spatiality—or what might be called in this context cultural geography—and the sort of expansionist, overseas programs pursued in the early modern period that perceived in the Atlantic a locus for an "enterprise of the Indies" (to invoke Columbus's famous expression) or an imperial "grand design" (to use the term favored by Dutch colonialists: *groot desseyn*) to extend Europe's reach into the newly discovered lands and seas to the west and south. It is an essay, thus, on Atlantic worlds, real and imagined, and on the possible correlation between the two.

This essay also seeks to address the broader thematic questions of this volume, albeit reformulated for a Dutch context. Does Atlantic history—leaving aside for the moment the question of what that term actually means—make sense in the case of the early modern Dutch Republic? Is it a useful category or idea that points down a sensible path of historical research and historiographic conceptualization? And if so, how does the case of the Netherlands fit into, and perhaps also comment upon, broader patterns suggested by other early modern instances of Atlantic history?[2]

As for the meaning of "Atlantic history," there are two ways, at least, to pose the implicit, central question of this volume. The first is to ask simply whether or not an "Atlantic history" existed: whether the term usefully describes (and, ideally, helps to explain) the political, social, economic, and cultural exchanges and configurations that took place in the regions bordering the Atlantic—the Americas, Africa, and (in this case) the Netherlands—in the period that, for the purposes of this essay, spans the late fifteenth through early eighteenth century. This approach seeks to identify what Horst Pietschmann has termed "Atlantic systems,"[3] and it endeavors to determine, if indeed such a phenomenon is detected, how such a system might pertain to various national or imperial contexts of the early modern world. Another approach is to ask not if the term and circumstances of an Atlantic system apply, but if they *were applied* at the time. Here the issue is not so much whether an Atlantic world of trade and expansion in fact existed, but whether an *idea* of the Atlantic existed and how this idea might have articulated a distinctively Dutch (in this case) sense of Atlantic space. This is a narrative of perceptions and conceptualizations, and it pertains less to economic and political configurations in the Atlantic than to an awareness of space itself. It investigates the geography, or better the cultural geography, of the Atlantic as perceived, in this case, by the early modern Dutch. This second line of inquiry seeks to determine, moreover, how such an idea of the Atlantic originated, what alternative conceptions may have developed, and how cultural geographies transformed over time. Above all, this approach recognizes the constructiveness of the category of "Atlantic history"—both then and now—and asks how the fashioning of geographic space relates to the formulation of policies pursued in that space. It investigates, in other words, the correlation between geographic ideas of and concrete actions—commercial, political, social—in the so-called Atlantic.

The dual approaches to the Atlantic that I am proposing are connected in subtle and revealing ways, and my goal in this essay is to juxtapose them in order to find patterns of correspondence and strategies of analysis that might enhance the study of Atlantic history. Some patterns appear neat; others, messy—yet all indicate the value of bearing in mind cultural perceptions of space as well as actions undertaken thereto. In the Dutch case, different Atlantic histories—ideas of and commercial-cum-colonial agendas in—can be seen as inversely related. Scholarly consensus contends that the Dutch Republic's "grand design" for the Atlantic failed grandly: its colonial initiatives of the early seventeenth century quickly fizzled out. Yet there is evidence, all the same, of an ongoing and productive fascination with the Atlantic world, an interest that expressed itself in abundant words and images. The one Dutch Atlantic fades rapidly from our textbooks, while the other ends up illustrating the covers of those books. That is, while the Dutch have not traditionally earned a place among the leading players in the early modern Atlantic world—the Dutch West India Company (WIC), it is often pointed out, was dissolved in 1674, following a period of sustained losses;

and this has prompted historians to dismiss or ignore whatever brief colonial moment in the West the Republic may have enjoyed—the Dutch, by contrast, produced some of the most enduring images of the Atlantic in the form of geographies, natural histories, atlases, maps, prints, paintings, and other sources that revealed the Americas and Africa to a growing market of European consumers. Even before this outpouring of Atlantic exotica, which took place preeminently in the mid-to-late seventeenth century, the Dutch wrote about and debated the meaning of America in scores of texts and prints—famously, those illustrating editions of Las Casas, which poured off Dutch presses.[4] These sources also comprise the political (and polemical) pamphlets that appeared in the wake of the Dutch Revolt and served to internationalize the rebels' struggle against Habsburg "tyranny," which (in the rebels' minds) infested the Atlantic world no less than the Netherlands. In this instance, cultural geography of the 1570s and 1580s *preceded* significant activity in the Atlantic by several decades. More generally, it would seem that even while Dutch engagements in the Atlantic may have been unremarkable, Dutch representations of the Atlantic have been nothing short of extraordinary. In truth, Dutch fortunes in the Atlantic were more extensive and impressive than historians have allowed; and cultural geographies produced in the Netherlands followed a more twisted and uneven path than is generally assumed. The varying Dutch Atlantics of the period have had disparate histories, and a preliminary assessment would suggest reframing the issue of *whether* there was a Dutch Atlantic to ask how the myriad Dutch Atlantics functioned and intersected, and how conceptions of space may have been shaped by, and were instrumental in shaping, events in the Atlantic world.

This essay seeks to combine these approaches with the aim of offering both an overview of the Dutch Atlantic and a methodological inquiry into conceptions of Atlantic space. It takes a two-pronged approach. It surveys the various, chiefly commercial and colonial, engagements of the Dutch in the Atlantic world during the early modern period—a narrative of "frustration and failure," as it has commonly been perceived by historians of European expansion.[5] And it also reviews the history of Dutch efforts to describe, conceptualize, and frame the Atlantic world in word and image, a story told from a rich corpus of literary and visual sources that have seldom received systematic comment. It proposes, ultimately, important correlations between these histories, if not directly causal connections. Early ideas of the Atlantic that developed in the Netherlands did not simply reflect or endorse the status quo, but effectively induced the new Dutch Republic to take action: to press for an aggressive Atlantic strategy and thereby join the ranks of colonial powers in the West. In later years, by contrast—after mid-seventeenth-century setbacks, by which time Dutch-controlled territories in the Atlantic had been mostly forfeited—geography played a role not so much by shaping imperial initiatives, as by offering a more open, fluid, and broadly "European" vision of the Atlantic. In this latter instance, Dutch-produced images *minimized* the Republic's place in the West. Rather than a "Dutch" Atlantic, Holland-made sources of this later period promoted a broadly internationalist view of the world, which contrasted with the otherwise restrictive, mercantilist, imperial models of this age of expansion. The image of the Atlantic produced in the Netherlands thus shifted from a provincial, idiosyncratic, and "local" perspective to a pluralistic, global, "universal" one. The Atlantic transformed itself, in the meantime, from a promising locus of Dutch empire to a lucrative venue for the Dutch transit trade.

The First Dutch Atlantic

The history of the Dutch Atlantic is a story best told in chapters, as there are several well-delineated moments of transition. What is striking, in fact, is how dramatically and abruptly the narrative could shift, and how closely domestic events could affect efforts overseas. These chapters are neatly divided by some of the signal events in Dutch history: the revolt of the Netherlands against Habsburg Spain (1568); the Twelve Years' Truce between Spain and the United Provinces (1609) and subsequent resumption of military hostilities (1621); the conclusion of this epic struggle for independence by the Peace of Westphalia (1648); the Republic's naval conflict against England, particularly the climactic Third Anglo-Dutch War and invasion of Dutch territory by the French army (1672–1674); the Union of Utrecht (1713) and reshuffling of the European balance of power; the assault and conquest of the Republic by French troops in 1795. In general terms, too, major trends in the history of the Dutch Atlantic developed over the course of neatly comparable seventy-to-eighty-year periods which parallel these key political events: from 1492 to 1570 (the revolt); from around 1570 to 1650 (Westphalia); from the mid-seventeenth to the early eighteenth century (War of the Spanish Succession); and from circa 1730 to the close of the century, when the vital political and commercial structures of the Republic, including the West India Company, collapsed under the weight of the French invasion and the Batavian Revolution (1795). What is not so neat is the way Dutch overseas strategies abruptly changed course and the way Dutch images of the Atlantic likewise hastily transformed. Celebration of the Habsburg Empire in the first half of the sixteenth century gave way to acerbic attacks by the close of the century. Notions of challenging Spain, and later England, in the Atlantic yielded to strategies of trading with these very same nations. And "grand designs" for a Dutch Atlantic ultimately led to programs less ambitiously imperial and more openly commercial and global than originally imagined. There were many and variable Dutch Atlantics.

The first chapter of the history of the Dutch Atlantic is the briefest and most straightforward, although it comes with a caveat: the Dutch did not, strictly speaking, become Dutch until they revolted against Habsburg Spain in the late 1560s. Until then traders, sailors, soldiers, missionaries, and other Dutch men and (less likely) women taking part in the evolving "enterprise of the Indies" would have labored for and pursued the goals of the larger Habsburg Empire, of which they were an integral part. Until then, too, one can hardly speak of "Dutch" initiatives in the Atlantic, let alone distinctly Dutch conceptualizations of Atlantic space. Certainly merchants from Antwerp participated in the Indies trade and profited from the circulation and sale of New World (less so African) goods to European markets. Many of these merchants would later migrate to cities in the northern provinces—Amsterdam above all—leaving behind the political violence and economic restrictions imposed by the war and the Spanish regime. With them they brought not only capital but also contacts within Iberian commercial circles, expertise on Atlantic products and markets, and even knowledge of Atlantic navigation and geography. As for ideas about the Atlantic world and cultural geographies of the Atlantic, here, too, Dutch sensibilities took their cue from Habsburg sources. Spanish news and, more important, publications swiftly became available in the north. Original histories of the *Conquista* were promptly translated into Dutch, French, and Latin; and some Spanish-language texts had their debut in Antwerp editions, a reflection of the superior printing facilities of the Netherlands as well as the restrictive rules of Spanish censorship.[6] Indeed, there was a relative abundance of early Americana in the Netherlands, in multiple media and genres—books, prints, paintings—indicating the considerable Dutch interest in the Atlantic world. The Low Countries by this time also occupied the center of the cartographic trade, and this meant that maps and (by 1570) atlases conveyed still further images of the Atlantic. As with literary sources, however, Dutch geographic texts tended to abet, rather than defy, Spain's imperial ambitions. The most famous of these, the *Theatrum orbis terrarum*, was dedicated by the Flemish mapmaker Abraham Ortelius to King Philip II of Spain in language

that was nothing less than effusive.[7] To many in the Netherlands, Spain's
Atlantic Empire was a source of unambiguous pride.

To many others, however, Spain's empire was increasingly a source
of unambiguous "tyranny," and this fissure reflects the outbreak of political tensions in that northern outpost of the empire also known as the
Netherlands. In the final third of the sixteenth century, as the Low Countries spiraled into chaos and as the Spanish-commanded Army of Flanders descended on the towns and countryside of the Netherlands, Dutch
notions of the Atlantic world shifted sharply, as did relations with the
primary superpower in the Atlantic, Habsburg Spain. This is the second
chapter of the story, and if it still does not involve major Dutch activities
in the Atlantic—while they continued to take part in Atlantic commerce,
either in the form of the carrying trade or in the service of Spanish fleets,
the Dutch did not yet launch any significant initiatives of their own—it
does signal a dramatic about-face in terms of cultural geography. The
Atlantic, and the "West Indies" in particular (the latter being a catch-all
phrase for the Americas, sometimes used to incorporate West Africa, too),
suddenly loomed ominously in the Dutch imagination, an oft-invoked and
highly charged site of cruelties and misconduct. How so? The transition
of the Dutch Atlantic from source of pride to invective can be dated fairly
precisely to the year 1568, when a group of Dutch nobles contested the
king's policies in the Netherlands, protesting that "the Spanish seek nothing but to abuse our Fatherland as they have done in the New Indies."[8]
This marked the commencement of the Dutch Revolt and the opening
salvo in the war of words waged against the "colonial" regime of Philip
II. It also pointed toward a new Dutch Atlantic. For even while the nobles'
geopolitical conceit might have seemed far-fetched—the Dutch conflict,
in the end, resembled something closer to a civil war than a genuine
rebellion against foreign, colonial occupiers—it turned out to be effective all the same, a potent form of propaganda used to tar the reputation
of the Habsburg-appointed government of the Low Countries. Over the
course of the Dutch Revolt—from the late 1560s through the Twelve-Year
Truce (1609–1621)—the rebels made repeated reference to "cruelties" in
the New World, the "destruction of the Indies," and the tragedy of the
Conquista—only to relate all this to events in the Netherlands. They raised
the specter of "Spanish tyranny" in the Atlantic to galvanize opposition to
the Habsburg regime in the Netherlands. The violent conquest of America,
no less than that of Antwerp, revealed the true character of "the Spanish
race," according to rebel polemicists. The shared experience of the Dutch
and the "Indians" (another catch-all phrase), both having directly felt the

yoke of Habsburg oppression, linked the two "nations" in a purported brotherhood of anti-Hispanism.

The pervasiveness and even preeminence in Dutch print of "the example of the Indies" is impressive. From the nobles' original complaint of colonial "abuses" there developed tropes of political "tyranny," which spread quickly among the opposition publicists. Philip Marnix van St. Aldegonde (1540–1598), the leading theorist and propagandist of the Calvinist party, made frequent mention of Spanish tyrannies ("In the newly discovered lands...they have murdered practically all of the natives"), as did the prince of pamphleteers, Prince William of Orange (r. 1544–1584). In his widely circulated *Apologie* of 1581, the leading grandee of the land painted the blackest of portraits of Spanish "barbarities," detailing how the king had "adjudged all you [the Dutch] to death, making no more account of you than of beasts...as they do in the Indies, where they have miserably put to death more than twenty million people and made desolate and waste thirty times as much land in quantity and greatness as the Low Country is with such horrible excesses and riots." The new ruling authority of the Netherlands, the States General, made much the same point a few months later in their official *Plakkaat van verlatinge* (declaration of independence), in which they complained that Philip II sought to "abolish all of the privileges of the country and have it tyrannically governed by Spaniards like the Indies and newly conquered countries"—a stunning reference to the Habsburg's Atlantic colonies. "All of this," concluded the States, "has given us more than enough legitimate reasons for abandoning the king of Spain and asking for another powerful and merciful prince to protect and defend these provinces." "All of this" demonstrates, moreover, how the image of the Indies served to validate the plight of the Netherlands, rhetorically linking the Dutch to the Atlantic world.[9]

The next move was colonial no less than rhetorical, and it illustrates the tight, effective correlation between the dual Dutch Atlantics. Two quick points need stressing: first, the distinctiveness of the Dutch conceit of the Atlantic; and second, the influence this conceit would have on strategies *for* the Atlantic. These two points are, of course, connected. By the turn of the seventeenth century, there had developed in the Netherlands an image of the Atlantic world that was as ubiquitous in the political discourse of the Republic as it was unique in that of Europe. The Dutch had aggressively promoted, over the course of their war against the Habsburgs, a notion of imperial "tyrannies" that deftly demonized the Spanish regime. The example of the Indies, as the rebels construed it, justified their insurrection insofar as it confirmed their adversary's abysmal record of colonial rule.

Such a rhetorical construction could not help but influence the actual colonial strategy of the Netherlands, as it began to contemplate its own enterprise in the West. And it was this peculiar picture of the Atlantic that set the Dutch Republic's efforts apart from those of its European cohorts. The late-sixteenth-century consumer of Dutch political literature envisioned in the Atlantic a familiar landscape of Spanish "cruelties"; the Indian featured as an innocent victim of Habsburg oppression, much like the beleaguered Dutch patriot. The Dutch projected themselves—in this sense very much unlike the English, the French, and certainly the Spanish—not as colonizers in the Atlantic but as the colonized, victims of imperial hostility. Their political situation encouraged them to see the Indians not as savage antagonists but as natural allies, even comrades, in the campaign against Habsburg "universal monarchy."[10]

These circumstances rendered Dutch formulations of the Atlantic distinctive and certainly exceptional among their early modern cohorts. They also induced initiatives that stand out in the history of Atlantic expansion.[11] Dutch schemes for the West Indies began to take serious shape around 1600, when leading promoters of an Atlantic enterprise proposed not so much to subdue, as to befriend, indigenous populations whom they imagined encountering; they would "ally" with the Indians. To reach such formulations involved a series of fascinating rhetorical maneuvers that converted the Indians from their enemy's enemy to the Dutch imperialists' friends. This occurred in the early seventeenth century, as the war against Spain began to cool down and calls for overseas expansion heated up. From the rebels' assumption of mutual suffering there evolved a more ambitious notion of a tactical alliance between those two "nations"—the Dutch Republic and "the Indies," the latter construed as a coherent political entity—most intimately familiar with the misrule of Spain. William of Orange's assertion of shared anguish contained a considerable degree of sympathy for the Indians. It also implied a singular affinity between the rebels and "Americans," who would be linked by their common hostility toward Spanish tyranny. To the polemically agile mind, this suggested the further possibility of an "alliance": if the natives could be construed as cousins in suffering, might they plausibly be represented as brothers in arms as well, or perhaps even partners in trade?

This was the tack taken by Willem Usselincx (1567–1647) and a group of like-minded colonialists who insisted that the Indians would welcome the Dutch as confederates and join with them in a campaign against Habsburg hegemony. Most of these political writers, to be sure, also advertised the religious and economic advantages of colonial programs: the traditional appeal to "God and gold." But they asserted, additionally, the moral duty of their readers (and potential investors) to aid those Atlantic "allies" whose experience had bonded them to the Republic. "The pitiless slaughter of over twenty million innocent Indians who did [Spain] no harm," quoted Usselincx directly from the rebels' propaganda, "[demanded] God's righteous judgment." A Dutch West India Company was not just an opportunity, in his view, but an obligation born of the pledges of fidelity made by the rebels to their Atlantic brethren. "Our friends and allies will lose all faith in us," wrote Usselincx in the wake of truce negotiations (circa 1606–1609), "if they see that we, but for the sake of a specious title [the truce], abandon our own inhabitants and the allied Indians who have been so faithful and done us such good service."[12]

As it turned out, that "specious title" undermined Usselincx's immediate plans, since the Twelve Years' Truce, signed in 1609, precluded Dutch activity in the Atlantic. Yet his efforts were not in vain. The Dutch West India Company, traditionally viewed as the product of hard-line Calvinist politics fueled by hard-nosed expansionist economics, had its roots in the ideological soil of the late sixteenth century and the rebels' conceit of an Atlantic alliance.[13] Usselincx's campaign for a West Indian enterprise had underscored the moral obligation of the Republic to "free" the Indians and grant them their "natural liberties"—by which he meant both freedom of conscience and freedom of trade (goals he presumed that the Indians shared with the Dutch). The promotional literature for the ultimately formed West India Company (WIC), founded upon the expiration of the truce in 1621, reveals the deep ambivalence of the company directors, who appealed simultaneously to their supporters' moral sensibilities—the company's mission to "save" the Indians—and their financial self-interest—the company's hope to *exploit* the Indians. Dutch rhetoric of "innocence" and "alliance" rivaled in this way the traditional rationales of imperial and commercial expansion. It also gave the WIC, even as it developed by the 1630s and 1640s in different directions, a distinctively Dutch profile.

The Exemplary Dutch Atlantic

The next chapter of the story narrates the rise of the Dutch West India Company, which enjoyed considerable, albeit short-lived, success in the first few decades after its foundation (a period that correlates to the final phase of the Eighty Years' War, 1621–1648). During this episode of commercial and colonial expansion, one can speak not only of a Dutch Atlantic—of a genuine, distinctive, and not insubstantial Dutch presence in the Atlantic—but also of an exemplary case of Atlantic history. In the space of two or three decades, the Dutch expanded ambitiously, extensively, effectively, and productively into the Atlantic. They established a prominent and profitable empire that reached into North and South America, the Caribbean, and West Africa; that moved peoples and products across sea routes and up river lanes; that supported several domestic and overseas industries; and that inspired the manufacture of widely admired cultural products depicting the extra-European world. They created, in short, a textbook case of what historians would seem to have in mind when they speak of early modern Atlantic systems. Historians, to be sure, rarely have the Dutch case in mind at all, and rarely mention the Dutch in their textbooks—so much so that the absence of the Dutch in studies of the early modern Atlantic has become almost a historiographic cliché: there is no such thing as a Dutch Atlantic. This scholarly cold shoulder notwithstanding, the exemplarity of the Dutch case should seem obvious in retrospect, and its habitual neglect derives as much from the distinctive origins as from the subsequent development of the WIC.[14]

The Dutch WIC took form against the backdrop of war and revolt, and it assumed a pronounced anti-Habsburg character from the start. This alone makes it distinctive: England and France, not to mention Portugal and Spain, did not launch their Atlantic empires primarily as acts of belligerence (against other Europeans, at least). A famous debate among Dutch historians weighs the relative importance of the martial origins of the WIC—its stated aim to take the war to Spain's American underbelly—and its commercial agenda to expand the Netherlands' assault on Iberian trade, as had lately been done with great success in the East Indies (at the expense of Portugal, which reverted to the Castilian crown in 1580).[15] A third motive, as Usselincx's writings make plain, was moral: to support Atlantic "allies" in their time of need. Wherever the emphasis lay, the fact of ongoing war and (not unrelated) the ongoing rhetorical onslaught against the Habsburg "colonial" regime, in the Netherlands and Spain's overseas empire alike, makes the Republic's Atlantic initiatives stand out.

So, too, does the early development of the Dutch West India Company and its swift expansion in the 1630s and 1640s. While this is no place to offer a full-scale overview of the WIC, a few quick points may help to contextualize the company's early fortunes and later reception.[16] To begin with, it is worth noting that the foundation of the WIC hardly inaugurated Dutch trade in the Atlantic. It simply brought together under a single charter several existing merchant groups and granted monopoly rights to this newly organized conglomerate. And though the States General granted these privileges, the state's role in the Dutch Atlantic was otherwise relatively limited in comparison with the Spanish, French, and (to a lesser degree) English Crowns' involvement in their countries' respective Atlantic endeavors. The WIC, like the Republic itself, was sui generis in this regard. That said, there was more symbiosis between state and company than is commonly recognized: the WIC helped conduct the war against Spain, and the States General contributed ships and soldiers to the WIC at critical junctures. Another distinction derives from the orientation of Dutch overseas trade in this period. In contrast to most other European empire builders of the seventeenth century, the Dutch looked east in preference to west (and well beyond the Levant) when they contemplated overseas expansion and profits. (The VOC, or United East India Company, had been in operation since 1602.) They also favored the fort-and-factory model learned from their early Asian experience—from the Portuguese—rather than the more ambitiously territorial programs pursued by Spanish *encomenderos* and English planters. Even in their briefly held Brazil colony, sometimes referred to as New Holland, the Dutch did better at trading and processing sugar than growing the raw product and operating the mills that pressed it. In fact, Dutch merchants continued to do well trading Brazilian sugar even after the loss of their colony in 1654. And this points to one more distinction: the remarkable dynamism of the Dutch Atlantic trade, a commerce that included WIC merchants and private (often illicit) traders alike, and carried Dutch colonial goods as well as products of other (non-Dutch) imperial powers in the Atlantic. This broad-reaching commercial network renders the Dutch Atlantic, on the one hand, notably different from the Iberian, English, and French mercantilist systems of the seventeenth century. It reflects fairly well, on the other hand, patterns of Dutch commerce back in Europe—and in some regards in Asia, where VOC merchants also profitably plied the transit trade. The Dutch sent over comparatively fewer migrants than the English in the mid-seventeenth century—or the Spanish a century earlier—yet they financed relatively more ships, the latter laden with the widely sought riches of Atlantic commerce.

None of this should detract from the basic fact that the Dutch did expand territorially in the early-to-mid seventeenth century, while simultaneously integrating into their overseas empire an impressive network of trade. More to the point, the Dutch extended their growing imperial reach to an array of settlements that touched the major promontories of the Atlantic world. In the 1620s, they settled in the center of coastal North America: the colony of New Netherland, with its superbly situated harbor of New Amsterdam, its deep and navigable inland rivers, and its richly wooded interiors with abundant supplies of beavers and pelts. In the 1630s, they assumed control of large sections, also centrally located, of South America (New Holland in

Brazil), placing themselves a quick sail from Africa and Europe. In West Africa they wrested control of Elmina from the Portuguese in 1637, and thereafter they used it as a clearing house for the Guinea slave trade, as well as trade in gold and ivory; and they captured Luanda (in present-day Angola), which likewise operated as a center of the slave trade. They colonized several Caribbean islands in this period, too, including the entrepôts of Curacao and St. Eustatius; and they gained possession of several smaller settlements on the Wild Coast (between the Orinoco and Amazon deltas), which would later develop into plantation colonies.[17]

Much of this expansion took place in the two decades directly following the WIC's foundation, and this process culminated in the appointment of the most distinctive European colonial governor of the century, Johan Maurits of Nassau-Siegen, who took the baton of power in Dutch Brazil in 1637. An exceptionally highborn figure in the context of colonial government (his father's uncle was William of Orange), a patron to the single greatest assemblage of artists and scientists in the early modern New World, a superb administrator of the multicultural population of Recife and its surroundings—where Portuguese and Dutch, Christian and Jewish, African and Brazilian men and women of diverse faiths and backgrounds all intermingled—Johan Maurits presided over one of the most impressive Baroque societies, in the Old World or the New. Under his rule, a truly exemplary Atlantic world flourished. Johan Maurits supervised the extension of the Brazilian colony, the conquest of African forts, the movement and mixture of colonial populations, the exploration and description of tropical *naturalia*, the study of exotic peoples, and, not least, the expansion of the Dutch Atlantic trade (especially in sugar) and other commercial ventures that linked the African, American, and European economies.[18]

Why, then, the scholarly disregard and omission? Why, if the Dutch Atlantic enjoyed such indubitable success and exemplified the sort of interconnected social, economic, and colonial system implied by the term "Atlantic history," with an added cultural overlay, is the case for the Dutch Atlantic so meekly made? Why, in short, no Dutch Atlantic? The history of the Dutch Atlantic suffers from at least double, if not triple, neglect. First, from the perspective of Dutch historiography, Atlantic history, and that of the WIC in particular, has always had to cede ground to the better-known legacy of the Dutch East Indies and the history of the VOC (even if, as we now understand, the total Atlantic trade of the Dutch may have been no less profitable than Dutch Asian operations).[19] From at least the nineteenth century—by which time New Netherland, New Holland, and the WIC were long past, whereas Batavia and the Indonesian trade were not—Dutch scholarly attention has focused on the East, where the Netherlands retained strong imperial ties. Second, and from the vantage point of the other side of the Atlantic, the prevailing narrative of colonial American history (both North and South) has all but ignored the Dutch, since history gets written by the winners, in this case the longer-lasting powers of England, Spain, and (to a lesser extent) Portugal. This has meant that the brief Dutch *imperial* moment of the mid-seventeenth century—the zenith of the WIC's might and influence, and the period of its greatest territorial reach—merits at best passing mention in narratives of Brazil and New York. Otherwise, however, the presence of Dutch traders in the Atlantic and their dynamic commercial networks, extending well into the eighteenth century, tend to be ignored.

And this brings up a third factor, less obvious at first glance: the distinctiveness of the Dutch Atlantic enterprise, which began, developed, and endured in ways that do not well match other European models. If the Dutch entered the Atlantic world with military and commercial motives (and perhaps vaguely imperial aspirations), they also embraced the "moral" imperative of aiding their indigenous Atlantic "allies" and joining these hypothetical brothers in arms in their shared struggle against Habsburg "tyranny." Such were hardly the origins of the British and French programs for the Atlantic. Once launched and organized under the direction of the WIC, the "grand design" for the Dutch Atlantic achieved rapid success by establishing an empire that was notably far-reaching and diversified. By the mid-seventeenth century, the WIC coordinated and consolidated colonies throughout the Atlantic—their northern operations in New Netherland extended beyond those of Spain and Portugal, and their southern presence (Brazil) exceeded that of the British and French—and they earned profits by plantation economy and transit trade alike. Their eggs were in several baskets—again, anomalously. The simple fact that all Dutch trade in the Atlantic came under the supervision (theoretically) of a single company—thus neither the state, which controlled the Spanish Atlantic, nor the private companies that competed in the English Atlantic—makes their Atlantic enterprise distinctive as well, although this characteristic became increasingly problematic as the seventeenth century progressed. Indeed, the later development of the Dutch Atlantic, over the second half of the seventeenth century and into the early eighteenth, took an altogether different direction, as Dutch merchants came to dominate the carrying trade that served other major Atlantic powers—yet was never matched by them. This shift—again, distinctive—marks a wholly new chapter in the history of the Dutch Atlantic, its organization, and its identity.

The Un-Dutch Atlantic

The "exemplary" Dutch Atlantic did not last long. Indigenous populations failed to ally with, or even welcome, their putative brethren from the Netherlands; and the widespread Atlantic empire built over the 1630s and 1640s attracted equally widespread attacks from competing European powers. The Dutch Atlantic went from zenith to nadir-like crisis soon after Johan Maurits returned to Europe, and the carefully pieced-together Atlantic edifice of the WIC came apart as quickly as it had been formed. A revolt of Portuguese planters cost the WIC its Brazilian colony in 1654; attacks from the English navy led to the forfeiture of New Netherland in 1664; and crippling debt coupled with gross mismanagement brought about the end of the original West India Company in 1674.[20] At this point, a new Dutch Atlantic company was chartered with much diminished powers and greatly restricted monopolies. Among the chief opponents of the original WIC, in fact, were merchants who favored a looser organization of commerce and greater access to markets. And the newly reconfigured WIC—and, accordingly, newly embraced model for the Dutch Atlantic—reflected this open-market approach. Only the African trade, which comprised the traffic in slaves and commerce in gold and ivory, was retained, along with certain administrative duties related to a few African forts and the relatively modest Dutch colonies in the Caribbean and on the Wild Coast. Otherwise, the new WIC assumed a sharply scaled-back role.

The decline of the Dutch Atlantic in the mid-seventeenth century was a decline in terms of Dutch imperial hegemony, the Republic's territorial reach, and the WIC's profitability (even if the latter would ultimately rebound under the new arrangement). Yet it does not denote the demise of the Dutch Atlantic per se. Rather than a *decline*, one might better speak of a *reconfiguration* of the Dutch Atlantic, or a new conception of its strategic value. For if the Republic had lost control of its premiere colonies, its merchants did not lose their appetite for profitable trade or their nose for fresh market opportunities. Dutch commerce consequently resumed in the Atlantic and in many ways flourished under this new system, which encouraged, on the one hand, a leaner WIC with a clearer market focus and, on the other hand, greater leeway for the unfettered (non-WIC) merchant. To start at the alleged end, private Dutch merchants continued to participate in the sugar trade, even in Brazil, by extending credit to local (Portuguese) planters; financing several plantations (particularly those administered by Sephardic Jews); and delivering sugar-producing technology throughout the Caribbean. They also transported sugar itself, along with other Atlantic products, utilizing the ever-busier entrepôt of Curaçao. Above all, Dutch merchants profited from the transit trade: the movement of goods from port to port, which facilitated the various Atlantic economies rather than any specifically Dutch colonial presence. "The Dutch are more fortunate in their trade than in their colonies," wrote an English official around this time (circa 1670), offering a perfectly apt observation of the revised Dutch operations in the Atlantic.[21] Dutch merchants—not "the Dutch" per se, let alone the WIC, but rather private merchants, mostly of Holland and Zeeland, working collaboratively with a range of colonial planters, Atlantic traders, chartered companies, and, by extension, English, French, and Spanish agents— participated in this "hardy commercialism," which entailed trafficking with multiple and multinational Atlantic entities.[22] The "Dutch" Atlantic had become conspicuously cosmopolitan.

As with these commercial shifts, this period also witnessed a series of conceptual adjustments in the Dutch Atlantic, which dictated a similar expanding and enhancing of Atlantic vistas. The Dutch conception of the Atlantic "loosened" in the second half of the seventeenth century, as it was made to accommodate a newer, more pluralistic vision of the region, a worldview less parochially Dutch and more broadly European. This shift pertains to sources of geography, and yet another distinction of the Dutch Atlantic experience is the outstanding role they played in the production of cultural materials that depicted the Atlantic world. The Dutch excelled in the field of geography, broadly defined, and this led to their extraordinary manufacture of textual, visual, and cartographic sources that represented the places, peoples, and products of the West. This, in some sense, had long been the case. Printers, engravers, and mapmakers, first in Antwerp and later in Amsterdam, had dominated the business of geography since at least the mid-sixteenth century (the Dutch produced some of the earliest maps and finest printed accounts of America).[23] What had changed by the mid-seventeenth century, however, was the nature of the images and the message they conveyed; what had shifted was the Dutch conception of their particular place in the Atlantic and their broader, global vision. The Atlantic world transformed from a distinctly "Dutch" space to one that, by the final decades of the seventeenth century, assumed a generically "European" appearance and endeavored to disguise even the Dutch presence in the Atlantic.

Two brands of Atlantic image-making prevailed in the earlier (pre-1650) period, one of which correlates to the "first" Dutch Atlantic, and the second of which speaks to the "exemplary" Dutch Atlantic, and both of which impressed a pronouncedly Dutch visage on the region. The first has been

broached: the recurring image of "Spanish tyranny in America," which dates
back to the revolt and the early years of the WIC. Once the Dutch had successfully established themselves in the Atlantic, however, the use of this
motif subsided, and a second manner of describing the region developed.
The sources in this case are less polemical if no less proud in their enuncia-
tion of a "Dutch" Atlantic. They are the stupendous and justly admired works
of Dutch art and scholarship produced in the 1630s and 1640s, a fair number
of which came into being under the patronage of Johan Maurits: Willem
Piso's natural history of Brazil, Caspar Barlaeus's heroic narrative of Johan
Maurits's colonial reign, the early landscape paintings of Frans Post, the
exotic portraits of Albert Eckhout, and so on.[24] These offer an unabashedly
celebratory, assertively Dutch picture of the region and, together with the
larger corpus of Dutch materials produced at this time—the exultant poems
of Jacob Steendam ("In Praise of New Netherland"), the epic *Mauritias* by
Franciscus Plante, the decorative maps of Johannes Janssonius and Willem
Blaeu (of *Nova Belgica* and the provinces of Brazil)—present a multimedia
view of the Republic's Atlantic world.[25] Dutch sources of this period produce
a plainly partisan image of the Atlantic, underscoring the colonial progress
of the Republic through the mid-seventeenth century.[26]

When the Republic's colonial progress halted at mid century and
abruptly changed course, so, too, did representations of the Dutch Atlantic.
Or rather, so did representations of the *European* Atlantic, since Dutch-
made materials of the later seventeenth and early eighteenth centuries tend
to underplay the Dutch presence in the region, which, after all, had become
far less conspicuous in terms of colonial control and imperial dominion.
Sources do not disappear—this is the very moment when the sumptu-
ous volumes of Olfert Dapper on Africa (1668), Arnoldus Montanus on
America (1671), and Johan Nieuhof on the West Indies (1682) debuted
and became the most sought-after works on their respective subjects.[27]
Yet the *Dutch* disappear, seeming to shrink into the background of the
Atlantic world. This entailed, first, a process of effacement. When Piso's
study of Brazilian *naturalia* originally appeared in 1648, at the height
of Dutch colonial power, it contained an appended section in praise of
the WIC empire. When reissued in 1658, however, the patriotic message
had been expunged, its place now taken by a poetic admiration of tropical wonders. Frans Post's landscapes underwent a comparable change of
course. His early works, commissioned by Johan Maurits and painted in
Brazil from 1637 through the early 1640s, depict Dutch forts and settlements; they are topographical and attentive to local, strategic concerns.
Upon returning to Holland, by contrast, Post painted well over a hundred

exotic landscapes for the open market, the lush flora and fauna of Brazil crowding his picture planes and all but subsuming the human landscape. The mid- and background elements of Post's brightly colored canvases typically contain smaller scenes of indigenous peoples, African slaves, and the occasional European, who is not necessarily or commonly Dutch (a fact revealed by the dress and manner of riding horseback). Rather than the colonial presence of the Dutch—or of the Portuguese, for that matter, who are subtly invoked by the cloisters and plantations frequently seen in the background—Post's landscapes celebrate the natural wonder and strangeness of the Atlantic world. They are generically exotic images rather than specifically Dutch ones.[28]

The new Dutch vision entailed, second, a process of dilution. The Atlantic world of these sources appears more global, in the sense that Dutch-made materials tend to expand their horizons, combine their colonial regions, and even mix their oceans. Narratives that previously might have harbored a Dutch imperial focus—on specific settlements in the Atlantic or on regions of strategic value—now attend to a broadly exotic world, looking east as well as west, with no colonial core. Piso's Brazilian study appeared in its later edition (1658) with an added section on the East Indies; it now described tropical *naturalia* in a global, rather than a Dutch–Brazilian, setting. A similar process shaped the publication of Johan Nieuhof's travels to the Indies. An original manuscript from the 1640s, which detailed the author's service in Dutch Brazil, was augmented with other materials to produce, on publication in 1682, a more fluid, international itinerary through the Atlantic, Pacific, and Indian oceans. The Dutch in this period also excelled in the publication of global geographies—sprawling, folio volumes, with lavish illustration programs, fold-out maps, intricate paratexts, and the like—which incorporate the Atlantic into a wider exotic world. And the Dutch published the Atlantic worlds of others. Not only were Dutch-language materials regularly translated into French, English, German, and Latin, but entrepreneurial publishers of the Netherlands also manufactured among the finest and most ubiquitous editions of works by Charles de Rochefort (on the Caribbean), Louis Hennepin and the Baron de Lahontan (each covering North America and especially French America), and, even into the eighteenth century, Walter Ralegh (on Guiana) and John Smith (on Virginia).[29] They produced the "remarkable voyages and travels into the best provinces of the West and East Indies," as the English editor of Nieuhof phrased it; and they thereby made the Dutch Atlantic at once less Dutch and less Atlantic.[30]

Conclusion

By the early eighteenth century, one might claim—with only mild exaggeration and conceptually speaking—that there was no such thing as a Dutch Atlantic. This is not to say that there were no Dutch merchants profiting in the Atlantic; no Dutch ports and plantations thriving along the margins of the Spanish, English, and French Atlantics; and no Dutch attention bestowed on the rich products and natural wonders of the Atlantic: all of this was certainly the case. Yet Dutch sources of this period engage with the Atlantic in ways that had become less provincial and "national" than might otherwise have been the case; and this produced a conception of the Atlantic that was more openly multinational, and ultimately more global, than it once had been. There had been a profound shift over the course of the early modern period in the ways the Dutch imagined the Atlantic, particularly during the middle decades of the seventeenth century, when the Republic's presence in the Atlantic altered appreciably. This involved a transformation not only in the Netherlands' colonial and commercial engagement in the Atlantic but also in the way the Dutch conceptualized Atlantic space: it entailed a move from "local" perceptions to "universal" ones, from a parochial Atlantic that served domestic discourses ("Spanish tyrannies") to a broadly appealing vision—and a widely salable image, too, insofar as the Dutch did a good business in geography—that served various constituencies. The Dutch Atlantic changed from a *Dutch* space to a more generically European one, and from an *Atlantic* space to a more fluidly global one, which could accommodate the East as well as West Indies with little more than the turn of a page.

How do early modern Dutch patterns fit larger European ones? The case of the Dutch Atlantic reflects its own particular contingencies (as all individual cases invariably must), and its distinctiveness points to the similarly idiosyncratic contours of Dutch history. Yet Dutch developments also highlight certain Atlantic patterns, whether they match them or not, and these might be usefully extrapolated. The history of the Dutch Atlantic points ultimately toward a Dutch *Sonderweg*—not unusually for the history of the early modern Republic—in the sense that the Netherlands' engagement with the Atlantic fits only awkwardly, if at all, in the prevailing paradigms of Atlantic history. The latter is almost axiomatically taken to be the British model (or perhaps some Anglo–Spanish amalgam, applying the Habsburg case for the sixteenth century and the English for the seventeenth), which underscores the steadily intensifying contacts across the Atlantic that laid the foundation for a future American empire (Africa is frankly left out).[31]

The Dutch initially and ultimately turned their back on this imperial model. Somewhat exceptionally, they approached the Atlantic from the perspective of "colonial" subjects—so, at least, they assiduously portrayed themselves at that vital, sixteenth-century moment when they became "Dutch"—and they viewed any Habsburg imperial advance with great alarm. The nascent Dutch Republic perceived the Atlantic world, accordingly, as a locus of *anti*-imperial alliances; they imagined it to be a site to roll back the "tyranny" of their archantagonist, Spain. This changed, of course, when Dutch colonialists more systematically entered the Atlantic and endeavored themselves to pursue an imperial agenda. Yet their very success in the middle years of this enterprise—above all, during the tenure of Johan Maurits—sets the Dutch model apart: they experienced an extraordinarily intensive Atlantic moment. In these years, arguably, no other early modern effort in the Atlantic matches that of the Dutch, in terms both of the WIC's extensive imperial reach and control over a mutually supportive constellation of colonies, scattered throughout the Atlantic; and of the impressive Dutch manufacture of scholarly and artistic products, which offered the finest available studies of the Atlantic's geography and natural world. The Dutch Atlantic of the mid-seventeenth century stands out, paradoxically enough, for its exemplarity.

The final chapter of the early modern Dutch Atlantic also suggests distinctiveness, yet without any of the earlier parochialism. If the Dutch had originally conceived of the Atlantic in terms of domestic discourses and political concerns, they later reformulated their ideas in ways that underemphasized and even disguised the Dutch presence in the Atlantic. They moved, that is, from a provincial sense of Atlantic space, which played to local debates and bolstered colonial ambitions, to an expansive vision of the Atlantic, which declined to highlight any single imperial strategy and thus appealed to a broadly European community of consumers. They created a "universal" form of knowledge (from Europe's perspective, to be sure), which offered a non-national, non-imperial image of the Atlantic. This conceptual adjustment took place in tandem with a practical shift in Dutch Atlantic engagements—from imperial "grand designs" to commercial networks of trade—and in both commercial and cultural shifts, the emphasis lay on a fluid conception of Atlantic space: more open in terms of economic exchange and less particularistic in terms of geographic focus. It was no longer a "Dutch" Atlantic, but a sphere of European activity. Indeed, it was no longer even an "Atlantic" space per se, but part of the larger, exotic, non-European world.

It is this last point that may be most useful to the study of Atlantic history. The Atlantic surely has had many histories, and, in the Dutch case, one can observe several transformations over the course of the early modern period. And even while these shifts may include some particularly "Dutch Atlantic" moments, they lead, in the end, to an abnegation of a Dutch Atlantic per se. By the early eighteenth century not only had the Dutch given up on an expansive Atlantic empire (even while trade continued to flourish), they also had, in their widely consumed works of geography, natural history, ethnography, and more, ceased to distinguish an Atlantic sphere; they dealt with a generically exotic world. In the context of Dutch global trade and Dutch global geography, the Atlantic no longer made sense. This is not to suggest that the Dutch perspective was any less imperial or colonial; but rather that it took a hyperimperial, or pancolonial, approach which effectively lumped Europeans and their disparate colonial subjects together. The Dutch Atlantic was supranational. Their conceptual model may not be any less Eurocentric than alternative models, it may not be any less imperial, and it may not be indicative of any bona fide Atlantic history. Yet it does show how the Dutch struggled with the conceptual problem of the Atlantic and solved it in a manner to their liking: by finally letting its waters flow into those of the other oceans of the world.

Acknowledgments

Thanks are due to the editors and to Wim Klooster and Peter Arnade, each of whom offered generous comments on earlier drafts. I am also grateful to the Institute for Advanced Study, Princeton, which provided the best setting imaginable to think about both globalism and provincialism.

NOTES

1. The allusive reference here is to Steven Shapin's opening gambit in *The Scientific Revolution* (Chicago: University of Chicago Press, 1996), p. 1, where the wobbly state of that historiographic model is also knocked around. The somewhat paradoxical argument proposed here is echoed—albeit for slightly different reasons and invoking somewhat different data—in a few revisionist studies of the Dutch Atlantic, including Pieter Emmer and Wim Klooster, "The Dutch Atlantic, 1600–1800: Expansion Without Empire," *Itinerario* 23 (1999): 48–69; Pieter Emmer, "The West India Company, 1621–1791: Dutch or Atlantic?," in Emmer, *The Dutch in the Atlantic Economy, 1580–1880* (Aldershot, U.K.: Ashgate, 1998), pp. 65–90; and Jan de Vries, "The Dutch Atlantic Economies," in Peter Coclanis, ed., *The Atlantic Economy During the Seventeenth and Eighteenth Centuries: Organization,*

Operation, Practice, and Personnel (Columbia: University of South Carolina Press, 2005), pp. 1–29. Most of these essays take an economic approach, whereas this essay makes its case also with reference to contemporary ideas of Atlantic space. More generally, see the Atlantic-skeptical approaches of Alison Games, "Atlantic History: Definitions, Challenges, and Opportunities," *American Historical Review* 111 (2006): 741–757; Peter Coclanis, "Atlantic World or Atlantic/World?," *William and Mary Quarterly* 63 (2006): 725–742; Pieter Emmer, "The Myth of Early Globalization: The Atlantic Economy, 1500–1800," *Europe Review* 11 (2003): 37–47; Peter Coclanis, "*Drang Nach Osten*: Bernard Bailyn, the World-Island, and the Idea of Atlantic History," *Journal of World History* 13 (2002): 169–182; and Alison Games, "Beyond the Atlantic: English Globetrotters and Transoceanic Connections," *William and Mary Quarterly* 63 (2006): 675–692.

2. A comparative historiographic approach is addressed more particularly in an earlier essay: Benjamin Schmidt, "American Allies: The Dutch Encounter with the New World, 1492–1650," *Working Papers of the International Seminar on the History of the Atlantic World*, 3rd ser., 32 (1998): 1–30.

3. Horst Pietschmann, "Atlantic History: History Between European History and Global History," in Pietschmann, ed., *Atlantic History: History of the Atlantic System, 1580–1830* (Göttingen: Vandenhoeck & Ruprecht, 2002), pp. 11–54. See also Pieter Emmer, "The Dutch and the Making of the Second Atlantic System," in Emmer, *Dutch in the Atlantic Economy*, pp. 11–32.

4. These sources are discussed below; on Las Casas more particularly, see Benjamin Schmidt, "The Purpose of Pirates, or Assimilating New Worlds in the Renaissance," in Willem Klooster and Alfred Padula, eds., *The Atlantic World: Essays on Slavery, Migration, and Imagination* (Upper Saddle River, N.J.: Prentice Hall, 2004), pp. 160–177.

5. De Vries, "Dutch Atlantic Economies," p. 18 (and see his similarly alliterative assessment that "[the Dutch Atlantic] has long appeared both unimpressive and unimportant," p. 1).

6. Hernán Cortés's letters to Charles V, Francisco López de Gómara's chronicle of Mexico, and Pedro de Cieza de León's description of Peru all came off the presses of the Low Countries virtually simultaneously with their publication in Spain;while the narratives of Agustín de Zárate (Peru) and Hans Staden (Brazil) went through more editions in Dutch than any other language, including that of their original composition. See further Benjamin Schmidt, *Innocence Abroad: The Dutch Imagination and the New World, 1570–1670* (Cambridge: Cambridge University Press, 2001), pp. 5–6.

7. Abraham Ortelius, *Theatrum orbis terrarum* (Antwerp, 1570), which also appeared in a Spanish edition, *Theatro de la tierra universal* (1588).

8. "Verbintenis van eenige eedelen," in J. W. Te Water, *Historie van het verbond en de smeekschriften der Nederlandsche edelen ter verkrijging van vrijheid in den godsdienst en burgerstaat in de jaren 1565–1567*, 4 vols. (Middelburg, 1779–1796), vol. 4, p. 61.

9. H. Wansink, ed., *Apologie of Prince William of Orange Against the Proc-lamation of the King of Spaine* (Leiden: Brill, 1969), esp. pp. 53–59; M. E. H. N. Mout, ed., *Plakkaat van verlatinge 1581* (The Hague, 1979), especially pp. 97, 99, 105, 117. Marnix's case and further samples of American "tyranny" are discussed in Benjamin Schmidt, "Tyranny Abroad: The Dutch Revolt and the Invention of America," *De zeventiende eeuw* 11 (1995): 161–174.

10. As Nicolas Canny has pointed out, the English began their colonization of America in the wake of their subjugation of Ireland—as seasoned colonialists, in other words: *Elizabethan Conquest of Ireland: A Pattern Established* (New York, 1976); see also James Muldoon, "The Indian as Irishman," *Essex Institute Historical Collections* 111 (1975): 267–289. If there was a degree of English hostility toward the Spanish model of colonization (especially in the 1580s and 1590s), the level of criticism never reached the shrill anti-Hispanism in the Netherlands. Although he criticized Spain's treatment of the natives, Ralegh aspired to *outdo*—not undo—Cortés as a conquistador (see his *Discovery of Guiana*, 1596). Uniquely among the early modern colonial players, the Dutch had first-hand experience of what they perceived as colonial rule.

11. Among the most impressive of these was a Chilean initiative to ally with the Araucanians: see Benjamin Schmidt, "Exotic Allies: The Dutch–Chilean Encounter and the (Failed) Conquest of America," *Renaissance Quarterly* 52 (1999): 440–473.

12. *Levendich discours vant ghemeyne lants welvaert, voor desen de oost, end nu de West-Indische Generale Compaignie aenghevanghen* (1622), sig. [C4]-v; *Memorie vande ghewichtighe redenen die de heeren Staten Generael behooren te beweghen, om gheesins te wijcken vande handelinghe ende vaert van Indien* (1608), sig. iij-r; and see *Onpartydich discours opte handelinghe vande Indien* ([1608?]), sig. Aij-r, which speaks of an "*alliante*" with the Indians. On Usselincx, a fascinat-ing figure in the history of free-trade discourse, see J. Franklin Jameson, *Willem Usselinx: Founder of the Dutch and Swedish West India Companies* (New York, 1887); and C. Ligtenberg, *Willem Usselinx* (Utrecht, 1914).

13. The Calvinist case was made by W. J. van Hoboken, "The Dutch West India Company: The Political Background of Its Rise and Fall," in. J. S. Bromley and E. H. Kossmann, eds., *Britain and the Netherlands* (London, 1960), pp. 41–61; while the economic brief was argued by J. G. van Dillen, "De West-Indische Compagnie, het Calvinisme, en de politiek," *Tijdschrift voor Geschiedenis* 74 (1961): 145–171. This debate was revisited by Emmer, "West India Company," pp. 68–70.

14. The neglect of the Dutch in standard narratives of Atlantic history has been pointed out early—from the 1980s—and often, most energetically perhaps by Joyce Goodfriend. See Goodfriend, "The Historiography of the Dutch in Colonial America," in Eric Nooter and Patricia Bonomi, eds., *Colonial Dutch Studies: An Interdisciplinary Approach* (New York, 1988), pp. 6–32; "The Dutch Colonial Leg-acy: 'Not Hasty to Change Old Habits for New,'" *De Haelve Maen* 65 (Spring 1992): 5–9; and "Writing/Righting Dutch Colonial History," *New York History* 80 (1999):

5–28. See also Karen Ordahl Kupperman, "Early American History with the Dutch Put In," *Reviews in American History* 21 (1993): 195–201; Joyce Goodfriend, ed., *Revisiting New Netherland: Perspectives on Early Dutch America* (Leiden: Brill, 2005); and Johannes Postma and Victor Enthoven, eds., *Riches from Atlantic Commerce: Dutch Transatlantic Trade and Shipping, 1585–1817* (Leiden: Brill, 2003), which approaches the topic from a South Atlantic perspective.

15. See note 13.

16. On the WIC, see Henk den Heijer, *De geschiedenis van de WIC* (Zutphen: Walburg, 1994); idem, "The Dutch West India Company, 1621–1791," in Postma and Enthoven, eds., *Riches from Atlantic Commerce*, pp. 77–112; and Emmer, "West India Company." Still useful are Charles Boxer's classic studies, *The Dutch Seaborne Empire, 1600–1800* (New York: Knopf, 1965), and *The Dutch in Brazil, 1624–1654* (Oxford: Clarendon Press, 1957).

17. On economic matters, see Emmer, *Dutch in the Atlantic Economy*; Jonathan Israel, *Dutch Primacy in World Trade, 1585–1740* (Oxford: Clarendon Press, 1989); and Postma and Enthoven, *Riches from Atlantic Commerce*. Dutch Brazil is surveyed in Boxer, *Dutch in Brazil*; José Antônio Gonsalves de Mello, *Tempo dos flamengos: Influência da ocupação holandesa na vida e na cultura do norte do Brasil*, 3rd ed. (Recife: Fundação Joaquim Nabuco, 1987); and P. Herkenhoff, ed., *Brazil and the Dutch, 1630–1654* (Rio de Janeiro: GMT, 1999). For New Netherland, see Jaap Jacobs, *New Netherland: A Dutch Colony in Seventeenth Century America* (Leiden: Brill, 2005); and Goodfriend, *Revisiting New Netherland*. On Africa and the slave trade, see Henk den Heijer, *Goud, ivoor en slaven: Scheepvaart en handel van de Tweede Westindische Compagnie op Afrika, 1674–1740* (Zutphen: Walburg, 1997); Pieter Emmer, *The Dutch Slave Trade, 1500–1850*, trans. Chris Emery (New York: Berghahn, 2006); and Johannes Postma, *The Dutch in the Atlantic Slave Trade, 1600–1815* (Cambridge: Cambridge University Press, 1990). And for the Caribbean, see Willem Klooster, *Illicit Riches: The Dutch Trade in the Caribbean, 1648–1795* (Leiden: KITLV, 1998); and Cornelis Goslinga, *The Dutch in the Caribbean and on the Wild Coast, 1580–1680* (Assen: Van Gorcum, 1971).

18. See E. van den Boogaart, H. R. Hoetink, and P. J. Whitehead, eds., *Johan Maurits van Nassau Siegen: A Humanist Prince in Europe and Brazil* (The Hague: Stichting Johan Maurits, 1979).

19. On the relative neglect of the WIC, see Henk den Heijer, *Geschiedenis van de WIC*: "Nog steeds wordt in de geschiedschrijving de Westindische Compagnie als een stiefkind [van de VOC] behandeld" (p. 9). And on the relative profitability of the Atlantic trade (compared to the commerce of the VOC), see Victor Enthoven and Johannes Postma, "Introduction," in *Riches from Atlantic Commerce*, 1–13; and de Vries, "Dutch Atlantic Economies," which notes the "leakage" that occurred throughout the WIC's history, making the Dutch Atlantic trade (including non-WIC trade) appear less profitable than it actually was.

20. By the mid-seventeenth century, the WIC had a debt approaching 20 million guilders on top of the original investment of 17 million guilders; in 1674 it effectively

declared bankruptcy. See den Heijer, "West India Company," pp. 97–100. Note that New Netherland was briefly recaptured by the Dutch in August 1673, only to revert permanently to the English in November 1674.

21. William Byam, governor of Antigua, to William Lord Willoughby, governor of Barbados, quoted in Willem Klooster, "An Overview of Dutch Trade with the Americas, 1600–1800," in Postma and Enthoven, *Riches from Atlantic Commerce*, pp. 365–383 (quote on 365, slightly revised).

22. De Vries, "Dutch Atlantic Economies," pp. 8–9, which also discusses the problems of trade within the "mercantilist box" that was the late seventeenth-century Atlantic economy.

23. See Kees Zandvliet, *Mapping for Money: Maps, Plans and Topographic Paintings and Their Role in Dutch Overseas Expansion During the Sixteenth and Seventeenth Centuries* (Amsterdam: Batavian Lion, 1998). The first engraved map to explicitly indicate the western discoveries appeared in Cornelius Aurelius, *De cronycke van Hollandt Zeelandt ende Vrieslant* ([Leiden, 1517]); the first atlas devoted exclusively to the new continents was Cornelis Wytfliet's *Descriptionis Ptolemaicae augmentum sive Occidentis notitia* (Louvain, 1597). Some of this corpus of sources is illustrated in Willem Klooster, *The Dutch in the Americas, 1600–1800* (Providence: John Carter Brown Library, 1997).

24. Willem Piso et al., *Historia naturalis Brasiliae* (Leiden, 1648); Caspar Barlaeus, *Rerum per octennium in Brasilia* (Amsterdam, 1647); Joaquim de Sousa-Leão, *Frans Post, 1612–1680* (Amsterdam: Van Gendt, 1973); Rebecca Parker Brienen, *Visions of Savage Paradise: Albert Eckhout, Court Painter in Colonial Dutch Brazil, 1637–1644* (Amsterdam: Amsterdam University Press, 2006); P. J. P. Whitehead and M. Boeseman, *A Portrait of Dutch Seventeenth-Century Brazil: Animals, Plants and People by the Artists of John Maurits of Nassau* (Amsterdam: North Holland, 1989).

25. Jacob Steendam, *'t Lof van Nuw-Nederland* (Amsterdam, 1661); Franciscus Plante, *Mauritiados libri XII* (Leiden, 1647). On the superabundant cartographic materials, see Zandvliet, *Mapping for Money*.

26. An important exception may be De Laet's sweeping history of America, which, even though composed by a WIC director, is less Dutch-centered than these other materials. By contrast, De Laet's *Jaerlijck verhael*, a thorough account of WIC affairs, reads like full-blown "patriotic scripture." See Joannes de Laet, *Nieuwe Wereldt oft Beschrijvinghe van West Indien* (Leiden, 1630), which also appeared in Latin, and his *Historie, ofte Iaerlijck verhael van de verrichtinghen der geoctroy-eerde West-Indische Compagnie* (Leiden, 1644). On "patriotic scripture," see Simon Schama, *The Embarrassment of Riches: An Interpretation of Dutch Culture in the Golden Age* (New York: Knopf, 1987).

27. Olfert Dapper, *Naukeurige beschrijvinge der Afrikaensche gewesten* (Amsterdam, 1668); Arnoldus Montanus, *De nieuwe en onbekende weereld, of, beschryving van America en 't Zuid-land* (Amsterdam, 1671); Johan Nieuhof,

Gedenkwaerdige zee en lantreize door de voornaemste landschappen van West en Oostindien (Amsterdam, 1682). All appeared in multiple editions and languages.

28. Peter Sutton is too hasty in calling these images "patriotic," a reading that fails to account for their appeal to such decidedly non-Dutch patriots as Louis XIV, who happily accepted twenty-seven landscapes presented to him in 1678: compare Sutton, *Dutch and Flemish Seventeenth-Century Paintings: The Harold Samuel Collection* (Cambridge: Cambridge University Press, 1992), p. 159.

29. Charles de Rochefort's *Histoire naturelle et morale des Îles Antilles de l'Amérique* (Rotterdam, 1658), primarily a product of Dutch publishing, is discussed in Everett Wilkie, Jr., "The Authorship and Purpose of the *Histoire naturelle et morale des Îles Antilles*, an Early Huguenot Emigration Guide," *Harvard Library Bulletin* 2nd ser., vol. 2, no. 3 (1991): 26–84. The chief publications of Louis Hennepin— the *Nouvelle découverte* and *Nouveau voyage*—both appeared in several handsome Dutch-made editions, which are sorted out in A. H. Greenly, "Father Louis Hennepin: His Travels and His Books," *Papers of the Bibliographical Society of America* 51 (1957): 38–60. And for the many versions of Baron de Lahontan's "New Voyages to North-America," see A. H. Greenly, "Lahontan: An Essay and Bibliography," *Papers of the Bibliographical Society of America* 48 (1954): 334–389. Smith's and Ralegh's narratives appeared in early-eighteenth-century editions done by the publishing impresario Pieter van der Aa. On the bibliographic voyages of Ralegh's *Discovery of Guiana*, see Benjamin Schmidt, "Reading Ralegh's America: Texts, Books, and Readers in the Early Modern Atlantic World," in Peter Mancall, ed., *The Atlantic World and Virginia, 1550–1624* (Chapel Hill: University of North Carolina Press, 2007), pp. 454–488.

30. See *Mr. John Nieuhoff's Remarkable Voyages and Travels into ye Best Provinces of ye West and East Indies*, in Awnsham Churchill, ed., *A Collection of Voyages and Travels*, 6 vols. (London, 1704), vol. 2.

31. Volumes on Britain are too plentiful to list, yet see the much-cited collection of David Armitage and Michael Braddick, eds., *The British Atlantic World, 1500–1800* (New York: Palgrave, 2002); and, for a comparative approach, John Elliott, *Empires of the Atlantic World: Britain and Spain in America, 1492–1830* (New Haven: Yale University Press, 2006). Perhaps the present volume, which explores the obvious exceptions to this pattern—the Portuguese and the Dutch— will disprove the British and Spanish rule.

PART II

Old Worlds and the Atlantic

7

INDIGENOUS AMERICA AND THE LIMITS
OF THE ATLANTIC WORLD, 1493–1825

AMY TURNER BUSHNELL

Atlantic history is that subset of European expansion in which the caravels and galleons sail west to the Americas or hug the west coast of Africa instead of rounding the Cape of Good Hope and sailing east to Asia. It is in essence the old seaborne empires minus Asia and East Africa.[1] The Atlantic world concept, which in theory deals with the connectedness of four continents, in practice concentrates on those regions where Europeans turned their claims into colonies fronting on the Atlantic.[2] The concept is intrinsically Eurocentric because, as those who favor it explain, it focuses on the mastery of space. American Indians, like Africans, enter that world laterally, as adjuncts or obstacles to the work of colonization and improvement. But the areas of neo-European mastery in the Americas were small and slow-growing: until the late nineteenth century more than half of the habitable hemisphere (defined as everything this side of the permanent frost line) remained under indigenous control. Meanwhile, between the island-like settler enclaves and the Indian nations' vast territories, closed to outsiders, lay the frontiers, where neo-European and Indian societies met on relatively even terms, neither side having a monopoly of violence and each side trying to change the other for the better.

Early efforts to define the Atlantic world in the Americas concentrated on regions where Indians were sparse and labor was imported, instead of where Indians were numerous and settlers lived off their tribute and labor.[3] Students of Atlantic history thus focused on the societies, plantations, and commerce of English, French, Dutch, and Portuguese colonists and on enslaved Africans, leaving Spanish colonists to their own historians and Indians to the ethnohistorians, pioneers in the use of nontraditional sources. Had Spanish America been included in the original Atlantic world, incorporated Indians and perhaps enslaved Indians might have been part of the Atlantic perspective. And had the "new Indian history" taken off before the mid-1980s, Indians who made the best of their own New World might have been accepted as producers, traders, and political innovators, instead of faulted for abandoning the ways of their fathers.[4]

The impassioned debate over how many people lived in the Americas on the eve of Columbus's first voyage subsided soon after the Quincentenary of 1992. A recent conservative estimate puts the hemispheric population between 46,800,000 and 53,800,000. Regional estimates suggest that 15 percent of this total lived in lowland South America, 28 percent in the Andes, between 4 and 6 percent in the Caribbean, 11 percent in Central America, 34 percent in Mexico, and a mere 6 to 8 percent in upper North America.[5] North of Mexico, the highest population densities were west of the Rockies, in California and on the Northwest coast. The arid Southwest contained more people per square mile than the forested eastern woodlands, south or north, and the population densities of the plains and Great Basin were barely double those of the Arctic and Subarctic.[6] The parts of North America destined to draw English, French, and Dutch settlers were especially thinly inhabited. Since the 1980s, woodland Indians have been the subject of a groundswell of innovative studies and are making their way into the colonial and early national narratives.[7] But Atlantic North America is not normative for the hemisphere. For the descendants of nineteen out of twenty people living in the Americas in 1492, the Atlantic world was to be Iberian, and its centers, Spanish.

The pathogens introduced by Spaniards caused the populations of incorporated Indians to decline alarmingly, reaching a nadir in the Andean world between 1600 and 1650 and in Mexico a century after the conquest.[8] Smallpox led the assault. In the century and a quarter before the English, French, and Dutch settled in the hemisphere, the population centers and peripheries of Spanish and Portuguese America suffered three major pandemics, and epidemics continued thereafter. Smallpox visited the Sabana de Bogotá six times during the seventeenth century alone.[9] In remoter regions, epidemic disease was slower to arrive, with virgin soil epidemics occurring for up to three centuries, but the advent of Europeans everywhere accelerated the death rate in Indian country. The Puritans who poured into New England in the 1630s concluded that God was smiting the Canaanites to make room for his chosen people.[10] Throughout the Americas, survivors amalgamated, speeding the normal processes of ethnogenesis, confederation, and lingua franca formation.

Indigenous peoples played different roles in different places, not because the neo-Europeans of their respective vicinities differed in national character, but because the natural world dictated the form that a native society must take to procure food and survive. The key variable was not the country from which the settlers came, nor even what they sought, but the character of the society they encountered. In the two regions of most intensive cultivation, and thus of greatest population density and political centralization, the victorious Spanish established contractual relationships with native rulers and incorporated the common people into a plural, caste-based society as peasant producers and a labor enclave. Spain kept a firm hold on its overseas empires and monitored the seaways that led to them. But the Americas were immense, and with or without Spain, the Atlantic world's domain ended where that of the autonomous nations began, in the shared space of the frontiers. And in these zones of smaller populations, simpler hierarchies, and shifting cultivation, the Spanish did their best to "reduce" the Indians to more permanent settlements.

Sixteenth-century Spanish explorers encountering new groups of Indians immediately, if unscientifically, classified them on a scale of mobility, with people of fixed settlements (*gente de razón*) at one end and wandering nations (*gente sin razón*) at the other. In their experience, only village-based farmers had the discipline to live "under the bell" as Christians, supporting their betters; people who hunted and gathered without accumulating a surplus were useless.[11] The polities of sedentary peoples ranged in complexity from empires to provinces to chiefdoms. Empires came preorganized, with systems for mobilizing peasant production, tribute, and labor; provinces had fewer such mechanisms; and chiefdoms managed with a minimum. Though Spaniards preferred the imperial peoples accustomed to authority, any people of fixed settlements could serve their ends, including those of provinces and chiefdoms.

Spain's viceroyalties, resting on a combination of agriculture, mining, and cheap native labor, fall into a category of their own. So do the plantation colonies of the Brazilian northeast, the West Indies, and English North America, resting on the institution of chattel slavery, which consumed Indians as well as Africans.[12] Setting the viceroyalties and the plantation colonies aside leaves the frontiers, or fringes of European empire. On the Spanish American frontiers, Spain made a valiant effort to retire the conquest by the sword and replace it with pacification, a kind of compact based upon trade, alliance, and indoctrination.[13] When the process of pacification stalled or went into reverse, whether a frontier colony would be abandoned or reinforced depended upon its strategic importance, its baptismal count, and its economic potential, measured in the rate of Spanish settlement. On the non-Spanish frontiers, colonists were more on their own, and expected to be.

The polities of semisedentary Indians were more varied than those of sedentary Indians and harder to subdue, as Europeans of every nationality, including Spaniards, discovered. But if the peoples of the frontier zones did not exactly join the Atlantic world, they did interact with it. Some of the indigenous nations bartered dyewood, pelts, and deerskins that they themselves extracted and processed. Some held the balance of power when European empires clashed, negotiating subsidies at a level approaching tribute for their friendship or neutrality. Some fled to mission reductions to escape expeditions of slave catchers or to recover from the effects of environmental degradation, thus making temporary use of mission resources. Some responded to depopulation and outside pressures by forming new collectives, or tribes. Others lived encapsulated, guarding their lands and their autonomy on all sides. Beyond the pale, the nonsedentary nations tended to increase in strength as the sedentary and semisedentary nations declined. Keeping the neo-Europeans at lance's length, the "wild" Indians took to piracy or horse nomadism, expanded their hunting and gathering grounds at the expense of their neighbors, and raided the frontiers of colonial settlement.[14]

Indigenous peoples shaped the course of Atlantic history in the Americas by subordination, interaction, or opposition. From the perspective of colonial history, they can be divided into three categories. In the first group were the incorporated peoples inside of empire, occupying niches in colonial centers and peripheries. In the second group were the peoples on the frontiers of empire, reconciled or contested, the difference being that on a reconciled frontier, pacified natives interacted with pacified missionaries, traders, and soldiers, both sides achieving their ends without resorting to violence, whereas on a contested ground, negotiation was apt to give way to armed conflict. For convenience, this essay separates the second group into peoples of the extractive frontiers and of the mission frontiers, although many had elements of both. The third group consisted of the autonomous peoples outside of empire, opposing the neo-Europeans with their own weapons. There were, of course, peoples outside of empire who were too remote for systematic contact and observation, but such peoples fall outside of history, a European construct that has lately begun to be based on data.[15]

Resisting the urge to hoist a pre-Columbian backdrop with informative panels about projectile points, language families, ethnobotany, cultivars, blood types and DNA, and ancient civilizations, this essay will begin in 1493, when Columbus made his first transatlantic voyage from the Indies to Spain, and end in 1825, after the wars of neo-European and neo-African independence and before the conquests of the plains and the pampas.

Truncated at both ends, it still spans a third of a thousand years. No interpretive essay of this scope can be comprehensive. The groups mentioned herein are exemplars, and no effort has been made to describe them completely.

Incorporated Peoples

The island people whom Columbus labeled "Indians" were not the simple savages that their nudity and strange speech suggested to those who in 1493 saw a handful of them paraded at court as curiosities. Culturally and linguistically related to the Arawakans living along the Orinoco River, the Taínos had spread across the Caribbean from central Cuba to the Leeward Islands. They had a four-level social structure of caciques, nobles, commoners, and dependents, and a dense population based upon the cultivation of maize and cassava. They were also great seafarers who traded with the South American mainland, journeying in dugout canoes (*piraguas*) that held up to 150 persons. As Spanish colonists poured into the Antilles, they divided the natives into *encomiendas*, a kind of tributary wardship developed by Spain in the Canaries, and set them to panning for placer gold. Only the Taínos' high rate of mortality when exposed to Old World pathogens, and Queen Isabella's scruples about the enslaving of her new subjects, saved them from being shipped to Spain wholesale. Acting as regent after Isabella's death, Ferdinand, Machiavelli's model for an amoral prince, was readier to countenance exploitation. Within twenty years, most of the surviving inhabitants of the Greater Antilles had been commended to Spaniards, and licensed expedition leaders like Juan Ponce de León had to look to the mainland for Indians to enslave.[16]

Hernán Cortés's conquest of the Aztec Empire of central Mexico from a base in Cuba, and Francisco Pizarro's conquest of the Inka Empire of Peru from a base in Panama, were Atlantic world epics, celebrated in chronicles and memoirs. Montezuma's and Atahuallpa's warriors were formidable, but the Spaniards had superior technology on their side—and smallpox, the pale horseman at the siege of Tenochtitlán and the Plain of Cajamarca. Charles I elevated the conquests of his self-appointed champions into overseas kingdoms, appointing viceroys in Mexico City (1535) and Lima (1544).[17] Tales of gold and glory fired the blood of Englishmen such as Sir Walter Ralegh and Captain John Smith and Frenchmen such as Samuel de Champlain to adventure overseas, but the Americas yielded no further empires.

What the two great American empires had in common were tributary regimes based on provinces which had seen former empires come and go, as the impressive ruins of Teotihuacán and Tiwanaku could testify. Farming intensively on permanent sites, the Mexicas and the Andeans were members of communities (*calpulli, ayllu*) upon which a state could draw for tribute and public works labor. The two empires had official languages, Nahuatl and Quechua, and elaborate social structures, complete with dynastic rulers, noble lineages, commoners, dependents, and specialists in the form of priests, craftsmen, and traders. Cortés's and Pizarro's men inserted themselves into the second level of the defeated imperial societies as *encomenderos*, demanding a lord's share of native labor and tribute, which in the Andes took the form of yet more labor.[18]

Mechanisms to channel tribute and labor to elites also existed among the Chibchas of present-day Colombia, who had two kings and two capitals, and among the Mayas, presiding over the ruins of city-states that had retreated from centralization—the highland Mayas in Guatemala and the lowland Mayas in the Yucatan. Lieutenants fanned out to conquer these regions and others, fighting over the spoils. But city-states and provinces were rare, and in places of chiefdoms, such as Paraguay and Chile, conquerors were obliged to content themselves with *encomiendas* based on personal service.[19]

Change at the top had always signified new gods, and the conquered peoples took the conquerors' deities of a self-immolating hero and a mother goddess in stride: unseen gods to match an unseen emperor. Overwhelmed by the sheer numbers of unsaved souls, the first Franciscan apostles to New Spain baptized Indians en masse, to be indoctrinated if they survived the plagues that were descending on the land like judgments.[20] Spain's title to the Indies rested on the natives' need to be protected and kept in tutelage until they reached Christian maturity, argued the Dominican scholar Francisco de Vitoria, lecturing on "the Affair of the Indies" at the University of Salamanca in 1539, but the day of spiritual emancipation was slow to arrive.[21] When in 1562 the Franciscan Provincial Diego de Landa discovered that the lowland Mayas of the Yucatan were still worshipping their old gods, and when, in remote parishes of northern New Spain and the Peruvian highlands (*altiplano*), later priests uncovered and extirpated "superstitions and idolatries," they concluded that Indians were not only weak in the faith, but in league with the devil.[22]

Change at the top had also frequently involved resettlement. In Peru, the Inkas thought nothing of commandeering kin groups to colonize a new frontier.[23] The Spanish were equally ready to relocate a workforce, permanently or temporarily. The discoveries in 1545 and 1546 of large deposits of silver ore in both of Spain's American viceroyalties brought new peoples and territories into the Spanish orbit, as the centers extended their peripheries. At Potosí, in the highlands of present-day Bolivia, Andean miners served their labor obligations (*mita*) to the state. Supplying the Villa Imperial de Potosí, whose population of 160,000 in 1650 made it the largest urban concentration in the Americas, led to the development of the jurisdiction of Tucumán in the northwest of present-day Argentina and the production, with Indian labor, of great quantities of coca, yerba maté tea, and foodstuffs. The carrying trade absorbed thousands of mules yearly from the livestock fair in Salta.[24]

In Chile, the conquest went into reverse in the mid-1550s in the Lautaro rebellion, the inspiration for Alonso de Ercilla's epic *La Araucana*,[25] and again in 1598, when the Araucanos drove the Spanish north of the Bío Bío River. For 200 years, the border with Araucanía was dotted with forts and Chile had the status of a combat zone (*una tierra reputada por guerra viva*). Standing guard over the southern route to Potosí, the captaincy general was too strategic to be abandoned. The number of soldiers on the contested southern frontier rose to 2,000, and the colony's economy revolved around the military payroll and the sale or exchange of captives taken in slave raids (*malocas*) However, the troops' annual campaigns into forested Araucanía only expedited the transfer of Spanish goods into Indian hands, encouraging the three most numerous groups—Mapuches, Pehuenches, and Huilliches—to adopt Spanish material culture, even shifting from maize to wheat, without recognizing Spanish sovereignty.[26]

Compared to Peru's, New Spain's silver deposits were closer to the viceregal capital in leagues, but more distant culturally. The Gran Chichimeca was home to four nations that had long defied the Mexicas: Guachichiles, Zacatecos, Guamares, and Pames. Rainfall and warfare permitting, some of the Chichimecos grew maize and squash and built shelters, but most of them lived in caves or on the shelves of canyons in rugged, cactus-covered terrain. When prospectors discovered silver at Zacatecas and planted mining settlements deep inside their territory, the Chichimecos began to raid the wagon trains for clothing, food, and horseflesh. The Chichimeca War (1550–1590) waged on the hostiles (*indios de guerra*), which churchmen suspected of being a cover for slave raids, was brought to a close by a combination of gifts, Tlaxcaltecan settlers (*pobladores*), and permanent garrisons (*presidios*). Supplying the mining camps (*reales de minas*) stimulated wheat growing and ranching in the near north, and as the mining frontier advanced into northwestern New Spain in the seventeenth century, Indians left the newly founded Jesuit missions to work on contract at the mines.

Extractive Frontiers

The Atlantic world's interest in a given frontier tended to rise and fall as a function of the value and availability of its extractive products. Some of these fruits of the land or sea—such as codfish from the banks off Newfoundland and Massachusetts, or salt from the salt pan at Punta de Araya on the coast of present-day Venezuela—Europeans themselves processed, keeping a wary eye on the locals. Where they discovered products of high value in concentration, Spaniards made use of Indian labor: enslaved labor at the pearl fisheries, where a diver's life was short,[27] and drafted labor at the silver mines, which rapidly changed from frontiers to peripheries. Shipwreck salvage, an essentially extractive process in which Europeans of all nationalities engaged, yielded products of high value, high processing costs, and uneven distribution. Salvage involved Indians in two ways. An underwater site demanded a corps of divers that the salvors, operating hastily, supplemented with natives kidnapped from the nearest coast. But a ship that ran aground near land was a windfall to coastal Indians, who kept the goods and castaways they wanted and traded their discards to the next ship that landed boats for wood and water.[28]

Extractive products of lower value spread over a larger area, such as dyewoods, pelts, and skins, the Indians themselves processed and traded, and Europeans could find themselves jockeying for favored-nation status. The Atlantic forest of Brazil offered only one product valuable enough to justify a voyage: brazilwood, source of a red dye. According to the line of demarcation in the prescient Treaty of Tordesillas (1494, 1496), the land that Pedro Álvares Cabral "discovered" in 1500 on his way to India belonged to Portugal, but French vessels were soon frequenting the coast to barter iron tools and trinkets for dyewood, which the local Tupi Indians provided cut, stacked, and ready to load. Apprehensive that French corsair–traders might plant a settlement, the Portuguese Crown first granted fifteen captaincies, then appointed a governor-general, who landed in Bahia in 1549 with America's first Jesuits. France, not to be outdone, sent a rival expedition to Guanabara Bay with America's first Calvinist pastors (1555–1560). But France Antarctique did not endure, and when its Portuguese successor settlement, Rio de Janeiro, turned to raising sugarcane, the trade in dyewood declined, to be replaced by a trade in enslaved Tupis.[29]

The fur trade in northeastern North America grew out of the busy sixteenth-century fisheries, where Algonkian peoples discovered the utility of metal goods such as axes, kettles, fishhooks, and knives. The first known French voyage primarily for furs was in 1569.[30] By 1610, what the northeastern natives most wanted was firearms, and Europeans with a toe-hold in the region were drawn into an arms race. Samuel de Champlain's tiny outpost of Quebec on the St. Lawrence waterway traded guns to the Hurons and Montagnais, and the Dutch on the Hudson River traded guns to the League of the Iroquois, which the Hurons had refused to join. What the Indians offered in return were beaver pelts, used to make waterproof felt hats, and pelts quickly became the region's principal export.[31] The Iroquois played the role of middlemen, monopolizing the trade in guns, tools, and textiles to the nations farther from the coasts. Their wars would set whole nations in motion as refugees or armed invaders, launching ricochet migrations and producing contested grounds in Indian country up and down the woodlands and as far west as the plains.

Montreal, at the mouth of the Ottawa River, every summer hosted hundreds of birchbark canoes bringing beaver pelts and the occasional Pawnee captive (*paní*). From that center—part mission hub, part trading post—missionaries and forest traders (*coureurs de bois*) embarked to explore the lands upriver (*pays d'en haut*) to the Great Lakes and beyond. By the 1670s they had descended the Mississippi River, past the Illinois country, down to the Arkansas River. Farther north, on Hudson Bay, a parallel trade developed between the Cree people and the Hudson's Bay Company, chartered in 1670.[32] As Indians farther away became involved, the fur trade moved westward on two fronts, leaving settlements of biracial people (*métis*) on the prairies and reaching the Pacific northwest in the early 1790s.[33]

Meanwhile, the eastward advance of Russian sable hunters had taken them across Siberia to Kamchatka, from which Vitus Bering made the short sail to Alaska in 1741. By the 1760s, seagoing hunters (*promyshlenniki*) in wooden boats lashed together with leather thongs were visiting the Aleutian Islands in search of sea otter furs for the China market. The Russian American Company was chartered in 1799. Although St. Petersburg forbade the company to take hostages, the Russian fur traders, convinced that only Aleuts had the skills for otter hunting, interned their families to secure their cooperation.[34]

When English proprietors took up the grant of Carolina in 1670, deer-skins and captured Indians rapidly became the colony's two main exports. By the early 1700s Charles Town traders with strings of packhorses could be seen for a thousand miles inland, carrying strouds, blankets, iron tools, and firearms to Creek and Chickasaw towns. Greater Carolina exported some 100,000 deerskins in 1750 alone, and before the end of the eighteenth century, every deer hunter and slave raider in the South carried a smooth-bore musket. Establishing themselves on the Gulf of Mexico at the turn of the century, the French also exported deerskins and Indian slaves from their ports of Biloxi and Mobile. Chronic warfare between the Choctaws and the Chickasaws kept the stream of captives flowing to Louisiana and to Carolina slave buyers and exporters.[35] For seventy years, militaristic slaving societies turned the Southeast into a "shatter zone."[36] Colonial authorities backing their respective allies told themselves that they were weakening each other in proxy wars.

As neo-Europeans struggled to maintain their footing in an increasingly complex Atlantic world, various groups of Indians found it to their advantage to side with them, and no pan-Indian consciousness gave them pause. The Republic of Tlaxcala, whose warriors had fought beside Spaniards on the bloody causeways of Tenochtitlán, shared in the rewards of conquest as allies. When, in 1591, 400 Tlaxcaltecan families volunteered to move north to plant pockets of civility on the frontier, Philip II extended to them the privileges of gentle birth (*hidalguía*), including exemptions from tribute and personal services.[37] Throughout the hemisphere, Indians kept up their fighting skills as mercenaries: the Spanish employed Tarascan and Otomí warriors to fight the Chichimecos and, a century later, Opatas to fight the Pimas; the British used the Cherokees against the Yamasees.[38]

Europeans liked to represent their subsidies to allies as gifts. In Florida, where the chiefs of the mission provinces directed labor and agricultural produce to the support of the presidio and convents, treasury officials rewarded them out of the Indian expense (*gasto de indios*), one of the funds in the presidio's annual subvention from the defense budget in Mexico City.[39] In the Great Lakes region, Indian refugees looked to the governor of New France (*Onontio*) to keep the peace of the "middle ground" by generous gifts, and as long as New France needed their friendship, the governor obliged. During the eighteenth century the British reluctantly followed suit, accustoming their Indian allies and even some neutral natives to subsidies that would evaporate in times of peace.[40]

Sometimes, a group of Indians remained on their ancestral lands, accepted but not absorbed as a colony grew up around them. Each case of encapsulation was different. The Massachusetts, Nipmucs, and Pawtuckets of John Eliot's seven praying towns talked theology to their Puritan visitors and kept their enclaves from being overrun by Bay Colony expansion.[41] The Iroquois Mohawks of Kahnawaké, near Montreal, accepted Christianity but not subordination. Rejecting both French sovereignty and Jesuit management, they ran their own affairs under what amounted to diplomatic immunity.[42] In Louisiana, refugees and tribal remnants (*petites nations*) on the margins of colonial society bartered provisions and did odd jobs in Mobile, Biloxi, and New Orleans.[43] In Virginia and North Carolina, "settlement nations" maintained a degree of political autonomy and, when they could, of power, as when the queen of the Pamunkeys made a bid to reestablish the Powhatan Confederation by having the governor of Virginia recognize her as paramount over the Rappahannocks and Chickahominys.[44] In the Sierra Zapoteca of Oaxaca, isolated from the rest of New Spain by its rugged terrain, the one Spanish town, Villa Alta, had a supporting settlement, Analco, of Nahuatl-speaking Tlaxcaltecans. When the chief magistrate's collectors made the rounds of the villages to gather the tribute of cotton mantles and cochineal, or when the Dominicans visited their parishes, collecting altar fees, auxiliaries from Analco escorted them.[45]

Unless population losses due to Old World diseases, habitat destruction, warfare, and slaving brought them to utter extinction, the remnants of Indian societies on the frontier and elsewhere made valiant efforts to reconstitute their polities, employing traditional regenerative techniques that included amalgamation, ethnogenesis, confederation, and replenishment. Throughout Spanish America, *congregación*, the process of combining underpopulated hamlets into a town of optimal size, served bureaucratic purposes without being the social innovation that bureaucrats supposed.[46] Towns had always been aggregations, and before European intervention, groups of towns coalesced or broke apart continuously, cycling in and out of paramount chiefdoms. In the North American Southeast, none of the chiefdoms described in the three Hernando de Soto relations existed in the same form 150 years later. In their place were more egalitarian federations of towns that over time developed into tribes presenting a more or less unified front as the Choctaws, Chickasaws, Cherokees, Catawbas, Yamasees, Creeks, and, after the Red Stick War (1813–1814), the Seminoles.[47] The many languages a traveler might hear spoken in a single tribe, indeed in a single town, were proof of the ongoing processes of amalgamation and ethnogenesis. In North America's Northeast, the five nations (later, six) speaking related languages that confederated as the League of the Iroquois dealt with population loss by launching "mourning wars" against their neighbors, replenishing their numbers by adopting captives or resettling whole towns.[48] Their wars set whole nations in motion as refugees or armed invaders, launching ricochet migrations and ratcheting up the level of conflict throughout the woodlands and west to the plains.

Mission Frontiers

On dozens of frontiers throughout the Americas, missionaries labored to attract semisedentary peoples to reductions (*reducciones, reduções*) where they could be protected from their enemies, Christianized, and taught the skills of peasants and laborers.[49] Factors influencing the success or failure of such enterprises included the threat posed by enemies, often slave hunters; the attractions of trade and a stable food supply; and the natural environment, which could require a level of mobility incompatible with European ideas of civility. For a variety of reasons, missionaries might extend the period of indoctrination, postponing the day when their charges would be integrated into the Atlantic world.

Mission systems were typically maritime or riverine, accessed and supplied by water.[50] A map may of course suggest water access where there is none. The missions of California were on the Pacific coast, but they were not on a seaway: the pattern of winds and currents made a voyage from Mexico to Alta California take three to four months, longer than a transatlantic crossing.[51] More accessible were the maritime mission systems of southern Chile, Florida, the Mosquito Coast of present-day Honduras, and the Philippine Islands—the latter, despite their location in Latin Asia, being outposts of New Spain's.[52] Many Brazilian rivers were essentially unnavigable, being so full of cataracts that canoemen spent most of their time raising or lowering their heavy dugouts with ropes and pulleys.[53] And in the arid regions north of New Spain, rivers were obstacles to be crossed instead of aids to travel.

New France's widely dispersed converts kept missionaries in motion on two great waterways, the St. Lawrence and the Mississippi, and the Great Lakes in between. In Spanish South America, the Great Arc of Missions was entirely river-based. The Jesuit Republic of the Guaraní with its three mission systems was on the Uruguay River. The Chaco mission system was on the Paraguay; the Chiquitos missions lay between the Paraguay and tributaries of the Amazon. The mission systems known as Casanare, Meta, Upper Orinoco, Cumaná, and Guiana were all on the Orinoco. Mission systems in Amazonia ranged from the Llanos de Moxos on the Madeira River in eastern Bolivia, to the Maynas on the Marañon River in the Peruvian tropical forest (*montaña*), to the Omaguas on the middle Amazon, established in 1686 to halt the advancing Portuguese.[54]

The first Jesuits to set foot in the New World arrived on the coast of Brazil in 1550. They were disappointed in the natives gathered into villages (*aldeias*) at São Vicente and Espíritu Santo for them to evangelize. The Tupi peoples of the Atlantic forest, with their slash-and-burn cultivation and their anthropophagy, resisted refashioning and died of European diseases, half-indoctrinated.[55] And back of the forest, the peoples of the dry Northeast (*nordeste*), reinforced by runaway Africans and Indians from the sugar plantations of Pernambuco, commenced the guerrilla warfare that would

keep settlers, whether Portuguese or—during the occupation of Pernambuco by the Dutch West India Company (1630–1654)—Dutch, out of the
backland (*sertão*) until well into the eighteenth century.[56]

More promising candidates for conversion were the semisedentary, Tupi-
speaking Guaranís, preyed upon by the warlike Guaycuruans of the Gran
Chaco. When in 1588 Jesuits from Peru invited the Guaranís to move to
the upper Paraná, they accepted with relief, and within forty years had built
three systems of reductions in Guairá, Itatín, and Tapé. In Brazil, the demand
for plantation labor was growing acute, and São Paulo, high on the coastal
palisade from which the rivers ran inland, was well placed for slave hunting.
Explaining that "a good Indian is a mission Indian" (*indio bom é indio do
padre*), leaders of biracial paramilitary expeditions (*bandeirantes*) from São
Paulo attacked the reductions on the Paraná and returned with thousands of
Guaranís, mostly women and children. When Philip III, one of the Spanish
Habsburgs who doubled as kings of Portugal from 1580 to 1640, declared in
1609 that the Indians were free, his Brazilian subjects ignored him.[57]

Survivors from the three mission systems fled south to the Uruguay and
Tebicuary rivers and rebuilt, close enough to be consolidated. When the
São Paulo slave hunters (*paulistas*) followed, the Guairá Guaranís under
chief Nicolás Ñeengirú defeated them in the battle of Mbororé (1641), using
firepower provided by the Jesuits, with royal license. The thirty reductions
of the Jesuit Republic of the Guaraní—fifteen in present-day Argentina,
seven in Brazil, and eight in Paraguay—functioned as a federation of cities.
They produced yerba maté and textiles for export; created their own art,
music, and crafts; printed books in the common language (*lingua geral*)
of Tupi-Guaraní; and could field an army of 20,000. Their common herd
of wild cattle increased to a million head, turning the eastern shore of the
Río de la Plata into a culture hearth for horsemen and cattle hunters. In the
1750 Treaty of Madrid, Portugal and Spain attempted to settle their differences in the Platine littoral by agreeing to a territorial exchange, Portugal's
Colônia do Sacramento for Spain's Banda Oriental, giving the 29,000 Tapé
Guaranís four years to evacuate their seven reductions, relocate their herds,
and replant their yerba maté trees. The *Sete Povos* refused and took up
arms in the Guaraní War (1754–1756), an early but unsuccessful bid for
independence.[58]

Deep inside the continent, Amazonian societies had achieved high levels of population density and organization. Long before the Europeans
arrived, the Arawakan chiefdoms of the Llanos de Moxos had addressed
their region's flood–drought problem with massive earthworks, mounds,
causeways, reservoirs, and 50,000 acres of raised, ridged fields. By the end

of the sixteenth century, slave hunters from Santa Cruz de la Sierra, on the eastern slopes of the Andes, were making regular forays into the savanna despite the Crown's prohibitions against Indian slavery. When the Moxos leaders accepted Jesuit missionaries in 1674, they were making a bargain with Spain. In return for protection from the *cruceños* and access to European goods, they would hold the line against the Portuguese, a role that the Crown recognized with subsidies and firearm licenses.[59]

On the northern coast of Brazil, where missionaries and settlers competed for control of the peoples of the lower Amazon, their activities produced similar results. Missionary expeditions "descended" vulnerable Indians to reductions near the population centers of Belém and São Luiz de Maranhão, where those who survived their exposure to Old World diseases were indoctrinated and hired out. At the same time, state-sponsored "ransom troops" (*tropas de resgate*) "rescued" Indians captured by other Indians and brought them to the coast to work off their ransoms, a way of getting around legal prohibitions that was also common in Chile and New Mexico, where detribalized Indians formed a caste of *genízaros*. Although the papal brief *Veritas Ipsa* (1537) granting freedom to Indians reached Brazil in 1640, anyone who spoke out against Indian slavery ran the risk of being poisoned or blown up. In response to the protests of Father António Vieira, the king of Portugal gave the Jesuits nominal control over Indian affairs in 1655, but the colonists defied the priests with impunity, and after 1688 the Jesuits settled for overseeing the distribution of captives. By 1700, the lower Amazon was a ghost land (*despovoado*).[60]

The first Jesuits to set foot in Spanish America went to the new colony of Florida in 1566, sponsored by its founder. After Powhatan Indians killed five of their number at the mission of Axacán in the Chesapeake, they withdrew, and Franciscans took their place in 1573. Traveling where possible by boat, the friars first evangelized the tidewater, then added a freshwater district, *Agua Dulce*.[61] The three mission provinces of Timucua, Guale, and Apalache reached their peak in the mid-1650s, only to come under assault by pirates out of Jamaica and Indian slavers armed in Carolina. The violence was by no means limited to Florida. In a five-year period, the eastern woodlands was shaken by the Chacato Revolt (1675), King Philip's War (1675–1676), Bacon's Rebellion (1676), and the Westo War (1680).[62] But Florida lay within the Southeast shatter zone. By the end of Queen Anne's War (1702–1713), all that was left of the missions was a handful of refugee pueblos under the guns of the fort in St. Augustine.[63]

New France owes its heroic place in mission history to the voluminous Jesuit Relations, with their candor about hardship and martyrdom. The

Jesuits who arrived in Quebec in 1625, like the Franciscan Recollects who had been there since 1615, were stymied by natives who lived beyond the range of agriculture. After a miserable winter following one band of hunters, Father Paul Le Jeune advised his superiors that the Montagnais would never be converted until they settled down under Jesuit direction. However, the first Montagnais to sample a life of discipline at the village of Sillery hurried back to the forests, and later arrivals succumbed to alcoholism. The Jesuits turned to the 30,000 Hurons 700 miles away, who lived in semipermanent villages, growing maize in ridged fields. To their consternation, half of the Hurons died of disease in the 1630s, and the Iroquois carried off most of the rest in mourning wars to offset their own losses.[64]

New England was as hegemonic as Iroquoia. The English settlers' conquest of the southern Algonkians in the Pequot War (1637) and their arrogance toward the peoples to their north encouraged the Abenaki of the Northeast to ally themselves with the French, first religiously and then militarily. Refugees from King Philip's War formed the nucleus of Abenaki communities on the St. Lawrence, where the Jesuits, having learned cultural tolerance, acted as shamans and brokers, arguing that the Indians had a right to be hunters and defending them against Francization.[65]

Attempts to establish mission systems north of New Spain produced mixed results. The sedentary Pueblos of New Mexico, who had accepted Franciscans in the early seventeenth century, expelled them along with the other colonists in the Pueblo Revolt (1680) and lived for thirteen years in apostasy.[66] Meanwhile, Jesuits were establishing missions among the freshly subdued, semisedentary Xiximes, Acaxees, Conchos, Tepehuanes, and Tarahumaras of Nueva Vizcaya, gaining Crown support for their endeavors by supplying labor to the silver mines and Spanish haciendas and riding out a series of "first-generation" rebellions, subsumed into the Great Northern Revolt (1680–1698).[67]

In New Spain's far west, beyond the limits of civil colonization, Jesuit missionaries worked their way northward, valley by valley, from Sinaloa into Sonora, encouraging the Opatas, Seris, and Pimas of the sierra to live in settlements, and the Yaquis and Mayos of the coast to combine into larger towns. Despite the widespread revolts of the 1690s, repeated in the 1740s, the Sonora missions were successful enough to serve as a springboard for a new mission field in Baja California, across the dangerous Sea of Cortez.[68]

The Indians of Texas, described by Álvar Núñez Cabeza de Vaca as early as 1542, were left in peace until the late seventeenth century. Once the French began to show interest in the Gulf of Mexico, alarmed Spanish officials sent an expedition from Coahuila in 1690, complete with a Franciscan missionary. The first missions in Texas were not, however, on the coast, but on the Trinity River in East Texas. The place was inaccessible by sea and more than 600 miles by land from the nearest supply point, but its Caddo inhabitants were farmers, always a draw. Other missions that appeared in San Antonio in the 1720s provided nonfarming Coahuiltecans with a refuge from raiding Apaches. A generation later, when the Apaches were being harassed by the Comanches, some of the eastern bands made peace with the Franciscans and used the San Antonio missions as food depôts and places to leave their families and horses while they raided the frontiers of Spanish settlement in Nueva Vizcaya and Nuevo León.[69]

The long struggle between colonists and missionaries over Indian labor in South America came to a head in the 1750s, when inspection of the regions disputed by Spain and Portugal, by order of the Portuguese minister now known as the Marquis of Pombal, revealed the extent, wealth, and autonomy of the mission systems: a virtual Jesuit Atlantic. Long suspected of transmontane loyalties, the Jesuits fell victim to the rising tide of regalism, being expelled from the Portuguese Empire in 1759, from the French in 1764, and from the Spanish in 1767.[70] Franciscans, not Jesuits, would head the Jesuit-style reductions of Alta California.

Mission systems were already in disrepute in 1769 when José de Gálvez, Spain's minister of the Indies, revived the reduction as an economical way to plant outposts on the Pacific coast and head off the challenge of Russian and British traders.[71] The conquest of Alta California was ecological: epidemics devastated the villages and an "ungulate irruption" of livestock degraded the environment. Ecological and demographic data answer at last the vexing question of why wave after wave of Indians continued to enter the reductions, where syphilis and other diseases were endemic. Family reconstitution findings for the Mission of San Carlos, near the presidio of Monterey, are bleak. A majority of Indian couples were infertile, less than a quarter of mission-born infants lived to be fifteen, and fewer than one in ten mission-married women reached the age of fifty.[72]

Whether Indians were better or worse off in Catholic missions is a question that has been debated for 250 years, with those in favor citing the idyllic Guaraní Republic and those opposed, the death camps of Alta California.[73] In defense of California, its mortality rate was high because it had been unusually isolated. In places where directed settlement was generations old and disease was endemic, mission Indians often became integral to their region's defense and economy and made the transition into the postcolonial period with their communities intact. Sonora, in northwestern Mexico, and

Chiquitos, in the lowlands of eastern Bolivia, are examples of places where missions evolved successfully.[74]

Protestant efforts to convert indigenous peoples were more modest in scale and less institutionalized than Catholic efforts, but Protestants shared the Catholic conviction that semisedentary Indians must be reduced and civilized. The high point of missionary activity in New England came in 1674, with hundreds of converts at Plymouth Colony, Martha's Vineyard, and Nantucket and fourteen model "praying towns" near Boston, presided over by the linguist John Eliot.[75] The German Moravians who settled at Bethlehem, Pennsylvania, in 1741 were avid ethnographers and linguists who established a relationship of mutual respect with the Lenape Indians, called Delawares.[76]

Autonomous Peoples

The domain of the Atlantic world ended where that of the autonomous peoples began. The peoples outside of empire, in areas of intermittent contact and observation, adopted elements of the European material culture and used them to advantage. In the Atlantic world's technology kit were tools and weapons that any culture could see the point of, and autonomous Indians were quick to comprehend their value. Fishhooks, knives, and iron-tipped projectiles simplified the work of hunting, gathering, and fishing. Hoes, iron and copper pots, needles, scissors, and awls shortened the tasks of cultivating, cooking, and sewing. Iron axes and adzes eased the labors of forest farmers felling a tree, hollowing a dugout, or building a lean-to. The material culture exchange worked both ways. Half of the settlers of New Sweden, on the Delaware River, were actually Savo–Karelian Finns with a thousand-year history of forest colonizing. As comfortable with the Lenapes as they had been with Lapps, they helped to create the mixed culture of the backwoodsman, complete with log cabin, plant lore, buckskin clothing, "rights in the woods," and the all-important rifle.[77] Firearms conferred power. The Spanish, who did not participate in the North American fur trade, at first tried to keep guns out of the hands of Indians, but Dutch, French, and English colonists readily supplied their own trading partners with firearms and ammunition for the hunt and for war, and by the 1680s the governors of Florida were defending their decision to do likewise.[78]

As revolutionary as the new technology were the new plants and animals. In large areas of northern New Spain—where, as in Spain, sheep pastoralism trumped agriculture—overgrazing turned farmlands into thorny scrub,[79] while in California, invasive animals and plants destroyed a hunting and gathering habitat. In other parts of the hemisphere, however, new species brought positive results. Nonnative fruit trees were a welcome addition to the biota, and feral livestock filled an ecological niche. Herds of wild cattle multiplied on the savannas of South America, replicating the herds of bison on the prairies of North America, and the reintroduction of horses to the hemisphere made it easier to hunt both. The cattle hunters and hide traders of the transfrontiers developed distinctive biracial cultures with a rough appeal to parlor readers. The vaqueros north of the old Chichimec frontier, the *boucaniers* of the "useless" islands, the *llaneros* of present-day Venezuela, the *caboclos* of the Brazilian *sertões*, and the gauchos ranging from southern Brazil into Uruguay, Paraguay, and Argentina—all served the needs of historical romance.[80]

It is no accident that the Indian groups labeled indomitable and barbarous were people of either horses or canoes, similarly mobile. The Island Caribs in their great dugouts dominated the eastern Caribbean from strongholds on the islands of Martinique and Guadeloupe, gathering resources on the depopulated islands and harassing the nearer mainland. Despite their name, they were Arawakan in origin, and only the men spoke the Carib-based trade language. Guerrilla action by Caribs in alliance with Maroons was the "Indian problem" that delayed the permanent English and French occupation of much of the Lesser Antilles until 1660, when the Caribs were confined to reservations on Dominica and St. Vincent.[81]

Canoe people added to the risks of Brazil's gold rush. The Paiaguás, a Guaycuruan group from the Chaco, controlled the Paraná–Paraguay river system, covering long distances in their war canoes and raiding Guaraní settlements, Viking-like, for women and food. After prospectors discovered gold in the far west in the 1720s, the miners, mostly enslaved Africans, traveled upriver in convoys (*monções*) of up to 400 dugouts to reach the goldfields in present Goiás and Mato Grosso. Between the delays waiting for rains to bring high water and the portages around the rapids, the journey to Cuiabá, the center of Mato Grosso gold mining, took five months, and the Paiaguás exacted a high toll, annihilating three expeditions in fifteen years. The Karajás and other river pirates harassed convoys on the Tocantins and the Araguaia, two other rivers communicating with the goldfields, until the 1780s and 1790s.[82]

Where Indians took to horses, the change in their lifestyle was dramatic. Controverting Western ideas of stages in cultural evolution, semisedentary people became nomadic, turning from part-time farming to full-time hunting and raiding, for, like the new technologies of firearms and iron-tipped projectiles, horses made them more effective at both. Some of the mounted nations kept the supply lines to European goods open by periodic raids on soldiers and settlers. Others increased their territories at the expense of their neighbors.

The Guaycuruans of the Gran Chaco, who acquired horses in the late 1500s, scorned their agricultural neighbors, enserfing the Arawakan Guanás and raiding the Guaranís. After the *paulistas* destroyed the missions of Itatín, Guaycuruan bands known as Abipones, Mocovís, Tobas, and Mbayás moved across the Paraguay River and into the vacated region. Reaching the height of their military prowess in the early 1700s, they pushed back the frontiers of the Spanish provinces of Tucumán, Paraguay, and Río de la Plata. After 1740, the push factors of punitive expeditions, epidemics, and ecological damage, and the pull factors of subsidies and access to iron-tipped weapons, induced the Guaycuruans to spend some time at missions, but strictly on their own terms. The women neglected their plantings when carob pods and palm berries were in season, and the men spent their time drinking maize beer (*chicha*), gambling, and rustling cattle.[83]

Horses had been multiplying on the pampas since 1537, and by 1600 great herds of feral cattle could be found there as well. Crossing the Andes on ancient trading paths, the Araucanians rounded up herds of cattle and drove them back across low, well-watered passes for sale to the Spanish. By 1700, most of the beef consumed in Chile was trans-Andean. In a drift migration known as "the araucanization of the desert," many Araucanians stayed in the east to raid, trade, and intermarry, making Mapuche the lingua franca of the Pampas Indians and even of the Tehuelches, whose territory in northern Patagonia was too arid for horses.[84]

When the Spanish first arrived in New Mexico, the high plains belonged to the bison and a few bands of Athapaskan hunter-gatherers known as Apaches, who followed the herds and traded with the Pueblos. The prairie plains were home to Caddoan and Siouan horticulturalists, who planted the fertile bottomlands near rivers and streams and ventured onto the prairie seasonally to hunt bison. In the mid-seventeenth century other Siouans arrived, pushed westward domino-fashion by waves of Algonkian peoples with French guns, who in turn were in flight from Iroquoians whose guns were Dutch or English. The livestock that the Spanish introduced affected every Indian group on or near the plains, starting with the sheep-herding Navajos and the Apaches, who counted their wealth in horses. The Comanches moved onto the plains from the Great Basin and began to raise mules and horses, trading them to would-be horse nomads—Algonkian, Caddoan, and Siouan—who were moving onto the plains from the north, east, and south.[85] By 1700, most of the Siouan peoples had left the woodlands and were colonizing the plains. Various nations of the Sioux, obtaining guns from the British in the fur trade, were the dominant power on the Missouri River, while the Siouan Osage and Quapaw dominated the southeastern plains—and the outliers of French, Spanish, and British empires—from the Arkansas River valley.[86]

The most powerful nations on the southwestern plains continued to be the Apaches and Comanches. The two groups competed for pasturage in the same narrow valleys, but the Comanches had the advantage of access to French guns and ammunition, obtained through intermediaries such as the Kansas and the Ouachitas. Gradually, they drove the Apaches southward into the *Gran Apachería*, stretching from present-day Sonora into Texas, to block the northward advance of the Spanish frontier with a true raiding economy, while they themselves made and honored a peace treaty with Spain.[87]

Rebalancings

In the non-Indian history of the hemisphere, the seventy-year period between the first battle of the French and Indian War in North America and the last battle of the wars for independence in South America is packed with exciting events. In a single pivotal year, 1776, thirteen of the thirty-one extant British American colonies declared their independence from Great Britain in eastern North America; the Spanish Crown separated the *Provincias Internas* from New Spain in southwestern North America; and Spain forced the boundary issue with Portugal in South America by making Buenos Aires the capital of a new viceroyalty.

Indians within or on the fringes of empire were living through a different, darker history of disease, thwarted nativism, and removal. The North American smallpox pandemic (1775–1782) recognized no boundaries. The rapid diffusion of *Variola* from Boston to Georgia, Virginia, Quebec, and Nova Scotia by means of Continental soldiers, and from Mexico City to Texas, New Mexico, the plains, the Northwest coast, and on up into Russian Alaska by means of missionaries, horse nomads, and fur traders makes a powerful case for continental history.[88] Disease and famine weakened the Chiricahua Apaches of the western plains, and New Spain was at last able to reduce these raiders of the northern frontier to exile and slavery, sending the women and children to Sonora and the men to Cuba.[89]

Pan-Indian movements were slow to develop—the Nahuatl language spoken in Mexico did not even have a word for "Indian"—but by the same process that created composite ethnic identities for Europeans and Africans transplanted to the Americas, indigenous peoples began to view themselves as Indians. They had come to the aid of their imperial allies during the French and Indian War in North America (1754–1763) and the Luso–Spanish boundary conflicts in South America (1762–1777), only to have their interests ignored in postwar treaties that made a mockery of the middle ground, and Nativist movements sprang up in the polyglot communities where the dispossessed gathered.[90]

Pontiac's War (1763–1764) in the Great Lakes region was a climactic episode in a long struggle for unity which reshaped the eastern woodlands, changing reconciled frontiers to contested grounds. The Great Rebellion in Upper Peru (1780–1783), which began with the uprising of Túpac Amaru II, was the culmination of a long struggle for justice for Indians and *castas* and cost 100,000 lives.[91] Unthinkable race and class wars followed, when a political dispute in St. Domingue metamorphosed into the Haitian Revolution (1791–1804), a stunningly effective slave rebellion, and when Father Miguel Hidalgo y Costilla's following of more than 80,000 Mexican Indians and mestizos fell upon New Spain's elites, both peninsular and creole (1810–1811).[92] The horrors of these two revolts and of the French Revolution (1789–1799) explain why Spanish South American elites feared social unrest more than they desired independence, until liberators with armies made the decision for them.

In the postcolonial period, creoles who had dared to sweep away empires and found republics on the slimmest of precedents would look at the Indians in their midst and on their frontiers and see in Indianness nothing but intractable opposition to the progress of mankind toward political and economic freedom. What the citizens of the new American republics, the subjects of the new Brazilian emperor, and the residents of the American colonies loyal to Great Britain and Spain failed to understand was that the Indians outside of empire were naturally free.

The free peoples in Spanish South America included the *bárbaros* of Tierra del Fuego and Patagonia, the Mapuches of Araucanía, and the eponymous Pampas. Brazil had three areas of unsubdued tribes—in the Amazon forest, in the basin of the Paraná–Paraíba, reaching into Mato Grosso and Goiás, and in the eastern *sertão* of Minas Gerais, where the Kayapós and descendants of the Gê-speaking Aimorés, called Botocudos, delayed internal colonization.[93] Maps of North America depicted the plains as split between the United States and the Republic of Mexico, but these claims were chimerical, for the Comanches dominated the Southwest and the Sioux grew strong on the prairies. In the far north, the Inuit lived as they had for millennia in an abundant land that nobody else wanted. The grasslands, deserts, forests, and tundra of the hemisphere have no colonial past, for they were outside of empire when the British, Portuguese, and Spanish Americans declared themselves independent. What these regions have is a past of warrior nations, invigorated by the existence of settlements beyond their borders, ripe for raiding.

Atlantic history focuses on European and African Atlantic-crossers and their creole descendants. The settlers occupy the stage; the natives stand in the wings. When the colonial era came to a close in 1825, indigenous peoples who had come to terms with empire faced a new challenge in the expanding nation-state. Peoples who had sided with royalists shared in their defeat; peoples outnumbered to the tipping point lost their lands to settlers bent on ethnic cleansing. From an Atlantic perspective, the new settler republics and empires were the masters of all the space that mattered. A hemispheric perspective, however, reveals that from Brazil to Alaska and from Patagonia to Newfoundland, indigenous people held sway over an abundance of habitable land. Unbroken to the yoke of the Atlantic world, if willing to use what it had to offer, the autonomous nations beyond the frontiers continued to hunt, trade, fight, and make peace in revised standard versions of the old ways. Their independence would not last forever, but in 1825 it was good for another fifty years.

NOTES

1. See C. R. Boxer, *The Dutch Seaborne Empire: 1600–1800* (New York: Alfred A. Knopf, 1965); J. H. Parry, *The Spanish Seaborne Empire* (New York: Alfred A. Knopf, 1966); C. R. Boxer, *The Portuguese Seaborne Empire: 1415–1825* (New York: Alfred A. Knopf, 1969); Jeremy Black, *The British Seaborne Empire* (New Haven: Yale University Press, 2004).

2. Though the Viceroyalty of Peru faced the Pacific, a well-traveled road across the Isthmus of Panama gave it access to the Atlantic and made it a part of that world.

3. The small Program in Atlantic History, Society, and Culture that began at the Johns Hopkins University in 1968 had specialists in the Caribbean and Brazil, but not in Peru or Mexico.

4. See James H. Merrell, *The Indians' New World: Catawbas and Their Neighbors from European Contact Through the Era of Removal* (Chapel Hill: University of North Carolina Press, 1989). On ethnohistory and the "new Indian history," see Amy Turner Bushnell, "The First Southerners: Indians of the Early South," in

John B. Boles, ed., *A Companion to the American South*, 2nd ed. (Malden, Mass.: Blackwell, 2004), pp. 3–23, especially pp. 3–4.

5. Suzanne Austin Alchon, *A Pest in the Land: New World Epidemics in a Global Perspective* (Albuquerque: University of New Mexico Press, 2003), pp. 147–172. For an acerbic analysis of the literature, see David Henige, *Numbers from Nowhere: The American Indian Contact Population Debate* (Norman: University of Oklahoma Press, 1998).

6. Shepard Krech III, *The Ecological Indian: Myth and History* (New York: W. W. Norton, 1999), pp. 93–94.

7. An example of the new approach is Daniel K. Richter, *Facing East from Indian Country: A Native History of Early America* (Cambridge, Mass.: Harvard University Press, 2001).

8. Alchon, *A Pest in the Land*, pp. 75–79.

9. Noble David Cook, *Born to Die: Disease and New World Conquest, 1492-1600* (New York: Cambridge University Press, 1998), pp. 95–216; Juan A. Villamarín and Judith E. Villamarín, "Epidemic Disease in the Sabana de Bogotá, 1536–1810," in Noble David Cook and W. George Lovell, eds., *"Secret Judgments of God": Old World Disease in Colonial Spanish America* (Norman: University of Oklahoma Press, 1991), pp. 113–141.

10. Cook, *Born to Die*, pp. 198–200.

11. Amy Turner Bushnell, "'None of These Wandering Nations Has Ever Been Reduced to the Faith': Missions and Mobility on the Spanish-American Frontier," in James Muldoon, ed., *The Spiritual Conversion of the Americas* (Gainesville: University of Florida Press, 2004), pp. 142–168. See also Bushnell, "The Sacramental Imperative: Catholic Ritual and Indian Sedentism in the Provinces of Florida," in David Hurst Thomas, ed., *Columbian Consequences*, vol. 2: *Archaeology and History of the Spanish Borderlands East* (Washington, D.C.: Smithsonian Institution Press, 1990), pp. 475–490.

12. See Stuart B. Schwartz, "Indian Labor and New World Plantations: European Demands and Indian Responses in Northeastern Brazil," *American Historical Review* 83(1) (February 1978): 43–79; and Alchon, *A Pest in the Land*, pp. 135–139.

13. See Amy Turner Bushnell, "A Requiem for Lesser Conquerors: Honor and Oblivion on a Maritime Periphery," in Raquel Chang-Rodríguez, ed., *Beyond Books and Borders: Garcilaso de la Vega and La Florida del Inca* (Lewisburg, Penn.: Bucknell University Press, 2006), pp. 66–74, and Bushnell, "Spain's Conquest by Contract: Pacification and the Mission System in Eastern North America," in Michael V. Kennedy and William G. Shade, eds., *The World Turned Upside Down: The State of Eighteenth-Century American Studies at the Beginning of the Twenty-first Century* (Bethlehem, Penn.: Lehigh University Press, 2001), pp. 289–320.

14. See Donna J. Guy and Thomas E. Sheridan, eds., *Contested Ground: Comparative Frontiers on the Northern and Southern Edges of the Spanish Empire* (Tucson: University of Arizona Press, 1998); and David J. Weber, *Bárbaros:*

Spaniards and Their Savages in the Age of Enlightenment (New Haven: Yale University Press, 2005).

15. For attempts to systematize frontier theory, see Christine Daniels and Michael V. Kennedy, eds., *Negotiated Empires: Centers and Peripheries in the Americas, 1500–1820* (New York: Routledge, 2002), especially Amy Turner Bushnell and Jack P. Greene, "Peripheries, Centers, and the Construction of Early Modern American Empires: An Introduction," pp. 1–14, and Bushnell, "Gates, Patterns, and Peripheries: The Field of Frontier Latin America," pp. 15–28.

16. Kathleen Deagan and José María Cruxent, *Columbus's Outpost Among the Taínos: Spain and America at La Isabela, 1493–1498* (New Haven: Yale University Press, 2002), pp. 33–45, 60–61; Jayme A. Sokolow, *The Great Encounter: Native Peoples and European Settlers in the Americas, 1492–1800* (Armonk, N.Y.: M. E. Sharpe, 2003), pp. 91–94; Cook, *Born to Die*, pp. 15–59; Paul E. Hoffman, *Florida's Frontiers* (Bloomington: Indiana University Press, 2002), pp. 21–26.

17. Matthew Restall, *Seven Myths of the Spanish Conquest* (New York: Oxford University Press, 2003); Cook, *Born to Die*, pp. 60–94; James Lockhart and Stuart B. Schwartz, *Early Latin America: A History of Colonial Spanish America and Brazil* (Cambridge: Cambridge University Press, 1983), pp. 86–92.

18. Lockhart and Schwartz, *Early Latin America*, pp. 37–49. On the expansion and organization of the Inka empire, see Juan Villamarín and Judith Villamarín, "Chiefdoms: The Prevalence and Persistence of 'Señoríos Naturales' 1400 to European Conquest," and María Rostworowski and Craig Morris, "The Fourfold Domain: Inka Power and Its Social Foundations," in Frank Salomon and Stuart B. Schwartz, eds., *The Cambridge History of the Native Peoples of the Americas*, vol. 3: *South America* (Cambridge: Cambridge University Press, 1999), part 1, pp. 577–667, especially pp. 628–653, and part 1, pp. 769–863. On the Aztec Empire, see Inga Clendinnen, *Aztecs: An Interpretation* (Cambridge: Cambridge University Press, 1995); and Ross Hassig, "Aztec and Spanish Conquest in Mesoamerica," in R. Brian Ferguson and Neil L. Whitehead, eds., *War in the Tribal Zone: Expanding States and Indigenous Warfare* (Santa Fe: School of American Research Press, 1992), pp. 82–102.

19. On Spain's sixteenth-century conquests, see Mark A. Burkholder and Lyman L. Johnson, *Colonial Latin America*, 6th ed. (New York: Oxford University Press, 2008), pp. 52–92; Lyle N. McAlister, *Spain and Portugal in the New World 1492–1700* (Minneapolis: University of Minnesota Press, 1984), pp. 96–107; and Lockhart and Schwartz, *Early Latin America*, pp. 138–140, 260–265, 283–288. See also Inga Clendinnen, *Ambivalent Conquests: Maya and Spaniard in Yucatan, 1517–1570* (Cambridge: Cambridge University Press, 1987); Mary W. Helms, *Middle America: A Culture History of Heartland and Frontiers* (Englewood Cliffs, N.J.: Prentice Hall, 1975), pp. 143–146; and Luis F. Calero, *Chiefdoms Under Siege: Spain's Rule and Native Adaptation in the Southern Colombian Andes 1535–1700* (Albuquerque: University of New Mexico Press, 1997).

20. John Leddy Phelan, *The Millennial Kingdom of the Franciscans in the New World*, 2nd ed., rev. (Berkeley: University of California Press, 1970); Robert Ricard,

The Spiritual Conquest of Mexico: An Essay on the Apostolate and the Evangelizing Methods of the Mendicant Orders in New Spain, 1523–1572, trans. Lesley Byrd Simpson (Berkeley: University of California Press, 1966).

21. On the Spanish debate about the rights of "barbarians," see pp. 289–301 of Bushnell, "Spain's Conquest by Contract."

22. Clendinnen, *Ambivalent Conquests*, pp. 72–111; Fernando Cervantes, *The Devil in the New World: The Impact of Diabolism in New Spain* (New Haven: Yale University Press, 1994); Kenneth Mills, *Idolatry and Its Enemies: Colonial Andean Religion and Extirpation, 1640–1750* (Princeton: Princeton University Press, 1997).

23. Kenneth J. Andrien, *Andean Worlds: Indigenous History, Culture, and Consciousness Under Spanish Rule, 1532–1825* (Albuquerque: University of New Mexico Press, 2001), pp. 24–26.

24. Jeffrey A. Cole, *The Potosí Mita 1573–1700: Compulsory Indian Labor in the Andes* (Stanford: Stanford University Press, 1985); Burkholder and Johnson, *Colonial Latin America*, pp. 157–162.

25. D. A. Brading, *The First America: The Spanish Monarchy, Creole Patriots, and the Liberal State, 1492–1867* (Cambridge: Cambridge University Press, 1991), pp. 55–57.

26. Álvaro Jara, *Guerra y sociedad en Chile: La transformación de la guerra de Arauco y la esclavitud de los indios* (Santiago, Chile: Editorial Universitaria, 1971), pp. 46–47; Kristine L. Jones, "Warfare, Reorganization, and Readaptation at the Margins of Spanish Rule: The Southern Margin (1573–1882)," in Salomon and Schwartz, *South America*, part 2, pp. 138–187; Margarita Gascón, *Naturaleza e imperio: Araucanía, Patagonia, Pampas (1598–1740)* (Buenos Aires: Editorial Dunken, 2007), p. 26.

27. Mark Kurlansky, *Cod: A Biography of the Fish That Changed the World* (New York: Walker, 1997); Cornelis Ch. Goslinga, *The Dutch in the Caribbean and on the Wild Coast 1580–1680* (Assen, The Netherlands: Van Gorcum, 1971), pp. 116–140; Lockhart and Schwartz, *Early Latin America*, pp. 282–285.

28. See Amy Turner Bushnell, "Escape of the Nickaleers: European–Indian Relations on the Wild Coast of Florida in 1696, from Jonathan Dickinson's Journal," in Richmond Brown, ed., *Coastal Encounters: The Transformation of the Gulf South in the Eighteenth Century* (Lincoln: University of Nebraska Press, 2007), pp. 31–58.

29. Bailey W. Diffie, *A History of Colonial Brazil 1500–1792* (Malabar, Fla.: Krieger, 1987), pp. 1–114; Warren Dean, *With Broadax and Firebrand: The Destruction of the Brazilian Atlantic Forest* (Berkeley: University of California Press, 1995), pp. 41–65.

30. Kenneth M. Morrison, *The Embattled Northeast: The Elusive Ideal of Alliance in Abenaki–Euramerican Relations* (Berkeley: University of California Press, 1984), pp. 14–28.

31. Bruce G. Trigger, *Natives and Newcomers: Canada's "Heroic Age" Reconsidered* (Kingston, Ont.: McGill-Queen's University Press, 1985), pp. 172–183;

Wim Klooster, *The Dutch in the Americas 1600–1800: A Narrative History with the Catalogue of an Exhibition of Rare Prints, Maps, and Illustrated Books from the John Carter Brown Library* (Providence, R.I.: The John Carter Brown Library, 1997), pp. 51–55; W. J. Eccles, *The French in North America 1500–1783* (East Lansing: Michigan State University Press, 1998), pp. 18–32, 88.

32. Eccles, *The French in North America*, pp. 103–112; William H. Goetzmann and Glyndwr Williams, *The Atlas of North American Exploration from the Norse Voyages to the Race to the Pole* (Norman: University of Oklahoma Press, 1992), pp. 60–63. The large white birch, used for birchbark canoes, grew only in the St. Lawrence valley and on the north shores of the Great Lakes.

33. Goetzmann and Williams, *The Atlas of North American Exploration*, pp. 66–69, 96–97, 103–116; Tanis C. Thorne, *The Many Hands of My Relations: French and Indians on the Lower Missouri* (Columbia: University of Missouri Press, 1996); Sylvia Van Kirk, *Many Tender Ties: Women in Fur-Trade Society, 1670–1870* (Norman: University of Oklahoma Press, 1980).

34. James R. Gibson, *Otter Skins, Boston Ships, and China Goods: The Maritime Fur Trade of the Northwest Coast, 1785–1841* (Montreal: McGill-Queen's University Press, 1992), pp. 2–18; Gwenn A. Miller, " 'The Perfect Mistress of Russian Economy': Sighting the Intimate on a Colonial Alaskan Terrain, 1784–1821," in Ann Laura Stoler, ed., *Haunted by Empire* (Durham, N.C.: Duke University Press, 2006), pp. 297–322. The reference to hostage-taking is on p. 304.

35. Alan Gallay, *The Indian Slave Trade: The Rise of the English Empire in the American South, 1670–1717* (New Haven: Yale University Press, 2002); D. W. Meinig, *The Shaping of America: A Geographical Perspective on 500 Years of History*, vol. 1: *Atlantic America, 1492–1800* (New Haven: Yale University Press, 1986), pp. 172–184; J. Leitch Wright, Jr., *The Only Land They Knew: The Tragic Story of the American Indians in the Old South* (New York: Free Press, 1981); Krech, *Ecological Indian*, pp. 153–165; Daniel H. Usner, Jr., *Indians, Settlers, and Slaves in a Frontier Exchange Economy: The Lower Mississippi Valley Before 1783* (Chapel Hill: University of North Carolina Press, 1992).

36. Robbie Ethridge, "Creating the Shatter Zone: Indian Slave Traders and the Collapse of the Southeastern Chiefdoms," in Thomas J. Pluckhahn and Robbie Ethridge, eds., *Light on the Path: The Anthropology and History of the Southeastern Indians* (Tuscaloosa: University of Alabama Press, 2006), 207–218.

37. David Frye, "Native Peoples of Northeastern Mexico," in *Richard E. W. Adams and Murdo J. MacLeod, eds., The Cambridge History of the Native Peoples of the Americas*, vol. 2: *Mesoamerica* (New York: Cambridge University Press, 2000), part 2, pp. 89–135. Oakah L. Jones, Jr., *Los Paisanos: Spanish Settlers on the Northern Frontier of New Spain* (Norman: University of Oklahoma, 1979), pp. 22–23.

38. Cynthia Radding, *Wandering Peoples: Colonialism, Ethnic Spaces, and Ecological Frontiers in Northwestern Mexico, 1700–1850* (Durham, N.C.: Duke University Press, 1997), pp. 2, 281–282; Gregory Evans Dowd, " 'Insidious Friends': Gift Giving and the Cherokee-British Alliance in the Seven Years' War," in Andrew

R. L. Cayton and Fredrika J. Teute, eds., *Contact Points: American Frontiers from the Mohawk Valley to the Mississippi, 1750–1830* (Chapel Hill: University of North Carolina Press, 1998), pp. 114–150.

39. Amy Turner Bushnell, *Situado and Sabana: Spain's Support System for the Presidio and Mission Provinces of Florida*. American Museum of Natural History, Anthropological Papers, no. 74 (Washington, D.C.: Smithsonian Institution Press, 1994).

40. Richard White, *The Middle Ground: Indians, Empires, and Republics in the Great Lakes Region, 1650–1815* (Cambridge: Cambridge University Press, 1991); Cornelius J. Jaenen, "The Role of Presents in French–Amerindian Trade," in Duncan Cameron, ed., *Explorations in Canadian Economic History: Essays in Honour of Irene M. Spry* (Ottawa: University of Ottawa Press, 1985), pp. 234, 245–246; James Taylor Carson, *Searching for the Bright Path: The Mississippi Choctaws from Prehistory to Removal* (Lincoln: University of Nebraska Press, 1999), p. 29; Joel W. Martin, *Sacred Revolt: The Muskogees' Struggle for a New World* (Boston: Beacon Press, 1991), p. 84.

41. Daniel R. Mandell, *Behind the Frontier: Indians in Eighteenth-Century Eastern Massachusetts* (Lincoln: University of Nebraska Press, 1996), pp. 12–23; Alden T. Vaughan, *Roots of American Racism: Essays on the Colonial Experience* (New York: Oxford University Press, 1995), pp. 213–227.

42. Eccles, *The French in North America*, pp. 77–79; Allan Greer, *The People of New France* (Toronto: University of Toronto Press, 1997), pp. 79–80.

43. Usner, *Indians, Settlers, and Slaves*, pp. 60–65.

44. Martha W. McCartney, "Cockacoeske, Queen of Pamunkey: Diplomat and Suzeraine," in Peter H. Wood, Gregory A. Waselkov, and M. Thomas Hatley, eds., *Powhatan's Mantle: Indians in the Colonial Southeast*, rev. and expanded ed. (Lincoln: University of Nebraska Press, 2006), pp. 243–266.

45. John K. Chance, *Conquest of the Sierra: Spaniards and Indians in Colonial Oaxaca* (Norman: University of Oklahoma Press, 1989).

46. For a typology of Spanish terms for missionization and directed settlement, see Bushnell, *Situado and Sabana*, pp. 20–23.

47. Patricia Galloway, "Confederacy as a Solution to Chiefdom Dissolution: Historical Evidence in the Choctaw Case," in Charles Hudson and Carmen Chaves Tesser, eds., *The Forgotten Centuries: Indians and Europeans in the American South, 1521–1704* (Athens: University of Georgia Press, 1994), pp. 393–420; James R. Atkinson, *Splendid Land, Splendid People: The Chickasaw Indians to Removal* (Tuscaloosa: University of Alabama Press, 2004); Theda Perdue, *Slavery and the Evolution of Cherokee Society, 1540–1866* (Knoxville: University of Tennessee Press, 1979); Merrell, *The Indians' New World*; Steven J. Oatis, *A Colonial Complex: South Carolina's Frontiers in the Era of the Yamasee War 1680–1730* (Lincoln: University of Nebraska Press, 2004); Robbie Ethridge, *Creek Country: The Creek Indians and Their World* (Chapel Hill: University of North Carolina Press, 2003); James W. Covington, *The Seminoles of Florida* (Gainesville: University of Florida Press, 1993).

48. On the seventeenth-century Iroquois wars, see José António Brandão, *Your Fyre Shall Burn No More: Iroquois Policy toward New France and Its Native Allies to 1701* (Lincoln: University of Nebraska Press, 1997).

49. See David G. Anderson, "Fluctuations Between Simple and Complex Chiefdoms: Cycling in the Late Prehistoric Southeast," in John F. Scarry, ed., *Political Structure and Change in the Prehistoric Southeastern United States* (Gainesville: University of Florida Press, 1996), pp. 231–252.

50. The Boltonian mission, landlocked and isolated, was atypical. See Herbert E. Bolton, "The Mission as a Frontier Institution in the Spanish American Colonies," *American Historical Review* 23(1) (1917): 42–61; and Bushnell, *Situado and Sabana*, pp. 23–28.

51. Goetzmann and Williams, *The Atlas of North American Exploration*, pp. 124–125.

52. Jorge Pinto Rodríguez et al., eds., *Misioneros en la Araucanía, 1600–1900: Un capítulo de historia fronteriza en Chile* (Temuco, Chile: Imprenta Universidad de la Frontera, 1988); Bushnell, *Situado and Sabana*, pp. 113–116; Troy S. Floyd, *The Anglo–Spanish Struggle for Mosquitia* (Albuquerque: University of New Mexico Press, 1967), pp. 39–54; John Leddy Phelan, *The Hispanization of the Philippines: Spanish Aims and Filipino Responses 1565–1700* (Madison: University of Wisconsin Press, 1967 [1956]).

53. Candice Millard, *The River of Doubt: Theodore Roosevelt's Darkest Journey* (New York: Doubleday, 2005).

54. McAlister, *Spain and Portugal in the New World*, pp. 320–321, 328–329, map 5; Weber, *Bárbaros*, p. 111, map 8.

55. Dean, *With Broadax and Firebrand*, pp. 58–62.

56. John M. Monteiro, "The Crises and Transformations of Invaded Societies: Coastal Brazil in the Sixteenth Century," in Salomon and Schwartz, *South America*, part 1, pp. 973–1023; Diffie, *A History of Colonial Brazil*, pp. 221–253; Pedro Puntoni, *A guerra dos bárbaros: Povos indígenas e a colonização do sertão nordeste do Brasil, 1650–1720* (São Paulo: Hucitec/Editora da Universidade de São Paulo, 2002).

57. Dean, *With Broadax and Firebrand*, pp. 58–65, 80–83; Lockhart and Schwartz, *Early Latin America*, pp. 196–197; Barbara Ganson, *The Guaraní Under Spanish Rule in the Río de la Plata* (Stanford: Stanford University Press, 2003), pp. 17–45; Diffie, *A History of Colonial Brazil*, pp. 207–216.

58. Ganson, *The Guaraní Under Spanish Rule*, pp. 1–5, 45–116; Diffie, *A History of Colonial Brazil*, pp. 255–262.

59. Lockhart and Schwartz, *Early Latin America*, pp. 273–282; David Cleary, "Towards an Environmental History of the Amazon: From Prehistory to the Nineteenth Century," *Latin American Research Review* 36(2) (2001): 64–96; David Block, *Mission Culture on the Upper Amazon: Native Tradition, Jesuit Enterprise, and Secular Policy in Moxos, 1660–1880* (Lincoln: University of Nebraska Press, 1994); Anne Christine Taylor, "The Western Margins of Amazonia from the

Early Sixteenth to the Early Nineteenth Century," in Salomon and Schwartz, *South America*, part 2, pp. 188–256.

60. Diffie, *A History of Colonial Brazil*, pp. 258–259, 271–293; Cheryl English Martin, *Governance and Society in Colonial Mexico: Chihuahua in the Eighteenth Century* (Stanford: Stanford University Press, 1996), pp. 2, 43; Weber, *Bárbaros*, pp. 234–241.

61. Hoffman, *Florida's Frontiers*, pp. 47–99; John E. Worth, *The Timucuan Chiefdoms of Spanish Florida*, vol. 1: *Assimilation* (Gainesville: University of Florida Press, 1998), pp. 44–76.

62. On the repercussions of the Chacato Revolt, see Amy Turner Bushnell, "That Demonic Game: The Campaign to Stop Indian Pelota Playing in Spanish Florida, 1675–1684," *The Americas* 35 (July 1978): 1–19.

63. For the rise and decline of the Florida missions, see Bushnell, *Situado and Sabana*.

64. James Axtell, *The Invasion Within: The Contest of Cultures in Colonial North America* (New York: Oxford University Press, 1985), pp. 23–127; Greer, *The People of New France*, pp. 76–83; Eccles, *The French in North America*, pp. 35–59; Brandão, *Your Fyre Shall Burn No More*; Trigger, *Natives and Newcomers*, pp. 226–297; Thomas S. Abler, "Beavers and Muskets: Iroquois Military Fortunes in the Face of European Colonization," in Ferguson and Whitehead, *War in the Tribal Zone*, pp. 151–174; Morrison, *The Embattled Northeast*, p. 93.

65. Morrison, *The Embattled Northeast*, pp. 88–99, 102–107.

66. David J. Weber, *The Spanish Frontier in North America* (New Haven: Yale University Press, 1992), pp. 123–141, 187; John L. Kessell, *Kiva, Cross, and Crown: The Pecos Indians and New Mexico 1540–1840* (Washington, D.C.: National Park Service, 1979), pp. 101–297.

67. Susan M. Deeds, "First-Generation Rebellions in Seventeenth-Century Nueva Vizcaya," in Susan Schroeder, ed., *Native Resistance and the Pax Colonial in New Spain* (Lincoln: University of Nebraska Press, 1998), pp. 1–29.

68. Evelyn Hu-DeHart, *Missionaries, Miners and Indians: Spanish Contact with the Yaqui Nation of Northwestern New Spain 1533–1820* (Tucson: University of Arizona Press, 1981); Radding, *Wandering Peoples*; Weber, *The Spanish Frontier in North America*, pp. 240–241.

69. Weber, *The Spanish Frontier in North America*, pp. 152–155, 192–195.

70. Diffie, *A History of Colonial Brazil*, pp. 413–431; Lockhart and Schwartz, *Early Latin America*, pp. 388–392.

71. Weber, *The Spanish Frontier in North America*, pp. 236–265.

72. Steven W. Hackel, *Children of Coyote, Missionaries of Saint Francis: Indian–Spanish Relations in Colonial California, 1769–1850* (Chapel Hill: University of North Carolina Press, 2005), especially pp. 106–113, 215–216.

73. For the historiography of attitudes toward the Guaraní and California reductions, see Ganson, *Guaraní under Spanish Rule*, pp. 6–9, and Hackel, *Children of Coyote*, pp. 1–12.

74. Cynthia Radding, *Landscapes of Power and Identity: Comparative Histories in the Sonoran Desert and the Forests of Amazonia from Colony to Republic* (Durham, N.C.: Duke University Press, 2005).

75. Henry Warner Bowden, *American Indians and Christian Missions: Studies in Cultural Conflict* (Chicago: University of Chicago Press, 1981), pp. 111–133; Axtell, *The Invasion Within*, pp. 130–267, 273–276; Dane Morrison, *A Praying People: Massachusett Acculturation and the Failure of the Puritan Mission, 1600–1690* (New York: Peter Lang, 1995).

76. Earl P. Olmstead, *Blackcoats Among the Delaware: David Zeisberger on the Ohio Frontier* (Kent, Ohio: Kent State University Press, 1991); A. G. Roeber, ed., *Ethnographies and Exchanges: Native Americans, Moravians, and Catholics in Early North America* (University Park: Pennsylvania State University Press, 2008).

77. Terry G. Jordan and Matti Kaups, *The American Backwoods Frontier: An Ethnic and Ecological Interpretation* (Baltimore: Johns Hopkins Press, 1989); Stephen Aron, "Pigs and Hunters: 'Rights in the Woods' on the Trans-Appalachian Frontier," in Cayton and Teute, *Contact Points*, pp.175–204.

78. Bushnell, *Situado and Sabana*, pp. 146, 169–179 passim.

79. Elinor G. K. Melville, *A Plague of Sheep: Environmental Consequences of the Conquest of Mexico* (Cambridge: Cambridge University Press, 1994).

80. On societies of cattle hunters in the transfrontier, see Philip D. Curtin, *The Rise and Fall of the Plantation Complex: Essays in Atlantic History* (Cambridge: Cambridge University Press, 1990), pp. 86–97. For an unromantic view of the South American transfrontier, see Dean, *With Broadax and Firebrand*, pp. 23, 75, 91–116.

81. Louis Allaire, "The Caribs of the Lesser Antilles," in Samuel M. Wilson, ed., *The Indigenous People of the Caribbean* (Gainesville: University of Florida Press, 1997), pp. 177–185; Philip P. Boucher, *Cannibal Encounters: Europeans and Island Caribs, 1492–1703* (Baltimore. Johns Hopkins Press, 1992); Neil L. Whitehead, "The Crises and Transformations of Invaded Societies: The Caribbean (1492–1580)," in Salomon and Schwartz, *South America*, part 1, pp. 864–903.

82. Diffie, *A History of Colonial Brazil*, pp. 370–377; Mary Karasch, "Periphery of the Periphery? Vila Boa de Goiás, 1780–1835," in Daniels and Kennedy, *Negotiated Empires*, pp. 143–169. See also Karasch, "Interethnic Conflict and Resistance on the Brazilian Frontier of Goiás, 1750–1890," in Guy and Sheridan, *Contested Ground*, pp. 115–134.

83. James Schofield Saeger, *The Chaco Mission Frontier: The Guaycuruan Experience* (Tucson: University of Arizona Press, 2000).

84. Weber, *Bárbaros*, pp. 62–68.

85. Dean R. Snow, "The First Americans and the Differentiation of Hunter–Gatherer Cultures," in Bruce G. Trigger and Wilcomb E. Washburn, eds., *The Cambridge History of the Native Peoples of the Americas*, vol. 1: *North America* (Cambridge: Cambridge University Press, 1996), part 1, pp. 125–199; Loretta Fowler, "The Great Plains from the Arrival of the Horse to 1885," in Trigger and Washburn, *North America*, part 2, pp. 1–55.

86. Thorne, *The Many Hands of My Relations*, pp. 13–63; Kathleen DuVal, *The Native Ground: Indians and Colonists in the Heart of the Continent* (Philadelphia: University of Pennsylvania Press, 2006).

87. On the relations of Apaches and Comanches with the Spanish, see Weber, *Bárbaros*, pp. 71–75; Weber, *The Spanish Frontier in North America*, pp. 204–235; James F. Brooks, *Captives and Cousins: Slavery, Kinship, and Community in the Southwest Borderlands* (Chapel Hill: University of North Carolina Press, 2002); and Kristine L. Jones, "Comparative Raiding Economies, North and South," in Guy and Sheridan, *Contested Ground*, pp. 97–114.

88. Colin G. Calloway, *New Worlds for All: Indians, Europeans, and the Remaking of Early America* (Baltimore: Johns Hopkins University Press, 1997), pp. 33–39; Elizabeth A. Fenn, *Pox Americana: The Great Smallpox Epidemic of 1775–82* (New York: Hill and Wang, 2001).

89. H. Henrietta Stockel, *Salvation Through Slavery: Chiricahua Apaches and Priests on the Spanish Colonial Frontier* (Albuquerque: University of New Mexico Press, 2008).

90. James Lockhart, *Nahuas and Spaniards: Postconquest Central Mexican History and Philology* (Stanford: Stanford University Press, 1991), p. 9; James H. Merrell, "Shamokin, 'the Very Seat of the Prince of Darkness': Unsettling the Early American Frontier," in Cayton and Teute, *Contact Points*, pp. 16–59.

91. Gregory Evans Dowd, *A Spirited Resistance: The North American Indian Struggle for Unity, 1745–1815* (Baltimore: Johns Hopkins University Press, 1992); Richard Middleton, *Pontiac's War: Its Causes, Course and Consequences* (New York: Routledge, 2007); Andrien, *Andean Worlds*, pp. 199–228; Burkholder and Johnson, *Colonial Latin America*, pp. 322–323.

92. Burkholder and Johnson, *Colonial Latin America*, pp. 384–388. Laurent Dubois, *Avengers of the New World: The Story of the Haitian Revolution* (Cambridge, Mass.: Harvard University Press, 2004).

93. Hal Langfur, *The Forbidden Lands: Colonial Identity, Frontier Violence, and the Persistence of Brazil's Eastern Indians, 1750–1830* (Stanford: Stanford University Press, 2006); Caio Prado, Jr., *The Colonial Background of Modern Brazil*, trans. Suzette Macedo (Berkeley: University of California Press, 1969), pp. 110–115; Dean, *With Broadaxe and Firebrand*, p. 102.

8

AFRICA AND THE ATLANTIC,
C. 1450 TO C. 1820

PHILIP D. MORGAN

Before the arrival of Europeans, the Atlantic Ocean played little role in most Africans' lives. There were few Atlantic ports, and most contact with the outside world was overland rather than by sea (less true of African-Asian interactions via the Indian Ocean). In some regions of West Africa, people ventured out to sea to fish (but usually no more than a few miles offshore), and some ethnic groups traded products such as kola and salt lengthy distances along the coast. But, for the most part, a combination of prevailing winds and currents, lack of sheltered seas, few natural harbors, treacherous offshore bars, and heavy surf inhibited an indigenous seafaring tradition. Furthermore, extensive river and lagoon systems in many parts of West Africa facilitated both north–south and east–west transportation without hazarding the ocean. Africans used waterways, but generally not the sea. They developed the technology of the dugout, a canoe hollowed and shaped from a single tree trunk, which could be large in size and seaworthy, but generally lacked more sophisticated boatbuilding techniques, sails, and navigational devices that would have permitted greater familiarity with the ocean. Africans also lacked the incentives, most notably the population pressures (for Africa was under- rather than overpopulated), that might have pushed them to overcome these geographical and technological hurdles. Significantly, West Africans did not attempt to colonize offshore islands such as São Tomé, Príncipe, or the Cape Verdes. Moreover, through a process of long-term internal migration, a number of African ethnic groups were recent newcomers to the coast, another reason for their unfamiliarity with the sea. In many parts of West Africa, then, people avoided the open ocean, and in most areas the divide between land and sea—the former viewed as inhabited by the living, and the latter belonging to the dead—seemed daunting and insurmountable.[1]

By the early nineteenth century, large parts of Africa had been pulled firmly into the Atlantic orbit. Most obviously, by 1820, about 10 million Africans had been transported across the ocean, the largest forced movement of peoples in history. Prior to 1820, about four Africans arrived in the Americas for every European. In terms of migration, Africa, not Europe, dominated the Atlantic. Furthermore, a large infrastructure had developed within Africa to mobilize and transport such large numbers of people. Tens of thousands of African intermediaries—interpreters, soldiers, guards, porters, itinerant peddlers (known as *pombeiros* in Portuguese Angola), canoemen, and *grumetes* (castle or fort slaves)—were the indispensable lubricants of the slaving system. By the seventeenth and eighteenth centuries, many Africans had extensive maritime experience. Europeans took Gold Coast canoemen and their canoes to the Slave Coast (or Bight of Benin) so that they could ferry slaves across the treacherous surf to the European ships anchored a few miles offshore. The Kru of the Malaguetta Coast became famous for their maritime expertise. Africans now manned vessels with sails. In the early eighteenth century, a European saw a canoe with sails capable of carrying 200 passengers sailing northward between Kongo and Cabinda Bay on the Loango Coast. Villages that had once served as bases for fishing or salt production expanded to become ports, where much trade centered. Luanda, Cabinda, and Benguela on the West-Central African coast, Bonny and Old Calabar in the Bight of Biafra, Ouidah (a lagoonside port) in the Bight of Benin, Anomabu and Cape Coast on the Gold Coast, and James Fort and St Louis in Senegambia dominated Africa's Atlantic trade. Between the 1680s and the 1780s the value of Africa's Atlantic trade rose sixfold. In the latter decade, the peak years in the Atlantic slave trade, it was worth about 47 millions pounds sterling.[2]

Four central questions about this striking transformation will be explored in this essay. First, how much agency did Africans have in bringing about these changes? Second, how significant were regional differences? Third, what was the overall impact of Atlantic contact on Africa? Finally, what role did the African diaspora play in the broader Atlantic world? These are significant, complex questions, each of which has generated many books and essays, so inevitably answers here must be sketchy. My basic argument is that although Africa's integration into the Atlantic world over three and a half centuries was impressive, it was still quite limited. Even by 1820, Atlantic influences were unequally diffused throughout Africa; much of the continent had hardly been penetrated by them.

Agency

Since Europeans initiated contact with Africans and dominated the sea routes that connected their two continents, the latter might be thought to lack any agency whatsoever. Africa became underdeveloped, some historians have argued, largely because Europeans drained it of resources. According to this view, the superior resources of Europeans overwhelmed the inherent weaknesses of Africans, and the appropriate term is pillage (as well as genocide). In some ways, Europeans did get the better of their exchanges with Africans, particularly in the long term, but in the short, and even medium, term (as Europeans constantly bemoaned) Africans seemed, and in fact were, much in control. By no means were all Africans victims or dupes. Indeed, a voluntary partnership best captures the relationship between African traders and rulers and European merchants and ship captains. Africans called the tune in many aspects of this relationship, even if overall Europeans benefited the most from their exchanges.[3]

The conduct of trade generally followed African dictates. Indigenous rulers largely kept the trading process offshore, on small islands or trading hulks, or aboard transient ships. If they permitted Europeans to set up bases on land, these were usually confined to the littoral. Europeans perched precariously on the edge of the shore, as it were, at the mercy of their hosts. The only exception to the marginality of the European presence in Africa was Portuguese Angola, but in truth its territory was confined to a small area near Luanda, a few outposts in the interior, and a small trading post at Benguela. In any case, most Europeans were so susceptible to the virulent African disease environment that few lasted many years on the coast. The constant turnover in European personnel was just one indication of their weakness. Africans, not Europeans, took the initiative in learning the others' languages; and the grammar of the various trading languages (or pidgins) that emerged on the coast owed most to African languages. Europeans paid rent, customs and excise duties, as well as other tributes and fees for the privilege of trading in Africa. For the most part, then, Africans were landlords; Europeans, tenants. The term "subordinate symbiosis" has been coined to describe European dependence on Africans in routine commercial relationships. So-called European factories and forts were in reality, as one historian notes, "joint African-European ventures" rather than "outposts of European power." Europeans ran the forts, but Africans dominated their personnel.[4]

Bonds of credit and trust arose between African and European merchants. European ship captains often returned to the same African port because of the ties that they had established and the access to market information those contacts supplied. African and European traders therefore formed, in the words one historian, "a 'moral community,' which was held together not only by obvious economic ties but also by cross-cultural links, which helped to create a climate of understanding." Along some parts of the coast, consolidation of state authority was critical in enforcing credit arrangements. Europeans with grievances over the nonpayment of debts had to seek redress in royal courts. In such places, political centralization was the key to safeguarding credit. In other parts of the coast, decentralized and sometimes unstable political environments facilitated the growth of pawnship or panyarring, essentially private-order mechanisms, as instruments to protect imported credit. In the first, African merchants secured credit by giving people as pawns (collateral) to European ship captains, who could take them as slaves if the merchant failed to deliver on his promises. In the second, a European trader could seize a "panyarred" person to enforce payment of a debt; and, if not redeemed, that person then became a slave. These various credit arrangements were vital to the efficient running of the slave trade.[5]

Africans were eager, discriminating consumers, not easily satisfied with shoddy baubles or worthless trifles. Chicanery was certainly present in Afro-European exchanges, particularly in the earliest years, but neither side possessed a monopoly on trickery, and over time both sides found it in their interests to strive for accommodation. Africans certainly knew what they wanted from the relationship. Above all, they sought textiles, followed by, in no particular order, metalwares, alcoholic spirits, tobacco, firearms, and currencies. Textiles accounted for about half the value of Africa's imports, and Africans were highly selective in their preferences, concerned about colors, patterns, weaves, and textures. Increasingly Africans desired brightly colored Indian cottons from their European suppliers. Cloth, rather than firearms, therefore constituted the most attractive imports to most Africans; and, although Africans wanted both luxuries intended for their elites and cheaper goods aimed at a broader cross section of the people, most textiles aimed at mass consumption. In general, Africans received much the same kinds of goods as American colonists.[6]

To get these goods, Africans were willing to sell, first of all, gold, then ivory, hides, malaguetta pepper, beeswax, various tropical gums and dye-woods (highly valued by Europeans for their textile industries), and finally—and most lastingly—slaves. For the first 250 years of African-European commercial relations, gold formed the main basis of exchange, and not until the beginning of the eighteenth century did the value of slaves begin to exceed that of gold and all other produce. Europeans wanted gold rather than slaves; indeed, initially they made do with slaves because African suppliers were often keen to sell them in place of gold. In fact, Europeans regularly took slaves from one part of the West African coast and sold them to African purchasers on the Gold Coast in return for gold; these African buyers then put those slaves to producing more gold. Even in the eighteenth century, Africans exchanged much more than slaves. In some years in the eighteenth century, for example, the value of gum arabic exports exceeded that of slaves in the Senegambia region. A significant reverse trade in gold existed in the Bight of Benin region during the first half of the eighteenth century. It was not a local product but a re-export, brought from Brazil by Portuguese traders to exchange for slaves. By the late eighteenth century, palm oil, which was in growing demand in Europe as an industrial raw material (mainly in soap-making), was being exported from Africa in fairly large amounts, although its heyday would come in the following century. Still, despite the diversity of trading, the traffic in slaves came to dwarf all other items; by the 1780s slaves comprised over 90 percent of the value of all African exports. The transatlantic slave trade first became significant at the end of the sixteenth century, tripled in volume over the course of the seventeenth century, and then doubled again during the eighteenth century. The 1780s was the acme of the trade, when about 866,000 enslaved Africans crossed the Atlantic.[7]

Why did Africans sell slaves? In general, Africans—like many other peoples throughout the world—accepted the legitimacy of enslavement of captives taken in war. Most slaves were the unintended by-products of warfare mainly carried out for reasons other than seizing captives, although dedicated slave raiding did occur. The captors would retain some slaves, but offered others for sale, because restive captives were dangerous in large numbers. In addition, prior to European contact, Africa possessed a well-developed institution of slavery, with quite sophisticated marketing and delivery systems. In many ways, Indian Ocean and trans-Saharan trades in slaves, which had ancient origins and amounted to about the same overall volume as the transatlantic trade (albeit over a much longer period), made the latter possible. Europeans tapped into existing supply networks even as their growing demands reoriented and greatly expanded them. Furthermore, the reason why Africa had a long history of slavery (longer than Europe, for instance) is that, unlike Europe, rights in slaves rather than in land were the primary form of revenue-producing property. Slaves constituted a store of wealth and a corps of trusty dependents, many of whom were soldiers and administrators; accordingly, they were a vital medium of exchange. The short answer to the question why Africans sold slaves, then, is that

African enslavers did not see their victims as fellow brothers and sisters, but rather as aliens, separated by ethnic, political, religious, linguistic, and other cultural differences. Few societies in the world have enslaved people they consider their own; African polities were no exception. In principle, Africans sold foreigners, enemies, not their own subjects, unless in punishment for a serious offense or because of a dire emergency (such as a famine). Still, though selling "strangers" (or nonbelievers in Islamic societies) was the norm, some Africans under duress sold subordinate members of their own communities and/or families, either clandestinely or to defray debts. Finally, of course, Africans received valuable products in return for their slaves. Otherwise why would they have sold them, for people comprised the basis of all wealth and power in Africa?[8]

A general acceptance of slavery could coexist, at certain times and in particular places, with opposition to its practice. Some African kingdoms, usually for limited periods, prohibited enslavement and refused to sell slaves. Occasionally Muslim societies in West Africa objected to the sale of their religious brethren. Many non-Muslim African societies distinguished between legal and illegal forms of enslavement: the sale of someone born in a kingdom outside of that polity might be banned; banditry and kidnappings were usually regarded as illegitimate. Thus, in parts of West Africa—most notably Upper Guinea and Gabon—where weak governments led to extensive kidnapping and illegal seizures, opposition surfaced in widespread attacks on European slaving vessels. Within Africa more generally, people in small-scale societies resisted conquest and slave raiding by more powerful and centralized societies by fleeing to hills, forests, and swamps, building walled villages, and engaging in various defensive strategies. The growing practice of pawning and panyarring was open to abuse, and sometimes aggrieved Africans retaliated against European ship captains whom they felt acted illegally. On occasion, Europeans seized free persons as slaves, leading their African relatives to go to great lengths to have them returned.[9]

Resistance to the trade is dramatic evidence of African agency, but it was exceptional; better testimony to the upper hand that Africans established—precisely because it was a general phenomenon—is the way in which the terms of trade shifted inexorably in their favor. By 1800, for each slave they sold, African traders generally received at least three or four times as much as a century earlier. Demand outstripped supply; and African rulers and merchants took advantage of their strong position. Not only did they secure better prices for their slaves over time, they also increased port charges, customary tributes, and other fees. Of course, they could not raise prices so high as to lose customers; but the degree of European competition meant that Africans usually found a ship captain willing to meet their demands. At least before the early nineteenth century (when British-imposed abolition began to curtail demand), the Atlantic slave trade was largely a sellers' market.[10]

Regionalism

Africa was no homogeneous land. The variations along a 5,000-kilometer expanse of Atlantic coast were enormous. Europeans did not idly bestow such names as Ivory, Gold, or Slave Coast on parts of the African littoral; they reflected distinct trading environments. The more scholars have studied Africa's integration into the Atlantic world, the more they have realized that the process varied markedly from one place to another. Depending on their propensity to lump or split and their primary unit of analysis, scholars divide Atlantic Africa differently. If cultural zones are the focus, perhaps it can be separated Gaul-like into three: Upper Guinea, Lower Guinea, and West-Central Africa. If political formation is the issue, the division might even be a simple binary—centralized and decentralized polities—although mapping this bifurcation onto Atlantic Africa is no easy task. A common-sense way of conceiving key regions is to follow contemporary opinion, which, though it may give too much priority to European conceptions, undoubtedly involved African input. Essentially, Atlantic traders saw seven major regions, moving from north to south: Senegambia (Senegal River to Rio Nunez); Sierra Leone (Rio Nunez to Cape Mount); Windward Coast (Cape Mount to Assini River); Gold Coast (Assini River to Volta River); Bight of Benin (Rio Volta to Rio Nun); Bight of Biafra (Rio Nun to Cape Lopez); and West-Central Africa (Cape Lopez to Kunene River).[11]

The way the transatlantic slave trade operated reveals the importance of these regions. Europeans soon realized that African customers had distinct regional preferences. Textiles were important in almost all regional markets, the exception being the Bight of Biafra, but English woolens sold best on the Gold Coast, and East Indian textiles dominated sales on the Slave Coast and in West-Central Africa. Almost all cowries went to the Bight of Benin, and almost all metal ended up in Senegambia and the Bight of Biafra. Manillas (or wristlets) sold only in the Bight of Biafra. Roll tobacco from Bahia in Brazil was much in demand along the Slave Coast. Almost no beads went to Angola, but they formed between 10 and 20 percent of cargoes destined for the Cameroons. African preferences dictated distinct regional assortments of goods.[12]

The age and sex ratios among the captives of a slave ship also varied greatly from one African region to another. It was a very different migration from Senegambia, where the slave complements had few children—about 6 percent, on average—than from West-Central Africa, where children usually comprised more than a fifth of the slaves. Similarly, women were almost as numerous as men in shipments from the Bight of Biafra region, whereas men outnumbered women heavily in ships leaving Upper Guinea. The differences in the age and sex ratios of slaves drawn from the various African coastal regions can be attributed to many factors: bringing captives a long distance from the interior, thereby increasing transportation costs, might account for a premium on men and an avoidance of children; the more a region was involved in the trans-Saharan trade, which absorbed large numbers of females, the more it was likely to export men in the transatlantic trade; warriors taken in war were always likely to be exported, so modes of enslavement shaped who was offered for sale; and the degree to which a regional economy depended on female labor helps account for the availability of women. Whatever the explanation—and it was primarily African-centered—the ages and sexes of captives varied far more by African region than by the European nation buying the slaves or by American destination.[13]

Although slave mortality in the Atlantic crossing declined over time, significant African regional differences persisted throughout the history of the traffic. Mortality varied markedly not just by African region of origin but also between ports, even within the same region. Apparently, different slaving hinterlands, as well as greater or shorter distances from inland point of capture to port, with slaves moving through greater or fewer epidemiological zones, were critical in determining death rates on board ship. Mortality was 120 percent greater on ships leaving the Bight of Biafra than on those from West-Central Africa. Perhaps it is no coincidence that the latter was the largest supplier of slaves across the Atlantic. Perhaps, too, the reason why Anomabu on the Gold Coast was the second-ranking port to which the British traded in the second half of the eighteenth century owed something to the relatively low mortality rate of slaves shipped from there.[14]

Patterns of slave revolts on board ships at the African coast and in the Atlantic also reveal large regional differences. Compared to ships trading in West-Central Africa or the Bight of Biafra, those trading in Upper Guinea were much more likely to experience a revolt. Rebellions on ships trading at places in Upper Guinea were four times greater than might be expected from their share of slave shipments from Atlantic Africa to the Americas. Again it seems hardly coincidental that the places with the most rebellions shipped the fewest Africans; and that the great majority of slaves came from regions with the lowest rates of insurrections.[15]

Upper Guinea stands out as the region least integrated into the Atlantic economy. Why did this area, which was closest to Europe and the Americas, with the best natural harbors, probably the most skilled indigenous mariners, the longest history of Euro-African contact, the presence of a sophisticated Euro-African merchant class, and the shortest Middle Passage, send the fewest slaves to the Americas? No doubt it had much to do with the degree of political fragmentation, the influence of Islam, the demand for slaves within the Upper Guinea economy, a high incidence of illegal seizures of free Africans, and a correspondingly strong African resistance to European encroachments, but the effectiveness of delivery systems and the resulting effect on prices may well have been determinative. Indeed, contemporary traders believed that African dealers in this region simply could not purchase enough slaves because of the high costs of transportation from hinterland to coast.[16]

West-Central Africa was the opposite of Upper Guinea. This region exported the most people—almost half of all Africans—across the Atlantic. They went to all parts of the Americas, although Brazil garnered the vast majority. Why was this region so much more integrated into the Atlantic economy than any other? Part is explained by the Portuguese presence, for they were the only group to establish a long-standing colony in Africa in the early modern era, and they shipped slaves for the longest period, beginning early and stopping late. Furthermore, the transatlantic passage from Angola to southeast Brazil and Bahia was far shorter than any routes from Africa to the Caribbean and North America. The sophisticated delivery systems that Africans developed in this region were also important, as was the centralized, unified character of the region. Compared to West Africans, who were divided into many groups, Central Africans shared, as one of the region's leading authorities puts it, "a single overarching culture." True, there were regional cultures—Kongo, Mbundu, and Ovimbundu—and separate languages, but there was much contact between them, and all were closely related within a larger Bantu culture. Whatever the explanation for this region's importance, its impact on the Atlantic world was undoubtedly immense. So central was the Central African component to Atlantic migration as a whole, one scholar contends that it "provided the common glue, the cultural background common to African American communities everywhere."[17]

Impact

The impact of growing Atlantic integration on African societies was undoubtedly significant, but its effects were mixed. Dislocations and disruptions there certainly were, but not all changes were destructive. The calculus of gain and harm is difficult to apportion, and varied much by strata of African society. Clearly, there were winners, such as rulers and merchants, and losers, most notably the ordinary Africans who ended up as victims of the slave trade. In general terms, however, the volume of Atlantic trade, no matter how rapidly it was growing, was not large enough to have transformed Africa's economy, although arguably the social and political effects of Atlantic integration were more dramatic than the economic—and more negative than positive. But even so, much of the continent's development continued along lines dictated by its own traditions and imperatives.

A major effect of increasing Atlantic integration was reorientation of African trade networks and stimulation of the economy. Merchants rose to prominence by specializing in the new trade. Especially in areas near the coast, new commercial groups came to exercise increasing power. In some cases, these new dynasties consisted of the bicultural descendants of mixed marriages between European men and African women; in others African widows themselves (*signares* in Senegal, *nhara* in Portuguese Guinea) became highly influential commercial intermediaries. Specialized merchant networks, such as the Aro trading community in the Bight of Biafra region, arose to organize large caravans of people from major inland trading centers to the coast. Thousands of small traders ventured into interior regions in search of captives to buy. With much greater access to currencies—whether expanded supplies of cowry shells and iron bars or new currencies such as copper and brass rods or *manillas*—local economies were not just monetized but commercialized. Monetary bottlenecks were much reduced; and inland trade expanded in volume and reach.[18]

Some imported goods replaced domestic products, but for the most part they supplemented and complemented rather than stifled local industries. African production did not collapse in the face of foreign competition. In inland markets in particular, imported textiles had to compete with locally made cloth, and the cost of transporting it overland did not always make it competitive. Imported iron bars boosted the work of African blacksmiths, who fashioned them into all types of useful objects. More abundant and efficient iron tools probably increased agricultural output. Foreign tobacco imports went hand in hand with a growing ability of Africans to supply the product locally. The higher status and stronger alcoholic content of imported drinks challenged but did not totally displace local beverages. In short, native industries were remarkably resilient.[19]

In general, Africa's involvement in Atlantic trade probably had only a modest effect on its overall economy (economies would be a more accurate term), although coastal areas felt the impact much more so than interior regions. Imports of alcohol and tobacco were small on a per capita basis. Even imported textiles supplied less than half a yard per person in the 1780s, at a time when a two-yard wrapper clothed one person. Unquestionably, Africans coveted the ever increasing flood of commodities Europeans made available; nevertheless, as one historian has noted, "the ratio of overseas trade to domestic economic activity was far lower for the majority of Africans than for the typical inhabitant of Europe or the Americas." In the mid-1780s the average value of overseas trade per person in West Africa was only £0.10 per year, compared with £1.4 in the United States of America, £2.3 in Britain, and £5.7 in the British West Indies. In large part, Africans fed, clothed, and housed themselves without overseas economic exchange. Changes in West African material culture were predominantly additive rather than substitutive.[20]

Imports of firearms grew substantially in many parts of Africa—amounting to a total of about 20 million guns in the second half of the eighteenth century—encouraging a view that Africans were increasingly trapped in a vicious "guns-for-slaves" cycle. Unquestionably, some predatory states in Africa used guns to capture slaves, and the growing availability of firearms buttressed the power of warrior aristocracies whose class interests lay in perpetuating wars and slave raids. Nevertheless, guns were not always or even generally a major factor in warfare or enslavement throughout Africa; they played a secondary role in most African armies. Furthermore, even at their peak, the per capita impact of guns was never large. In addition, the militarization of African states sometimes preceded or paralleled the importation of firearms. As one historian puts it, "guns were a component of a process of military transformation that was already underway." Finally, Africans used firearms for positive as well as negative purposes: for hunting and protecting crops and persons. In all these ways, firearms were not quite the destructive force once imagined, even if they were "the most significant technological innovation to arrive from the Atlantic."[21]

New states and political arrangements arose to meet the demands of Atlantic trade. Typically, weak authorities in older kingdoms nearer the coast were the first to consolidate their power internally and to mount attacks on their neighbors. Then the peoples inland organized in self-defense and created new polities from the refugees they attracted. They consolidated their new states by integrating still more peoples whom they then conquered. The famous military states of eighteenth-century West Africa—Asante inland of the Gold Coast and Dahomey inland from Ardra on the Bight of Benin— took shape in this way. Atlantic integration encouraged a centralization of power in many polities, although political fragmentation was still the dominant feature of Atlantic Africa. Furthermore, larger states did not nec- essarily defend their interests all that much better than smaller chiefdoms and village groups, the "stateless societies" that prevailed in many parts of Atlantic Africa. Small and decentralized polities protected themselves much more effectively than once thought. Atlantic trade was not, of course, the only catalyst for political transformation. Many of the centralized states that rose and fell in West Africa were only remotely linked to the Atlantic slave trade.[22]

The forced movements of people had obvious adverse effects, but Africans were resilient. The slaving frontier tended to be intense for a gen- eration or two before moving on, usually allowing a region's population to rebound. The ethnographic map of Atlantic Africa displays impressive con- tinuities, indicating that the disappearance of ethnic groups was rare. With much guesswork, the overall population of Atlantic Africa (from Senegal to Angola) has been estimated at about 22–23 million from the late seventeenth to the late eighteenth century, perhaps dropping to no more than 20 million in 1820, reflecting the peak years of the slave trade. For the most part, then, the overall population of western Africa appears to have remained fairly stable, despite the losses of millions of people through the process of enslavement and forced migration across the Atlantic. Of course, another way of view- ing these totals, if (and it's a big if) they approximate reality, is to point out that the population of western Africa stagnated at a time when most other continents were beginning to undergo demographic growth. On the other hand, Africa largely avoided the demographic disaster that engulfed Native Americans. Indeed, African population levels may well have been affected more by climatic and epidemiological variations than by losses attributable to slaving. Yet another possibility is that the introduction of high-yield, and in some cases drought-resistant, New World cultigens—maize in the grain-growing areas and manioc, or cassava, in the forest areas—helped offset losses from the slave trade by providing Africans with a more reliable diet. Less prone to malnutrition, Africans perhaps increased their fertility. Moreover, that Africans generally retained nearly twice as many females as males among their slaves at least limited the overall demographic effect of transatlantic exports. Quite possibly, birthrates rose to compensate for the losses of men and boys. In short, not much can be said definitively about the demographic effects of the slave trade, other than that it undoubtedly slowed, even halted or reversed, population growth at least in the short term.[23]

If Africa's overall population was not drastically reduced, it was structurally altered; the social impact of the slave trade was probably more important than the purely demographic. For one thing, slavery increased in Africa as the continent was brought into greater contact with the Atlantic economy. Africans kept more of the people taken captive as slaves than they sold. Thus, the procurement of slaves for the Americas led to an enlargement of slavery within Africa. Furthermore, as slavery became an even more central institution, the status of slaves became more depersonalized, reducing the assimilative tendencies of traditional African lineage slavery. Since most of these retained slaves were women and children, the burden of work on those groups, which was already heavy, became even heavier. Furthermore, patriarchy was enhanced, as the general surplus of women encouraged the spread of polygyny. A gerontocracy emerged in which young men were the most vulnerable members of society. Societies organized around kinship, with concepts of authority resting on consensus and tradition, gave way to societies dominated by individuals who had wealth and power through their possession of followers, whether clients, servants, or slaves. The rich became richer; the poor, poorer. Social stratification intensified.[24]

The greatest direct impact of Atlantic integration on Africa was, of course, the people who were uprooted, often violently, and shipped off to the Americas. Ripped from their societies of birth, stripped of their ancestry, they encountered displacement, dishonor, and dislocation. Their fate represented a colossal human tragedy. For them, there could be no mitigation of their loss.

Diaspora

In the past couple of decades, the big question in studies of Africa's Atlantic diaspora has been the degree to which Africa or America should be placed center stage. The debate—whether construed as continuity versus discontinuity, persistence versus creation, Africa-centered versus creole-oriented models, or "homeland plus diaspora" versus "diaspora apart" approaches—has become unnecessarily polarized. African continuities were indisputably important; Africans were not entirely shorn of their cultural heritage when they stepped ashore in the New World. Yet, equally true, Africans and their descendants created much that was new in the Americas; many homeland institutions simply could not be transferred across the ocean. Africanist scholars need not be pitted against their Americanist colleagues. There is no need to label one group "survivalist" or the other "creationist." Africans did not come to the New World in uniformly homogeneous groupings or as totally heterogeneous crowds. The persistence of African elements in the New World did not have to take the form of specific ethnic institutions and rituals as opposed to more generalized beliefs and practices. Similarly, one does not have to choose between Africans as either wholly fragmented or at best generic peoples. There is considerable middle ground between the recognition of African diversity and of African shared understandings. In some places, at certain times, African ethnicities (and other aspects of their homeland heritages, it might be added) played an important role in the New World. In other places, at particular times, creolization—the rapid formation of a new hybrid culture, associated with the growth of an American-born population—was powerfully evident. To understand the history of Africans in the Americas, it is vital to study both sides of the Atlantic. Nevertheless, getting the balance right, attending to all the many variables that shaped cultural development in the New World, and paying attention to temporal and spatial variations is remarkably difficult.[25]

For one thing, there was much fluidity and dynamism in Atlantic Africa. In most early modern societies, people tended to identify with their local village, neighborhood, or larger kinship grouping, not necessarily an ethnic or protonational identity. People voluntarily entered into "supple groupings" based on everything from economic collaboration to political clientage. Most African captives arrived in the Americas, one scholar rightly notes, "not with visions of stable institutions of 'state' in their heads but rather thinking in metaphors of protective powers exercised by strong, personal patrons on behalf of loyal clients through continual *ad hoc* demonstrations of efficacy, often through metaphorical reliance on ancestors and other spiritual figures." Such political sentiments were "more flexible and transferable to the New World than...structured concepts of institutionalized states." In addition, as bases for self-identification, age, gender, skills, rank, and religion—to mention just some of the more obvious categories—might have mattered as much as ethnicity. Wolof rarely thought of themselves as Wolof, or Yorubas as Yorubas, or Igbos as Igbos. Such terms hardly existed, particularly among the respective peoples themselves. As groups came into greater contact with one another through their involvement in Atlantic trade (and, of course, through Atlantic migration), self-consciousness and cohesiveness no doubt grew; but ethnic identities still tended to be flexible and inchoate. Many Africans were bilingual or multilingual. In a sense, then, many could choose among a variety of self-identifications, and they might even switch from one to the other. In short, Africans in the early modern period had no fixed, stable sense of ethnic identity.[26]

The Middle Passage—and the process of enslavement, more generally— compounded the complications of self-identification. On the one hand, that most European slavers tended to embark slaves from just one coastal region provided a foundation for a measure of solidarity in the New World. In addition, that particular regions of the African coast established close connections with certain parts of the New World reinforced these possibilities. On the other hand, as one historian notes, slaves in Africa "experienced no single 'uprooting' through extraction from a secure, single, stable background..., but rather a series of transfers and partial and ephemeral integrations," especially as distances lengthened from increasingly remote interior regions to the coast. Why define oneself against a "home" background alone, given all these experiences? Other aspects of loading slaves along the African coast—the increased time spent acquiring a consignment of captives, the greatly widened geographic range, the preponderance of small group purchases, movements of the enslaved along the coast from one port to another—introduced a significant measure of randomization into the process. Even though most Africans (on average seven out of every eight) survived the Middle Passage, its conditions of emotional shock, physical deprivation, and cultural disorientation were profound. There is no minimizing the trauma of the Middle Passage. The development of a strong shipmate bond in many parts of the New World is a testament to the formative character of this most infamous voyage.[27]

Most ethnic identity labels were crude approximations of the complex realities of most Africans' lives. Some names such as "Coromantee" originally came from a port (in this case Kormantyn), but came to signify a broad region (the Gold Coast) where most people shared a common language (Akan). There were many Akan variants (Fante, Twi, etc.), no common name for the language in contemporary parlance, and its speakers lived in dozens of independent states. Alternatively, the label "Angola" referred to a huge region that meant different things to different people. For the Portuguese, Angola signified the area south of the Zaire River (or "Congo" River, as it was often known), most particularly the area served by the Kwanza River, with its principal port of Luanda (although also extending to the port of Benguela farther south); for northern Europeans, it was anywhere south of Cape Lopez, but most particularly the Loango Coast north of the Zaire River (the ports were Mayumba, Loango, Malimbo, Cabinda, and the Congo River mouth itself). Some identity markers such as "Ibo" or "Mandingo" referred to linguistic and cultural backgrounds much broader and vaguer than the actual communities in which people lived. The term "Mina" is perhaps the most complicated ethnic label of them all. Like "Coromantee," it originally referred to a specific town—the Portuguese São Jorge da Mina (St. George of the Mine, referring to a place where gold was exchanged, which was then corrupted to Elmina when the Dutch occupied it)—and then to the broader Gold Coast region (Costa da Mina or Coast of the Mine). In the Atlantic world, "Mina" could refer to people from the Gold Coast (mostly Akan speakers, much like Coromantee), but it also might include speakers of the Ga-Adangme languages of the eastern Gold Coast, and over time, especially in Brazil, came to refer to peoples from the Slave Coast (or Bight of Benin) to the east who were "Gbe" speakers (such languages as Ewe, Adja, and Fon), although in parts of Brazil "Minas" was an even more inclusive term, referring to all Africans or to those from Lower Guinea (western Ivory Coast to Cameroon). As one exceptionally detailed study of two ships that arrived in Costa Rica has found, the label "Mina" encompassed "members of numerous ethnic and linguistic groups."[28]

In the Americas, at particular times and in certain places, specific African backgrounds were undoubtedly salient. In the late sixteenth century, over half of all African, and two-thirds of Upper Guinea, slaves in Peru came from a 20,000-square-kilometer area stretching from the Lower Casamance to the River Kogon. The century spanning roughly 1650 to 1750 saw a strong West-Central African connection to Brazil. Accordingly, in their new Brazilian setting, Mbundu and BaKongo slaves re-created specific ritual practices such as divination ordeals, spirit possession, and funeral ceremonies that owed much to their homelands. In some cases, the connections were remarkably direct. Thus, prominent war captives from the Akan state of Akwamu in the early 1730s later led a slave revolt in Danish St. John; their plans drew on their knowledge of Akwamu statecraft. Similarly, the rebels in the Stono Rebellion in South Carolina of 1739 were probably from Kongo (not the generic "Angola," which British slave traders generally used), and their dancing, music making, and military strategies can be attributed to homeland practices. Their making for Spanish St. Augustine also might be traced to their prior homeland conversions to Catholicism. Indeed, the African escapees from the Low Country who founded Gracia Real de Santa Teresa de Mose outside St. Augustine were predominantly "Congo."[29]

In other places, African ethnicities were much less important and faded quickly. Even in seventeenth- and eighteenth-century Brazil, broad understandings transcended ethnic groups, thereby facilitating a process of

"Africanization" or inter-African syncretism that preceded or paralleled creolization, the process by which African beliefs and practices became Americanized. Such was certainly the case for the Saramakas, a Maroon group in Surinam, very much in touch with their African past, but for whom African ethnicities soon lost importance as a way of identifying individuals or as group markers. The same process applied even more thoroughly to most North American slaves. Rather than clinging to specific ethnic traits, Africans everywhere throughout the Americas inevitably drew on widely shared cultural principles, ranging from the aesthetic to the religious. These deep-level, in some cases unconscious, principles were vital resources, facilitating exchanges among Africans from many regions and ethnic groups, shaping everything from hairstyles to clothing, woodcarving to blacksmithing, music to dance, healing to conjuring.[30]

The processes by which Africans became African Americans were never simple or uniform. In many places, the earliest migrants formed a charter generation that had undue influence on later arrivals. Conversely, other groups, who arrived late in the migration process—the Yoruba are perhaps the best example—had an impact disproportionate to their numbers. Large concentrations of slaves, in towns or in certain plantation neighborhoods, facilitated the retention of African traditions. In urban centers such as Havana or Salvador in Brazil, "neo-African ethnic identities" emerged via social clubs and mutual aid societies organized along ethnic lines and through ritual events such as carnivals. Where Africans were dispersed widely in rural neighborhoods and on small farms, the process of creolization was hastened. In general, however, Africans everywhere acted pragmatically, opportunistically, and *bricoleur*-like in constructing new identities, integrating elements from many cultures.[31]

One last feature of Africa's Atlantic diaspora is notable. It was not just one-way; there was always a trickle—in some cases, more than a trickle—of Africans or people of African descent who moved east as well as west. Many Africans who went to Europe as ambassadors, traders, or students returned to their homeland, bringing their acquired knowledge of European languages and culture with them. American influences also were notable: a Brazilian, more specifically Bahian, diaspora arose on the Slave Coast. Indeed, the ethnic terminology that emerged in both Africa and the Americas actually evolved in a process of mutual interaction. It has been best documented on the Slave Coast, where Brazilian usages, particularly the use of the term "Nago," fed back into the homeland; conceivably it happened elsewhere to a lesser degree. In short, as two scholars have noted, "a dynamic and continuous movement of peoples east as well as west across the Atlantic forged diverse and vibrant reinventions and reinterpretations of the rich mix of cultures represented by Africans and peoples of African descent.on both continents."[32]

Conclusion

Africans played an important role in the early modern Atlantic. Even though Europeans initiated Atlantic trade, organized it for their benefit, and under-pinned it with their shipping technology and financial institutions, Africans participated willingly and powerfully in the new commerce. Not passive victims or unwitting dupes, they were active agents, voluntary partners, major shapers, if not actual originators, of Atlantic trade. African involve-ment in the Atlantic also affected many aspects of their world, stimulat-ing their economies, reshaping forms of social and political organization, widening the use of slaves, and heightening insecurity. Furthermore, the African diaspora was by far the largest in the early modern Atlantic. Large parts of the tropical Americas depended on the labor of Africans and their descendants. People of African descent predominated in most areas of Latin America and the Caribbean, and were significant minorities almost every-where. Small enclaves of Africans even emerged in Europe. Some of them, along with an even greater number of returnees from the Americas, made it back to Africa, further integrating the Atlantic.

At the same time, the connections between Africa and the Atlantic should not be exaggerated. For one thing, some coastal regions of Atlantic Africa were much more fully integrated into the Atlantic world than others. Furthermore, in all regions, Atlantic influences did not reach deeply into the interior. For many Africans, domestic activities went on much as before. The per capita impact of Atlantic commerce was modest, leading one expert to argue that in this period "the economy of western Africa remained little affected by trade with the Atlantic." Africans retained as many or more cap-tives within their continent as they exported. Thus an internal diaspora, at least equal in size to its Atlantic counterpart, existed within Africa. Moreover, in addition to the Atlantic diaspora, two other external diasporas existed: one across the Sahara and into the Mediterranean, and the other across the Indian Ocean into the Middle East. The Atlantic diaspora was the largest in the early modern period, but the other two were also significant. Thus, from the fifteenth to the nineteenth century, for every 100 persons who went across the Atlantic, about 50 left sub-Saharan Africa for the Mediterranean and the Indian Ocean. The Atlantic diaspora was one of many. Africa was a full partner in the emerging Atlantic world, but much of the continent was unaffected by Atlantic influences and, indeed, was oriented in other directions. In the early modern era, Africans were more important to the Atlantic world than the Atlantic world was to Africans.[33]

NOTES

1. Robert Smith, "The Canoe in West African History," *Journal of African History* [hereafter, *JAH*], 11, 4 (1970): 515–533; Jeffrey C. Stone, ed., *Africa and the Sea: Proceedings of a Colloquium at the University of Aberdeen, March 1984* (Aberdeen: Aberdeen University African Studies Group, 1985); Jean-Pierre Chaveau, "Une histoire maritime africaine est-elle possible? Historiographie et histoire de la navigation et de la pêche africaines à la côte occidentale depuis le Xve siècle," *Cahiers d'études africaines* 26 (1986): 101–102, 173–235; Robin Law, "Between the Sea and the Lagoons: The Interaction of Maritime and Inland Navigation on the Precolonial Slave Coast," *Cahiers d'études africaines* 29 (1989): 209–237; Wyatt MacGaffey, "Dialogues of the Deaf: Europeans on the Atlantic Coast of Africa," in Stuart B. Schwartz, ed., *Implicit Understandings: Observing, Reporting, and Reflecting on the Encounters Between Europeans and Other Peoples in the Early Modern Era* (New York: Cambridge University Press, 1994), pp. 249–267, especially pp. 255–257.

2. For the most up-to-date estimate, see David Eltis and David Richardson, "A New Assessment of the Transatlantic Slave Trade," in Eltis and Richardson, eds., *Extending the Frontiers: Essays on the New Transatlantic Slave Trade Database* (New Haven: Yale University Press, 2008). For just a few representative works on African infrastructure, see George E. Brooks, *Eurafricans in Western Africa: Commerce, Social Status, Gender and Religious Observance from the Sixteenth to the Eighteenth Century* (Athens: Ohio University Press, 2003); Joseph C. Miller, *Way of Death: Merchant Capitalism and the Angolan Slave Trade 1730–1830* (Madison: University of Wisconsin Press, 1988); and Phyllis M. Martin, *The External Trade of the Loango Coast, 1576–1870: The Effects of Changing Commercial Relations on the Vili Kingdom of Loango* (Oxford: Clarendon Press, 1972), and "Cabinda and Cabindans: Some Aspects of an African Maritime Society," in Stone, ed., *Africa and the Sea*, p. 84. For African ports, a useful general work is Robin Law and Silke Strickrodt, eds., *Ports of the Slave Trade (Bights of Benin and Biafra)* (Stirling, Scotland: University of Stirling Press, 1999). The best single study is Robin Law, *Ouidah: The Social History of a West African Slaving "Port" 1727–1892* (Athens: Ohio University Press, 2004). For the best estimates of Africa's Atlantic trade, see David Eltis, "Precolonial Western Africa and the Atlantic Economy," in Barbara L. Solow, ed., *Slavery and the Rise of the Atlantic System* (New York: Cambridge University Press, 1991), pp. 97–119.

3. Walter Rodney, *How Europe Underdeveloped Africa* (Washington, D.C.: Howard University Press, 1982 [1972]), especially pp. 75–113; Ralph Austen, *African Economic History: Internal Development and External Dependency* (London: J. Currey, 1987), especially pp. 81–108; see John Thornton, *Africa and Africans in the Making of the Atlantic World, 1400–1800* (New York: Cambridge University Press, 1998 [1992]), pp. 6–7, 43–71. It is not useful to assign blame, though I agree with Lansiné Kaba when he says that "white businessmen, ship owners, mariners, and plantation owners played the dominant role," but that "African merchants and rulers... actively participated in the slave trade as middlemen whose services reduced the risks for white dealers": "The Atlantic Slave Trade Was *Not* a 'Black-on-Black Holocaust,'" *African Studies Review* 44 (2001): 1–20 (quotes on 2, 8).

4. There is a large literature on this subject. For good overviews, see David Northrup, *Africa's Discovery of Europe, 1450–1850* (New York: Oxford University Press, 2002), pp. 50–69 (quotes on pp. 54–55); and David Eltis, *The Rise of African Slavery in the Americas* (New York: Cambridge University Press, 2000), pp. 137–163. For one especially fine regional perspective, see Robin Law, " 'Here Is No Resisting the Country': The Realities of Power in the Afro–European Relations on the West African 'Slave Coast,' " *Itinerario* 18 (1994): 50–64; and for an interesting snapshot of African traders at one part of the coast, see Stephen D. Behrendt and Eric J. Graham, "African Merchants, Notables, and the Slave Trade at Old Calabar, 1720: Evidence from the National Archives of Scotland," *History in Africa* 30 (2003): 37–61.

5. A. G. Hopkins, *An Economic History of West Africa* (New York: Columbia University Press, 1973), p. 109; Toyin Falola and Paul Lovejoy, eds., *Pawnship in Africa: Debt Bondage in Historical Perspective* (Boulder, Colo.: Westview Press, 1994); Paul E. Lovejoy and David Richardson, "Trust, Pawnship, and Atlantic History: The Institutional Foundations of the Old Calabar Slave Trade," *American Historical Review* [hereafter, *AHR*] 104 (1999): 333–355, "The Business of Slaving: Pawnship in Western Africa, c. 1600–1810," *JAH* 42 (2001): 67–89, and " 'This Horrid Hole': Royal Authority, Commerce, and Credit at Bonny, 1690–1840," *JAH* 45 (2004): 363–392; Robin Law, "Finance and Credit in Pre-colonial Dahomey," in Endre Stiansen and Jane Guyer, eds., *Credit, Currencies, and Culture: African Financial Institutions in Historical Perspective* (Uppsala, Sweden: Nordiska Afrikainstitutet, 1999), pp. 15–37; and Law, *Ouidah*, pp. 133–135.

6. Northrup, *Africa's Discovery of Europe*, pp. 50–106; Stanley B. Alpern, "What Africans Got for Their Slaves: A Master List of European Trade Goods," *History in Africa* 22 (1995): 5–43; George Metcalf, "A Microcosm of Why Africans Sold Slaves: Akan Consumption Patterns in the 1770s," *JAH* 28 (1987): 377–394.

7. James L. A. Webb, Jr., *Desert Frontier: Ecological and Economic Change Along the Western Sahel, 1600–1850* (Madison: University of Wisconsin Press, 1995), pp. 97–131, and "The Mid-eighteenth Century Gum Arabic Trade," *Journal of Imperial and Commonwealth History* 25 (1997): 35–58; Joseph E. Inikori, *Africans and the Industrial Revolution in England: A Study in International Trade and Economic*

Development (New York: Cambridge University Press, 2002), pp. 395–402; Law, *Ouidah*, p. 125, and "The Gold Trade of Whydah in the Seventeenth and Eighteenth Centuries," in David Henige and T. C. McCaskie, eds., *West African Economic and Social History* (Madison: University of Wisconsin Press, 1990), pp. 105–118; Paul E. Lovejoy and David Richardson, "From Slaves to Palm Oil: Afro-European Commercial Relations in the Bight of Biafra, 1741–1841," in David Killingray, Margarette Lincoln, and Nigel Rigby, eds., *Maritime Empires* (Rochester, N.Y.: Boydell Press, 2004), pp. 13–29; Ernst van den Boogaart, "The Trade Between Western Africa and the Atlantic World, 1600–1690: Estimates of Trends in Composition and Value," *JAH* 33 (1992): 369–385; and David Eltis, "The Relative Importance of Slaves and Commodities in the Atlantic Trade of Seventeenth-Century Africa," *JAH* 35 (1994): 237–249.

8. Thornton, *Africa and African*, pp. 72–125; Eltis, *Rise of African Slavery*, pp. 15–28, 57–84.

9. Winston McGowan, "African Resistance to the Atlantic Slave Trade in West Africa," *Slavery and Abolition* 11 (1990): 1–29; Ismail Rashid, "Escape, Revolt, and Marronage in Eighteenth and Nineteenth Century Sierra Leone Hinterland," *Canadian Journal of African Studies* 34 (2000): 656–683; Walter Hawthorne, "Nourishing a Stateless Society During the Slave Trade: The Rise of Balanta Paddy-Rice Production in Guinea-Bissau," *JAH* 42 (2001): 1–24; Martin A. Klein, "The Slave Trade and Decentralized Societies," *JAH* 42 (2001): 49–65; David Richardson, "Shipboard Revolts, African Coastal Violence and the Structure of the Atlantic Slave Trade," *William and Mary Quarterly* [hereafter, *WMQ*] 3rd ser. 48 (2001): 69–92; James F. Searing, " 'No Kings, No Lords, No Slaves': Ethnicity and Religion Among the Sereer-Safèn of Western Bawol, 1700–1914," *JAH* 43 (2002): 407–429; Robin Law, "Legal and Illegal Enslavement in West Africa, in the Context of the Trans-Atlantic Slave Trade," in Toyin Falola, ed., *Ghana in Africa and the World: Essays in Honor of Adu Boahen* (Trenton, N.J.: Africa World Press, 2003), pp. 513–533; Sylviane A. Diouf, ed., *Fighting the Slave Trade: West African Strategies* (Athens: Ohio University Press, 2003); Randy L. Sparks, *The Two Princes of Calabar: An Eighteenth-Century Atlantic Odyssey* (Cambridge, Mass.: Harvard University Press, 2004).

10. David Eltis and Lawrence C. Jennings, "Trade Between Western Africa and the Atlantic World in the Pre-colonial Era," *AHR* 93 (1988): 936–959, especially 942–944.

11. Thornton, *Africa and Africans*, pp. 186–192; David Eltis, "African and European Relations in the Last Century of the Transatlantic Slave Trade," in Olivier Pétré-Grenouilleau, ed., *From Slave Trade to Empire: Europe and the Colonisation of Black Africa 1780s–1880s* (London: Routledge, 2004), pp. 21–46. For slightly different groupings, see Austen, *African Economic History*, pp. 83–85; and Paul E. Lovejoy, "Ethnic Designations of the Slave Trade and the Reconstruction of the History of Trans-Atlantic Slavery," in Paul E. Lovejoy and David V. Trotman, eds., *Trans-Atlantic Dimensions of Ethnicity in the African Diaspora* (New York: Continuum, 2003), pp. 34–37.

12. David Richardson, "West African Consumption Patterns and Their Influence on the Eighteenth-Century English Slave Trade," in Henry A. Gemery and Jan S. Hogendorn, eds., *The Uncommon Market: Essays in the Economic History of the Atlantic Slave Trade* (New York: Academic Press, 1979), pp. 303–330; Eltis, *Rise of African Slavery*, pp.167–178, 299–301; for an excellent account of the African regional factors that needed to be taken into account by European traders, see Stephen D. Behrendt, "Markets, Transaction Cycles, and Profits: Merchant Decision Making in the British Slave Trade," *WMQ*, 3rd ser., 58 (2001): 171–204. For Europeans trading at one place on the African coast for items they would sell elsewhere, see Silke Strickrodt, "A Neglected Source for the History of Little Popo: The Thomas Miles Papers ca. 1789–1796," *History in Africa* 28 (2001): 293–330, especially 301; and David Eltis and Paul Lachance, "The Voyage of Venture Smith and the Historical Record of Transatlantic Slave Trading," *Slavery and Abolition* (forthcoming).

13. David Eltis and Stanley L. Engerman, "Fluctuations in Sex and Age Ratios in the Transatlantic Slave Trade, 1663–1864," *Economic History Review* 46 (1993): 308–323; G. Ugo Nwokeji, "African Conceptions of Gender and the Slave Traffic," *WMQ*, 3rd ser., 58 (2001): 47–67.

14. Herbert S. Klein et al., "Transoceanic Mortality: The Slave Trade in Comparative Perspective," *WMQ*, 3rd ser., 58 (2001): 93–117.

15. Richardson, "Shipboard Revolts."

16. Eltis, *Rise of African Slavery*, pp. 164–172, and "The Volume and Structure of the Transatlantic Slave Trade: A Reassessment," *WMQ*, 3rd ser., 48 (2001): 42; Behrendt, "Markets, Transaction Cycles, and Profits," pp. 189, 191; see some of the literature cited in note 9 for Upper Guinea resistance; for key regional studies, see Walter Rodney, *A History of the Upper Guinea Coast, 1545–1800* (Oxford: Clarendon Press, 1970); James F. Searing, *West African Slavery and Atlantic Commerce: The Senegal River Valley, 1700–1860* (Cambridge: Cambridge University Press, 1993); Boubacar Barry, *Senegambia and the Atlantic Slave Trade* (New York: Cambridge University Press, 1998); Robert M. Baum, *Shrines of the Slave Trade: Dioula Religion and Society in Precolonial Senegambia* (New York: Oxford University Press, 1999); Walter Hawthorne, *Planting Rice and Harvesting Slaves: Transformations Along the Guinea-Bissau Coast, 1400–1900* (Portsmouth, N.H.: Heinemann, 2003); and Brooks, *Eurafricans in Western Africa*.

17. Jan Vansina, "Foreword," in Linda M. Heywood, ed., *Central Africans and Cultural Transformations in the American Diaspora* (Cambridge: Cambridge University Press, 2002), pp. xi–xii; Miller, *Way of Death*.

18. Northrup, *Africa's Discovery of Europe*, pp. 56, 64–69; for a fascinating story of one female intermediary in a South African context, see Julia C. Wells, "Eva's Men: Gender and Power in the Establishment of the Cape of Good Hope, 1652–74," *JAH* 39 (1998): 417–437; Marion Johnson, "The Cowrie Currencies of West Africa," *JAH* 11 (1970): 17–49, 331–53; Law, "Finance and Credit."

19. Northrup, *Africa's Discovery of Europe*, pp. 77–90; L. M. Pole, "Decline or Survival? Iron Production in West Africa from the Seventeenth to the Twentieth

Centuries," *JAH* 23 (1982): 503–513; Marion Johnson, "Technology, Competition, and African Crafts," in Clive Dewey and A. G. Hopkins, eds., *The Imperial Impact: Studies in the Economic History of Africa and India* (London: Athlone Press, 1978), pp. 259–269.

20. Eltis, "Precolonial Western Africa," p. 118.

21. Northrup, *Africa's Discovery of Europe*, pp. 90–98 (quotes on pp. 90, 97) is an excellent summary; also see W. A. Richards, "The Import of Firearms into West Africa in the Eighteenth Century," *JAH* 21 (1980): 43–59; Robin Law, "Warfare on the West African Slave Coast, 1650–1850," in R. Brian Ferguson and Neil L. Whitehead, eds., *War in the Tribal Zone: Expanding States and Indigenous Warfare* (Sante Fe, N.M.: School of American Research Press, 1992), pp. 103–126; Thornton, *Africa and Africans*, pp. 98–125, and *Warfare in Atlantic Africa 1500–1800* (London: UCL Press, 1999), pp. 5–6, and passim.

22. Paul E. Lovejoy, *Transformations in Slavery: A History of Slavery in Africa* (New York: Cambridge University Press, 2000 [1983]), pp. 68–90; Martin Klein, "Slave Trade and Decentralized Societies," *JAH* 42 (2001): 49–65.

23. P.E. H. Hair, *Africa Encountered: European Contacts and Evidence, 1450–1700* (Brookfield, Vt.: Variorum, 1997), vol. 7, pp. 247–268, vol. 8, pp. 32–70, and vol. 9, pp. 47–73, 225–256; the demographic effects of the slave trade on Africa are controversial, and almost impossible to resolve satisfactorily—for contrasting perspectives, see Patrick Manning, *Slavery and African Life: Occidental, Oriental, and African Slave Trades* (Cambridge: Cambridge University Press, 1990), pp. 38–85; David Eltis, *Economic Growth and the Ending of the Transatlantic Slave Trade* (Oxford: Oxford University Press, 1987), pp. 64–71; and David Henige, "Measuring the Immeasurable: The Atlantic Slave Trade, West African Population and the Pyrrhonian Critic," *JAH* 27 (1986): 295–313; for the role of climate, see Joseph C. Miller, "The Significance of Drought, Disease, and Famine in the Agriculturally Marginal Zones of West Central Africa," *JAH* 23 (1982): 17–62; for food crops, see James C. McCann, *Maize and Grace: Africa's Encounter with a New World Crop 1500–2000* (Cambridge, Mass.: Harvard University Press, 2005), pp. 23–49; and James D. La Fleur, "The Culture of Crops on the Gold Coast (West Africa) from the Earliest Times to Circa 1850" (Ph.D. dissertation, University of Virginia, 2003).

24. Manning, *Slavery and African Life*, pp. 110–125, 131–134; Lovejoy, *Transformations in Slavery*, pp. 112–139; Jan Vansina, "Ambaca Society and the Slave Trade, c.1760–1845," *JAH* 46 (2005): 1–27. See also some of the essays in Joseph E. Inikori and Stanley L. Engerman, eds., *The Atlantic Slave Trade: Effects on Economies, Societies, and Peoples in Africa, the Americas, and Europe* (Durham, N.C.: Duke University Press, 1992).

25. Thornton's *Africa and Africans*, especially pp. 129–303, is the classic text emphasizing African continuities; for recent works in similar vein, see Paul E. Lovejoy, ed., *Identity in the Shadow of Slavery* (London: Continuum, 2000); James H. Sweet, *Recreating Africa: Culture, Kinship, and Religion in the African–Portuguese World, 1441–1770* (Chapel Hill: University of North Carolina Press,

2003); Lovejoy and Trotman, eds., *Trans-Atlantic Dimensions of Ethnicity*; Toyin Falola and Matt D. Childs, eds., *The Yoruba Diaspora in the Atlantic World* (Bloomington: Indiana University Press, 2004); and Gwendolyn Midlo Hall, *Slavery and African Ethnicities in the Americas: Restoring the Links* (Chapel Hill: University of North Carolina Press, 2005). For an emphasis on creolization, the classic text is Sidney W. Mintz and Richard Price, *The Birth of African–American Culture: An Anthropological Perspective* (Boston: Beacon Press, 1992); but also see Richard Price, "On the Miracle of Creolization," in Kelvin A Yelvington, ed., *Afro–Atlantic Dialogues: Anthropology in the Diaspora* (Sante Fe, N.M.: School of American Research Press, 2006), pp. 113–145, and *Travels with Tooy: History, Memory, and the African American Imagination* (Chicago: University of Chicago Press, 2007). For some recent work on diasporas, see Emmanuel Akyeampong, "Africans in the Diaspora: The Diaspora and Africa," *African Affairs* 99 (2000): 183–215; Isidore Okepewho, Carole Boyce Davies, and Ali A Mazrui, eds., *The African Diaspora: African Origins and New World Identities* (Bloomington: Indiana University Press, 2001); Kristin Mann and Edna G. Bay, eds., *Rethinking the African Diaspora: The Making of a Black Atlantic World in the Bight of Benin and Brazil* (London: Frank Cass, 2001); Patrick Manning, "Africa and the African Diaspora: New Directions of Study," *JAH* 44 (2003): 487–506; and David Eltis, Philip Morgan, and David Richardson, "Agency and Diaspora in Atlantic History: Reassessing the African Contribution to Rice Cultivation in the Americas," *AHR* 112 (2007): 1329–1358.

26. See, in particular, Joseph C. Miller, "Retention, Reinvention, and Remembering: Restoring Identities Through Enslavement in Africa and Under Slavery in Brazil," in José C. Curto and Paul E. Lovejoy, eds., *Enslaving Connections: Changing Cultures of Africa and Brazil During the Era of Slavery* (Amherst, N.Y.: Humanity Books, 2004), pp. 81–121 (quote on p. 86), and "Central Africa During the Era of the Slave Trade, c. 1490s–1850s," p. 42; Martin A. Klein, "Ethnic Pluralism and Homogeneity in the Western Sudan: Saalum, Segu, Wasulu," *Mande Studies* 1 (1999): 109–124. Pier M. Larson, *Ocean of Letters: Language, Literacy, and Longing in the Western Indian Ocean* (New York: Cambridge University Press, 2009) has implications for the Atlantic.

27. Miller, "Retention, Reinvention, and Rembering," p. 89. For the sanguine view of the Middle Passage, see Thornton, *Africa and Africans*, pp. 153–162. Most of the recent statistical work on the slave trade, sterile as it may seem, actually heightens its horror, revealing how distinctive it was in terms of crowding and mortality rates. No other migrants left with so little: Jerome S. Handler, "On the Transportation of Material Goods by Enslaved Africans During the Middle Passage: Preliminary Findings from Documentary Sources," *African Diaspora Archaeology Newsletter* (December 2006). Available at http://www.diaspora.uiuc.edu.

28. John Thornton, "The Coromantees: An African Cultural Group in Colonial North America and the Caribbean," *Journal of Caribbean History* 32, 1 and 2 (1998): 161–178, and "War, the State, and Religious Norms in 'Coromantee' Thought: The Ideology of an African American Nation," in Robert Blair St. George, ed., *Possible*

Pasts: Becoming Colonial in Early America (Ithaca, N.Y.: Cornell University Press, 2000), pp. 181–200; David Northrup, "Igbo and Igbo Myth: Culture and Ethnicity in the Atlantic World, 1600–1850," *Slavery and Abolition* 21 (2000): 1–21; also see Douglas B. Chambers, "The Significance of Igbo in the Bight of Biafra Slave-Trade: A Rejoinder to Northrup's 'Myth Igbo,'" *Slavery and Abolition* 23, 1 (2002): 101–120; Robin Law, "Ethnicities of Enslaved Africans in the Diaspora: On the Meanings of 'Mina' (Again)," *History in Africa* 32 (2005): 247–267; Hall, *Slavery and African Ethnicities*, pp. 112–125; Russell Lohse, "Slave-Trade Nomenclature and African Ethnicities in the Americas: Evidence from Early Eighteenth-Century Costa Rica," *Slavery and Abolition* 23, 3 (2002): 73–92; and Falola and Childs, *The Yoruba Diaspora*, pp. 77–110, 130–156, 231–247.

29. Stephan Bühnen, "Ethnic Origins of Peruvian Slaves (1548–1650): Figures for Upper Guinea," *Paideuma* 39 (1993): 57–110; Sweet, *Recreating Africa*, pp. 119–188; Ray A. Kea, "'When I Die, I Shall Return to My Own Land': An 'Amina' Slave Rebellion in the Danish West Indies, 1733–1734," in John Hunwick and Nancy Lawler, eds., *The Cloth of Many Colored Silks: Papers on History and Society, Ghanian and Islamic in Honor of Ivor Wilks* (Evanston, Ill: Northwestern University Press, 1996), pp. 159–193; John K. Thornton, "African Dimensions of the Stono Rebellion," *AHR* 96 (1991): 1101–1113; Mark M. Smith, ed., *Stono: Documenting and Interpreting a Southern Slave Revolt* (Columbia: University of South Carolina Press, 2005); Jane Landers, *Black Society in Spanish Florida* (Urbana: University of Illinois Press, 1999), pp. 29–60, and "The Central African Presence in Spanish Maroon Communities," in Heywood, ed., *Central Africans*, pp. 227–241.

30. Sweet, *Recreating Africa*, especially pp. 131–132; Richard Price, *First-Time: The Historical Vision of an Afro–American People* (Baltimore: Johns Hopkins University Press, 1983); for North America, compare Michael Gomez, *Exchanging Our Country Marks: The Transformation of African Identities in the Colonial and Antebellum South* (Chapel Hill: University of North Carolina Press, 1998); and Philip D. Morgan, *Slave Counterpoint: Black Culture in the Eighteenth-Century Chesapeake and Lowcountry* (Chapel Hill, University of North Carolina Press, 1998).

31. For the early formation of slave cultures and some discussion of these processes, see Mintz and Price, *The Birth of African–American Culture*; and Philip D. Morgan, "The Cultural Implications of the Atlantic Slave Trade: African Regional Origins, American Destinations, and New World Developments," *Slavery and Abolition* 18 (1997): 122–145; and Linda M. Heywood and John K. Thornton, *Central Africans, Atlantic Creoles, and the Foundation of the Americas, 1585–1660* (New York: Cambridge University Press, 2007). For the role of some latecomers, see Falola and Childs, *The Yoruba Diaspora*, pp. 1–55 and passim; Stephan Palmié, "Ethnogenetic Processes and Cultural Transfer in Afro–American Slave Populations," in Wolfgang Binder, ed., *Slavery in the Americas* (Würzburg, Germany: Königshausen & Neumann, 1993), pp. 337–363, and *Wizards and Scientists: Explorations in Afro–Cuban Modernity and Tradition* (Chapel Hill: University of North Carolina Press,

2002), especially pp. 135–144; and David H. Brown, *Santería Enthroned: Art, Ritual, and Innovation in an Afro–Cuban Religion* (Chicago: University of Chicago Press, 2003), especially pp. 25–74. Much can be learned from the processes undergone by African recaptives. For excellent accounts, see David Northrup, "Becoming African: Identity Formation Among Liberated Slaves in Nineteenth-Century Sierra Leone," *Slavery and Abolition* 27 (2006): 1–21; G. Ugo Nwokeji and David Eltis, "Characteristics of Captives Leaving the Cameroons for the Americas, 1822–37," *JAH* 43 (2002): 191–210, and "The Roots of the African Diaspora: Methodological Considerations in the Analysis of Names in the Liberated African Registers of Sierra Leone and Havana," *History in Africa* 29 (2002): 365–379.

32. Robin Law and Kristan Mann, "West Africa and the Atlantic Community: The Case of the Slave Coast," *WMQ*, 3rd ser., 56 (1999): 307–334; Robin Law, "Ethnicity and the Slave Trade: 'Lucumi' and 'Nago' as Ethnonyms in West Africa," *History in Africa* 24 (1997): 205–219; J. Lorand Matory, "The English Professors of Brazil: On the Diasporic Roots of the Yorùbá Nation," *Comparative Studies in Society and History* 41 (1999): 72–103, and *Black Atlantic Religion: Tradition, Transnationalism, and Matriarchy in the Afro–Brazilian Candomblé* (Princeton: Princeton University Press, 2005), especially pp. 1–72, 267–300; Northrup, *Africa's Discovery of Europe*, pp. 1–23, 141–185; Mann and Bay, *Rethinking the African Diaspora*, p. 1.

33. Eltis, "Precolonial Western Africa," p. 103; Pier M. Larson, "African Diasporas and the Atlantic," in Jorge Cañizares-Esguerra and Erik R. Seeman, eds., *The Atlantic in Global History 1500–1800* (Upper Saddle River, N.J.: Pearson Prentice Hall, 2007), pp. 129–149.

9

EUROPE AND THE ATLANTIC

CARLA RAHN PHILLIPS

Much of the work published by scholars of the Atlantic world has focused on the impact of European expansion—including exploration, colonization, and trade—on the other areas bordering the Atlantic Ocean. Nonetheless, the experience of that expansion also affected Europe and European peoples in profound as well as mundane ways. Examining that experience reveals numerous links between events and developments in the Atlantic world and events and developments in Europe. The problem then becomes how best to examine those links.

One useful approach might begin with important aspects of European history and then move to their relationship with the Atlantic world. This approach would focus the analysis and allow for depth as well as breadth, whether dealing with one or more European countries or with Europe as a whole. There are many aspects of European history that might lend themselves to such an approach. For example, the social and cultural structures that evolved in ancient and medieval Europe helped to shape the later experiences of Europeans overseas.[1] At the same time, the encounter with new peoples, cultures, and ecological systems overseas profoundly affected European thought and life, as did the new geographic and anthropological knowledge gained from those encounters. Experiences across the Atlantic—even if they came as hearsay rather than personal histories—inspired Europeans of all social levels to reimagine their own political and social possibilities. Many of them acted on that inspiration to emigrate to the New World, and the subsequent flows of people back and forth across the Atlantic also affected Europeans' perceptions of themselves and others. Unfortunately, the diversity of European peoples makes it very difficult to generalize about the region as a whole in matters of society and culture. For example, although Christian evangelization was a strong component of the transatlantic activities of some European states—most notably Spain—it

was much less important to others. Because of that diversity, this chapter
will instead concentrate on matters related to political and economic developments that affected the whole of Europe and that were linked closely to
the Atlantic world.

Deciding on the chronological limits of the analysis presents similar
dilemmas. The Atlantic Ocean as a physical reality and a venue for human
history can be traced back into geological time, just as Fernand Braudel so
memorably demonstrated for the Mediterranean Sea.[2] Traditionally, however, historians tend to focus on the Atlantic world from the voyages of
Christopher Columbus, or his precursors in the earlier fifteenth century,
to the end of the eighteenth century. With the political upheavals of the
late eighteenth and early nineteenth centuries—which are often dubbed the
period of the "Atlantic Revolutions"—the relationship between Europe and
newly independent lands in the Americas changed fundamentally. At the
same time, the relationship between Europe and Africa also changed, moving toward increasing European dominance of African societies. For example, during the nineteenth century automatic weaponry such as the Gatling
gun put even the strongest African monarchies at a serious disadvantage
militarily and opened the way to European conquests in parts of Africa that
had resisted European incursions in earlier times.[3] Although the concept of
an Atlantic world remains useful for understanding the nineteenth century
and beyond, it was a far different Atlantic world from the one bracketed at
one end by the fifteenth-century voyages of exploration and at the other end
by the era of the Atlantic revolutions. For that reason, this chapter will focus
on the period from about 1450 to about 1825.[4]

Politics and International Rivalries

Rivalries among European powers were present from the earliest days of
Atlantic exploration. Rulers in late medieval and early Renaissance Europe
sponsored voyages down the African coasts in hopes of finding a way eastward toward Asia and its legendary spices and other luxury goods. These
Asian dreams gained in appeal after the capture of Constantinople by the
Ottoman Turks in 1453. During the late fifteenth century, the kingdoms of
Portugal and Castile vied with one another in sponsoring voyages into the
great "Ocean Sea" that bordered their western coastlines, with Asia as their
ultimate goal. In the short term, however, those voyages had to turn a profit
one way or another, or they could not continue. Decades before Columbus
came on the scene, both monarchies sponsored expeditions that claimed

islands in the Ocean Sea in their names—Portugal in the Azores, the Cape Verdes, and the Madeiras, and Castile in the Canaries. Both Castile and Portugal would develop sugar plantations on the islands that they claimed. Similarly, both powers vied for trading opportunities with Africa in fish, grain, gold, and slaves. Without understanding that long rivalry in the Atlantic, we cannot fully understand the hard-fought wars between Portugal and Castile in the fifteenth century.

The last of those wars, occasioned by a disputed succession in Castile, ended with the Treaty of Alcáçovas-Toledo in 1479 that temporarily sorted out their rival claims in the Atlantic. Portugal agreed to restrict future exploration to the area south and east of the Canaries; Castile agreed to restrict its efforts to the area west of the Canaries. That is one of the reasons that Columbus's scheme to sail westward toward Asia had little hope of success in Portugal, where he first sought backing, and much better prospects in Castile, where Queen Isabel finally agreed to sponsor him. She and Columbus shared a vision of spreading Christianity to all peoples, as well as finding new markets and products to benefit Europe. When Columbus returned from his historic 1492–1493 voyage and was forced by a storm to sail into Lisbon, the king of Portugal carefully interrogated him to ascertain whether the lands he had found might possibly lie in the Portuguese sphere. Both Portugal and Castile subsequently appealed to Pope Alexander VI to adjudicate the matter, but the four papal bulls that he issued added to the uncertainty by responding alternately to pressure from one side or the other. The well-known Treaty of Tordesillas in 1494—the result of direct and indirect diplomacy rather than papal intervention—had more staying power and effectively regulated exploration and territorial claims in the Atlantic by the two Iberian powers. The Asian dimension of those claims need not concern us here, but it continued to shape Iberian diplomacy for several more decades.

Elsewhere in Europe, Atlantic exploration in the late fifteenth century also sprang from the desire of centralizing monarchs to enhance their prestige and diplomatic bargaining power and to develop new opportunities for production and trade. England's Henry VII had a keen interest in exploration in the North Atlantic, but he had little luck in persuading English merchants and mariners to replicate the exploratory voyages by Bristol merchants in 1480–1481. Instead, the king backed the efforts of Italians such as John Cabot and his son Sebastian, and Portuguese such as João Fernandes, João Gonsales, and Francisco Fernandes. In the first few years of the sixteenth century two Englishmen who had worked with the Cabots—Hugh Eliot and Robert Thorne—collaborated with the Portuguese in further English voyages to North America. Thus began the English quest for a northwest passage to Asia that would last well into the twentieth century and consume thousands of lives in the process. The history of English efforts to explore and colonize lands across the Atlantic brought England into persistent and unavoidable conflict with Spain and France and—to a lesser extent—Portugal and the Netherlands. The political history of England from the times of Henry VII Tudor onward can hardly be understood without considering those Atlantic rivalries.[5]

Similarly, the political history of France had an important Atlantic dimension. The Habsburg-Valois wars during the first half of the sixteenth century pitted Francis I of France against the Holy Roman Emperor Charles V Habsburg—who also reigned as King Charles I of Spain. Although historians generally focus on the European battles during those wars, French voyages of exploration across the Atlantic, and French attempts to found colonies in areas claimed by Spain, carried that struggle across the ocean. As Charles V consolidated support for his tenure as emperor, he allowed German explorers and venture capitalists into Spanish America. Revenues from the Americas allowed Charles to keep his bankers interested in extending credit and loans to him as he fought the French, the Ottomans, and the German Protestants in the 1530s and 1540s. In a very real sense, Habsburg hegemony in sixteenth-century Europe rested on the foundation of Spain's transatlantic empire; the emperor could not have maintained his ambitious and costly foreign policy in Europe without the promise of American revenues and taxes on transatlantic trade. Resistence to Habsburg power in Europe had a transatlantic dimension as well. Rival European rulers sponsored voyages of exploration, piratical raids, contraband trade, and other challenges to Spain's American claims, forcing the emperor to expend resources to meet those challenges.

Under Charles's son Philip II, that pattern continued—with variations. French rivalry became less important as France descended into civil war in the 1560s. English challenges, by contrast, became the most serious threat to Spanish claims in the Americas, as Queen Elizabeth I struggled to create a powerful state despite the divisions that resulted from England's break with the Roman Catholic Church. Challenging the power of Catholic Spain was far easier across the Atlantic, away from the European base of that power. The queen sponsored and profited handsomely from marauding ventures of men such as Francis Drake and John Hawkins that included piracy in peacetime and privateering and official naval actions in wartime. It is no exaggeration to say that the ill-fated armada that Spain sent to invade England in 1588 had its genesis in the raids of Drake, Hawkins, and other like-minded and daring Englishmen on the seas. Although not all the raids occurred in the Atlantic, their activities disrupted the Atlantic fleet system that held Spain's empire together and that enabled Philip II to acquire even greater power than his father had exercised.

In short, the Atlantic world played a key role in the late-sixteenth-century struggle between Spain and England. The converse is true as well: Anglo-Spanish rivalry played a key role in the history of the Atlantic world in the sixteenth century. English raids in the Caribbean and England's success in thwarting the 1588 armada helped the English population to define themselves as a nation and to unite in support of their charismatic queen. Whatever their differences internally, on the international scene the English nation became anti-Spanish and anti-Catholic, and the struggle with Spain for colonies and trade in the Atlantic world was crucial to that self-definition.

As for France, her merchants and mariners had launched small expeditions to Brazil since the early years of its discovery, mostly to collect brazilwood, the source of a red dye much prized in Europe's textile industries. Although Portugal's monarchs repeatedly tried to oust the French from Brazil, the demands of Portuguese trade with Africa, India, and the Spice Islands in Asia left few resources to protect claims in the Americas. French logging interests therefore remained in northeast Brazil, which the French crown called "La France Antartique," allying with Indian groups that were enemies of Portugal's local allies. Farther north, the French tried to establish a presence in Florida, but Spanish forces under Pedro Menéndez Avilés ousted them in the 1560s and established the town of St. Augustine as a permanent Spanish settlement. French merchants and explorers had far greater success in Canada, attracted by the rich fishing grounds around Newfoundland that English, Portuguese, and Spaniards were also exploiting.

After the death of Portugal's young, unmarried King Sebastian in an ill-fated expedition to Africa in 1578, the European political situation changed. Sebastian's uncle, Philip II of Spain, had the strongest dynastic claim to the Portuguese crown through his own Portuguese ancestors. He had to back up that claim militarily, in addition to confronting a rebellion in the Netherlands and trying to thwart Ottoman expansion in the Mediterranean. Nonetheless, he deemed the overlordship of Portugal and its empire important enough to make the effort. With Spain distracted and overextended, rivals such as France and the Netherlands expected less opposition across the Atlantic. Instead, Philip II grew even more determined to defend Iberian claims in the Americas. A Spanish fleet expelled the French temporarily from northeast Brazil in 1581, though they soon returned. Despite efforts by successive Habsburg kings of Spain and Portugal to thwart their incursions into Ibero-America, the French continued to work toward establishing an Atlantic empire of their own.

During the seventeenth century, the Spanish Empire continued to be firmly established in Central and South America, and the Habsburg monarchy claimed additional lands that extended far into North America. Spain's rivals in Europe knew, however, that Spanish resources and manpower were stretched too thin to defend and colonize the whole area claimed across the Atlantic by the Habsburg monarchy. Even in Europe, those resources would reach the breaking point during the Thirty Years' War (1618–1648), as Spain's kings Philip III and Philip IV poured men and money into efforts by the Austrian Habsburgs to defend their authority in central Europe and to bring Protestant Europe back into the Catholic fold. Although the major battles of the Thirty Years' War occurred in Europe, English, Dutch, and— after 1635—French vessels carried out attacks in the Americas as well. For that reason, as well as for its strong religious dimension, the Thirty Years' War is often called both the last European religious war and the first global war. In 1640 the start of a Portuguese rebellion against Habsburg rule separated the two Iberian empires and left Portuguese Brazil even more vulnerable to foreign incursions.

The upheavals of the seventeenth century in Europe provided an ideal opportunity for various European powers to amplify their presence across the Atlantic. English colonization in North America began in earnest in 1607 with the settlement of Jamestown in Virginia, after repeated earlier failures. French colonization began with Port Royal (Nova Scotia) in 1605 and Quebec in 1608, which served as a base for the fur trade. In the following decades, both English and French adventurers would establish a presence in the Caribbean as well, eventually founding permanent settlements for trade and privateering on the fringes of Spanish America. Later in the century, religious dissidents would lead several successful English colonizing efforts—for example, the Puritans in New England, the Quakers in Pennsylvania, and the Catholics in Maryland. The French government, by contrast, prevented religious minorities from settling in France's American colonies. Like the Spanish and Portuguese governments before them, Catholic France feared that the introduction of beliefs heretical in their view could endanger the souls of the local inhabitants whom they hoped to convert to Catholic Christianity.

The English Civil War in mid-century gave an added boost to English colonization overseas. Under the Protectorate established after the execution of King Charles I, Oliver Cromwell's Western Design led to the English capture of the island of Jamaica in 1655. Strategically located in the Caribbean, Jamaica served as a base for further challenges to the Spanish Empire and for the development of English trade and colonization across the Atlantic. In the last half of the century, France also exploited new opportunities to develop its presence in the Americas, promoted by King Louis XIV and able bureaucrats such as the Count of Pontchartrain. Over the course of the seventeenth century, France effectively claimed a dozen Caribbean islands, the most promising of which became plantation economies producing for the European market.

Huge deposits of gold and gems were discovered in Portuguese Brazil late in the seventeenth century, and Europe as a whole would eventually profit from the infusion of new wealth mined in Brazil. Here again, the history of Europe cannot easily be divorced from European endeavors across the Atlantic. Nowhere was that clearer than in the War of the Spanish Succession (1701–1714). Although fought mostly in Europe, this global conflict arguably had Atlantic concerns at its center. On his deathbed in 1700, the last Habsburg king of Spain, Charles II, wrote a will designating the teenaged Duke of Anjou, one of Louis XIV's grandsons, as his successor, in the hope that French power would keep the Spanish Empire intact. An anti-Bourbon coalition feared that France would gain unprecedented access to that empire and went to war to prevent the Bourbon succession. The coalition members favored an Austrian Habsburg pretender, planning to divide up the Spanish Empire if he gained the throne with their support. The allies viewed Spain itself as little more than an additional pawn in the game. Against the odds, and despite the on-again, off-again participation of France in the war, the Duke of Anjou retained the Spanish throne as Philip V, the first of the Spanish Bourbon dynasty. Under Philip V (d. 1746) and his sons Ferdinand VI (d. 1759) and Charles III (d. 1788), the Spanish Empire remained intact and attained its greatest territorial extent at the end of the eighteenth century. This required close attention to defense as well as to the bureaucratic structures that administered more than 12 million square miles of territory in the Americas. The Bourbon monarchy in Spain asserted greater control in the American empire than their Habsburg precursors, even as colonial societies gained their maturity and began to chafe at control from Europe. That same evolution marked the British colonies in the Atlantic world, though they included far fewer people and far less territory.[6] The French colonies remained more tightly linked to the mother country as political dependencies, which may have affected the evolving colonial societies they created in America.

The areas claimed by various European powers in North America and the Caribbean held a diverse mix of peoples and ethnicities, trading with one another across the indistinct and permeable borders between colonies. Modern approaches often stress the intertwined histories of those colonies, relegating their connections with one European power or another to secondary importance. Nonetheless, European states in the eighteenth century continued to project their rivalries across the Atlantic, working to undercut the authority of rival powers, and enticing settlers from outside their own colonies to shift their residence and their loyalties. This dynamic process characterized British, French, and Spanish territories in North America and the Caribbean through much of the eighteenth century. In the heart of the vast Spanish Empire, rivals were in no position to challenge Spain's political authority, but commercially Spain's rivals, especially Britain, came to dominate much of the trade to and from Spanish America.

In North America, the rivalry between Britain and France gained intensity as both countries grew in wealth, population, and power. Repeated skirmishes in what would become Canada, in the Ohio Valley, and in the Mississippi Valley, marked the first half of the century. In 1756 the global conflict called the Seven Years' War in Europe, and the French and Indian War in North America, began with Anglo-French engagements in the Ohio Valley. When the war ended, Britain took over all of French North America, gained Florida at the expense of Spain, and ousted the French from India, half a world away, setting the stage for British hegemony in the nineteenth century. Some of the French colonists in Canada went to the Caribbean at the end of the Seven Years' War. Others, captured and forced into exile, ended up in Louisiana, which France had ceded to Spain in 1762.

When Britain's North American colonies rebelled in 1776, France supported the rebels and brought its treasury close to bankruptcy in the process. The French government's financial embarrassment thereafter was a major precipitant of the French Revolution, which arguably affected all of subsequent European history. Spain also aided the North American rebels, both because of diplomatic alliances between the two Bourbon powers, and because both defined Britain as the enemy. Because Spanish forces won crucial engagements against the British in Florida and the Gulf Coast, Spain was able to demand the return of Florida by the terms of the treaty that ended the American Revolution in 1783. Spain's Count of Aranda negotiated the treaty in Paris, but he nonetheless feared that the new American colossus would soon view Spain's American colonies as likely candidates for takeover. Aranda was correct in the long run. In the short run, a more imminent threat loomed. The disruptions and wars entrained by the French Revolution and the rise of Napoleon Bonaparte had an important transatlantic dimension, involving rival pretensions to islands in the Caribbean,

Spanish Florida, and the huge Louisiana Territory. During those wars, Spain came to rely heavily on loans from New Spain (Mexico), a pattern that had begun several decades earlier.[7] When the Napoleonic Wars ended in 1815, Spain had lost Louisiana and several Caribbean islands, and several political leaders in parts of Spanish America had declared their independence. Others would follow, disillusioned with the restored constraints of empire. Devastated politically and economically by decades of global warfare, Spain could not stem the rebellions. Britain, France, and other European countries watched the unfolding drama across the Atlantic with great interest, as did the United States, looking for ways to profit from the upheaval, or at least to prevent their rivals from profitting. In 1819, Spain ceded Florida to the United States, and by the 1820s nearly all of Spanish America had broken away, after more than three centuries of imperial rule. Eventually, some two dozen republics, with upwards of 15 million people, would take form in the former Spanish empire, politically independent but still linked in important ways to European politics and transatlantic trade and diplomacy.[8]

The colonial map of the Americas took shape with reference to the political and diplomatic map of Europe, along with its spatial contours. Spain and Portugal were ideally placed—geographically, politically, and historically— to pioneer in the exploration of the Central and South Atlantic. They got to the Americas first, defended their exclusive claims to the lands in the Southern Hemisphere, and managed to hold off rival claimants for more than three centuries. Their European rivals did not establish a serious presence in the Americas until the seventeenth century, and then only beyond the borders of the Iberian sphere. Little changed on the colonial map of the Americas until the colonies broke free from their European overlords.

This brief survey of the period from the mid-fifteenth century to the early nineteenth century has traced the connections between the Atlantic world and the political and diplomatic history of Europe. Although it has concentrated on the actions of a few major rivals for colonies in the Americas—Spain, Portugal, France, and Britain—the Atlantic world involved virtually every European state to one degree or another. The political and diplomatic history of Europe as a whole was linked inextricably to rivalries and conflicts in the transatlantic world.

European Economic Trends and Atlantic Interactions

From the earliest days of Atlantic exploration, trade generated the profits that allowed European colonial ventures to continue, even as they enriched the home economies. That was as true for Portuguese voyages down the Atlantic coast of Africa in the early fifteenth century as it was for later transatlantic voyages. Once regular contacts developed connecting Europe, Africa, and the Americas, the trades related to the Spanish and Portuguese empires were far and away the most important to the Atlantic world as a whole. Virtually all of Europe participated in those trades to some extent, however indirectly. In other words, from decades before Columbus, the European economy was linked to ventures into the Atlantic world.

Three long periods of development in European economic history provide ideal cases in point: the unprecedented expansion of the sixteenth century; the depression of the seventeenth century; and the explosive boom of the eighteenth century. Although these developments have sometimes been discussed with minimal reference to the Atlantic world, transatlantic trade was intimately connected to all of them, and a new generation of scholarship is discovering the complexity of those connections. Europe's economic history also includes the movement of peoples across the Atlantic, both as permanent migrants to the Americas and as temporary sojourners who brought their experiences across the ocean into the European consciousness. The transatlantic movements of goods and peoples shaped European economy and society as much as they shaped the evolution of America.

In 1503, between Columbus's third and fourth voyages, the Spanish monarchs founded the House of Trade in Seville to oversee all aspects of transatlantic commerce, migration, and communication to what they called "the Indies." By the 1520s nearly a hundred ships each year carried cargoes and migrants to and from colonies in New Spain (Mexico) and Tierra Firme (South America). Together, the ships represented about 9,000 *toneladas* of carrying capacity, each *tonelada* being about 1.42 cubic meters. By the late sixteenth century, a yearly average of 150–200 ships participated in the Indies trade each year, with a total capacity of about 30,000–40,000 *toneladas*. In other words, the number of ships had doubled since the 1520s, and their average size had also doubled, leading to a fourfold increase in carrying capacity. For comparison, Fernand Braudel estimated that there were about 350,000 tons of shipping capacity in the Mediterranean in the late sixteenth century, and 600,000–700,000 tons in the Atlantic for all maritime activities, including fishing.[9]

In the late sixteenth and early seventeenth centuries, a regular guard squadron of six to eight armed warships called *galeones* (galleons) usually accompanied the Tierra Firme fleet; the New Spain fleet had a smaller escort of two galleons. After a trade fair at Portobelo in Panama, the Tierra Firme squadron carried royal tax revenues back to Spain, escorting the previous year's merchant fleet on that dangerous route and trying to evade the pirates and privateers that lay in wait at both ends. Although the system of convoys and escorts was not as all-inclusive as its planners intended, it still accounted for about 85 percent of the trade. Even when Spain abolished the convoys in the late eighteenth century, 85–90 percent of the trade continued to follow the same timing and trajectories, which had proven ideal for sailing conditions in the Atlantic.[10]

Spain's Atlantic trading system was fed by production in the Indies, which the colonizers had reorganized from traditional patterns to suit the needs of international commerce. Livestock introduced from Europe multiplied easily in the New World, which had few domestic animals, and no cattle, horses, pigs, or sheep, before Spaniards brought them across the Atlantic. Soon hides and tallow became major exports for the transatlantic trade. Other important exports eventually included sugar, indigo (a blue vegetable dyestuff), cochineal or *grana* (a red dyestuff derived from small insects), exotic woods for construction and dyemaking, and a wide range of aromatic and medicinal plants, either native to the Americas or introduced there for export production.[11]

The total value of all European trade with the Spanish Indies is very difficult to quantify, because the volume of goods shipped could fluctuate widely from year to year as merchants tried to adjust supply and demand in a trade that required one to three years for a round trip. The volume of bullion and coinage shipped for the Spanish Crown and private individuals could also vary considerably from year to year. To provide a gross estimate of the volume and value of Spain's transatlantic trade, the modern French historian Pierre Chaunu used figures for taxes on imports and exports. A generation after Chaunu, scholars in Spain such as Modesto Ulloa, Eufemio Lorenzo, and Antonio García-Baquero also relied heavily on those tax figures. They suggest a total value for the transatlantic trade of nearly 450 million *maravedís* a year in the early 1560s, rising to about 850 million in the early 1590s. To put the figures in context, the ordinary tax revenue collected by the Spanish Crown in Castile in the mid-sixteenth century was about 500 million *maravedís* a year.[12] The merchandise, treasure, and foodstuffs shipped back and forth in Spain's Atlantic trading system involved all of Europe and added an imporant component to Europe's commercial life.

Official figures for individual products allow historians to document the trade from about 1550 on. By the early 1560s, the Caribbean islands and New Spain exported about 30,000 hides a year to Europe. By the early 1570s, the number had risen to about 83,000, and by the early 1580s, to perhaps 150,000, with an average value of 78 million *maravedís* a year. The imported hides ended up not only in footwear, saddlery, furniture, and other traditional manufactures, but also as wall coverings—tanned and intricately tooled. Exports of sugar from Spanish America at the same time were worth a bit more than half as much as hides—some 40 million *maravedís* per year. The exports of sugar from Spanish America in the 1580s show a yearly average of about 32,000 *arrobas*[13] in 1581–1585, but only about 10,000 in 1586–1590, at a time when the Spanish colonies were under attack from pirates. Figures for indigo exports do not become available until the late 1570s, averaging between 1,000 and 2,000 *arrobas* each year until the end of the century, but they were worth nearly as much as sugar in an ordinary year—about 30 million *maravedís*. One of the most valuable single items exported from Spanish America to Europe was cochineal, estimated at about 125 million *maravedís* a year in the late sixteenth century, or nearly 42 percent of all the trade goods (not including treasure) shipped from the Indies. The price of cochineal varied from year to year, but the quantity sent to Europe rose fairly steadily, from about 1,800 *arrobas* in the late 1550s to about 8,000 in the late 1580s. The rapidly growing textile industries of Europe provided a ready market for the dyestuffs in Iberian America, from the brazilwood of Brazil and the Campeche wood of New Spain, to cochineal, indigo, and other plant-based materials. Some textile areas in Europe prohibited the import of these new products because they competed with traditional sources for textile dyes, but the market found a way around the prohibitions.

The most valuable, as well as the most famous, exports from the Indies were not trade goods, but the gold, silver, pearls, and precious stones that constituted the "treasure" of the Indies. Gold dominated treasure exports during the early sixteenth century, based at first on plunder during the conquest of the Aztec and Inca empires and then on panning operations and mining. Several important goldfields were discovered in northern South America in the 1530s and 1540s, and exports of gold reached a peak in the 1550s, with a registered volume of over 4,200 kilos per year entering Spain and passing from there into the monetary system of Europe as a whole. Gold production and exports fell off sharply in the late sixteenth century. Some of the gold produced in the Indies stayed there to finance the growth of the colonies, but, judging from the large gap that scholars have found between estimates of production and figures for registered imports, considerable gold presumably was smuggled into Europe outside the official registers. By the nature of things, it is very difficult to estimate the magnitude of the smuggling, though generations of scholars have tried to do so.[14]

Along with gold, several deposits of silver were discovered in northern South America in the 1530s and 1540s, leading to registered exports of nearly 18,000 kilos per year in the early 1540s. Then in 1545, discovery of the mountain of silver at Potosí in the Viceroyalty of Peru (modern Bolivia) ushered in the silver cycle of Spain's transatlantic trading system. The Potosí mines proved to be among the richest the world has ever known, although their location above 12,000 feet in the Andean highlands made mining extremely difficult for the miners and expensive for the mine owners. The initial flush of the Potosí discovery produced nearly 85,000 kilos of silver each year during the late 1540s, and production reached a peak of nearly 280,000 kilos in the late 1580s. Silver exports to Europe began modestly in the 1520s, rising to some 18,000 kilos per year in the 1540s, before the great boom. Once Potosí went into production, silver exports surged to 94,000 kilos, in the 1560s, 112,000 in the 1570s, and 271,000 in the 1590s, far outstripping gold in both volume and value.

About 20–30 percent of the registered bullion that crossed the Atlantic belonged to the Spanish Crown. The single most valuable source of royal income was the tax called "the royal fifth" on mining production in Tierra Firme, plus fees for assay and coinage, which together made up about 60 percent of the royal share between 1555 and 1600. Another 8 percent of the royal share came from ecclesiastical taxes that had been transferred to the Crown by the Roman Catholic Church. Penalties and condemnations for smuggling, the sale of offices, and various minor taxes made up the balance of the 20–30 percent of registered treasure that belonged to the Crown. The other 70–80 percent of the bullion crossing the Atlantic belonged to merchants and other private individuals.

Unregistered private treasure undoubtedly added to those totals. Private individuals were anxious to avoid taxes, but even more, they wanted to avoid the possibility of confiscation of their trading profits. From time to time in the mid-sixteenth century and thereafter, successive kings of Spain confiscated incoming treasure to pay pressing bills in wartime. The owners of the treasure were compensated with interest-paying government bonds, but that hardly made good the loss of their capital. Although this drastic action did not happen often, the threat was enough to make many private individuals risk dire penalties to avoid registration. The law-abiding citizens who dutifully registered their treasure were thus left to pay a larger share of taxes for defense of the Indies fleets. That inequity induced even more private citizens to become smugglers. The total of smuggled bullion and other valuables is ultimately unknowable, though many scholars have tried to estimate it for various periods. One careful investigation of fraud concluded that about 10 percent of the treasure that arrived in Europe in the late sixteenth century never appeared in the registers. Other estimates range far higher, and it is clear that the level of smuggling could vary widely, depending on changing circumstances. By the late sixteenth century, increasing amounts of treasure mined in Spanish America stayed there to fund both public and private needs in the growing colonies. Moreover, from the late 1560s, much American silver flowed toward Asia to finance the new trans-Pacific trade.[15] With these points in mind, the estimate of a 10 percent underregistration for treasure remittances to Spain in the late sixteenth century seems plausible enough, but that generalization cannot be extended to other periods.

Spain's ambitious foreign policy in Europe during the reigns of Charles V and Philip II would have been impossible to fund without revenues from the Atlantic world, even though they constituted less than 20 percent of the Crown's total income. The enormous growth in the European economy during the sixteenth century was also related to the profits from transatlantic trade, but historians and economists continue to argue about the nature of that relationship. An earlier generation of economic historians credited the boom above all to infusions of bullion from the Americas, following the work of Earl J. Hamilton. Later research has complicated that picture considerably, in particular by considering the effects of population growth and production within Europe. Some historians have argued against any important role for transatlantic trade in fostering European growth. Nonetheless, the creation of the Atlantic world undoubtedly provided new venues for trade and colonization for Europe's rising population, and American bullion undoubtedly added to the European money supply. During the sixteenth century, Europe experienced an unprecedented fivefold inflation (often called the "Price Revolution"), and it seems likely that American bullion enabled prices to rise that high in response to the pressure generated from increased population, production, and the intensification of markets in Europe.[16]

As for migration, the pioneering work of Peter Boyd-Bowman and others calculated that some 450,000 people registered to emigrate from Spain to Spanish America from the late 1400s to about 1650, with the highest rates occurring in the late sixteenth century. Some scholars estimate that unregistered emigration could bring the total several times higher, but the general consensus is that some 4,000–5,000 migrants each year crossed the Atlantic from Spain during the early colonial period. Most of the registered migrants came from the heartland of the Kingdom of Castile in the center, west, and south of the Iberian Peninsula.[17] Spain had a population of about 8.5 million in 1600, and it is arguable that migration to Spanish America helped relieve some of the population pressure that had built up by the late sixteenth century.

The earliest migrants from Spain to Spanish America were almost exclusively male, most of them unmarried and relatively young, and many of them ecclesiastics, sent across the ocean to convert the Indians to Christianity as well as to serve the religious needs of Spaniards in the colonies. Nonetheless, contrary to persistent assumptions, women and families played a continuing and important role in Spanish migration across the Atlantic. From the earliest days, the Crown encouraged whole families to migrate and urged bureaucrats, in particular, to bring their wives and families with them. This policy not only fostered social stability in the colonies, but it also discouraged Crown officials from dividing their loyalties by marrying into local families. Women accounted for 5.6 percent of legal emigrants for 1493–1519, 6.3 percent for 1520–1539, 16.4 percent for 1540–1559, 28.5 percent (60 percent single) for 1560–1579, and 26 percent (59.5 percent single) for 1580–1600. There was considerable regional variation in these numbers; for example, in the seventeenth century, women accounted for 51 percent of registered emigrants from southern Spain.[18] The large number of migrants, and natural increase among peoples of mixed Spanish, Indian, and African heritage in Spanish America, helped to offset the early catastrophic mortality in the Indian population due to conquest and disease.

Economic and migratory trends for Portuguese Brazil followed a somewhat different trajectory from Spanish America. Through much of the sixteenth century, Portuguese trading profits from Brazil centered on forest products such as brazilwood, but the total volume of that trade was minuscule compared to Portuguese trade with Asia for spices and other luxury goods. Moreover, very few permanent settlers migrated from Portugal to Brazil in the first few decades after 1500. In the 1530s, there were only about 2,000 Portuguese in Brazil, along with some 4,000 African slaves. As the sixteenth century progressed, the Portuguese began to use increasing numbers of African slaves in an expanding plantation economy, producing largely for the European market. By the late sixteenth century the total population of Brazil numbered about 57,000—some 44 percent of them Portuguese—but it is not clear how many—if any—native peoples figured in that count.[19]

As other Europeans expanded their presence in the Atlantic world, they participated in trade with the Iberian colonies through official channels in Seville and Lisbon; they also found ways to avoid the official channels through interloping into Spanish and Portuguese colonial trade. English and French explorers and merchants, with the support of their governments, tried to establish their own profitable ventures in both North and South America, despite having to contend with attacks from hostile Indians and from Spanish and Portuguese forces. By the late sixteenth century, ships from England, the Netherlands, and France made regular voyages across the Atlantic, and a few had managed to make their way into the Pacific as well, challenging the control claimed by Spain and Portugal over all contact with the Americas. However, very few Europeans from outside Iberia migrated as settlers to the Americas during the sixteenth century.

The first expansive phase of Atlantic trade lasted until about the first decade of the seventeenth century. Figures for Spain's Indies fleets reached their peak in 1609; thereafter, the total size of the fleets and their cargoes entered a steep decline that lasted for much of the rest of the century. As bullion imports into Europe fell, a Dutch writer observed that combined plant and animal products from the Indies exceeded the more famous gold and silver in value.[20] Nonetheless, the flow of silver from the Americas to Europe remained impressive. It continued to play a major role in Europe's internal and external trade and in funding the periodic wars among European states.

The downturn in transatlantic trade coincided with what is often called the "seventeenth-century crisis" in the European economy. Scholars generally use the term "crisis" to mean a turning point, or a reversal of fortunes, and they seem to understand it as a temporary condition. Controversy about the characteristics of the seventeenth-century crisis—and even about its existence—is ongoing in debates that often center on the divide between economic (generally Marxian) and political historians.[21] Political and economic realities were inextricably connected in the seventeenth century, however, and it makes little sense to exclude one or the other from the analysis. Depending on where we look in Europe, the crisis varied in magnitude and duration; some areas may have escaped its effects altogether, while a few others prospered as their neighbors faltered—for example, the northern Netherlands.

Many economic historians who think there was a seventeenth-century crisis, or at least some sort of economic downturn, have sought its explanation in bullion flows and price differentials. The long European inflation of the sixteenth-century, fueled in part by bullion flows from the New World, meant that the relative value of silver in Europe declined. As silver lost value, New World mines eventually became less profitable to operate, and production declined. Other historians focus on trade rather than bullion as the crucial variable, seeing prices largely as reflections of shifts in trade. According to this argument, the migration of Europeans around the globe encouraged long-distance trade to take advantage of global price differences. Once regular trade was established, price differences tended to even out. That created a situation in which the diminished value of silver in Europe discouraged transatlantic exchanges. Explanations based primarily on bullion flows and prices can be misleading, given the complexities of the Atlantic world as a whole. There is little question, however, that the volume and value of trade between Europe and Spanish America suffered a decline in the early seventeenth century, and that many areas in Europe experienced an economic crisis at more or less the same time. It is reasonable to conclude that the two phenomena were related, though historians continue to debate the issue, focusing on themes as diverse as climate change and consumer preferences.

Economic developments in Europe related to Brazil followed a somewhat different path. During the period of Spanish-Portuguese union (1580–1640), Brazil was effectively developed as a colony and linked by intensified trade to Europe and Africa.. Portuguese bureaucrats viewed outward migration with great misgivings, because the total population of Portugal numbered only about two million in 1600. Nonetheless, they encouraged permanent settlement, especially of family units, to develop the colony. Recent scholars estimate that some 100,000 Portuguese migrated across the Atlantic in the period from 1500 to 1700, and nearly all of them settled in Brazil. Unlike the Portuguese luxury trades to Asia, the Brazilian trade continued to feature high-volume, low-priced goods, especially brazilwood and various aromatic woods and construction timber. Settlers developed sugar production on large plantations during the late sixteenth century, and sugar rapidly became the most valuable item among Brazil's exports, even more valuable than gold. Sugar production had a multiplier effect on the development of the colony as a whole, because it required capital investment for mills and slave labor. Ordinarily, labor is considered an expense, not a capital investment. In the case of a slave economy, however, the labor force is owned like other capital goods. In addition to profiting from the labor of slaves in Brazil, Portugal held the contract (*asiento*) for supplying slaves to Spanish America on and off from 1573 to 1676, which generally produced profits for the contractors.[22]

In Europe, speculation based on sugar prices generated profits and new plantations in Brazil. Although individual plantations were not always profitable, the trade in sugar provided a bright spot in a transatlantic economy that was generally depressed in the middle third of the seventeenth century. As their Brazilian colony developed, the Portuguese increased their domestic production of salt, fish, wine, and oils to keep up with rising demand at home and abroad, and financed purchases to cover shortfalls in their wheat and meat production with the profits from imperial trade. In other words, the Portuguese domestic economy became closely linked to the world of Atlantic exchanges.

Portuguese control of Brazil did not go unchallenged, however. The Dutch captured and held important sugar-producing areas in the northeast from about 1624 to about 1654, exporting some 48,000 *arrobas*[23] annually in 1631–1635 and about 298,000 *arrobas* annually in 1641–1645. Dutch exports of sugar from Brazil fell abruptly to about 40,000 *arrobas* in 1646–1651. In the areas remaining under Portuguese control, production and exports likely declined as well, but the data are too sparse to be sure. Nonetheless, the figures available suggest that the profitability of Brazilian sugar production and trade in general were affected by the crisis in the European economy. For the most part, early Dutch settlements in the Americas were commercial enclaves rather than permanent colonies, and they were treated as interlopers by Spanish and Portuguese authorities. The Dutch presence in the Atlantic world never surpassed 15,000 settlers, even at its peak, and only 10,000 of those settlers came from the Netherlands.

The cultivation of tobacco in Brazil followed many of the same patterns as sugar, although it began later. Seventeenth-century Europeans quickly developed a liking for tobacco, which Columbus and his men first encountered in Cuba. In the seventeenth century, tobacco fetched a good price in Europe, as well as in the West African slave trade, then dominated by the Dutch. As long as the Dutch remained in northeast Brazil, they took full advantage of their position, producing for the European market, preying on Portuguese and Spanish shipping in the Caribbean, and importing slaves from their bases in West Africa. These efforts seem to have been repaid by handsome profits in the short term, but they could not be sustained in the face of revolts, rising costs, and pressure from Spain and Portugal. When the Dutch left Brazil in 1654, they carried their sugar and tobacco operations with them to the Lesser Antilles.[24]

France, in addition to having its own ambitions in Brazil, was the most important trading partner of Portugal for most of the seventeenth century, especially in the 1670s. Although Portugal and France exported many of the same products, for a time their bilateral trade prospered. France sent grain and hides south in exchange for salt and exotic re-exports from Brazil and the Far East. Once France established tropical colonies of its own in the Caribbean, it had no further need for Portugal's colonial production, and their bilateral trade declined. Portugal then turned to other countries, especially England, for the cloth, hides, and agricultural products formerly supplied by France. English support for Portugal's rebellion against Habsburg rule (1640–1668) laid the groundwork for increasing English influence in the trade with Brazil, and an increasing influence in Portuguese affairs as well.

By about 1670, the growth in colonial production by other European states seems to have had a downward effect on prices in Lisbon. Sugar prices fell by more than half between 1650 and 1688, and tobacco prices fell by almost three-quarters. Although European prices in general were falling at the same time, the declines for sugar and tobacco were much steeper. Portugal's trade also suffered because of the general downturn in Spanish–American trade. With less silver entering Seville, less went to Lisbon as well, and Dutch vessels made fewer stops in Lisbon and Setúbal than before. The Portuguese government had little success in trying to keep foreign goods out of Lisbon. Efforts to stimulate internal manufactures were more effective, and a devaluation of the currency made Portuguese goods cheaper for foreign buyers. The Portuguese also founded a company in 1685 for the purchase of slaves, one of the few still-profitable aspects of their transatlantic trade in that period.

One of the early comprehensive analyses of the seventeenth-century crisis—the Marxian interpretation of Eric Hobsbawm—defined a key role for the transatlantic context and for the long-term importance to the European economy of profits from colonial trade and exploitation. As settlers in British America increased both their own population and its integration into transatlantic trade, merchants and entrepreneurs on both sides of the Atlantic prospered, but especially those in England.[25] In addition to trade with her own colonies, England benefited from both official and clandestine trade with Spanish America and Portuguese Brazil. According to Hobsbawm, the combined profits from colonial trade allowed England to emerge from the crisis of the seventeenth century—which he defined as a crisis in "feudal production"—strengthened and ready to industrialize.[26]

Following Hobsbawm's lead, André Gunder Frank and Immanuel Wallerstein developed models of a coercive and extractive relationship between Europe and other areas around the globe. According to those models, immense profits flowed into European hands, providing the capital that led in the long term to European industrialization, and locking areas overseas into a pattern of dependency and underdevelopment.[27] Although such all-inclusive models held a certain appeal among scholars for a decade or more, they also attracted a steady barrage of criticism for their broad generalizations. More recent work has used a variety of statistics and other concrete evidence to analyze the profitablility of European empires and the role that imperial profits played in European economic development. Scholars now recognize that imperial profits must be examined in their full context, particularly during difficult periods such as the seventeenth-century. With regard to the start of industrialization in Britain, in 1982 Patrick O'Brien took the extreme view that transatlantic profits played a minor role in the industrializing process, whereas Kenneth Pomeranz and others later reverted to the older notion that Britain derived substantial benefits from colonial production all over the Americas. As for the Spanish Empire, the available figures suggest that, although Spain clearly benefited from empire over the long term, the level of profits was far lower and more erratic than historians used to assume.[28]

The issue is further complicated by the ups and downs of the European economy and the volume of transatlantic trade, both of which turned upward again toward the end of the seventeenth century. The two phenomena were presumably related, though here again historians continue to debate the precise nature and timing of that relationship. Properly speaking, European economic expansion in the eighteenth century related more to global trade than to transatlantic trade alone, though the eighteenth century saw particularly important changes in the Atlantic world. One such change was the discovery of gold and diamonds in Brazil in the 1680s and 1690s, notably in the district that would become Minas Gerais.[29] The development of mining production in Brazil had immediate and far-reaching consequences for the Atlantic world, one of which was to increase the market demand for slaves from Africa. The rapid development of Brazil in the eighteenth century also attracted a greatly increased flow of migrants from Portugal. Scholars estimate that as many as a half million Portuguese emigrated to Brazil in the eighteenth century. Even allowing for exaggeration, the quickened pace of emigration may help to explain why the Portuguese population rose from two million in 1700 to only two and three-quarter million by 1800, while populations in other European countries soared.

In addition to Brazil, the plantation economies elsewhere in North and South America and the Caribbean also increased their demand for slave labor in the eighteenth century. As a consequence, the transatlantic trade in slaves rose enormously, integrating West Africa more fully into the Atlantic world, but at a terrible human cost. Efforts to analyze the volume and impact of the slave trade have occupied generations of scholars. Current estimates for the forced migration of Africans to the Americas range from about five million to ten million or more in the period before 1800, the vast majority of them in the eighteenth century.[30] European merchants reaped much of the benefit from that dismal traffic in human beings, and their profits flowed toward further expanding the slave economies in the Americas and the agrarian and manufacturing economies in Europe.

The volume of shipping traffic in Lisbon provides clear evidence for the expansion of overall trade in the eighteenth century, when Portugal's capital served as an emporium for all of Europe, and indeed for the world. In the early 1720s, an average of 609 ships a year visited the port; in the early 1730s, an average of 945 ships sailed in and out of Lisbon each year. Although the Portuguese benefited from the trade that passed through their capital city, they were by no means in sole control of it. In a typical year, at least half of the ships frequenting Lisbon were English, and English merchants acquired an estimated two-thirds of the gold that arrived in Portugal, in exchange for cloth and other trade goods.[31]

Brazilian gold also flowed into Amsterdam and Seville to finance trade, and from there to the rest of Europe, altering the relative value of gold and silver in the process. In 1703 alone, imports of Brazilian gold surpassed the total that the Portuguese had ever obtained in Mina and Guinea in West Africa, or that Spain had obtained annually from its American colonies in the sixteenth century. By the second decade of the eighteenth century, Brazilian gold far surpassed all of those sources combined. At the peak of the gold trade in 1741–1760, Brazil sent an average of 14,600 kilos of gold to Europe each year.[32] This enormous influx of bullion would continue from 1695 to about 1770, when it entered a half-century of depression. The imports of Brazilian gold presumably helped to fuel the expansion of European production and trade in the eighteenth century.

The benefits that Europe derived from the output of mines, agricultural and manufacturing production, and trade to and from America varied greatly from country to country. For example, although the Spanish Empire in America was huge, by the late eighteenth century far less tax revenues and profits from production were sent to Spain than remained in Spanish America, where they supported the economic development of colonies that by then included some 15 million people. By contrast, exports from the single French plantation colony of Saint-Domingue were worth nearly as much as the exports from all of Spanish America, because Saint-Domingue was a slave economy producing almost exclusively for the European market.[33]

In the French Caribbean, slaves from Africa and their descendants made up some 90 percent of the population by the late eighteenth century, and their production had fueled an eighteenfold increase in French colonial trade. Given the huge population of France—some 22 million in 1700—French migration to the Americas presumably had little effect on demographic development in France, except perhaps to slow the effects of rapid growth in the eighteenth century. When Great Britain took over French Canada at the end of the Seven Years' War in 1763, there were perhaps 60,000 people living there, a population that had grown fourfold since 1700. Very little of that growth came from migration, however, but instead resulted from the natural increase of a resident population willing to adapt to the harsh climate. On the French islands in the Caribbean, by contrast, tropical diseases took such a high toll that only a steady stream of new arrivals allowed the European settler population to grow. By the end of the eighteenth century, there were perhaps 50,000 French settlers in the Caribbean, though as many as 200,000 French may have immigrated there in the course of the seventeenth and eighteenth centuries.

Migration to the Americas from Great Britain and other areas in Europe showed a similar disparity between mainland and island destinations. Mainland destinations in British America were farther to the south and much more hospitable to European migrants than French Canada. With abundant land, the population in British America, as in Spanish and Portuguese America, grew largely through natural increase, with a small infusion of new migrants from Europe and a much larger infusion of migrants from Africa. Overall, during the seventeenth and eighteenth centuries, some 425,000 migrants left the British Isles for North America—an average of about 2,000 per year, plus smaller numbers from elsewhere in Europe, notably the Germanies (103,000).[34] By the end of the eighteenth century, the fledgling United States included about 3.9 million people, over half of British ancestry. Considering that the British Isles held about 6.25 million people in 1600 and 16 million in 1800, the out-migration of a few thousand people each year presumably did not have much effect on the sending areas. The economic importance of migration lay, rather, in the formation of a lucrative and growing market that linked both sides of the Atlantic.[35]

In the last half of the twentieth century, Hobsbawm, Frank, Wallerstein, and a host of others argued that the first three centuries of transatlantic trade funneled extraordinary profits into European coffers, laying the groundwork for European industrialization, first in Britain and then elsewhere in western Europe. Others denied the importance of transatlantic profits for European economic development. Few scholars today would agree with either of those unnuanced views, arguing instead for the complexity of transatlantic exchanges, and the active participation and profit-making of peoples in the Americas and Africa, as well as in Europe. At this juncture, most scholars seem to accept the notion that the Atlantic world was important for the political and economic development of Europe in the early modern centuries, though they continue to debate the magnitude and character of that importance. It seems fair to say that many of the changes in European political and economic development in the extended period between 1450 and 1825 were linked to overseas exploration, colonization, trade, and the international rivalries they fomented. In other words, the creation of the Atlantic world in the aftermath of European voyages of discovery had profound repercussions on both sides of the ocean.[36]

NOTES

1. See Carla Rahn Phillips, "The Organization of Oceanic Empires: The Iberian World in the Habsburg Period," in Jerry Bentley, Renate Bridenthal, and Kären E. Wigen, eds., *Seascapes, Maritime Histories, Littoral Cultures, and Transoceanic Exchanges* (Honolulu, University of Hawaii Press, 2007), pp. 71–86.

2. Fernand Braudel, *The Mediterranean and the Mediterranean World in the Age of Philip II*, trans. Siân Reynolds, 2 vols. (New York: Harper & Row, 1972).

3. See Daniel R. Headrick, *The Tools of Empire: Technology and European Imperialism in the Nineteenth Century* (New York: Oxford University Press, 1981).

4. Helpful discussions regarding definitions and chronology appear in Bernard Bailyn, "The Idea of Atlantic History," *Itinerario* 20, 1 (1996): 19–44; and Alison Games, "Atlantic History: Definitions, Challenges, and Opportunities," *American Historical Review* 111, 3 (June 2006): 741–757.

5. For comprehensive overviews of Atlantic exploration in its global context, see Felipe Fernández-Armesto, ed., *The Times Atlas of World Exploration* (London: Times Books, 1991); and David Buisseret, ed., *The Oxford Companion to World Exploration* 2 vols. (Oxford and New York: Oxford University Press, 2007).

6. See the magisterial comparison of the two empires by J.H. Elliott, *Empires of the Atlantic World: Britain and Spain in America, 1492–1830* (New Haven: Yale University Press, 2006), as well as Jack P. Greene, *The Intellectual Construction of America: Exceptionalism and Identity from 1492 to 1800* (Chapel Hill: University of North Carolina Press, 1993).

7. Carlos Marichal, *Bankruptcy of Empire: Mexican Silver and the Wars Between Spain, Britain, and France, 1760–1810* (Cambridge: Cambridge University Press, 2007).

8. Articles by James Epstein, Rafe Blaufarb, and Eliga Gould, with a commentary by Jorge Cañizares-Esguerra, explore the interconnectedness of the Atlantic world in the eighteenth and early nineteenth centuries, in the *AHR* Forum, "Entangled Empires in the Atlantic World," *American Historical Review* 112, 3 (June 2007): 710–799.

9. Pierre Chaunu and Huguette Chaunu, *Séville et l'Atlantique 1504–1650*, 8 vols. in 12 (Paris: S.E.V.P.E.N., 1955–1960), vol. 6, part 1, pp. 168, 337; Braudel, *Mediterranean*, vol. 1, pp. 445–448.

10. The following discussion of the volume and value of transatlantic trade relies on Chaunu and Chaunu, *Séville et l'Atlantique*; Eufemio Lorenzo Sanz,

Comercio de España con América en la época de Felipe II, 2 vols. (Valladolid: Diputación Provincial de Valladolid, 1980); Antonio García-Baquero González, *Cádiz y el Atlántico (1717–1778)*, 2 vols. (Cádiz: Diputación Provincial, 1976); Modesto Ulloa, *La hacienda real de Castilla en el reinado de Felipe II* (Madrid: Fundación Universitaria Española, 1977); Michel Morineau, *Incroyables Gazettes et fabuleux métaux: Les retours de trésors américains d'après les gazettes hollandaises (XVIe–XVIIIe siècles)* (Cambridge and New York: Cambridge University Press, 1985); and Frédéric Mauro, *Le Portugal, le Brésil et l'Atlantique au XVIIe siècle (1570–1670)* (Paris: Fondation Calouste Gulbenkian, 1983). For overviews of transatlantic trade to and from various areas of Europe, as well as Africa, see the "Round Table Conference: The Nature of Atlantic History," *Itinerario* 23, 2 (1999): 48–173.

11. In addition to the works cited above, see Alfred W. Crosby, *The Columbian Exchange: Biological and Cultural Consequences of 1492* (Westport, Conn.: Greenwood, 1972); and Crosby's *Ecological Imperialism: The Biological Expansion of Europe* (Cambridge and New York: Cambridge University Press, 1986).

12. The Spanish *maravedí* in these centuries was a money of account, as was the *ducado*, or ducat; the *real* was a silver coin. Monies might be issued in multiple *reales*, such as the *peso de ocho*, known in English as a "piece of eight." Each *real* was worth 34 *maravedís*, and each *ducado* was worth 375 *maravedís*, or 11 *reales*. To give some idea of the relative value of these sums, a sailor on Spain's Indies fleets in the late sixteenth century earned 44.1 *reales* a month, the equivalent of 1,500 *maravedís*. His monthly food ration, supplied by the government, cost slightly more than that—about 1,800 *maravedís*.

13. The Spanish *arroba* weighed about 25 pounds.

14. The classic work on the issue of bullion imports to Europe is Earl J. Hamilton *American Treasure and the Price Revolution in Spain, 1501–1650* (Cambridge, Mass.: Harvard University Press, 1934; repr. New York: Octagon, 1964). The discussion of mining production is based on Peter Bakewell, "Mining in Colonial Spanish America," in Leslie Bethell, ed., *The Cambridge History of Latin America* (Cambridge and New York: Cambridge University Press, 1984), vol. 2, pp. 105–151; and Richard L. Garner, "Long-term Silver Mining Trends in Spanish America: A Comparative Analysis of Peru and Mexico," *American Historical Review* 93, 4 (October 1988): 898–935.

15. Dennis O. Flynn and Arturo Giraldez, eds., *Metals and Monies in an Emerging Global Economy* (Aldershot, U.K.: Variorum, 1997); and Dennis Owen Flynn and Arturo Giraldez, "Cycles of Silver: Global Economic Unity Through the Mid-Eighteenth Century," *Journal of World History* 13, 2 (Fall 2002): 391–427.

16. Hamilton, *American Treasure*, pp. 42–45, 283–306. J. H. Elliott, *The Old World and the New 1492–1650* (Cambridge and New York: Cambridge University Press, 1970), pp. 55–68, provides a useful summary of the debate over bullion and inflation in the sixteenth century.

17. Magnus Mörner, "Immigration into Latin America, Especially Argentina and Chile," in *European Expansion and Migration: Essays on the Intercontinental Migration from Africa, Asia, and Europe* (New York: Bert, 1992), pp. 211–243.

18. Peter Boyd-Bowman, "Patterns of Spanish Emigration to the Indies, 1579–1600," *The Americas* 33, 1 (1976): 78–95. Boyd-Bowman's pathbreaking work with the official passenger registries in Seville established a whole subfield of inquiry and has produced a wealth of published work. See also Antonio Eiras Roel, "Introducción: Consideraciones sobre la emigración española a América y su contexto demográfico," in *Emigración española y portuguesa a América: Actas del II Congreso de la Asociación de Demografía Histórica* (Alicante: Instituto de Cultura Juan Gil Albert, 1991), pp. 9–32. See also the pioneering work of C. R. Boxer, *Women in Iberian Expansion Overseas 1415–1815* (New York: Oxford University Press, 1975). The best entry point into modern scholarship on this theme is Ida Altman and James Horn, eds., *"To Make America": European Emigration in the Early Modern Period* (Berkeley: University of California Press, 1991).

19. H. B. Johnson, "The Portuguese Settlement of Brazil, 1500–1580," in Leslie Bethell, ed., *The Cambridge History of Latin America* (Cambridge and New York: Cambridge University Press, 1984), vol. 1, pp. 268–275.

20. Willem Usselincx, cited in C. R. Boxer, *The Dutch in Brazil, 1624–1654* (Oxford: Clarendon Press, 1957), pp. 2–3.

21. Trevor Aston, ed., *Crisis in Europe* (London: Routledge & Kegan Paul, 1965); Geoffrey Parker and Leslie M. Smith, eds., *The General Crisis of the Seventeenth Century* (London: Routledge & Kegan Paul, 1978); Peter A. Coclanis, ed., *The Atlantic Economy During the Seventeenth and Eighteenth Centuries: Organization, Operation, Practice, and Personnel* (Columbia: University of South Carolina Press, 2005); David Hackett Fischer, *The Great Wave: Price Revolutions and the Rhythm of History* (New York: Oxford University Press, 1997).

22. For Portugal and its overseas empire, as well as broader concerns, see the monumental work of Vitorino de Magalhães Godinho, *Os descobrimentos e a economia mundial*, 4 vols., 2d ed. rev. (Lisbon: Editorial Presença, 1981–1982). See also Stuart B. Schwartz, *Sugar Plantations in the Formation of Brazilian Society: Bahia, 1550–1835* (Cambridge and New York: Cambridge University Press, 1985); and Daviken Studnicki-Gizbert, *A Nation upon the Ocean Sea: Portugal's Atlantic Diaspora and the Crisis of the Spanish Empire, 1492–1640* (Oxford and New York: Oxford University Press, 2007).

23. The Portuguese *arroba* weighed about 32 pounds.

24. Boxer, *Dutch in Brazil*, pp. 277–290; Pierre Verger, *Bahia and the West African Trade, 1549–1851* (Ibadan: Ibadan University Press, 1970), pp. 5–6. See also Wim Klooster, *Illicit Riches: Dutch Trade in the Caribbean, 1648–1795* (Leiden: Koninklijk Institut voor Taal-Land en Volkenkunde, 1998).

25. For the increase in population in New England, see Richard Archer, "New England Mosaic: A Demographic Analysis for the Seventeenth Century," *William and Mary Quarterly* 3rd ser., 47, 4. (October 1990): 477–502. For trade, see

Jacob M. Price, *Perry of London: A Family and a Firm on the Seaborne Frontier, 1615–1753* (Cambridge, Mass.: Harvard University Press, 1992.

26. E. J. Hobsbawm, "The General Crisis of the European Economy in the 17th Century," *Past and Present* no. 5 (May 1954): 33–53, and no. 6 (November 1954): 44–65.

27. Andre Gunder Frank, *Capitalism and Underdevelopment in Latin America: Historical Studies of Chile and Brazil* (New York: Monthly Review Press, 1967); Immanuel Maurice Wallerstein, *The Modern World-system*, 3 vols. (New York: Academic Press, 1974–1989).

28. Patrick O'Brien, "European Economic Development: The Contribution of the Periphery," *Economic History Review* 25 (1982): 1–18; Patrick Karl O'Brien and Leandro Prados de la Escosura, "The Costs and Benefits of European Imperialism from the Conquest of Ceuta, 1415, to the Treaty of Lusaka, 1974," in Clara-Eugenia Núñez, ed., *Debates and Controversies in Economic History* (Madrid, 1998), pp. 9–69; Kenneth Pomeranz, *The Great Divergence: China, Europe, and the Making of the Modern World Economy* (Princeton: Princeton University Press, 2000).

29. In addition to the sources on Brazil cited above, see A. J. R. Russell-Wood, "Colonial Brazil: The Gold Cycle, c. 1690–1750," in Leslie Bethell, ed., *The Cambridge History of Latin America* (Cambridge and New York: Cambridge University Press, 1984), vol. 2, pp. 547–600.

30. For comprehensive overviews of the field, see David Eltis, David Richardson, Stephen D. Behrendt, and Herbert S. Klein, eds., *The Atlantic Slave Trade: A Database on CD-ROM Set and Guidebook* (New York: Cambridge University Press, 1999); Herbert S. Klein, *The Atlantic Slave Trade: A History and Analysis* (New York: Cambridge University Press, 1999); and Paul Finkelman and Joseph C. Miller, eds., *Macmillan Encyclopedia of World Slavery* (New York: Macmillan Reference USA, 1998).

31. Virgilio Noya Pinto, *Ouro brasileiro e o comercio anglo-português: Uma contribução aos estudos da economia atlantica no seculo XVIII* (São Paulo: Companhia Editora Nacional, 1979), pp. 248–252, 296; Frédéric Mauro, "Portugal and Brazil: Political and Economic Structures of Empire, 1580–1750," in Leslie Bethell, ed., *The Cambridge History of Latin America* (Cambridge and New York: Cambridge University Press, 1984), vol. 1, pp. 461–463.

32. Vitorino Magalhaes Godinho, "Le Portugal, les flottes du sucre et les flottes de l'or (1670–1770)," *Annales: Economies, sociétés, civilisations* (April–June 1950): 184–193; Morineau, *Incroyables Gazettes*, pp. 190–197.

33. D. A. Brading, "Bourbon Spain and Its American Empire," in Leslie Bethell, ed., *The Cambridge History of Latin America* (Cambridge and New York: Cambridge University Press, 1984), vol. 1, p. 426.

34. For migration to British America in the eighteenth century, see Bernard Bailyn and Barbara DeWolfe, *Voyagers to the West: A Passage in the Peopling of America on the Eve of the Revolution* (New York: Knopf, 1986).

35. See David Hancock, *Citizens of the World: London Merchants and the Integration of the British Atlantic Community, 1735–1785* (Cambridge and New York: Cambridge University Press, 1995).

36. The study of transatlantic interactions is a vast and growing field. The notes to this chapter provide an indication of that literature, as do the articles in two recent forums in the *American Historical Review*: "The New British History in Atlantic Perspective," *American Historical Review* 104, 2 (April 1999): 426–500; and "Entangled Empires in the Atlantic World," *American Historical Review* 112, 3 (June 2007).

PART III

Competing and Complementary Perspectives

10

FROM ATLANTIC HISTORY TO
A CONTINENTAL APPROACH

PETER H. WOOD

For several centuries, chroniclers of the North American experience before 1800 have faced a basic dilemma—so basic, in fact, that it is rarely recognized or stated. Put bluntly, the familiar but vexing paradox is this: Should "early American history" concern the growth and expansion of European colonies, particularly those English-speaking ones along the east coast that eventually combined to form the United States and to push westward across the continent? Or should it concern all parts of the North American continent, and all the people living there before 1800?

Certainly the east coast orientation is the older and more familiar of these two approaches. After all, the rapid growth of the population along the eastern seaboard and the creation of the American Republic in the late eighteenth century paved the way for a massive demographic, political, and cultural push westward in the nineteenth century that transformed the North American continent.[1] That push was epitomized by cowboys on European horses herding European cattle, and by immigrant farmers from Europe planting wheat and raising hogs that had been brought from the Old World. Rapidly, it changed the heartland into what Alfred Crosby has called a "neo-Europe."[2] In addition, it fixed the way that future generations would look at American history, for the century of Euro-American expansion was also the formative era for writing about the American past. Ever since, the United States has cast its entire narrative in terms of "Westward the Course of Empire."

Granted, the well-known eastern seaboard narrative has been modified in recent decades. Most, though not all, survey courses now begin in North America well before Columbus's voyage; the rise of Native American history and ethnohistory has thankfully moved us beyond old "empty continent" and "virgin land" formulations. Most important, the evolving literature on colonial-era North America has been enriched, over the past generation, by the welcome growth of a self-conscious Atlantic history. Among other things, that worthwhile venture is erasing the invisible boundary used by several generations of scholars to separate their familiar North Atlantic from what seemed an all-too-foreign South Atlantic. A new cohort of early Americanists feel increasingly drawn to the well-known ports, peoples, and landscapes of Africa and Latin America. One can debate whether this more expansive approach has been adopted belatedly and reluctantly or swiftly and eagerly. But it is hard to deny the recent payoffs. Scholars who can conceptualize an early modern "Atlantic world" find themselves grappling with timely notions of globalization, intercultural contact, the growth of transnational capitalism, and the spread of European imperialism—ecological and religious, as well as economic and political.

But even as the gains of Atlantic history are being consolidated, historians are already peering over new horizons. Though an Atlantic-centered viewpoint remains dominant, scholars are beginning to question it in interesting ways.[3] What possibilities lie ahead? One inevitable next step, facilitated by the growth of an increasingly well-traveled and international generation of scholars, will be an increase in comparative history. Atlantic history should, as Jack Greene makes clear in an accompanying essay, give new life to a complementary hemispheric perspective of the kind that Herbert Bolton began to advocate and practice nearly a century ago. Not surprisingly, early Americanists are forging fresh links to the complex histories of Europe and Africa as well, and it is only a matter of time before the watery trails of the Atlantic lead them to see new connections and comparisons in the Indian and Pacific oceans.

But there is another prospect equally close at hand. It is linked to the broad paradox with which I began, and it can best be described as a "continental" approach to early America history. This different stance (looking broadly at the vast lands north of the Rio Grande without becoming drawn into tedious turf wars and definitional boundary debates) has gained adherents in recent years.[4] Only time will tell how productive or successful such a viewpoint will be over the long term. But it is already possible to suggest what a continental approach *is not*, and also what it could become. It is not, first of all, a wholesale substitute for existing models of colonial American history, including the expansive and useful Atlantic formulation. Nor is it in direct conflict or competition with hemispheric or comparative approaches; indeed, it is more readily seen as a precursor to such efforts, for future comparisons will differ and grow as we explore more fully all the rooms of our own house. Finally, it is definitely not presentist, nationalist, or anachronistic. On the contrary, it builds upward from a deep chronological foundation, rather than digging down to find the roots of the American republic; it challenges and traverses later geopolitical boundaries, rather than being defined by them; and it tends to underscore, rather than diminish, the huge contrasts between distant pasts and the surrounding present.

If the continental approach to early North America is not some sudden and dangerous replacement, it may still prove an increasingly logical and promising tool as the twenty-first century unfolds. What it becomes will depend on future scholars, but continental history already shows potential in several obvious ways. Far from precluding consideration of French and Spanish (and Dutch and Russian) colonial history, this approach invites it, while also demanding a far fuller understanding of the deep and diverse Native American presence. Also, while encompassing imperial and cultural boundaries, continental history gives importance, and sometimes precedence, to geographic and ecological variables. (It is no longer just ecologists and environmentalists who are demanding that we comprehend the interconnectedness of our continent's vast ecosystems and their significant long-term changes in response to invasive and escalating human presence.) Moreover, if the Atlantic and comparative approaches move horizontally into a wider early modern world, this complementary continental approach creates vertical, or chronological, links. It is by no means isolationist, but it stretches deep into the precolonial past and forward toward the North American present. It is a challenging asset, not a liability or pitfall, that this approach connects suggestively to the later chapters of American history, whether it is being studied in Hackensack or Honolulu, Fairbanks or Fort Myers.

It is now increasingly possible to start exploring, and teaching, early North American history from a broad continental perspective. To think about doing this, we need to plant ourselves in the West occasionally, and look east. *But which West?* When the historian Frederick Jackson Turner wished to "stand" in the late-eighteenth-century "West" and face east, he imagined himself at Cumberland Gap in southwest Virginia. In the current century, when ethnohistorian Daniel Richter conceived his recent book, *Facing East*, he was high up in a St. Louis hotel overlooking the Mississippi River, not far from the spot where Meriwether Lewis and William Clark set out for the Pacific in 1804.[5]

Despite suggestive recent work, the eighteenth-century West still lies just beyond the Alleghenies for most Americans. But a broader and more continental vision seems to be on the way. Eventually, in discussing America before 1800, we shall use the term "the West" to refer to the geographical, continental West rather to than the provincial, pre-Louisiana Purchase West of trans-Appalachia, located along the eastern side of the Mississippi river Basin.[6] That larger West begins at the Mississippi and ends in the Pacific (or vice versa). It is part of a continental vision for America's early modern era that embraces *two* oceans and puts Atlantic history into a very different perspective, as the following brief experiment may suggest.

Suppose that instead of standing at Cumberland Gap with Turner and Daniel Boone, or at St. Louis with Richter and the expectant Lewis and Clark, we situate ourselves far out over the North Pacific, at the very beginning of the eighteenth century.[7] If we hover there—roughly half way between the Aleutian Islands and Hawaii—in the year 1700, with our stationary spacecraft/time-capsule facing eastward (and if we assume clear weather, superhuman vision, and an altitude that overcomes the Earth's curvature), we can see, from that vantage point, a great deal that European mapmakers do not yet know.[8]

We can confirm, for instance, that Lower (Baja) California is clearly a peninsula rather than an island.[9] Likewise, looking far to the north, we can observe that easternmost Siberia's Chukchi Peninsula is not, in fact, linked to the western hemisphere, even though some in the court of young Peter the Great in Moscow still hope that a land connection may exist.[10] Glancing backward over our left shoulder and scanning the North Pacific below the Aleutians, eastward from Japan, we see no sign of the fabled isles of Rica de Oro (Rich in Gold) and Rica de Plata (Rich in Silver). Nearly a century earlier, in 1611, Sebastián Vizcaíno had been sent out from Mexico in a futile effort to locate these rumored islands. He expended valuable resources that the king of Spain had originally designated for the purpose of establishing the first colonial post along the coast of California. Vizcaíno spent several years in Tokugawa Japan, and when he returned eastward across the Pacific in 1613, he brought 180 Japanese with him to Mexico. These residents of Japan constituted a high-level trading and cultural delegation that moved on to Spain and Italy. But persecution of Christian foreigners in Japan increased soon afterward, and no lasting link ever developed.[11]

If it is late summer, we might be able to make out almost below us *Nuestra Señora del Rosario*, a large "Manila galleon" that left the Philippines in June 1700. The ship is riding the prevailing winds and currents eastward toward California. From there, it will sail south toward Acapulco, arriving in Mexico in December. The huge Spanish vessel, well over 300 tons and with a polyglot crew of more than 100 men, had sailed westward across the

Pacific the previous year, via a more southerly route, carrying silver and chocolate from Mexico. Now this galleon, one of several engaged in the trade, is returning from Manila, laden with cinnamon, pepper, gold, ivory, silk, and porcelain. By 1700, Spain's lucrative trans-Pacific commerce has been conducted on an annual basis for well over 100 years, and it will persist regularly for more than a century to come.[12]

Off to our right, in the south, we can see the Hawaiian Islands, settled some fourteen centuries earlier by experienced Polynesian ocean explorers sailing northward more than 2,000 miles from the distant Marquesas below the equator. And looking eastward, we scan the North American continent, inhabited for more than 15,000 years by the descendants of early migrants from Eurasia. In 1700, the ancient mesa-top pueblos along the upper Rio Grande have been reconquered again by the Spanish (and have revolted again) since the massive Pueblo Revolt of 1680. In the twenty years since that first successful uprising, a series of native rebellions has swept the northern frontier of New Spain.[13] There has also been a sudden acceleration in the distribution of Spanish horses among the Indian nations bordering the Great Plains.[14]

Farther east and more than twenty degrees to the north, in the great bay explored by Henry Hudson nearly a century before, the English trading posts at York Factory and Moose Factory have been in operation for several decades. In competition with France for furs from the interior, the English, like their more experienced French rivals, are trading guns to Indians bordering the northern plains west of Lake Superior. And French explorers are reacting to the disappointing and unexpected failure of La Salle's ambitious effort to launch a colony near the mouth of the Mississippi River in 1685.[15] Shaken by the news of La Salle's murder in 1687, potential successors, sometimes cooperating and sometimes competing, jostle for his mantle. Even before the eventual founding of the Louisiana colony by Iberville in 1699, others have moved quickly to pursue the new vistas laid open by La Salle's generation. Almost immediately, they begin probing west beyond the Mississippi; further research may show that several of them soon moved much further than we yet understand.

Even a brief glance eastward at North America above the Rio Grande in 1700 raises a basic question: What was the continent's overall population? Scholars are only beginning to piece together plausible information on this fundamental matter. We do know that the Native American population was declining and that the European colonial population was growing at an accelerating rate. North America's small African population of roughly

30,000 persons was about to expand exponentially in the decades ahead.[16] In 1698, England's Parliament had passed the Africa Trade Act, formally breaking the monopoly of the Royal African Company and opening the English slave trade to independent shippers, known as separate traders. "In the fifteen years prior to the 1698 act," William Pettigrew reminds us, "slavers transported close to fifty-five hundred slaves to the American mainland. In the fifteen years after, that figure increased by nearly 300 percent to more than fifteen thousand."[17]

Geographically, we know that the new European population was clustered almost entirely along the eastern seaboard, below the fall line of the major rivers. Most newcomers lived within fifty miles of the Atlantic Ocean; their communities still constituted a marginal foothold on a continent 3,000 miles wide. Granted, colonial outposts were being established at places such as Pensacola, Biloxi, Detroit, and Cahokia. But these new forts, along with older missions and settlements such as Santa Fe, prove statistically insignificant when their occupants are compared to the entire human population living north of the Rio Grande.

Moreover, the population of the English colonies in 1700 is generally estimated at 250,000 or slightly higher, and the North American colonies of France and Spain contained far fewer than 30,000 inhabitants between them.[18] Hence, the continent's overall European population in 1700 had not yet reached 300,000, and the entire colonial population (combining Europeans and Africans) was below 330,000 people. Meanwhile, the total population of indigenous Americans had been falling rapidly for generations.[19] In 1700, the declining Native American population, according to rough calculations, was still somewhere between 1.4 and 1.6 million people, using the most conservative estimates. This means that eight years after the Salem witch trials and six years before the birth of Benjamin Franklin, roughly five out of every six persons living in North America was a Native American.

It also means, significantly, that the North American population was still spread rather evenly across the entire continent in 1700. This would change dramatically by the end of the eighteenth century, with the rapid buildup of east coast population and the further decimation of native populations by nearly half a million, due to recurrent warfare and the ongoing spread of epidemic diseases. But in 1700, at the start of the eighteenth century, eastern populations remained relatively small, and in some areas east of the Mississippi (such as Florida, Georgia, southern Appalachia, and Mississippi, for example) the total population was actually declining.[20] Over the previous generation across the South, Indian deaths had more than offset all new colonial arrivals, by birth and immigration combined.[21]

If we use the admittedly speculative, but also rather conservative, estimates of Douglas Ubelaker regarding the changing size of Indian populations in each major North American region, we find that in 1700 there were more men, women, and children living in the Great Basin region of the mountain West (34,000) than were living in Maryland (31,000). At the same time, the number of indigenous people spread across the continent's northernmost regions was nearly three times larger than the colonial population rooted in Virginia's tidewater settlements. According to Ubelacker, there were nearly 160,000 people living in either the frigid Arctic (59,000) or the inhospitable Subarctic (100,000), whereas there were scarcely 60,000 persons inhabiting William Byrd's temperate Virginia.[22]

Such arbitrary but suggestive comparisons can be expanded. In 1700, for instance, more than twice as many people inhabited the Great Plains (189,000) as there were colonists in New England (92,000). Four times as many people resided in California (221,000) as there were settlers living in the Middle Colonies of New York, New Jersey, and Pennsylvania combined (53,000). There were nearly 50,000 people (the majority of them Indians) living in the Carolinas and Florida in 1700. At the same time there were an estimated 275,000 indigenous people—women and men, young and old—living in the Southwest, and another 175,000 residing on the salmon-rich Northwest Coast.[23]

These numbers—informed estimates rather than confirmed head counts—are eye-opening, to say the least. There were roughly equal numbers of Indians and non-Indians (a quarter of a million each) residing throughout the "East" (that is, the greater Northeast plus the greater Southeast) in 1700. But the rest of the continent (the vast region least familiar to most early American historians) was inhabited by an additional 1.15 million persons—almost all Native Americans. In other words, of an estimated 1.65 million people in North America in 1700, only about 15 percent of them were non-Indians.

This startling and unfamiliar demographic picture would change dramatically over the course of the eighteenth century. By the time of Jefferson's election as president, the native population, according to Ubelaker, had declined precipitously by 25 percent, from 1.4 million in 1700 to slightly over one million people in 1800. This decline affected all regions of the continent, as accelerated trade spread epidemic diseases more extensively, more rapidly, and more frequently across North America. Certain areas of increasing movement and expanding contact were particularly hard hit, such as the Southeast, the Great Plains, and the Northwest Coast.[24]

Conversely, the European and African populations in the East had grown dramatically; the federal census of 1800 counted roughly 5.3 million people. In 100 years, North America's population had roughly quadrupled in size, with almost the entire gain occurring in the East, thanks to high birth rates, steady immigration, and an almost unremitting traffic in enslaved Africans. In short, the demographic tables had been completely reversed. Of an estimated 6.6 million people in North America in 1800, only about 15 percent of them were Native Americans. Precisely how and why this great reversal came about is a story that has only begun to be explored on a continental scale.[25]

The logic of these surprising numbers would seem to point to a new research agenda. A provocative 1994 essay in the *William and Mary Quarterly* by James A. Hijiya, entitled "Why the West Is Lost,"[26] prompted the frontier scholar John Mack Faragher to observe cogently: "What we really need is a fundamental change in the way we think about the colonial history of North America, a change that re-envisions the field in continental perspective. The place to begin is with the agendas of colonial historians themselves."[27] In geographical terms, such a change would move early Americanists toward the center of the continent.[28] In disciplinary terms, it would move many of them in the direction of ethnohistory.

New research agendas always stem from complex shifts in the interests of scholars and the questions and priorities of their audiences. Still, such agendas must begin with practical reconsiderations. So it seems appropriate to list briefly half a dozen basic steps that will help to point the way. We need, first, to explore in greater detail what anthropologists and archaeologists have to tell us about a vast array of North American cultures. As we know, these indigenous groups differed greatly from one another, and they were in various stages of contact with the Europeans who were competing to control navigation on both the Atlantic and the Pacific. But we need to learn far more about these groups; they still seem as homogeneous and remote to most early American scholars as West Africa's diverse societies appeared to American teachers and students in the 1950s.

Second, we need to re-immerse ourselves in the multitude of Spanish sources that have been located and utilized by several generations of "Borderlands" historians, from Herbert Bolton to David Weber.[29] Many of these sources now exist in English translations; but many more await scholars with a reading knowledge of Spanish—something that should become a requirement for the next generation of early Americanists. Third, we also need to revisit the rich troves of French documentary material, such as the incomparable *Jesuit Relations*, translated and published a century ago in more than seventy volumes.[30] Fourth, we would profit from combing existent colonial documents on Russia's eastward expansion, many of which are now available in English translation.[31] To gain a better sense of what has already been done, as a fifth step we might do well to revisit certain surveys of cultural contact in the American West from recent generations.[32] Finally, while building upon past scholarship in all these areas, we need to intensify our work in published primary sources and in unpublished archival manuscript collections, both here and abroad.

Having listed possible approaches to this broader, transcontinental version of early American history, let me suggest half a dozen topics of ongoing research which are now only marginally familiar to most eighteenth-century Americanists, but which are rapidly becoming more widely known and deeply understood. These specific non-Atlantic subjects suggest some of the diverse dimensions of a general reexamination. I mention them here only by way of example. In each instance significant work has been done, much of it dated and most of it still scarcely integrated into standard treatments of early American history. Clearly, more remains to be done regarding these few illustrative topics (and a much longer set of research possibilities that is now emerging).

The first topic is the European exploration of the Pacific, beginning with Ferdinand Magellan.[33] This slow probing of the world's largest ocean stretched across two and a half centuries.[34] Though much work exists on the Pacific voyage of Sir Francis Drake,[35] scholarly attention to a wider early English presence in that ocean remains limited.[36] In contrast, the scholarly effort expended upon Cook and his voyages has been enormous, and an Australian-built replica of his ship, the *Endeavor*, continues to make its way around the world to publicize his exploits, some of which transformed the history of Hawaii and completed the mapping of the Northwest Coast.[37] Exploration remains a crucial aspect of the West Coast frontier, and a fuller understanding of the naval rivalries, geographic breakthroughs, and native contacts associated with eighteenth-century Pacific voyages remains overdue.

The second topic concerns Russian Alaska. No eighteenth-century Pacific voyages were more dramatic than those of Vitus Bering, the Danish-born explorer who gave his name to the strait separating Siberia from North America. On his deathbed in 1724, the Russian emperor, Peter the Great, sought to resolve the vexing scientific and political question of whether Russia "might be joined to America." It was a matter, he observed, "which has been on my mind for many years." Bering, an experienced officer in the Russian navy, was sent east in 1725, but when his extensive survey of the Siberian coast in 1728 failed to provide a definitive answer, he was sent back in the following decade to build more ships and explore again. In

1741 the navigator finally managed to outfit two small vessels on Siberia's Kamchatka Peninsula and set out for American shores. At first, he expended precious time sailing southeast rather than northeast, meandering through the North Pacific in hopes of finding the imaginary lands that had lured Vizcaíno 130 years before. After finally touching Alaska very briefly, he rushed his return voyage through uncharted waters as winter approached. During an ill-advised stopover on a frozen island that now bears his name, Bering suffered a harrowing death in December 1741 from what his physician described as "hunger, thirst, cold, vermin and grief."[38]

Along with Bering, thirty of his crewmen died of scurvy and exposure before their return, but forty-six survivors limped back to Kamchatka the following year with an enormous cargo of furs that would spark further exploration.[39] In 1991, to mark the 250th anniversary of the voyage, members of Russia's Merchant Marine Academy sailed replicas of Bering's tiny vessels, the *Saint Peter* and *Saint Paul*, from Vladivostok to Kodiak, Alaska. This feat received little attention beyond the Northwest Coast, even among early Americanists, but that is hardly surprising, for it is difficult to commemorate events that are unfamiliar. Fortunately, contact-period archaeology, document retrieval, and sophisticated ethnohistory are well under way in opening up this neglected chapter of North American colonization.[40]

As the Russians were moving southward along North America's Pacific coast, reaching California in the early nineteenth century, Spaniards were moving northward with very different kinds of Christian missionaries, European soldiers and imperial bureaucrats. The Spanish push into California constitutes a third topic of current and future study for early American historians. In contrast to the Russians, the Spanish had been present in America for centuries, and had long been the dominant naval and commercial force in the Pacific. The Spanish-speaking settlers who founded San Diego in 1769 and San Francisco in 1776 were operating in a more hospitable climate, and they had far easier access to the resources of Mexico and Madrid than Russian colonizers of Kodiak and Sitka had to Kamchatka and St. Petersburg.

It has been nearly 100 years since Irving Richman published *California Under Spain and Mexico*, lamenting that as yet "few critical monographs" had been devoted to the subject.[41] Eight decades have passed since Herbert Bolton published his volumes on the 1774 expedition of Juan Bautista de Anza and Father Garcés from Tubac in northern Sonora to San Gabriel (what is now Los Angeles).[42] Research and scholarship have proceeded steadily since Bolton's time.[43] An excellent work now exists on the general topic of Indian–Spanish relations along the vast boundaries of Spain's empire in the Americas in the late eighteenth century, and new books on the Spanish missions of Alta California are appearing frequently.[44] But the satisfactory linking of colonial California history to the wider framework of early North American history remains tenuous at best.

The same might be said for other aspects of the eighteenth-century Pacific frontier. The fatal impact of Captain Cook on Hawaii, and vice versa, has been dealt with frequently in various popular forms, and has been the focus of an extended and often bitter theoretical debate among anthropologists.[45] But it stands out as a fourth topic for further exploration and integration. So far early Americanists, preoccupied with the Revolutionary War when they get to the 1770s, have had little to say about the European "discovery" of the so-called Sandwich Islands in either comparative or ethnohistorical terms.

Similarly (and this remains a fifth appealing topic), there is an extensive, but somewhat specialized, literature about the arrival of American ships along the Northwest Coast after the Revolution. It relates to several topics already noted—Pacific exploration and eighteenth-century Hawaii—and it is often associated with the obscure diplomatic controversy of 1790 known as the Nootka Sound Crisis. But it is actually, among much else, a final chapter in the search for the Northwest Passage. Most early Americanists drop this subject after discussing Jacques Cartier and Henry Hudson. We are less familiar with the later endeavors of the Italian navigator Alejandro Malaspina, the Spanish captain Juan Francisco de la Bodega y Quadra, the French naval officer Jean-François de Galaup de la Pérouse, Cook's English successor George Vancouver, and Scottish fur trader Alexander Mackenzie.[46] This is not simply an unfamiliar chapter in "great man history"; it involves devastating interactions between natives and newcomers, as well as imperial conflict and commercial enterprise.[47]

Finally, a corollary to this Northwest Coast story involved the opening up of a lucrative commerce in Pacific whaling and in the exchange of sea otter pelts for China tea by east coast merchants and New England sailors.[48] Toward the end of the eighteenth century, many among North America's eastern elite, like their wealthier counterparts in England and France, developed growing economic and cultural interests in the Orient. Leading the way, the financier Robert Morris dispatched the American vessel *Empress of China* on its pioneering and lucrative voyage to Asia in 1784. Moreover, some of the same ships that once plied the Atlantic in the slave trade later sailed the Pacific in the China trade. For example, as John Brown of Providence was reducing his involvement in the African slave trade in 1787, he dispatched his 300-ton vessel, *General Washington*, to China.[49] Professor Sucheta Mazumdar and others are finding significant links between the curtailing of the Atlantic slave trade and the expansion of commerce with China.

Few of these topics are unknown, but all can be explored more deeply and integrated more fully than they have been. And this list, confined to the Pacific and its immediate North American coastline, is presented merely as an appetizer. As we begin to push our inquiries inland from Sitka, Nootka, and Monterey, moving east toward the distant Cumberland Gap, we approach the busy Atlantic world from an unfamiliar direction.

Interestingly, this fresh vantage point, different as it may seem, has an eighteenth-century precedent in the vision of John Ledyard, who had sailed with Captain Cook on his final voyage to the Pacific. After seeing the West Coast of North America, the Connecticut-born adventurer conceived an ambitious plan with Thomas Jefferson in Paris in 1786. As Jefferson explained admiringly, this intrepid traveler hoped to make his way, via Asia and the Pacific, "to the Western side of America, and penetrate through the Continent to our side of it."[50] Ledyard failed to realize this ambitious dream, and he is now all but forgotten. Yet several centuries later we are finally in a position to rediscover the world he hoped to explore.

If we dare to press eastward into the continent as it existed well before 1800, we shall encounter all of North America's peoples, and we stand to learn a great deal. One payoff could involve a greater attention to the land itself and to the slow evolution of geographical and cartographic understanding among foreigners. Another payoff would be a fuller understanding of the extensive networks which carried ever more numerous trade goods and ever more devastating diseases. Still another reward would involve a better awareness of the diverse Native residents—along with the few isolated traders, explorers, missionaries, and colonizers—who inhabited most of North America during the eighteenth century. It is too early to imagine all the other possibilities in such a reorientation. Already, however, it seems safe to say that as early American history becomes more continental in scope, the subject will become more diverse and more interdisciplinary, while taking on a fresh relevance as well.

NOTES

1. As late as 1875, a quarter of a century after the California gold rush, only 7 million Americans, out of a total of 44 million, lived west of the Mississippi. All but 2 million of those lived in states bordering that river. Fewer than 1 million people lived on the Pacific side of the Continental Divide. (Among 4 million Canadians,

scarcely 150,000 lived west of Sault Saint Marie.) Colin McEvedy, *The Penguin Historical Atlas of the Pacific* (New York: Penguin, 1998), p. 76.

2. Alfred W. Crosby, *Ecological Imperialism: The Biological Expansion of Europe, 900–1900* (New York: Cambridge University Press, 1986), pp. 171–194, and "Metamorphosis of the Americas," in Herman J. Viola and Carolyn Margolis, eds., *Seeds of Change: A Quincentennial Commemoration* (Washington, D.C.: Smithsonian Institution Press, 1991), pp. 70–89.

3. Trevor Burnard, "Only Connect: The Rise and Rise (and Fall?) of Atlantic History," *Historically Speaking* (July/August 2006): 19–21. Also see the useful collection, "Forum: Beyond the Atlantic," *William and Mary Quarterly* 3rd ser., 63 (October 2006): 675–742.

4. I use *continental* broadly and loosely here. We sensibly continue to employ national boundaries in teaching American history at all levels, but the presence of Alaska and Hawaii as the most recent states prompts greater awareness of U.S. relationships with Canada, Mexico, and the islands of the Caribbean and the Pacific.

5. Daniel K. Richter, *Facing East from Indian Country: A Native History of Early America* (Cambridge, Mass.: Harvard University Press, 2001), p. 1.

6. For a useful presentation of this broader, continental approach, see William H. Goetzmann and Glyndwr Williams, *The Atlas of North American Exploration: From the Norse Voyages to the Race to the Pole* (New York: Prentice Hall, 1992). See also John Logan Allen, ed., *North American Exploration*, 3 vols. (Lincoln: University of Nebraska Press, 1997), especially James R. Gibson, "The Exploration of the Pacific Coast," in vol. 2: *A Continent Defined*, pp. 329–396. An excellent issue of the online publication *Common-Place* [5, no. 2 (January 2005)] focused on bringing the Pacific into early American history.

7. See Ernest Stanley Dodge, *Islands and Empires: Western Impact on the Pacific and East Asia* (Minneapolis: University of Minnesota Press, 1976); Walter A. McDougall, *Let the Sea Make a Noise: A History of the North Pacific from Magellan to MacArthur* (New York: Basic Books, 1993); and the review article of Stefan Halikowski Smith, "The Pacific World, 1500–1900," *Itinerario*, 30, no. 1 (2006): 83–86.

8. For an introduction to the unfolding of this complex cartography, see Carl I. Wheat, *The Mapping of the Transmississippi West*, 5 vols. (San Francisco: Institute of Historical Cartography, 1957–1963)., vol. 1.

9. Dora Beale Polk, *The Island of California: A History of the Myth* (Lincoln: University of Nebraska Press, 1991).

10. Benson Bobrick, *East of the Sun: The Epic Conquest and Tragic History of Siberia* (New York: Poseidon Press, 1992), pp. 97–98.

11. W. Michael Mathes, *Vizcaíno and Spanish Expansion in the Pacific Ocean* (San Francisco: California Historical Society, 1968), p. 146; William Lytle Schurz, *The Manila Galleon* (New York: E. P. Dutton, 1959), pp. 230–234; Naojiro Murakami, "Japan's Early Attempts to Establish Commercial Relations with

Mexico," in H. Morse Stephens and Herbert E. Bolton, eds., *The Pacific Ocean in History* (New York: Macmillan, 1917), pp. 467–480.

12. Schurz, *The Manila Galleon*, pp. 50, 194, 209; H. Morse Stephens, "The Conflict of European Nations in the Pacific Ocean," in Stephens and Bolton, eds., *The Pacific Ocean in History*, p. 26. For Bruce Cruikshank's expanding Directory of Manila Galleon Voyages, 1565 through 1815, see http://home.windstream.net/cr33856/.

13. Roberto Mario Salmon, *Indian Revolts in Northern New Spain: A Synthesis of Resistance (1680–1786)* (Lanham, Md.: University Press of America, 1991): pp. 38, 41.

14. Richard White, *It's Your Misfortune and None of My Own: A History of the American West* (Norman: University of Oklahoma Press, 1991), pp. 20–21.

15. Peter H. Wood, "La Salle: Discovery of a Lost Explorer," *American Historical Review* 89 (April 1984): 294–323. For a sound introduction to the literature on La Salle, see the various works of Robert S. Weddle and William C. Foster.

16. On Africans, see Ira Berlin, *Many Thousands Gone: The First Two Centuries of Slavery in North America* (Cambridge, Mass.: Harvard University Press, 1998), p. 370. Berlin's table suggests that the slave population of mainland North America was just below 30,000 in 1700 and at least 900,000 by 1800. Not all Africans in North America were enslaved, and not all of those enslaved were of African ancestry, but these numbers suggest the proper range.

17. William A. Pettigrew, "Free to Enslave: Politics and the Escalation of Britain's Transatlantic Slave Trade, 1688–1714," *William and Mary Quarterly* 3rd ser., 64 (January 2007): 33.

18. See, for example, Morris Altman, "Economic Growth in Canada, 1695–1739: Estimates and Analysis," *William and Mary Quarterly* 3rd ser., 45 (October 1988): 707 (table VII).

19. Suzanne Austin Alchon, *A Pest in the Land: New World Epidemics in a Global Perspective* (Albuquerque: University of New Mexico Press, 2003); Charles C. Mann, *1491: New Revelations of the Americas Before Columbus* (New York: Knopf, 2005).

20. See Marvin T. Smith, "Indians of Mississippi, 1540–1700," in *Native, European, and African Cultures in Mississippi, 1500–1800* (Jackson: Mississippi Department of Archives and History, 1991), p. 35.

21. Peter H. Wood, "The Changing Population of the Colonial South: An Overview by Race and Region, 1685–1790," in Gregory A. Waselkov, Peter H. Wood, and Tom Hatley, eds., *Powhatan's Mantle: Indians in the Colonial Southeast*, 2nd ed., enl. (Lincoln: University of Nebraska Press, 2006), pp. 59–60.

22. Douglas H. Ubelaker, "North American Indian Population Size: Changing Perspectives," in John W. Verano and Douglas H. Ubelaker, eds., *Disease and Demography in the Americas* (Washington, D.C.: Smithsonian Institution Press, 1992), p. 173. I have rounded some of the figures slightly to underscore the fact that all of these numbers are estimates.

23. For the Carolinas and Florida, I have used Wood, "Changing Population," p. 59; for Maryland and Virginia, Robert V. Wells, *The Population of the British Colonies in America Before 1776* (Princeton, Princeton University Press, 1975), pp. 147, 161; for New England and the Middle Colonies, Wesley Frank Craven, *The Colonies in Transition, 1660–1713* (New York: Harper & Row, 1968), p. 288; for Native American regions, Ubelaker, "North American Indian Population Size," p. 173.

24. Ubelaker, "North American Indian Population Size," p. 173, estimates the following declines for these three regions over the eighteenth century: Southeast, from 105,125 to 60,370; the Great Plains, from 189,100 to 120,330; and the Northwest Coast, from 175,000 to 98,333. His overall North American Indian totals decline from 1,404,745 in 1700 to 1,051,688 in 1800. For a recent detailed study of mortality in the Pacific Northwest, see Robert Boyd, *The Coming of the Spirit of Pestilence: Introduced Infectious Diseases and Population Decline Among Northwest Coast Indians, 1774–1874* (Vancouver and Seattle: University of British Columbia Press and University of Washington Press, 1999).

25. See Elizabeth A. Fenn, *Pox Americana: The Great Smallpox Epidemic of 1775–82* (New York: Hill and Wang, 2001).

26. James A. Hijiya, "Why the West Is Lost," *William and Mary Quarterly* 3rd ser., 51 (April 1994): 276–292.

27. "Forum: 'Why the West Is Lost': Comments and Response," *William and Mary Quarterly* 3rd ser., 51 (October 1994): 727. On the relation of western history to global history, see Stephen Aron, "Returning the West to the World," *Magazine of History* 20, no. 2 (March 2006): 53–60.

28. Peter H. Wood, "North America in the Era of Captain Cook: Three Glimpses of Indian-European Contact in the Age of the American Revolution," in Stuart B. Schwartz, ed., *Implicit Understandings: Observing, Reporting, and Reflecting on the Encounters Between Europeans and Other Peoples in the Early Modern Era* (New York: Cambridge University Press, 1994), pp. 489–490.

29. See, for example, Herbert E. Bolton, *The Spanish Borderlands: A Chronicle of Old Florida and the Southwest* (New Haven: Yale University Press, 1921); John Francis Bannon, ed., *Bolton and the Spanish Borderlands* (Norman: University of Oklahoma Press, 1964); John Francis Bannon, *The Spanish Borderlands Frontier, 1513–1821* (New York: Holt, Rinehart and Winston, 1970; Albuquerque: University of New Mexico Press, 1974); David J. Weber, ed., *New Spain's Far Northern Frontier: Essays on Spain in the American West* (Dallas: Southern Methodist University Press, 1979); David J. Weber, *The Spanish Frontier in North America* (New Haven: Yale University Press, 1992).

30. Reuben Gold Thwaites, ed., *Jesuit Relations and Allied Documents, 1610–1791*, 73 vols. (Cleveland: Burrows Brothers, 1896–1903). Also see Louise Phelps Kellogg, ed., *Early Narratives of the Northwest, 1634–1699* (New York: Scribner's, 1917) (vol. 16 in the Original Narratives of Early American History series); and Theodore Calvin Pease and Raymond C. Werner, eds., *The French Foundations, 1680–1693*, vol. 23 in the Collections of the Illinois State Historical

Library (Springfield: Illinois State Historical Library, 1934). Among excellent new English-language resources, see Joseph L. Peysar (trans.) and José António Brandão, eds., *Edge of Empire: Documents of Michilimackinac, 1671–1716* (East Lansing: Michigan State University Press, 2008).

31. See the 3-vol. document series, Basil Dmytryshyn et al., eds. and trans., *To Siberia and Russian America: Three Centuries of Eastward Expansion* (Portland: Oregon Historical Society Press, 1985–1989).

32. Edward H. Spicer, *Cycles of Conquest: The Impact of Spain, Mexico, and the United States on the Indians of the Southwest, 1533–1960* (Tucson: University of Arizona Press, 1962); Elizabeth A. H. John, *Storms Brewed in Other Men's Worlds: The Confrontation of Indians, Spanish, and French in the Southwest, 1540–1795* (College Station: Texas A & M University Press, 1975); Warren L. Cook, *Flood Tide of Empire: Spain and the Pacific Northwest, 1543–1819* (New Haven: Yale University Press, 1973); William W. Fitzhugh and Aron Crowell, *Crossroads of Continents: Cultures of Siberia and Alaska* (Washington, D.C.: Smithsonian Institution Press, 1988); Wheat, *Mapping the Transmississippi West*; Donald A. Barclay, James H. Maguire, and Peter Wild, eds., *Into the Wilderness Dream: Exploration Narratives of the American West, 1500–1805* (Salt Lake City: University of Utah Press, 1994); and Ned Blackhawk, *Violence over the Land: Indians and Empires in the Early American West* (Cambridge, Mass.: Harvard University Press, 2006). Also, see forthcoming works by Michael Witgen (University of Michigan) and Paul W. Mapp (College of William & Mary).

33. Laurence Bergreen, *Over the Edge of the World: Magellan's Terrifying Circumnavigation of the Globe* (New York: William Morrow, 2003).

34. See John H. Parry, *The Discovery of the Sea* (Berkeley: University of California Press, 1974); Derek Howse, *Background to Discovery: Pacific Exploration from Dampier to Cook* (Berkeley: University of California Press, 1990); Stephen Haycox, James Barnett, and Caedmon Liburd, eds., *Enlightenment and Exploration in the North Pacific, 1741–1805* (Seattle: University of Washington Press, 1997). See also Mathes, *Vizcaíno*; Cook, *Flood Tide*; Ernest Stanley Dodge, *Beyond the Capes: Pacific Exploration from Captain Cook to the Challenger, 1776–1877* (Boston: Little, Brown, 1971); Oliver E. Allen, *The Pacific Navigators* (New York: Time-Life Books, 1980); John Dunmore, *Storms and Dreams: The Life of Louis de Bougainville* (Fairbanks: University of Alaska Press, 2007).

35. On Drake, see John Hampden, ed., *Francis Drake, Privateer: Contemporary Narratives and Documents* (University: University of Alabama Press, 1972); Derek Wilson, *The World Encompassed: Francis Drake and His Great Voyage* (New York: Harper & Row, 1977); Norman J. W. Thrower, ed., *Sir Francis Drake and the Famous Voyage, 1577–1580* (Berkeley: University of California Press, 1984); David Beers Quinn, *Sir Francis Drake as Seen by His Contemporaries* (Providence: John Carter Brown Library, 1996); Stephen Coote, *Drake: The Life and Legend of an Elizabethan Hero* (New York: St. Martin's Press, 2003); and R. Samuel Bawlf, *The Secret Voyage of Sir Francis Drake, 1577–1580* (New York: Walker, 2003).

36. On the English in the Pacific before Cook, see Glyndwr Williams, *The Great South Sea: English Voyages and Encounters, 1570–1750* (New Haven: Yale University Press, 1997); Peter Gerhard, *Pirates of the Pacific, 1575–1742* (Lincoln: University of Nebraska Press, 1990); and Glyndwr Williams, "The Pacific: Exploration and Exploitation," in P. J. Marshall, ed., *The Oxford History of the British Empire: The Eighteenth Century* (New York: Oxford University Press, 1998), pp. 552–575.

37. J. C. Beaglehole, *The Life of Captain James Cook* (Stanford: Stanford University Press, 1974); Daniel Conner and Lorraine Miller, *Master Mariner: Capt. James Cook and the Peoples of the Pacific* (Seattle: University of Washington Press, 1978); Adrienne L. Kaeppler, ed., *Cook Voyage Artifacts in Leningrad, Berne, and Florence Museums* (Honolulu: Bishop Museum Press, 1978); Robin Fisher and Hugh Johnston, eds., *Captain James Cook and His Times* (Seattle: University of Washington Press, 1979); Ròdiger Joppien and Bernard Smith, *The Art of Captain Cook's Voyages*, 3 vols. (New Haven: Yale University Press, 1988); Richard Hough, *Captain James Cook: A Biography* (New York: W. W. Norton, 1995); Andrew David, chief ed., *The Charts and Coastal Views of Captain Cook's Voyages*, 3 vols. (London: The Hakluyt Society, 1988–1997); Anne Salmond, *The Trial of the Cannibal Dog: The Remarkable Story of Captain Cook's Encounters in the South Seas* (New Haven: Yale University Press, 2003).

38. The quotations appear in Felipe Fernández-Armesto, *Pathfinders: A Global History of Exploration* (New York: W. W. Norton, 2006), pp. 269–275 (where Bering's death is mistakenly dated as 1742 rather than 1741).

39. Raymond H. Fisher, *Bering's Voyages: Whither and Why* (Seattle: University of Washington Press, 1977), p. 150. Cf. Gerhard Friedrich Müller, *Bering's Voyages: The Reports from Russia*, Rasmuson Library, Historical Translation Series, vol. 3, trans. Carol Urness (Fairbanks: University of Alaska Press, 1986); Georg Wilhelm Steller, *Journal of a Voyage with Bering, 1741–1742*, edited by O. W. Frost (Stanford: Stanford University Press, 1988); Corey Ford, *Where the Sea Breaks Its Back: The Epic Story of Early Naturalist Georg Steller and the Russian Exploration of Alaska* (Boston: Little, Brown, 1966; Anchorage: Alaska Northwest Books, 1992); Orcutt Frost, *Bering: The Russian Discovery of America* (New Haven: Yale University Press, 2003).

40. Fitzhugh and Crowell, *Crossroads of Continents*; Steve J. Langdon, *The Native People of Alaska*, rev. 2nd ed. (Anchorage: Greatland Graphics, 1989); S. Frederick Starr, ed., *Russia's American Colony* (Durham, N.C.: Duke University Press, 1987); Barbara Sweetland Smith and Redmond J. Barnett, eds., *Russian America: The Forgotten Frontier* (Tacoma: Washington State Historical Society, 1990); James R. Gibson, *Imperial Russia in Frontier America: The Changing Geography of Supply of Russian America, 1784–1867* (New York: Oxford University Press, 1976); Nikolai N. Bolkhovitinov, *The Beginnings of Russian–American Relations, 1775–1815*, trans. Elena Levin (Cambridge, Mass.: Harvard University Press, 1975); William R. Hunt, *Arctic Passage: The Turbulent History of the Land and People of the Bering Sea, 1697–1975* (New York: Scribner's, 1975). See also Erik

Hirschmann, "Empires in the Land of the Trickster: Russians, Tlingit, Pomo and Americans on the Pacific Rim, Eighteenth Century to 1910s" (Ph.D. dissertation, University of New Mexico, 1999); and the forthcoming book, *Kodiak Kreol*, by Gwenn A. Miller. Numerous important translations of Russian sources have been edited by Richard A. Pierce of the University of Alaska at Fairbanks and published by the Limestone Press, Kingston, Ontario.

41. "The Atlantic Coast of North America has been dealt with in works elaborate and minute. The Pacific Coast, on the contrary, is as yet nearly a virgin field, few critical monographs having been devoted to it. The consequence is that in this field it is necessary for the historical writer to use the sources directly; and these sources are almost wholly manuscript." Irving Berdine Richman, *California Under Spain and Mexico, 1535–1847* (reprinted New York: Cooper Square, 1965 [1911]), p. v.

42. Herbert E. Bolton, *Anza's California Expeditions*, 5 vols. (Berkeley: University of California Press, 1930). Cf. Father Francisco Garcés, *A Record of Travels in Arizona and California, 1775–1776*, trans. John Galvin (San Francisco: John Howell, 1965).

43. See, for example, Donald C. Cutter, *California in 1792: A Spanish Naval Visit* (Norman: University of Oklahoma Press, 1990); Joseph P. Sánchez, *Spanish Bluecoats: The Catalonian Volunteers in Northwestern New Spain, 1767–1810* (Albuquerque: University of New Mexico Press, 1990); and Robert H. Jackson and Edward Castillo, *Indians, Franciscans, and Spanish Colonization: The Impact of the Mission System on California Indians* (Albuquerque: University of New Mexico Press, 1995). See also Donald Cutter and Iris Engstrand, *Quest for Empire: Spanish Settlement in the Southwest* (Golden, Colo.: Fulcrum Publishing, 1996); Dennis Reinhartz and Gerald D. Saxon, eds., *The Mapping of the Entradas into the Greater Southwest* (Norman: University of Oklahoma Press, 1998).

44. David J. Weber, *Bárbaros: Spaniards and Their Savages in the Age of Enlightenment* (New Haven: Yale University Press, 2005); James A. Sandos, *Converting California: Indians and Franciscans in the Missions* (New Haven: Yale University Press, 2004); Steven W. Hackel, *Children of Coyote, Missionaries of St. Francis: Indian–Spanish Relations in Colonial California, 1769–1850* (Chapel Hill: University of North Carolina Press, 2005); Kent G. Lightfoot, *Indians, Missionaries, and Merchants: The Legacy of Colonial Encounters on the California Frontiers* (Berkeley: University of California Press, 2005); Alison Lake, *Colonial Rosary: The Spanish and Indian Missions of California* (Athens: Ohio: Swallow Press/Ohio University Press, 2006).

45. Marshall Sahlins, *Historical Metaphors and Mythical Realities: Structure in the Early History of the Sandwich Islands Kingdom* (Ann Arbor: University of Michigan Press, 1981), and his *Islands of History* (Chicago: University of Chicago Press, 1985); Gananath Obeyesekere, *The Apotheosis of Captain Cook: European Mythmaking in the Pacific* (Princeton: Princeton University Press, 1992).

46. John Kendrick, *Alejandro Malaspina: Portrait of a Visionary* (Toronto: McGill-Queens University Press, 1999); Herbert K. Beals, ed. and trans., "The 1775

Journal of Juan Francisco de la Bodega y Quadra," in Beals et al, eds., *Four Travel Journals* (London: Hakluyt Society, 2007), pp. 1–139; John Dunmore, ed., *The Journal of Jean-François de Galaup de la Pérouse, 1785–1788*, 2 vols. (London: Hakluyt Society, 1994–1995); W. Kaye Lamb, ed., *The Voyage of George Vancouver, 1791–1795*, 4 vols. (London: Hakluyt Society, 1984), and *The Journals and Letters of Sir Alexander Mackenzie* (Cambridge: Cambridge University Press for the Hakluyt Society, 1970). See also Donald C. Cutter, *Malaspina and Galiano: Spanish Voyages to the Northwest Coast, 1791–1792* (Seattle: University of Washington Press, 1991); Robin A. Fisher and Hugh Johnston, eds., *From Maps to Metaphors: The Pacific World of George Vancouver* (Vancouver: University of British Columbia Press, 1993); John Dunmore, *Where Fate Beckons: The Life of Jean-François de la Pérouse* (Fairbanks: University of Alaska Press, 2007); and Derek Hayes, *Historical Atlas of British Columbia and the Pacific Northwest* (Vancouver, B.C.: Cavendish Books, 1999).

47. Richard Batman, *The Outer Coast* (New York: Harcourt Brace Jovanovich, 1985); John Kendrick, *Men with Wooden Feet: The Spanish Exploration of the Pacific Northwest* (Toronto: University of Toronto Press, 1986); Erna Gunther, *Indian Life on the Northwest Coast of North America, as Seen by the Early Explorers and Fur Traders During the Last Decades of the Eighteenth Century* (Chicago: University of Chicago Press, 1972); Derek Pethick, *First Approaches to the Northwest Coast* (Seattle: University of Washington Press, 1979); Alexander Walker, *An Account of a Voyage to the North West Coast of America in 1785 & 1786*, ed. Robin Fisher and J. M. Bumsted (Seattle: University of Washington Press, 1982); José Mariano Moziña, *Noticias de Nutka: An Account of Nootka Sound in 1792* (Seattle: University of Washington Press, 1970; 2nd ed., 1991); John Kendrick, trans., *The Voyage of Sutil and Mexicana, 1792: The Last Spanish Exploration of the Northwest Coast of America* (Spokane: Arthur H. Clark, 1995).

48. Alfred Tamarin and Shirley Glubok, *Voyaging to Cathay: Americans in the China Trade* (New York: Viking Press, 1976); Margaret C. S. Christman, *Adventurous Pursuits: Americans and the China Trade, 1784–1844* (Washington, D.C.: Smithsonian Institution Press, 1984); Samuel Eliot Morison, *The Maritime History of Massachusetts, 1783–1860* (Boston: Houghton Mifflin, 1921); Ernest Stanley Dodge, *New England and the South Seas* (Cambridge, Mass.: Harvard University Press, 1965); Arrell Morgan Gibson, with John S. Whitehead, *Yankees in Paradise: The Pacific Basin Frontier* (Albuquerque: University of New Mexico Press, 1993); James R. Gibson, *Otter Skins, Boston Ships, and China Goods: The Maritime Fur Trade of the Northwest Coast, 1785–1841* (Seattle: University of Washington Press, 1992).

49. Charles Rappleye, *Sons of Providence: The Brown Brothers, the Slave Trade, and the American Revolution* (New York: Simon and Schuster, 2006), p. 247. See also Captain John DeWolf, *A Voyage to the North Pacific* (Fairfield, Wash.: Ye Galleon Press, 1998).

50. Jefferson to Ezra Stiles, 1 September, 1786, quoted in James Zug, *American Traveler: The Life and Adventures of John Ledyard, the Man Who Dreamed of Walking the World* (New York: Basic Books, 2005), p. 172. See also William C. Gifford, *Ledyard: In Search of the First American Explorer* (New York: Harcourt, 2007); Stephen D. Watrous, ed., *John Ledyard's Journey through Russia and Siberia, 1787–1788: The Journal and Selected Letters* (Madison: University of Wisconsin Press, 1966).

11

HEMISPHERIC HISTORY AND ATLANTIC HISTORY

JACK P. GREENE

Historians of the early modern Americas have always been open to the broader approach. Already by the closing decades of the nineteenth century, they had recognized and sought to subvert the tendency of emerging national histories to reduce the colonial past to little more than the pre-history of the independent nations that formed in the Americas after the mid-1770s. By insisting that colonial histories be contextualized, both as parts of the empires to which they belonged and as subsets of the greater process of European expansion, they called attention to the larger worlds in which early modern colonies took shape and to which they were intimately and immediately attached. Considering themselves what we might now call *cosmopolitan contextualists*, colonialists regarded those who tried to shoe-horn colonial histories into the mold of the new states that were consequent to decolonization as *parochial anachronists*.

In this spirit, early modern colonialists have been at the forefront of the rush to adopt still larger perspectives over recent decades. Including the whole of the Atlantic basin—Europe, Africa, the Americas, and adjacent seas and islands—the *Atlantic perspective*, first articulated in the early 1970s and energetically pushed by fresh proselytes in the early 1990s, has been enthusiastically embraced by students of the colonial British world and has begun to gain considerable currency among scholars working in other areas of the early modern world that formed around the Atlantic. As a result, few early modern Americanists remain unconverted to the idea that developments throughout the Americas can be more fully understood when placed within the broader transatlantic, inter-atlantic, or intra-atlantic settings in which they occurred. One of the central attractions of this perspective has been the prospect that, by calling attention to social, economic, political, and cultural commonalities and interactions among areas that either were not connected by national allegiances or did not remain within the same national state system, it would help to break the hold of the national frameworks within which history traditionally has been written, frameworks that have operated not just to parochialize specific histories but also to obscure the larger patterns and processes within which the several societies around the Atlantic functioned and of which they were integral parts.[1]

Even more recently, a second, broad, and complementary movement toward a *multicultural perspective* has exhibited considerable vigor. Among early American historians within the United States, this perspective seems to have been the immediate consequence of a growing consciousness that some portions of the United States had a "prenational" history that was neither English nor exclusively indigenous. Like the Atlantic perspective, this consciousness is not exactly new. Herbert Bolton was an ardent exponent of this point of view more than three-quarters of a century ago,[2] and his influence upon a few English colonialists—particularly Max Savelle, who produced one of the best and most widely used texts in colonial British American history—was by no means insignificant.[3] But the proliferation of interest in the Spanish, French, and Russian origins of the United States among pre-United States historians is relatively recent and arises largely and logically out of two impulses in historical studies: an older impulse, deriving from the *annalistes'* ambitious goal of constructing a *histoire totale* decentering elite white males, and a newer and more parochial impulse to give all cultures and regions space within the United States historical narrative. The latest manifestation of this multicultural, multiregional impulse has been the emergence of a demand for the creation of a *continental history* that would place the indigenous inhabitants at the center of the story and give as much attention to Spanish, French, and Russian colonies in the middle and western edges of the continent as to British provinces on the east coast.[4]

So far, I think it is fair to say that the recent interest of pre-United States historians in non-British areas has been largely confined to those regions that would subsequently become part of the United States. At least in its earliest stages, this development was a potential boon to those scholars who, having been marginalized in their own field of early modern Latin American history precisely because the areas upon which they worked—Florida, New Mexico, Texas, California, Louisiana—were no longer a part of Spanish or French America, now suddenly found a home in pre-United States history and a new and enthusiastic audience for their work.[5] But it is also fair to say, I think, that the new multicultural interest in the non-British roots of United States civilization has not moved far beyond the borders of the present United States and has remained relatively unconcerned with the larger cultural worlds to which the areas of Spanish or French penetration were attached. Indeed, calls for a continental history often turn out to exclude significant portions of the North American continent to the south of the Rio Grande and to the north of the later boundary between Canada and the United States.[6] As a result, the United States community of early American historians has continued to be largely uninformed about the extensive and rich historiography produced, especially over the last half century, on those larger Spanish and French cultural worlds. Incorporation into the national history of the United States has thus effectually disattached areas with non-British origins from the national cultural areas with which they were associated for lengthy periods of their early histories. Such decontextualization cannot be expected to produce comprehensive understandings of the histories of the areas that suffer it, much less to enrich them.

While the emergence of the Atlantic perspective has served to undermine traditional national frameworks, the multicultural turn has thus largely functioned to reinforce them. The central contention in these brief reflections is that this need not be the case, that the new interest in the non-English colonial histories of areas in the United States points logically in the direction of the desirability of a broad *hemispheric perspective* that, by promoting broad comparative analysis across both the South and North American hemispheres and their adjacent islands, might actually enhance the prospects for transcending national frameworks. Moreover, a hemispheric perspective also seems to offer better prospects for achieving one of the unfilled promises of the Atlantic perspective, the possibility of drawing comparisons. The developing field of Atlantic history has tended to concentrate on identifying and elaborating the connections that tied the Atlantic together, and, as J. H. Elliott remarked, will probably "always...remain a history framed more in terms of connections than of comparisons."[7]

The primary obstacle to the development of a hemispheric perspective is, of course, the dense historiographies that, especially in recent decades, have emerged in the study of all areas of the Americas, historiographies that require enormous time and energy to master.[8] In 1999, at a conference of historians primarily concerned with the history of those parts of colonial British America that became the United States, James Lockhart and Stuart Schwartz, two of the most distinguished contributors to the literature on colonial Latin America and coauthors of an acclaimed synthesis, *Early Latin America*,[9] endeavored to guide their audience into this wholly different and unusually rich terra incognita.[10] Their remarks provide a foundation for the following speculations about the possible benefits of a broad hemispheric approach.

As both Lockhart and Schwartz made clear, the historiographies they represent stand in no need of intellectual colonization by pre-United States historians. Indeed, as Lockhart pointed out, pre-United States historians working on Spanish areas should not expect to make a significant contribution to this literature until they have mastered it. Devoted to the exposition of cultural complexes radically different from the British, with different laws, different if sometimes parallel institutions, and different social dynamics, those historiographies are based on sources unfamiliar to students of the British American world. The two presenters provided a powerful sense of how much there was to learn and how demanding such an enterprise might be. They made it clear that those who aspire to advance a more inclusive version of the pre-United States past would do well to hie it to one of those rare universities at which it is possible to study the histories of all the colonial Americas with equal seriousness.

Superficially and on a general level, there seem to be many similarities between the historiographies of early Latin American and colonial British American history. At least until comparatively recently, both have been source-driven and both have followed Lockhart's well-known law of the conservation of the energy of historians: "always take the easiest, most synthetic source first."[11] In colonial British American history, the private narratives of settlement produced by such people as John Smith, William Bradford, John Winthrop, and Andrew White—the nearest equivalents to the Spanish chronicles of conquest—never acquired the historiographical importance of those chronicles, but both early American fields were dominated for many decades by studies based on official correspondence and metropolitan and provincial institutional records, an emphasis that grossly exaggerated the importance of the metropolis and provincial centers in the construction of colonies and empire. In pursuit of social history, both fields turned to legal records and notarial archives—or, in the British case, to probate records, deeds, and parish and church registers. The absence of notarial records in British America may have been responsible for what I perceive to have been a lag in the turn to social history among historians of the English-speaking world, who took a bit longer to devise ways to bring the methods of the *annalistes* to bear upon social history issues.

Between the earlier emphasis on institutional history and the advent of social history, historians of colonial British America used a rich cache of contemporaneously and locally generated and produced printed materials, including political tracts, political economy treatises, improvement literature, sermons, chorographies, civil and religious histories, natural histories, a variety of belletristic productions, and newspaper essays, as the foundations for an intellectual history stage that dominated colonial British American historiography for at least a generation in the wake of World War II and seems to have had no counterpart in early Latin American studies. Only during the last quarter-century have a few historians begun to use similar materials to explore the intellectual and cultural development of Hispanic America with a comparable level of detail and sophistication.[12]

Because British America, like the rest of the Americas outside greater Mexico and Peru, lacks the extensive indigenous language sources that scholars such as Lockhart and his students have exploited so brilliantly for the Nahuatl-speaking polities of central Mexico, it has, of course, missed the New Philology phase that has been so prominent in recent early modern Latin American studies. It has, however, participated fully in the eclecticism characteristic of much recent work on early Latin America: the rise of ethnohistory and the interest in indigenous peoples; the reexamination of African slavery; the focus on women's history and gender definitions; the exploration of transatlantic intellectual connections in political, economic, social, educational, and religious life; the turn to cultural history and the emergence of creole or American cultural systems and identities; and perhaps even the development of a new interest in the history of secondary centers and peripheral areas in the Americas. In both colonial Latin American and British American studies, moreover, much of this recent work has relied less upon the use of new kinds of sources than upon revisiting and requestioning documents that have long been familiar to historians. Indeed, some of this work is driven not by sources, but by the absence of sources and by the theory that scholars have generated to help them fill the historical silences present in the records.

In view of the fact that early Latin American and colonial British American historians are part of the same general historical community, these similarities in historiographical development are hardly surprising. No matter how different their sources or the cultures they study, both sets of historians are equally subject to the same professional intellectual fashions that makes social history the darling of one generation and cultural history the central interest of the next. And the parallels could be extended to the historiographies of the fragmented early modern American enterprises of both the French and the Dutch.[13]

As one dips even casually into the historiographies of the early modern colonial Americas, however, one senses that the parallels and correspondences extend beyond historiography to substantive issues involving structures and processes. The first impression is one of extraordinary and fundamental difference. Iberian American polities were established a full century before those of the north Europeans—*before* the Protestant and Catholic Reformations had occurred, before the chivalric model had lost its appeal, and before the international market system was well developed. Within a generation of contact, moreover, the Spanish happened upon, conquered, and occupied the two areas with the greatest mineral wealth and the largest concentrations of indigenous peoples in the Americas. The post-Conquest societies that the Spanish constructed in New Spain and Peru were the New World's great exceptions. Nowhere else was mineral wealth so readily accessible or native political and social development so complex. The presence of such numerous peoples required extensive adaptation on the part of the Spanish as well as of the indigenes. Although the Spanish used indigenous labor to work the mines, the ranches, and the agricultural settlements they established, they eventually negotiated the system of two republics—Spanish and Indian—that permitted the indigenes a degree of self-government under the Spanish Crown. At least in part because of the vast wealth they acquired through these conquests, the Spanish, moreover, were able to invest large sums of money and considerable manpower in evangelization. Through the mission system, combining civil and religious pacification, these efforts extended well beyond the sedentary indigenous empires of New Spain and Peru.

Encountering no similarly exploitable cultures, the Portuguese American settlements in Brazil exhibited quite different relationships with the indigenes, spent far fewer resources upon their evangelization, and established flourishing agricultural and cattle-raising societies before finding great mineral wealth a century and a half after their first effective settlement. In many respects, Spanish polities established in the late sixteenth and seventeenth centuries beyond the areas of highly developed indigenous states and great mineral wealth–in Central America, New Granada, Venezuela, Chile, Paraguay, Río de la Plata—were, like Brazil, the products less of conquest than of settlement, and focused on agriculture and livestock.

Despite these differences, the various Iberian polities were profoundly similar. They shared an attachment to Roman Catholicism, and they were unusually *in*clusionary, even fusionist, in two senses: first, they incorporated indigenes and Africans into the legal and political systems they established, and second, they generated the extensive mixed populations that by the early nineteenth century could credibly claim to be *the people* of Brazil or Mexico.[14] Established a full century later and also lacking mineral wealth and highly developed indigenous societies, the French colonies were similar to the Iberian colonies in their Catholicism, the extensiveness of their efforts at evangelization, their mixed-race populations, and the civil spaces those populations occupied.

In all these respects, the situation was far different in British and Dutch American polities established at roughly the same time as the French, after the Protestant Reformation, just as the new international trading system that would reach full flower in the early nineteenth century was taking off. Neither the Dutch nor the British encountered a densely populated indigenous empire or discovered any mines. They spent little energy and less funds on the evangelization of the indigenes, and they established polities that were—implicitly with regard to the indigenes and explicitly with regard to imported Africans and their descendants—much more *ex*clusionary than those established by the Iberians. The mixed populations they generated, though not insignificant, were never numerous or powerful enough to appropriate the title of *the people*.

As the above sketch suggests, there can be little doubt that within the vast Iberian American world, colonial outcomes were determined less by cultural differences among Europeans than by physical differences, economic potentialities, and the nature and density of indigenous populations in occupied areas. Spaniards and Portuguese shared a common religion, albeit one more heterodox and independent of Rome than historians from Protestant countries used to assume. They also shared a civil law tradition with Roman origins and scrupulous written records. To instruct them in their forays in the Americas, they both had had extensive contact with non-Christian peoples: Moors in Iberia and North Africa, Guanches in the Canary Islands, and, for the Portuguese, peoples along the West coast of Africa and around the Indian Ocean. Notwithstanding these and other broad cultural similarities, however, the colonial process produced a wide variety of different kinds of political societies in the Iberian American world, differences not just between Spanish and Portuguese colonies but within the Spanish Empire and within Portuguese Brazil.

If we extend the field of comparison to include the polities established by northern Europeans in the West Indies and North America, however, we may discover that cultural differences were more important. Certainly, considerations of what sort of resource environment and indigenous societies were encountered, and what the economic potential of an area was, were paramount in determining the nature of the polities created in northern European as well as in Iberian America. But the fact that the British and Dutch were mainly Protestant peoples, that the English functioned within a common-law tradition and the Dutch within a similarly customary one, and that the British operated within a political culture that was explicitly consensual and participatory may also have been deeply differentiating. Not just the languages spoken, the books read, and the national or ethnic styles of deportment or transactions exhibited, but also the underlying religious and, even more profoundly, legal and political cultures may have distinguished British and Dutch polities in America from those that were Spanish, Portuguese, or French. A comparison between Portuguese and British America is revealing in this regard. Despite the facts that neither of them encountered great sedentary indigenous empires, and that both of them imported large amounts of African labor and developed staple agricultural economies filled with a combination of plantations and smaller settlements, Brazil and the British polities of the West Indies and North America, so similar on the surface, exhibited important divergences—for instance, in the relationship of the slave and free colored populations to the law—that have to be marked down largely to cultural differences.

As interesting as these differences may be, even a casual review of the burgeoning literatures on the early modern Americas strongly suggests that there were also some remarkable commonalities. The various colonizing powers were all mutual participants in the colonial process that transformed the Americas in the centuries after 1492. As European agents, often assisted by African or indigenous auxiliaries, their subjects took the initiative in reconstructing the social order throughout the Americas. They all established a number of new societies shaped by a combination of local conditions and immigrant efforts to replicate the cultures they had left behind, societies that both deviated from metropolitan norms and were unmistakable offshoots of the national cultures they represented. They all involved transfers of people—substantial transfers in the case of Spain, Portugal, and Britain—drawn by the opportunities that the Americas offered, and they all participated in an aggressive European reconstruction and renaming of American spaces and a massive exploitation and economic, social, and political reorganization of American peoples and resources. To one degree or another, they all conceived of the changes they wrought as the working out of a providential design and part of an extensive civilizing project, and used their own legal inheritances and forms of governance to impose their mastery over large parts of the Americas. They all unwittingly introduced pathogens that destroyed vast numbers among the indigenous populations and addressed their labor problems through a resort to unfree labor, including slavery. They all participated in a profound cultural transformation by which a galaxy of indigenous groups were reduced to far fewer tribes or nations.

Nor were these the only commonalities. With the exception of the Dutch, who lost their foothold in North America and their principal holdings in South America during the seventeenth century, they all experienced impressive expansion and economic and social development, including, in the eighteenth century, considerable economic acceleration and diversification, a process that over time led to the transformation of some areas from fringes of the European world into colonial centers and peripheries. They all produced a wide variety of provincial political societies, each with a distinctive legal system and collective identity to fit its changing peculiarities, experiences, and circumstances. Over time, they all experienced a significant transfer of political authority to the creoles or native-born Americans who presided over these societies, and mid-eighteenth-century wars led in the cases of both the Spanish and the British to metropolitan policies that challenged settler autonomy and ultimately provoked or contributed to reluctant settler revolts and the establishment of independent nations. The identification of these many general similarities provides the additional advantage of calling attention to the remarkable extent to which the secondary centers and peripheries in the New World and the settler, indigenous, and enslaved populations who inhabited them were active participants in the construction of early modern empires and of the broader Atlantic and hemispheric worlds of which they were all a part.[15]

Yet these casual contrasts and parallels only beg the question of why pre-United States historians should be interested in the experience of early modern Latin America and vice versa. If pre-United States historians need instruction as they endeavor to contribute to a more inclusive prenational history, what is in it for Latin Americanists or Québecois? Most historians seem to be quite content to let national boundaries channel their research interests. Surely, however, there is more at stake here than bringing neglected areas and experiences into one or another national narrative. At best, that objective is an extremely modest one, and it creates many intellectual problems. In the case of pre-United State historians, for instance, focusing only on the Spanish borderlands not only reinforces the power of the nation-state paradigm in United States historical studies but also leaves the core areas of the Spanish American enterprise out of the picture altogether. Much more interesting are the possible benefits that may accrue from the adoption of a much wider perspective encompassing the entire western hemisphere.

A *hemispheric* approach that has for its long-range objective the development of a comprehensive, comparative analysis across both South and North America and their adjacent islands, and oriented toward the analysis of the encounter between the Old Worlds of Europe, America, and Africa;

the subsequent creation of many New Worlds in the Americas; and the ongoing development of those New Worlds has much to recommend it. Like the continental approach, it directs attention to both sides of that encounter: the invaded as well as the invaders. Unlike the continental approach as so far formulated, it avoids anachronism, not excluding contiguous and closely connected areas that happen to fall on the wrong side of a later national boundary. Furthermore, it encourages the contextualization of regions that during the colonial era formed part of the same national culture area. In all these ways, it offers an effective way to escape the distortions that subordination to the nation-state paradigm imposes upon colonial histories. Because it is infinitely broader than the continental approach, it also promises to yield the richest and most comprehensive understanding of the early modern Americas. In virtually every respect, a hemispheric perspective seems to be superior to a continental one.

A hemispheric perspective would complement an Atlantic perspective and in some respects be more effective, in that it keeps the focus on developments within American spaces rather than upon connections among them. A hemispheric perspective on the colonial process would identify the widest possible range of variations over time, place, and social type as those variations become evident, in the case of the settlers; in patterns of land occupation, relations with indigenous peoples, socioeconomic structures, forms of governance, and modes of religious and cultural life; and, in the case of the indigenous and the enslaved, in patterns of resistance, accommodation, amalgamation, or exclusion. To contextualize these and other subjects, a hemispheric approach, no less than an Atlantic approach, would need to be attentive to ongoing interactions between metropolis and provinces, between American provinces and the source cultures of their populations, and among and within the Americas. A hemispheric perspective thus promises to produce the fullest and most deeply contextualized understanding of the changing character of the early modern American world, as well as of the central elements in its formation. It has a greater capacity to generate comparative analysis and to free the study of the colonial era from the cage of national political boundaries.

Of course, this approach has deep historiographical roots. Bolton called for a hemispheric history in his 1933 presidential address,[16] which generated a lively debate over whether the Americas had a common history[17] and helped to inspire a collective project, supported by the Rockefeller Foundation and spearheaded by the Mexican historian Silvio Zavala and other historians from Latin America, to produce a multivolume hemispheric history in three broad parts, respectively covering the indigenous, colonial, and national eras. Simultaneously published in 1962 in both a Spanish edition and an English abridgement by Max Savelle, Zavala's *The Colonial Period in the History of the New World*, an insightful and extended discussion of the subjects to be covered in the second part of the project, was one of the initial fruits of this project, and remains perhaps the best single analysis of the issues inherent in a hemispheric approach and of the rich promise it holds for achieving an understanding of the full complexity of the colonial process in the early modern Americas. Only by investigating this process "in its totality," Zavala observed, could historians "obtain a more complete knowledge of each of the colonizations and regions in particular," with their many "similarities and diversities." His complaint that the early modern American hemisphere had "not received sufficient comparative attention" explicitly held out the hope that the project in which he was involved would produce not just a general history of the Americas but a comparative one.[18]

This project was finally brought to fruition in 1987, with the publication of an eleven-volume history of the colonial era under the editorship of the Venezuelan historian Guillermo Morón.[19] Each written by a specialist, the many chapters in these volumes provided authoritative accounts of their respective subjects as of the time they were written, but, as in the case of the multivolume histories now being produced for many areas by UNESCO,[20] the specialist authors rarely spoke across chapters to one another. As a result, the volumes failed to deliver on the promise of comparative history, providing instead what might better be thought of as parallel histories, and it is difficult to see how any similar undertaking would be more successful in facilitating, much less achieving, a comparative hemispheric history of the early modern Americas. Moreover, the logistics and publication delays of such massive projects mean that many of the chapters will be out of date before they are published.

But a multivolume, multiauthor project is not the only approach to the pursuit of a hemispheric history. One alternative might be for some younger scholar with extensive language proficiency to write a volume following the broad outlines Zavala laid out in the early 1960s. Whether any individual scholar is likely to complete a project of this magnitude, however, is doubtful. Few historians will ever be better equipped to do so than J. H. Elliott, whose *Empires of the Atlantic World: Britain and Spain in America, 1492–1830*[21] is a truly magnificent scholarly achievement. Demonstrating his extensive mastery over two rich and sophisticated historical literatures, this well-crafted synthesis provides a genuinely comparative history of the Spanish and British empires from the Columbian voyages during the closing decades of the fifteenth century through the independence era of

1770 to 1825. Elliott impressively accomplishes his objectives of transcending the atomization that has increasingly characterized colonial studies of the Americas and, through his comparisons, of throwing new light on the colonial process as it operated in the Americas. Whether his hefty volume will actually "help to shake historians out of their provincialisms" remains to be seen.[22]

Broad as his study is, however, Elliott makes no claim to comprehensiveness. As he acknowledges, he did not, by design, include the Portuguese, French, and Dutch empires, and he focused mainly on "the development of the settler societies and their relationship with their mother countries," treating indigenous peoples and the African enslaved only insofar as they related to that development. As he also acknowledges, he was selective in his choice of which settler societies to cover in detail, focusing heavily on the prominent Spanish kingdoms of New Spain and Peru and the older and more populous British colonies in Virginia and New England. He thus neglects the Caribbean colonies and gives scant attention to the British middle and lower southern colonies or to the Spanish territories in Central America, New Granada, Venezuela, Chile, Río de la Plata, Florida, or the northern borderlands of New Spain, the last two of which he characterizes as the "orphans of Spain's empire in America." One can scarcely disagree with Elliot's observation that "the number of colonizing powers...and the multiplicity of the societies they established in the Americas" make "a sustained comparison embracing the entire New World" a project "likely to defy the efforts of any individual historian."[23]

A third alternative might involve a cooperative undertaking involving just a few devoted scholars, each of whom has mastered segments of the increasingly extensive literatures on each of the Americas: not only South and North, island and continental, Spanish, Portuguese, French, Dutch, Scandinavian, and Russian, but also neo-African and indigenous America, as well as the populations, entities, and cultures that grew up and occupied the interstices between and within those worlds. The aim of such a project would be to produce not a comprehensive general history, but a systematic and authoritative comparative study of the early modern Americas, an analytic overview that would endeavor to identify the processual commonalities and the rich social and cultural variations throughout the hemisphere in the early modern era.[24]

The difficulties involved in all three of these strategies strongly suggest, however, that the ultimate goal of a hemispheric perspective should not be the production of a general history of the early modern Americas, nor even of a multiauthor comparative analysis. Since the 1960s, Atlantic history has

not managed to generate such a volume. Like Atlantic history, American hemispheric history should rather pursue a more incremental and diffuse approach, one that emphasizes the production of well-researched synthetic studies and monographs with a comparative dimension or a comparative promise. Accessible to those with the necessary linguistic skills, the rich monographic literature produced since the 1950s provides a sturdy foundation on which to build synthetic studies of many aspects of the early modern transformation of the Americas. However, the wide scope of a hemispheric approach strongly suggests that collaborative enterprises, made more manageable by Web-based networking and circumventing the linguistic deficiencies of individual scholars, may be the most promising way forward. Moreover, such studies would not have to be comprehensive to be useful. They could treat as few as two national spheres. The range of topics that could be illuminated by such undertakings is virtually limitless, including, to list only a few, the changing indigenous experience with and response to European intrusions; settler adaptations of inherited Old World values, institutions, and customs to New World conditions; the development of viable provincial economies; the recruitment and organization of labor; patterns of ethnic interactions; relations between colonial provinces and their respective European metropolises; and the emergence of provincial identities throughout the new American political units. Of course, collaborative studies would not have to be limited to such broad questions. They might, perhaps with more effectiveness, focus on particular aspects of such subjects, such as family formation, gender relations, wealth differentiation, inheritance practices, and patterns of land or resource utilization.

But the tried-and-true method of producing new knowledge is through new research and the publication of monographs. Depending on the extent of their linguistic skills, scholars have at least three strategies available to them. First, those able to do research in more than one language can design studies of the same phenomenon in two or more similar or contrasting places in different cultural areas. Mariana Dantas's carefully integrated study of urban laborers of African or biracial descent in the Brazilian town of Sabará in Minas Gerais and in Baltimore during the last decades of the eighteenth century and the early decades of the nineteenth century is a model of this type of study.[25] Second, teams of scholars with complementary expertises can collaborate on comparative projects that transcend national and linguistic historiographical boundaries. Thus, Trevor Burnard, a specialist on the British West Indies, and John Garrigus, a student of the French Antilles, have jointly undertaken a comparative study of Jamaica and Saint-Domingue, the two most prolific sugar regimes in the eighteenth-century Caribbean. Third, colonial historians, especially those who study either the Spanish, Portuguese, British, or French American colonies, each of which extended over a broad range of societies formed in a great variety of physical spaces, have always been implicit, and occasionally even explicit, comparativists, and scholars can do important and useful comparative studies without moving out of a specific imperial region. Elizabeth Mancke's rigorous comparison of the economic, community, and political development of two socioeconomically similar towns in Massachusetts and Nova Scotia, and Cynthia Radding's comparative study of the Sonora region of northwestern New Spain and the Chiquitos region of lowland Bolivia, two ecologically different Spanish frontier colonies, provide particularly good examples of this approach.[26]

Unfortunately, the pedagogical devices necessary to encourage new generations of colonialists to step outside nation-state paradigms and work within a hemispheric framework are not yet in place. Just as the proliferating interest in Atlantic history has led to the creation of programs to foster the study of that subject, however, we hope that the intellectual attractions of studying the internal histories of the new early modern American worlds may lead to the creation of similar programs to promote the analysis of those worlds and foster the intellectual interchange and comparative thinking necessary to enable scholars to cross traditional specialized fields.[27] The creation of a center devoted to bringing together younger scholars and advanced doctoral students who were working in various areas of the colonial Americas to discuss their work and exchange ideas within a broad hemispheric framework would also be an effective device for advancing this perspective.[28]

Having embraced the broader Atlantic perspective in recent years, pre-United States historians may now be ready to embrace—as a counterbalance—a complementary hemispheric one. While the Atlanticists continue to pursue connections and interactivity, Hemispherists can concentrate on developing comparisons. With these two broad perspectives before them, early Spanish American, colonial Brazilian, colonial British, and colonial French historians may manage finally to escape—and transcend—the *national* frameworks that have long channeled their work and inhibited broad comparative analyses. Early modern colonial history would then become something more than the prehistory of the adventitious nation-states of the contemporary American world. In the process, knowledge of the transformation of the American hemisphere following the Columbian encounter, surely one of the grandest and darkest subjects in the unfolding history of the human race, would be enormously deepened and enriched.

NOTES

1. See Jack P. Greene, "Beyond Power: Paradigm Subversion and Reformulation and the Re-creation of the Early Modern Atlantic World," in Jack P. Greene, *Interpreting Early America: Historiographical Essays* (Charlottesville: University Press of Virginia, 1996), pp. 17–42; and David Armitage, "Three Concepts of Atlantic History," in David Armitage and Michael J. Braddick, eds., *The British Atlantic World, 1500–1800* (New York: Palgrave, 2002), pp. 11–30.

2. Herbert E. Bolton, "The Epic of Greater America," *American Historical Review* 38 (1933): 448–474.

3. Max Savelle, *The Foundations of American Civilization, a History of Colonial America* (New York: Henry Holt, 1942).

4. Daniel H. Usner, Jr, "Borderlands," in Daniel Vickers, ed., *A Companion to Colonial America* (Malden, Mass.: Basil Blackwell, 2003), pp. 408–424, provides an excellent recent historiographical guide.

5. See Amy Turner Bushnell, "Gates, Patterns, and Peripheries: The Field of Frontier Latin America," in Christine Daniels and Michael V. Kennedy, eds., *Negotiated Empires: Centers and Peripheries in the New World, 1500–1820* (New York: Routledge, 2001), pp. 15–28.

6. A notable exception, Vickers, *Companion to Colonial America*, pp. 429–507, includes four chapters under the rubric "Comparisons" on the Caribbean, New Spain, New France, and Atlantic Canada, respectively by Verene Shepherd and Carleen Payne, Robert Ferry, Allan Greer, and Peter Pope.

7. J. H. Elliott, "Atlantic History: A Circumnavigation," in Armitage and Braddick, eds., *British Atlantic World, 1500–1800*, p. 237.

8. See the collection of articles reprinted in Amy Turner Bushnell, ed., *Establishing Exceptionalisms: Historiography and the Colonial Americas* (Brookfield, Vt.: Variorum, 1995).

9. James Lockhart and Stuart B. Schwartz, *Early Latin America: A History of Colonial Spanish America and Brazil* (New York Cambridge University Press, 1983).

10. James Lockhart, "Some Comments on Early Latin American Historiography," and Stuart B. Schwartz, "The Recent Historiography of Early Modern Brazil in a Comparative Perspective," both unpublished papers presented at the plenary session "Colonial America: Spanish and Portuguese Worlds," Fifth Annual Conference of the Omohundro Institute of Early American History and Culture, University of Texas at Austin (1999).

11. Lockhart, "Some Comments on Early Latin American Historiography," p. 4.

12. Superb examples include D. A. Brading, *The First America: The Spanish Monarchy, Creole Patriots, and the Liberal State 1492–1867* (Cambridge: Cambridge University Press, 1991), and *Merxican Phoenix: Our Lady of Guadalupe: Image and Tradition Across Five Centuries* (Cambridge: Cambridge University Press, 2002); Anthony Pagden, *The Fall of Natural Man: The American Indian and the Origins*

of Comparative Ethnology (Cambridge: Cambridge University Press, 1982); and Jorge Cañizares-Esguerra, *How to Write the History of the New World: Histories, Epistemologies, and Identities in the Eighteenth-Century Atlantic World* (Stanford: Stanford University Press, 2001).

13. Alan Greer, "Comparisons: New France," in Vickers, ed., *Companion to Colonial America*, pp. 469–488, provides a full discussion for New France, though not for the French settlements in the Caribbean and the West Indies.

14. Schwartz, "Recent Historiography of Early Modern Brazil in a Comparative Perspective," p. 26.

15. a. See Amy Turner Bushnell and Jack P. Greene, "Peripheries, Centers, and the Construction of Early American Empires: An Introduction," in Daniels and Kennedy, eds., *Negotiated Empires*, pp. 1–14; Schwartz, "Recent Historiography of Early Modern Brazil in a Comparative Perspective."

16. Bolton, "Epic of Greater America."

17. Lewis Hanke, ed., *Do the Americas Have a Common History? A Critique of the Bolton Theory* (New York: Alfred A. Knopf, 1964), collected much of this material.

18. Silvio Zavala, *The Colonial Period in the History of the New World,*, abridged by Max Savelle (Mexico City: Instituto Panamericano, 1962). The quotations are from p. x. A version of Zavala's penetrating and thoughtful introduction appeared as "A General View of the Colonial History of the New World," *American Historical Review* 66 (1961): 913–929.

19. Guillermo Morón, ed., *Historia general de América: Período colonial*, 11 vols. (Caracas: Academia Nacional de la Historia de Venezuela, 1987).

20. For instance, *The History of Humanity: Scientific and Cultural Development*, 7 vols. (Paris: UNESCO, 1999).

21. John H. Elliott, *Empires of the Atlantic World: Britain and Spain in America, 1492–1830.* (New Haven: Yale University Press, 2006).

22. Ibid., p. xvi.

23. Ibid., pp. xvi, xviii, 272.

24. This is precisely the sort of working group that James Lockhart, Stuart Schwartz, and I undertook to establish in the early 1990s at the Humanities Research Institute of the University of California. A combination of budgetary shortfalls and my departure from the University of California at Irvine sabotaged that particular effort, but any attempt to put together and finance a group of specialists to produce a genuinely comparative history of the early modern Americas would face similar obstacles.

25. Mariana Dantas, *Black Townsmen: Urban Slavery and Freedom in the Eighteenth-Century Americas* (New York: Palgrave Macmillan, 2008).

26. Elizabeth Mancke, *The Faultlines of Empire: Political Differentiation in Massachusetts and Nova Scotia, ca. 1760–1830* (New York: Routledge, 2004); Cynthia Radding, *Landscapes of Power and Identity: Comparative Histories of the*

Sonoran Desert and the Forests of Amazonia from Colony to Republic (Durham, N.C.: Duke University Press, 2005).

27. Earlier models for such a program include the Tropical History program that flourished at the University of Wisconsin in the 1960s and early 1970s and the interdisciplinary Atlantic History and Culture program that functioned so successfully at Johns Hopkins University in the 1970s and 1980s. The former required, and the latter strongly encouraged, doctoral students not to work entirely or even mostly within a single national boundary, and the latter offered the opportunity for doctoral students in early modern colonial history to trade a possible expertise in the national era of the United States or Latin America for a knowledge of a parallel segment of the early modern colonial enterprise.

28. Perhaps the relatively new Center for New World Comparative Studies at the John Carter Brown Library, the world's most extensive and comprehensive collection of published works on the Americas during the early modern period, will undertake to raise the funds necessary to enable it to play a catalytic role in the spread of the hemispheric approach.

12

ATLANTIC HISTORY AND
GLOBAL HISTORY

NICHOLAS CANNY

There have been so many recent advocates for Atlantic history that David Armitage has declared us all to be Atlanticists now.[1] While conceding Armitage's point that the subject of Atlantic history has become fashionable, and while saluting his effort to define a British Atlantic, there is such limited agreement over what the subject entails that it might be said that there are as many varieties of Atlantic history as there are Atlanticists.[2] This chapter seeks to bring clarity to the study of the subject in three ways. First, it provides a taxonomy of six prescriptions that have been advanced by various practitioners of Atlantic history so that the strengths and shortcomings of each can be considered; second, it discusses two books which, each in its own way, challenge the legitimacy or importance of Atlantic history; and third, it offers some counters to these challenges and justifies the continued study of Atlantic history once it has been clearly distinguished from global history.

First among those who have come to be considered Atlantic historians have been specialists of early modern Europe who study what was once called the history of European overseas expansion in a comparative context. They have favored comparisons between the endeavors of England and Spain in the Atlantic or between the achievements of England and France in North America (but strangely only occasionally in the Caribbean), but also recently have given some attention to comparisons between the attainments of the English and the Dutch in the New World. When it comes to the eighteenth century, the activities of the Portuguese in Africa and America are sometimes also drawn into such comparisons. The issues that principally concern these scholars are cultural encounters between the extraordinary range of peoples who were brought into contact or conflict with one another in the Atlantic basin, principally through the agency of Europeans, over the course of the early modern centuries; Europeans' promotion of new economic interests in the Atlantic; and different European groups' efforts to monopolize trade in certain areas and commodities and to command the labor of other peoples. These historians are particularly interested in how Europeans created societies and polities de novo in distant places or fashioned them out of what remained of those indigenous societies which Europeans had made subservient to their interests.[3] The work of these authors has aroused considerable interest among students of literature, who, in turn, have persuaded several historians to include within their purview the analysis of literary texts—both those composed in a colonial context and those written by European authors who may have had no direct experience of overseas voyaging.[4]

Those in category two are scholars interested in the comparative study of migrations across the Atlantic from the sixteenth to the twentieth centuries, with attention sometimes being given to the comparative study of the social configurations that resulted from these various migration streams. These scholars are mostly historians, but their empirical investigations have attracted increasing attention from social theorists who deploy historical evidence to enable generalizations about the phenomenon of human migration. One merit of this work, which justifies the appellation Atlantic, is that it links European with American and with African experiences, usually from the late seventeenth to the early nineteenth century, and, in doing so, it draws a clear distinction between slave migrations and voluntary free migrations. Also, insofar as the work of Frank Tannenbaum falls into this category, it may be credited with pioneering the comparative study of slavery in its North and South American configurations. Scholars of recent years tend to view the movement of peoples, whether free or unfree, also as a trading enterprise, with the result that historians increasingly attribute relativities in the always harsh treatment of passengers to the profit motives of both the carriers and the ultimate employers rather than, as in earlier scholarship, to supposed variations in the sensibilities of European traders and planters from different national or religious backgrounds.[5] Nonetheless, the investigation of the impact of both European Enlightenment ideas and those of Protestant evangelicals in discrediting first the slave trade, and then the institution of slavery itself, continues to attract the attention of scholars who also increasingly address their subject in a comparative Atlantic perspective.[6]

My third category includes economic historians interested more particularly in the history of trade, especially comparative intra-European trade of the early modern centuries. These address such questions as new trades, reexports, trading networks, and the relationship between long distance intercontinental trade and intra-European trade. These scholars generally query the impact of novel trades upon growing disparities in the commercial activity of various regions of Europe or of individual European countries. More particularly, some of these scholars are interested in the impact of such trades upon the development of an industrial revolution in England toward the close of the eighteenth century or, in more recent scholarship, their influence upon the emergence of what Jan de Vries has described as the industrious revolution. By this term de Vries means the dramatic increase in the production of marketable commodities within a traditional household context, which was stimulated by the desire of artisans to become consumers of the increasing range of luxury commodities that was becoming available to would-be consumers during the seventeenth and eighteenth centuries.[7]

Category four belongs to those who believe that there must be an Atlantic history, or at least a history of the Atlantic, to match that fashioned by Fernand Braudel for the Mediterranean and that outlined by Indian historians, several of them disciples of Braudel, who depict a flourishing trading world in the Indian Ocean long before the arrival there of European seaborne traders, a world that Asians continued to dominate for some centuries after Europeans had intruded upon that sphere. Those who are so inspired are obviously drawn to issues of geographical, geological, oceanographic, and, more generally, environmental constants that shaped, assisted, or constrained human endeavor. However, in the instance of the Atlantic they usually acknowledge that European, rather than African or American, peoples imagined the new worlds that might be fashioned within the limits set by nature, although they also give increasing attention to African, and, to a lesser degree, Native American inputs in molding these European-inspired constructs to better suit their ends.[8]

Another obvious scholarly group that falls within the ambit of Atlantic history includes historians of England or of Britain seeking to construct a wider focus for their subject. These can be social historians interested in witnessing how English or British social norms endured an Atlantic crossing; or disenchanted refugees from the so-called New British History whose protagonists decree that historical developments in England, Scotland, Ireland, and Wales should be interpreted as but several strands of a single process; or, more frequently, historians of British political thought of the seventeenth, eighteenth, and early nineteenth centuries who can recognize how ideas formulated in Europe to resolve particular problems there came to be applied in different transatlantic contexts by those who had conveyed these ideas across the Atlantic in their cultural baggage. These scholars seek to illustrate the unique characteristics of the particular threads of political discourse that informed the creation of political institutions both within England, Scotland, and Ireland, and within the societies that people from these jurisdictions established on the other side of the Atlantic both before and after the era of the American Revolution.[9] The apparently self-contained character of this subject is disturbed only by a few scholars' recognition that political discourse both within the British monarchies and in colonial British America was occasionally influenced by debates on the continent of Europe, or by the recognition that British-inspired political institutions may have emerged in a more pristine form in other British communities of white settlement throughout the world besides those on the Atlantic periphery.[10] The more wide-ranging of this group recognize that what they are investigating held implications also for groups of European colonists in the Americas other than the British, and to this extent we might credit them with inspiring the body of scholarly work associated with the so-called Atlantic Revolutions stretching forward from the American and French revolutions of the late eighteenth century to those in Latin America of the 1820s, and also embracing that in Haiti.[11]

The sixth category of aspirant Atlanticists belongs to historians of the United States wishing to counter the scholarly and popular tendency to depict North American achievements as exceptional. Their version of Atlantic history differs from most others in their concern to trace Atlantic interconnections over a long interval, including the nineteenth and twentieth centuries, and including such subjects as trade, comparative industrialization, labor demands, and the transatlantic migrations that resulted from these interconnections. This line of investigation usually concludes with a consideration of U.S. engagement in the first and second World Wars and of Marshall plan aid. This line, to my mind, is the least convincing variety of Atlantic history because once the attention of its proponents moves forward chronologically from the early modern centuries, it remains fixed spatially as they persist in privileging Atlantic over Pacific or global connections and comparisons, despite the fact that they are treating centuries when Western peoples generally (Euro-Americans and Americans as well as Europeans) had devised maritime technologies which made it possible for them to engage in exploration, trade, and settlement on a global scale and not just within the Atlantic basin.[12]

My description of these six categories of Atlanticists should, in itself, make clear that not all who would wish to be considered Atlantic historians are concerned with the same issues or even with the same centuries. Moreover, as this chapter proceeds, I will be arguing that a reasonably coherent and autonomous Atlantic world existed only from soon after 1492 until about the 1820s. The concern to define the period for which Atlantic history is meaningful is closely related to the other core issue requiring resolution for each group of authors; that is, where Atlantic history ends and where global, or world, history begins. This particular problem has been identified by other contributors to this volume and also by other scholars who have engaged in recent discourse on the range and nature of Atlantic history.[13] These issues raise the further question of what place remains for Atlantic history (if such has any legitimacy) within a larger framework of global history. These questions have assumed greater urgency in recent years by virtue of two publications that are breathtaking in scope and erudition, and that present challenges for Atlantic historians from all six defined categories. These challenges have seldom been confronted by Atlanticists, possibly because these books were not conceived within the paradigm of Atlantic history, but it is all the more necessary to address them because their theses are winning acceptance from historians of other subjects and scholars in other disciplines. The first book, by a German historian of labor and migration, is Dirk Hoerder's *Cultures in Contact: World Migrations in the Second Millennium*, and the second, by the foremost of Britain's historians of empire, is C.A. Bayly's *The Birth of the Modern World, 1780–1914*.[14]

Hoerder's book presents a major challenge to Atlanticists because it implicitly rejects one feature that they consider unique to their subject—the large movement of migrants from Europe and Africa which made possible the peopling or repeopling of the Americas in the aftermath of conquest and depopulation. By demonstrating the propensity of human communities in all centuries and from all known cultural backgrounds to migrate from their heartlands to populate new lands, Hoerder shows that the movement of people from the Old World to the New between the sixteenth and nineteenth centuries was, for all its magnitude, a normal element in the continuum of human history. He has also discounted its novelty by pointing to the concern of leaders from most human societies and in all centuries to commandeer labor—both voluntarily and under compulsion—to meet onerous and hazardous obligations defined by the would-be masters. His argument that the universality of the methods used in several societies to mobilize workforces cannot be attributed solely to imitation or cross-cultural contact is nicely illustrated by reference to how workers were assembled in pre-Columbian America: a society that had had no remembered contact with peoples outside the Americas at the point when Europeans stumbled upon it.[15]

When he focuses particularly on the movement of people across the Atlantic during the sixteenth, seventeenth, eighteenth, and nineteenth centuries, Hoerder neither questions its scale nor minimizes the atrocities, privations, and human suffering associated with it. However by situating these voluntary and forced migrations in global and wider chronological contexts, and by taking account of forced and voluntary human movements throughout the world during the course of the twentieth century (especially population movements within Europe and Asia both before and immediately after the Second World War), he seems to deprive Atlantic history of the one subject that was previously considered to render it distinctive. Moreover, he provides a geographic jolt to traditional presuppositions when he juxtaposes the dispersal of Chinese people throughout Asia over time with the so-called nineteenth-century "diaspora" of European migrants across the Atlantic, a subject that is important to the work of those in two of the six categories of Atlanticists I have defined.[16]

Chris Bayly's *The Birth of the Modern World* has relatively little to say about migration, at least in the statistical sense, but it presents a comprehensive challenge to Atlantic history because the book specifically denies the novelty and significance of most features that historians of the Atlantic have traditionally claimed as special to their subject. Bayly diminishes the subject's importance when he estimates the total outcome of European overseas endeavors of the early modern centuries as no more than the establishment of "networks" of "archaic globalization...created by geographical expansion of ideas and social forces from the regional level to the inter-regional and inter-continental level."[17] Such networks, he contends (and here he obviously has Asian trades with Europe in mind), preceded and continued to run in parallel with, but were in no way necessary to, the achievement of "the first age of truly globalized imperialism," which he associates with political developments in each of western Europe, Asia, and Africa during the period between 1760 and 1830. These decades, he contends, rather than the preceding centuries, led to "the market-driven uniformity of today's world." If European overseas endeavor of the early modern centuries is to be credited with promoting change, this contribution was, in Bayly's estimation, at most "transitional," leading into what he identifies as the profoundly innovatory decades, 1760–1830, which brought the world from a localized and technologically traditional past toward the infinitely complex and global transformation that it was to experience during the nineteenth century.[18] In assessing the importance of Europe's activity beyond its traditional frontiers during the early modern centuries, Bayly contends that only the development of "inter-regional" trades, especially that in slaves, can be considered a harbinger of modernity. Even then he describes the slave trade, for all its individualistic and brutal aspects, as but a "proto-capitalist industry."[19]

This carefully argued and powerfully documented book therefore falls slightly short of declaring the concerns of Atlantic historians to be of little more than antiquarian interest. In response to this challenge, I will first question the premise from which Chris Bayly proceeds, and second, seek to clarify, in a more systematic way than has been done heretofore, the particular achievements of the early modern centuries on which most Atlantic history has been written. And it also seems appropriate to stake a claim for the vitality of Atlantic history by demonstrating the extent to which the four traits of modernity, as Chris Bayly has defined these, had already been achieved in the Atlantic world before 1760, the date from which he would have the modern world proceed. This will suggest that the progression of human society toward a condition that might be described as "modern" was more gradual that Bayly admits and that developments within the Atlantic world of the sixteenth, seventeenth, and the eighteenth centuries were more essential to its attainment than he acknowledges.

A society is modern, according to Bayly's measurement, (1) when most (or a large number) of people there believe themselves to be modern; (2) when leaders of such societies abandon the ambition to achieve a universal monarchy that has been divinely ordained; (3) when it manifests the emergence of a national state representing centralization of power and loyalty to ethnic solidarity; and (4) when it is sustained by a massive explosion of global, commercial, and intellectual links.

When the Atlantic world of the early modern centuries is judged by the first of these standards, it becomes evident that for the sixteenth and much of the seventeenth century, those Europeans and their descendants of diverse nationalities who established themselves at several points around the Atlantic littoral, and within the continental areas of Central and South America, considered the various societies they shaped to be derivative of their particular societies in Europe—which, they all contended, set the standard for civil living. However, in several societies in the Americas (but not in those European implantations on the coastline of Africa with the possible exception of the Dutch settlement on the Cape of Good Hope), there emerged the phenomenon that historians refer to as creolization. This term describes the process whereby Europeans and their descendants placed in a colonial situation began to see and depict the society in which they were located as more moral than, and therefore superior to, the society from which their ancestors had departed for America. Historians have frequently explained the emergence of such an ideology as a colonial reaction to the patronizing attitude of government officials from the metropole and their agents in the colonies, especially when these agents sought to impose taxes to enable policies (including defensive policies) dictated from the center of power. However, there is also evidence that in some situations, colonials became increasingly proud of their own achievements, usually in the material, but sometimes also in the intellectual, sphere, and were coming to recognize their society as, in certain respects, more accomplished than the metropolitan society from which their forebears had come. Such manifestations might be dismissed as nothing more than colonial provincialism, but in those several instances where resentment of metropolitan rule led to resistance to that rule, and even to bids for political independence, the leaders of those newly independent jurisdictions that emerged displayed a ready willingness to declare their societies to be modern as opposed to that in the metropole whose authority they had discarded and which they could now portray as frozen in time.[20] When we take into account such developments, it becomes evident that the former colonial world of the Atlantic, rather than the Old World of Europe (with the possible exception of France), produced the first crop of self-consciously modern jurisdictions.

On the issue of universal monarchy, it is manifest that the first generation of Spanish colonists and some of their spiritual advisers accepted that they had been specially chosen by God to discover and evangelize New World peoples. Some even asserted that this opportunity had been made available to them to compensate for the loss of Catholic influence in Europe due to the advances made by the Protestant Reformation. Other religiously inspired European groups that became involved in the Atlantic, including French Huguenots and English Puritans, were equally convinced that God had chosen them to bring native Americans to Him. These latter, however, espoused no ambition to rule the world; on the contrary, they were determined to counter what they believed were the Spanish ambitions to achieve universal monarchy. Even this determination became increasingly irrelevant with the passage of time because, subsequent to the mid-seventeenth century, few in Spain or in Spanish America fostered universal ambitions. Also, from that point forward, most people in Europe who ventured into the Atlantic world were motivated by commercial, political, and even cultural, rather than spiritual, considerations, although some groups, Catholics as well as Protestants, sought intermittently to persuade colonial populations to return to the spiritual first principles of their founders.[21]

The issue of ethnic solidarity is more difficult to contemplate in the context of Atlantic history since groups within nations, rather than states or monarchies, were most responsible for advances into the Atlantic. Moreover, European concern to master and augment the existing populations of the Americas led everywhere to the emergence of more ethnically diverse populations than had existed anywhere previously. These were frequently composed of Native Americans, people from many familial and ethnic groups in Africa, and Euro-Americans drawn from a variety of European backgrounds, religions, and nationalities. Nonetheless, as European powers came to appreciate the commercial importance of possessions and control of trade in the Atlantic, many sought to control particular areas of that world to meet their individual needs. This effort persisted until several former colonies made bids to imagine themselves as, and constitute themselves into, new nations that would be recognizable as nation-states of a European kind. In the course of doing so, each subsumed several ethnic groups (usually with the exception of Native Americans and African slaves) residing within their frontiers into a single cultural group.

In the matter of commercial links, Chris Bayly is probably correct to portray the new trading networks that developed between Europe and Asia during the early modern centuries as "archaic," in that they were built upon, or were a substitution for, older trading connections and were primarily concerned (at least at the outset) with providing luxury goods for a wealthy elite who (as it happened) had little besides precious metal to offer in exchange.[22] However, such trade contributed but incrementally to the quickening of economic activity in the Western world. Insofar as the newly fashioned intercontinental networks of trade contributed immediately to an industrious revolution of the De Vries type, this would have been in certain sophisticated parts of Asia—areas such as Gujarat—which for most of the seventeenth and eighteenth centuries greatly increased the supply of Asian manufactured goods, notably Indian textiles and Chinese porcelains, so that they could obtain more American precious metals from European traders.

However the simultaneous trading activity in manufactured goods which developed on the Atlantic, to which Chris Bayly devotes scant attention, was the very obverse of the Asian developments because it stimulated the manufacture of goods in the more sophisticated parts of Europe and Africa, which were then exchanged for the variety of raw materials available in profusion from several regions of the Americas and which consumers in the Old World had come to covet. Atlantic trade was also different in character from that which developed between Europe and Asia, in that it aimed not only to satisfy the appetites of the rich but also was, at least from the early decades of the seventeenth century, aimed at creating a mass market for goods. It resulted both in the improvement in the quality of life of a broad spectrum of the population of the West, and in the quickening of the pace of economic activity in Europe and throughout the globe. The Atlantic trades, even more than their Asian counterparts, also provided goods for reexport throughout Europe and for their transmission to Asia and Africa, while they generated an ever increasing demand in the Americas for European produce and products ranging from such basic foodstuffs as wine and oil, livestock, grain, and poultry, to agricultural implements, house furnishing, cheap clothing for indentured servants and slaves, and luxury commodities for emerging elites. Such novel aspects of the Atlantic trades are attributable to the fact that they were generated by societies that, from the outset, were being newly fashioned by Europeans in the Americas, through the establishment of Western domination over indigenous populations, or the importation of African and European workers, or a combination of all three.

Another factor that made Atlantic trade different from any other was that it relied on the transport of people to cover marginal costs. Thus, though Dirk Hoerder is correct to insist that other human population movements were greater in scale than the mass one that passed from Europe and Africa to the Americas during the course of four centuries, there was none other where the carriage of people was essential to turning a profit on the entire trading transaction. The central importance of the transport of humans (free and unfree) to cover costs on the outward journey was as great for the conduct of the Spanish transatlantic trade in the sixteenth and seventeenth centuries as for that of the English and Portuguese during the seventeenth and eighteenth centuries.[23]

The boost given by Atlantic trade to innovation in manufacturing and marketing within Europe, and to European commercial contacts with Asia and Africa, becomes more apparent when account is taken of the economic benefits for the Old World populations that derived from the principal trades that were conducted across the Atlantic in successive centuries. These were silver, furs, and fish in profusion in the sixteenth century; these same commodities, together with sugar, tobacco, dyestuffs, and timber products in the seventeenth century; and these, together with massive food supplies in the eighteenth century, but with trade in Peruvian silver then giving way to Brazilian gold as the precious metal that lubricated an emerging global economy. Most of the output that led to these intercontinental trades, especially during the seventeenth and eighteenth centuries, were, as Chris Bayly acknowledges, enabled both by the African slave trade and (as Bayly hardly mentions) by the trade in indentured servants from Europe to America. More significantly, the seemingly insatiable demand for labor in all parts of the Americas was ultimately the result of the decimation of the Native American populations; a destruction of life on a scale without precedent in human experience that resulted from the various contacts that Native Americans had had with Europeans and Euro–Americans. When this population loss is calculated and placed beside the parallel endeavors of Europeans in all parts of the Americas to create a sequence of novel societies modeled on European-imagined constructs, it becomes evident that it was within the Atlantic basin of the early modern centuries that a complex society fashioned ultimately by a Western desire to achieve a "market-driven uniformity" first came into being.[24] Even if conceding the principal point of Chris Bayly's *The Birth of the Modern World*—that the Western drive to impose such uniformity on the world became manifest only after the political, military, and naval revolutions of the interlude 1760–1830—it strikes me that the Europeans of that generation had become confident that such market-driven uniformity was attainable at the global level only because they were already familiar with the prototype of the modern that had been fashioned after long centuries of travail in the Atlantic. I would also suggest that such previous experience in the Atlantic provided Europeans of the nineteenth century with the assurance to undertake the creation of European-like societies in Australia and New Zealand, with the same consequence for native populations as in the Americas. This suggestion is all the more plausible because nineteenth-century imperial apologists frequently used the same legal and moral rationalizations to legitimate their actions as had helped ease the consciences of those who were, in effect, the creators of human calamity in the Atlantic world of the sixteenth, seventeenth, and eighteenth centuries.

I am offering this response to the challenges presented by publications of Hoerder, Bayly, and several others who have likewise raised questions concerning the scope, coherence, and validity of Atlantic History,[25] with a view to promoting a better understanding of a vibrant world that flourished for the full duration of the early modern centuries. This had been fashioned by several European groups working in concert and in competition one with the other, but also in conjunction with Native American and African peoples. Work by several scholars working together and alone has defined a Hispanic, a French, a British, and even a Portuguese Atlantic (by which can be understood individual sections of the Atlantic basin dominated by one set of European actors). However, relatively few scholars explain that such spaces were but elements of a greater whole, since the settlers within any one sector relied ultimately upon those dominated by other European groups to supply it with goods or markets, or to help it in meeting its need for a labor force. Thus, for example, even an apparently self-sufficient Spanish Atlantic came to rely on Portuguese traders to supply it with African slaves after persistently high mortality rates among the native population had eroded the supply of indigenous labor Spanish settlers had previously taken for granted, and seventeenth-century French settlers in the West Indies relied heavily on

Dutch traders to supply them with European goods and produce as well as
with African slaves. I would also draw attention to the dynamic economy
that developed on the several Caribbean islands under various European
jurisdictions and to the dependency (licit and illicit) that the European settler populations on each island had upon traders and settlers associated with
islands (and even mainland settlements) controlled by European governments other than their own.

The reality of the Atlantic experience seems to have been that as European
traders, explorers, and officials familiarized themselves with the Atlantic
Ocean and the best means of traversing that body of water in either direction, as well as with the resources and opportunities which it, its islands,
and its coastlines provided them, they began to depict it as a place apart
even if they did not designate it the Atlantic world. For example, in 1707
Sir Hans Sloane included in the first volume of his comprehensive study of
the natural history of Jamaica what we today would describe as a map of
the Atlantic world but which he titled "A New Chart of the Western Ocean."
This particular chart was one of three, the other two being one of the island
of Jamaica and the other of the Caribbean; each designed to illustrate the
wider context within which its predecessor would be comprehended. But if
Sloane appeared to represent an apparently self-contained Atlantic world,
he, more than most of his generation, was also thinking universally, since
his primary purpose in studying and describing the natural resources of the
island of Jamaica was to make it possible for him to relate what he discovered to plants and animals already known to educated Europeans, with a
view to contributing to a classification of the world's resources that would
have universal application.[26]

In that sense Sloane was acknowledging what some recent historians
have been arguing: that, for all its size and the opportunities which it presented, the Atlantic world was but one of several interacting sectors of trade
and settlement spread across the globe to which Europeans had access.[27]
These spheres of influence have been best described in this volume, and
elsewhere, by Peter Coclanis, and few would disagree with his assertions,
like those of most commentators on this subject, that European activity in
the Atlantic must be considered in conjunction with European endeavors
in other parts of the world, particularly in Asia.[28] Most would also be persuaded by the argument, most recently articulated by Paul Mapp, that the
search for a direct route to Asia, which inspired Columbus to sail westward
into the Atlantic in the first instance, remained a prime motivating factor
for some explorers and the makers of charts of the Atlantic long after the
true circumference of the globe had been established and long after it had

been realized that fortunes, careers, and even dynasties could be achieved as readily within the Atlantic sphere as elsewhere.[29]

Thus, while many of Sloane's generation could think universally, and while some might even try to break through the geographic shackles that prevented them from seeking after opportunity on a global scale, they had to confront a reality that remained constant until the 1780s: that Western peoples (Americans as well as Europeans) could not be true global adventurers because they lacked the knowledge and skills systematically to navigate the Pacific in the way that they could navigate the Atlantic and Indian oceans. Despite this constraint, some Western people did move from one sphere of European trading influence to the other, and in doing so became, in a sense, world figures or at least figures with experience of a goodly part of the globe. Those who did so, however, always had to negotiate their way through a European conduit in order to move from one sphere of action to another, a fact that is nowhere better illustrated than in Linda Colley's outstanding reconstruction of the life of the previously obscure eighteenth-century figure Elizabeth Marsh. This character was conceived by her parents in Jamaica, experienced hardship in Morocco, spent a significant part of her career in India, but made the vital social and institutional connections in London that enabled her to translate herself from one sector of the world to another.[30]

While saluting Elizabeth Marsh, and also those other characters, ranging from clergymen and naval officers to common sailors and their women, whose intercontinental movements are being pieced together by Alison Games and others,[31] we must also acknowledge that previous to the 1780s, when a solution had been found to the problem of determining longitude with greater precision, such individuals were exceptional. During the three centuries before then, those who promoted trade and settlement beyond the confines of Europe usually limited their attention to one sphere of activity, not least because the truly long-distance trade by water between Europe and Asia around the southern tip of Africa was managed differently from trade within Europe and across the Atlantic and required greater creditworthiness, including the ability to invest in what, by the standards of the time, were extraordinarily large purpose-built craft.

Such impediments to human endeavor on a global scale confirm my opinion that the three centuries of the early modern period were those when what historians describe as an Atlantic world was shaped and flourished. I propose that those who would write the history of that world as a totality should concentrate on those centuries, and give attention also to the half-century that followed, when what previously had been a largely self-contained Atlantic world was absorbed into a global space. In this spirit

Sir John Elliott presents his magisterial *Empires of the Atlantic World: Britain and Spain in America, 1492–1830*, which can be recommended as an interesting case study of Atlantic history, first because it alludes to the limitations as well as to the merits of that subject, and second because it demonstrates how knowledge can be advanced through comparison; in this case, by comparing developments in the Spanish-dominated sector of the Atlantic, that Elliott knows best, with the area of North America which was brought under British influence over the course of the sixteenth, seventeenth, and eighteenth centuries, which has been studied most.[32] The big question that drives Elliott's inquiry is why two European-dominated transatlantic empires, which had functioned effectively for centuries, suddenly, and within a half- century of each other, fell apart.[33] However, in the course of seeking a resolution to that problem, Elliott develops several other comparisons that collectively sustain a comprehensive corrective to received wisdom (received, that is, within the Anglophone academic world) on the shaping of the two principal empires within the Atlantic world. This corrective holds that whether measured in terms of urban development, artistic achievement, the recruitment of a European workforce of talent (although not necessarily of ingenuity), the opportunities offered to European settlers to stay alive and make good, and even efforts made to advance the religious reform and partial assimilation of significant elements of the Native American population to Western norms, the achievements of those who went to the Spanish Empire in the Atlantic far outmatched those of their counterparts who shaped the Euro-American society that emerged in colonial British America.

Though it remains interesting in its own right, the Elliott book is especially important because it points to the enormous potential for acquiring further insights into the dynamic and varied character of the Atlantic world of the early modern centuries, once specialists on other domains of European interest in the Atlantic basin develop similar comparisons with the achievements of rival settler communities. Here one can think of comparisons that might be developed among Portuguese, Dutch, and English traders as conveyers and retailers of slaves; between the English and the French as promoters and managers of sugar plantations; between the evangelization efforts of Protestant and Catholic missionaries; or between the ways in which any two or several European dominant groups interacted with the indigenous populations they encountered.

To say this is not to suggest that progress in Atlantic history can occur only when research is undertaken in a comparative mode. Far from it: the subject is new, and has only begun to be studied. Much fundamental empirical research within particular spheres and areas of endeavor in the Atlantic world remains to be accomplished before some comparisons can be made. However, the fact that one can point to endless interesting potential comparative studies indicates that the totality of the Atlantic experience will be savored only when the achievements of the particular are placed in the context of the more general. Such comparisons (and they do require linguistic and archival competencies that practitioners of Atlantic history must be encouraged to develop) are certain to establish how rich, varied, cruel, and sublime were the human experiences lived out in the Atlantic world of the sixteenth, seventeenth, and eighteenth centuries, and also how developments there affected contemporary events in Europe and Africa and contributed to the shaping of the modern world. When such connections have been made, it will become equally clear that despite being a largely self-contained space, the Atlantic world of the early modern centuries remained susceptible to influences from the traditional Old World and other areas of the globe in which Europeans had established a presence. The best-known of such interactions was the introduction by Europeans of Asian crops which they strove to produce commercially in the Americas, particularly on the islands of the West Indies, or the stimulus to, or distortion of, traditional economic activity in the Americas produced by seemingly insatiable European and Asian appetites for precious metals and the other prime materials that America could supply in profusion. There were, of course, multitudinous other such connections, great and small, obvious and unexpected, and extending into the cultural field.

Thus, one of the principal attractions of Atlantic history is that the interactions that concern it have only begun to be investigated, which explains why the living subject, as I have delineated it, does not fit neatly with any of the six typologies with which this chapter commenced. Another factor that adds to its fascination is that while the Atlantic world of the early modern centuries, which I contend should be the subject of Atlantic history, was a largely self-contained space, it was not a hermetically sealed one. However, because of this I am concerned that the entire subject may be subsumed within increasingly fashionable global or world history, which is ultimately focused on the nineteenth, twentieth, and twenty-first centuries, with scant regard for any developments in previous centuries other than the extent to which these contributed to the achievement of a globalized world. Therefore, the essential purpose of this chapter has been to explain that Atlantic history can be associated with a particular place and with particular centuries, and is worthy of study in its own right rather than as an appendage to some other history. Moreover, I believe that when it is approached in this manner, the subject will prove interesting to scholars, students, and readers of other times and places because the commercial, political, and cultural problems encountered by actors of the sixteenth, seventeenth, and eighteenth centuries would recur as their imitators acted out their parts on a truly global scale in the centuries that lay ahead.

NOTES

1. David Armitage, "Three Concepts of Atlantic History," in David Armitage and Michael Braddick, eds., *The British Atlantic World, 1500–1800* (Basingstoke, U.K.: Palgrave Macmillan, 2002), pp. 11–27; the historiography of the subject is best treated in Bernard Bailyn, *Atlantic History: Concept and Contours* (Cambridge, Mass.: Harvard University Press, 2005).

2. Nicholas Canny, "Writing Atlantic History; or Re-Configuring the History of Colonial British America," *Journal of American History* 86 (1999): 1093–1114, and "Atlantic History: What and Why?" *European Review* 9 (2001): 399–411.

3. Felipe Fernando Armesto, *Millennium: A History of the last Thousand Years* (London: Bantam Press, 1995); Ralph Davies, *The Rise of the Atlantic Economies* (Ithica, N.Y.: Cornell University Press: 1973); J. H. Elliott, *The Old World and the New, 1492–1650* (Cambridge: Cambridge University Press, 1970); Martin Daunton and Richard Halpern, eds., *Empire and Others: British Encounters with Indigenous Peoples, 1600–1850* (London: University College London Press,, 1999); Donna Merwick, *Death of a Notary and Possessing Albany* (Ithaca, N.Y.: Cornell University Press, 1999), and *The Shame and the Sorrow: Dutch–Amerindian Encounters* (Philadelphia: University of Pennsylvania Press, 2006); Alan Gallay, *The Indian Slave Trade: The Rise of the English Empire in the American South* (New Haven: Yale University Press, 2002); Gilles Havard and Cécile Vidal, *Histoire de l'Amérique française* (Paris,: Flammarion, 2003); Horst Pietschmann, ed., *Atlantic History: History of the Atlantic System, 1500–1830* (Göttingen: Vandenhoeck & Ruprecht, 2002).

4. Stephen Greenblatt, *Marvelous Possessions: The Wonder of the New World* (Chicago: University Chicago Press, 1991); Anthony Pagden, *The Fall of Natural Man* (Cambridge: Cambridge University Press, 1982); Karen O'Brien, *Narratives of Enlightenment: Cosmopolitan History from Voltaire to Gibbon* (Cambridge: Cambridge University Press, 1997).

5. Bernard Bailyn, *The Peopling of British North America: An Introduction* (New York: Knopf, 1986), and *Voyagers to the West: Emigration from Britain to America on the Eve of the Revolution* (New York: Taurus, 1986); Frank Tannenbaum, *Slave and Citizen: The Negro in the Americas* (New York:, Knopf, 1946); James Horn, *Adapting to a New World: English Society in the Seventeenth-Century Chesapeake* (Chapel Hill: University of North Carolina Press, 1994); Alison Games, *Migration and the*

Origins of the English Atlantic World (Cambridge, Mass.: Harvard University Press, 1999); Patrick Griffin, *The People with No Name: Ireland's Ulster Scots, America's Scots Irish, and the Creation of a British Atlantic World* (Princeton: Princeton University Press, 2001); Marianne S. Wokeck, *Trade in Strangers: The Beginnings of Mass Migration to North America* (College Park: Pennsylvania State University Press, 1999); Philip D. Curtin, *The Atlantic Slave Trade: A Census* (Madison: University of Wisconsin Press, 1969); Ira Berlin, *Many Thousands Gone: The First Two Centuries of Slavery in North America* (Cambridge, Mass.: Harvard University Press, 1998); Olivier Pétré-Grenouilleau, *Les Traites négrières: Essai d'histoire globale* (Paris: Gallimard, 2004); David Eltis, Frank D. Lewis, and Kenneth Sokoloff, eds., *Slavery in the Development of the Americas* (Cambridge: Cambridge University Press, 2004); David Eltis et. al., eds., *The Trans-Atlantic Slave Trade: A Data-Base on CD-ROM* (Cambridge: Cambridge University Press, 1999); David B. Abernethy, *The Dynamics of Global Dominance: European Overseas Empires, 1415–1980* (New Haven: Yale University Press, 2000). It is interesting to note that the French study of slavery as represented by the book by Pétré-Grenouilleau is conceived as a contribution to global history; since then a conference on slavery organized at Nantes in June 2005 by the École des Hautes Études, was conceived "dans les espaces atlantiques"; and a conference held at Université Paris Diderot in December 2006 was titled "Des Colonies aux républiques dans un monde atlantique."

6. David Brion Davis, *The Problem of Slavery in Western Culture* (Ithaca, N.Y.: Cornell University Press, 1966), and *The Problem of Slavery in the Age of Revolution, 1770–1823* (Oxford: Oxford University Press, 1975); Seymour Drescher, *From Slavery to Freedom: Comparative Studies in the Rise and Fall of Atlantic Slavery* (New York:, New York University Press, 1999); Christopher Brown, *Moral Capital: Foundations of British Abolitionism* (Chapel Hill: University of North Carolina Press, 2006).

7. Jan de Vries. "The Industrial Revolution and the Industrious Revolution," *Journal of Economic History* 54 (1994): 240–270; David Hancock, *Citizens of the World: London Merchants and the Integration of the British Atlantic Community, 1735–1785* (Cambridge: Cambridge University Press, 1995); Wim Klooster, *Illicit Riches: Dutch Trade in the Caribbean* (Leiden: Kitvl Press, 1998); Ralph Davis, *The Rise of the Atlantic Economies* (Ithaca, N.Y.: Cornell University Press, 1973); Klaus Weber, *Deutsche Kaufluet im Atlantikhandel, 1680–1830* (Munich: C.H. Beck, 2004); Claudia Schnurmann, *Vom Inselreich zur Weltmacht* (Stuttgart: Kohlhammer, 2001); James D. Tracy, ed., *The Rise of Merchant Empires: Long Distance Trade in the Early Modern World, 1350–1750* (Cambridge: Cambridge University Press, 1990); Peggy Liss, *Atlantic Empires: The Network of Trade and Revolution, 1713–1826* (Baltimore: Johns Hopkins University Press, 1983); P. K. O'Brien, ed., *The Industrial Revolution in Europe*, 2 vols. (Oxford: Oxford University Press, 1994).

8. Fernand Braudel, *The Mediterranean and the Mediterranean World in the Age of Philip II*, trans. Sian Reynolds, 2 vols. (N.Y: Harper, 1972–1973); K.N.

Chaudhuri, *Trade and Civilization in the Indian Ocean: An Economic History from the Rise of Islam to 1750* (Cambridge: Cambridge University Press, 1985); O. Prakash, *European Commercial Expansion in Early Modern Asia* (London: Variorum, 1997); D. W. Meinig, *The Shaping of America: A Geographical Perspective on 500 Years of History* (New Haven: Yale University Press, 1986–1998); John Thornton, *Africa and Africans in the Making of the Atlantic World, 1400–1600* (Cambridge: Cambridge University Press, 1992).

9. Peter Laslett, *The World We Have Lost* (N.Y: Scribner, 1965); David Cressy, *Coming Over: Migration and Communication Between England and New England in the Seventeenth Century* (Cambridge: Cambridge University Press, 1987); Caroline Robbins, *The Eighteenth Century Commonwealthman* (Cambridge, Mass.: Harvard University Press, 1959); J. G. A. Pocock, *The Machiavellian Moment* (Princeton: Princeton University Press, 1975); Bernard Bailyn, *The Ideological Origins of the American Revolution* (Cambridge, Mass.: Harvard University Press, 1987); David Armitage, *The Ideological Origins of the British Empire* (Cambridge: Cambridge University Press, 2000), and *Greater Britain 1516–1776: Essays in Atlantic History* ((Aldershot, U.K.: Ashgate, 2004); Carla Gardina Pestana, *The English Atlantic in an Age of Revolution, 1640–1661* (Cambridge, Mass.: Harvard University Press, 2004); Andrew Fitzmaurice, *Humanism and America: An Intellectual History of English Colonization, 1500–1625* (Cambridge: Cambridge University Press, 2003); Armitage and Braddick, eds., *The British Atlantic World*; Elizabeth Mancke and Carole Shammas, eds., *The Creation of the British Atlantic World* (Baltimore: Johns Hopkins University Press, 2005); Colin Kidd, *British Identities Before Nationalism: Ethnicity and Nationhood in the Atlantic World, 1600–1800* (Cambridge: Cambridge University Press, 1999).

10. Pocock, *Machiavellian Moment*; Fitzmaurice, *Humanism and America*; J. G. A. Pocock, *The Discovery of Islands* (Cambridge: Cambridge University Press, 2005).

11. R. R. Palmer, *The Age of the Democratic Revolution: A Political History of Europe and America, 1760–1800*, 2 vols. (Princeton: Princeton University Press, 1959–1964); Jacques Godechot, *France and the Atlantic Revolution of the Eighteenth Century, 1770–1799*, trans. Herbert Rowen (New York: Macmillan, 1965); Lester D. Langley, *The Americas in the Age of Revolution, 1750–1850* (New Haven: Yale University Press, 1996); Laurent Dubois, *Avengers of the New World: The Story of the Haitian Revolution* (Cambridge, Mass.: Harvard University Press, 2004).

12. For examples, see some of the contributions to the special issue of *Journal of American History* on "The Nation State and Beyond," 86 (December 1999).

13. Canny, "Atlantic History: What and Why?"; "Forum: Beyond the Atlantic," with contributions by Alison Games, Philip J. Stern, Paul W. Mapp, and Peter A. Coclanis, in *William and Mary Quarterly* 3rd ser., 63 (2006): 675–742.

14. Dirk Hoerder, *Cultures in Contact: World Migrations in the Second Millennium* (Durham, N.C.: Duke University Press, 2002); C. A. Bayly, *The Birth of the Modern World, 1780–1914* (Oxford: Blackwell Publishing, 2004).

15. Hoerder. *Cultures in Contact*, pp. 188–189.

16. Ibid., pp. 5, 170–174, 369–373.

17. Bayly, *Birth of the Modern World*, pp. 44–47.

18. Ibid., pp. 44, 49–120.

19. Ibid., p. 44.

20. Nicholas Canny and Anthony Pagden, eds., *Colonial Identity in the Atlantic World, 1500–1800* (Princeton: Princeton University Press, 1987); Jack P. Greene, *Pursuits of Happiness: The Social Development of Early Modern British Colonies and the Formation of American Culture* (Chapel Hill: University of North Carolina Press, 1988); David A. Brading, *The First America: The Spanish Monarchy, Creole Patriots, and the Liberal State, 1492–1867* (Cambridge: 1991); Bailyn, *The Ideological Origins of the American Revolution*.

21. On the similarity between the preoccupations of fundamentalist Catholics and Protestants in the Atlantic, see Jorge Cañizares-Esguerra, *Puritan Conquistadors: Iberianizing the Atlantic, 1550–1700* (Palo Alto, California: Stanford University Press, 2006).

22. Niels Steensgaard, *Carracks, Caravans and Companies: The Structural Crisis in the European Asian Trade in the Early Seventeenth Century* (Copenhagen: Nordic Institute of Asian Studies, 1973).

23. Nuala Zahedieh, "Overseas Expansion and Trade in the Seventeenth century," in Nicholas Canny, ed., *The Origins of Empire* (Oxford: Oxford University Press, 1998), pp. 398–422.

24. The phrase is from Bayly, *Birth of the Modern World*, p. 44.

25. Jorge Cañizares-Esguerra and Erik R. Seeman, eds., *The Atlantic in Global History, 1500–2000* (Upper Saddle River, N.J.: Prentice Hall, 2007); see details on the *William and Mary Quarterly* issue in note 13.

26. The three maps were included together in one pull-out illustration in Hans Sloane, *A Voyage to the Islands of Madeira, Barbados, Nieves, S. Christophers and Jamaica*, vol. 1 (London, 1707); Sloane was aware of his being involved in a competition to become the recognized authority on the classification of plants, and he both cited and corrected others. One author to whom he referred persistently was Plumier, who must have been the Franciscan Charles Plumier, who had made significant progress in this domain in *Nova plantarum americanarum genera, authore P. Carlos Plumier...* (Paris, 1703).

27. See especially Alison Games, "English Globetrotters and Transoceanic Connections," and Philip J. Stern, "British Asia and British Atlantic: Comparisons and Connections," in *William and Mary Quarterly* "Forum: Beyond the Atlantic" issue, 3rd ser., 53 (October 2006): 675–712.

28. See Peter A. Coclanis, "Atlantic World or Atlantic/World?," in *William and Mary Quarterly* "Forum: Beyond the Atlantic" issue, 3rd ser., 53 (October 2006): 725–742; the approach he favors was also adopted in Nicholas Canny, "Asia, the Atlantic, and the Subjects of the British Monarchy," in Barry Coward, ed., *A Companion to Stuart Britain* (Oxford: Blackwell, 2003), pp. 45–66.

29. See Paul W. Mapp, "Atlantic History from Imperial, Continental and Pacific Perspectives," in *William and Mary Quarterly* "Forum: Beyond the Atlantic," 3rd ser., 53 (October 2006): 713–724.

30. Linda Colley, *The Ordeal of Elizabeth Marsh: A Woman in World History* (London: Pantheon: 2007).

31. Games, "English Globetrotters and Transoceanic Connections," and *The Web of Empire: English Cosmopolitans in an Age of Expansion, 1560–1660* (Oxford: Oxford University Press, 2008).

32. J. H. Elliott, *Empires of the Atlantic World: Britain and Spain in America, 1492–1830* (New Haven: Yale University Press, 2006).

33. Ibid., pp. xvii–xviii.

13

BEYOND ATLANTIC HISTORY

PETER A. COCLANIS

The fact that books assessing the state of Atlantic history are being written probably means that this field can no longer be considered trendy, much less edgy or *outré*. Indeed, given its huge popularity among historians, particularly younger ones, in recent years, Atlantic history is now an (if not *the*) official establishment approach, an approach deemed sufficiently mature and orderly—even well behaved—to be allowed to sit with the interpretive grown ups, as it were. Now sitting with the grown ups is not necessarily a bad thing—given the most likely alternative—but in contemplating this change in status, I can't help but to recall Gertrude Stein's famous quip about the establishment of the Museum of Modern Art: "Either you're a museum or you're modern." You can't be both, in other words.

Fads fade, trends have a shelf life—"that's so yesterday," as our students might say—but becoming part of the interpretive establishment, like the signal museum status emits, also comes at a cost. Over the past decade or two, Atlantic history has insinuated itself into the very depths of the discipline. For better or worse, or, more accurately, for better *and* worse.

Why, one might ask? What is it about Atlantic history that has made it so appealing? For one thing, the relative capaciousness of the approach represents a significant improvement, *ceteris paribus*, over narrower, national or proto-national alternatives. Second, the approach has proved attractive and enticing to some absolutely first-rate historians, which has had what economists would call a powerful "signaling effect" on others in the profession. Indeed, I'd be the first to admit that it's hard to improve on a roster led by sluggers such as Jack P. Greene and Bernard Bailyn.

And cultural capital helps, too. Through a variety of powerful institutional mechanisms—the Hopkins program in Atlantic History, Culture and Society, Harvard's International Seminar in the History of the Atlantic World, 1500–1825, and Leiden University's Institute for the History of European

Expansion (IGEER), to name three of the most obvious and important—scores of bright young scholars over the years have been exposed to, dazzled by, and initiated into Atlantic history. As these scholars (and other like-minded ones) have risen in the discipline, they have come to constitute a powerful cohort moving together, a cohort operating from many of the same Atlanticist premises and assumptions, if not always with the same perspectives, ideologies, and, dare I say, *world*views. Rather like an impala passing through the body of an African python. Very impressive (if a bit difficult to swallow).

What are these people talking about when they wax on about the history of the Atlantic world(s)? What does the concept "Atlantic world" mean? Most, if not all Atlanticists would probably agree with Bailyn's simple and direct proposition, put forth in the journal *Itinerario* in 1996, that during the "early modern" period (c. 1500–1800 CE) Western Europe, West Africa, and the Americas were sufficiently integrated in many ways as to lend themselves to treatment as a single unit: The Atlantic World.[1] To be sure, such scholars might disagree amongst themselves over what material and/or ideational concerns to include in such treatment, over just how unitary said treatment perforce needs to be, over the power dynamics within and historical consequences of the unit in question, and over the degree to which this unit was hermetic or subject to breach. But, by and large, members of the "Atlantic community" could live with this conceptual scheme. In truth, under its broad shelter, they have lived very well indeed.

So what's my beef with Atlantic history? Simply stated, in my view the levels of explanatory power and analytical acuity possible via the Atlantic history stratagem are beguiling, but ultimately limiting, because the stratagem artificially limits the field of vision of its devotees, often leaving them with their eyes wide shut to processes, developments, and conditions of central importance to understanding their "little corner of the world," speaking figuratively. Or to put it another way, Bobby Darin's way, we need to move "beyond the sea." Certainly *that* sea, but maybe others as well.

Of course, seas and oceans are very much in these days. We have Atlantic historians, and historians of the Indian Ocean "world." We've long known about Braudel, but there are new generations of scholars touting *la méditerannée* as organizing conceit. The Black Sea has its people, as do the Great Lakes (both those in East Africa and those in the U.S. Midwest). Others are studying the "world" of the North Sea, and there are Pacific basinites and rimmers galore.[2] Other scholars are even beginning to chant the mantra "ocean's connect, ocean's connect." [3] The problem with this mantra and other repetitive sacred formulae, including Atlantic history, is that such repetition has what economists call opportunity costs, that is to say, the costs foregone by not pursuing the best available alternative. And it is to that alternative that we now shall turn.

In a critique of Atlantic history, or, more properly, the "Atlanticist perspective," published in the *Journal of World History* in 2002, I made a four-part case against the approach, arguing that the perspective:

> ...however enriching, is constricting interpretively and somewhat misspeci-
> fied analytically, a halfway historiographical covenant as it were, nothing
> more, nothing less. By fixing our historical gaze so firmly toward the West,
> the approach may, anachronistically, give too much weight to the Atlantic
> Rim, separate Northwest Europe too sharply both from other parts of Europe
> and from Eurasia as a whole, accord too much primacy to America in explain-
> ing Europe's transoceanic trade patterns, and economically speaking, misrep-
> resent through overstatement the place of Europe in the order of things.[4]

Where do I stand today? Hopefully, a bit better informed, and, thus, a bit more nuanced and sophisticated in my critique. But I must admit that work done in the intervening years hasn't persuaded me to move at all toward the Atlantic camp.

Take my 2002 point about the Atlanticists' fixation toward the West. Now, admittedly, I probably should have used a different preposition here—*on* rather than *toward*—as important works such as Daniel Richter's *Facing East from Indian Country* clearly demonstrate.[5] But the obsession with the Atlantic world *qua* unit continues to impede our understanding of the degree to which this unit drew its life blood from—and hemorrhaged into—others. Virtually everywhere one looks in the "Atlantic World" in the "early modern" period, one finds other worlds impinging on and often shaping developments. I'm not necessarily talking about the ori-gins of many European and African foodstuffs—this isn't a game of "got-cha," after all—although even a cursory look at a work such as Andrew M. Watson's *Agricultural Innovation in the Early Islamic World* is enough to give pause to even the most ardent Occidentalists.[6] The problems result-ing from a fixation on origins—"the idol of origins," as March Bloch famously put it—were laid out long ago.[7] So for the record I'm not call-ing for us to focus here on the manner in which wind from the East, as it were, affected "Western" social developments well before the early modern period: for that we can look to that famous scholarly double-play combination Hodgson to Bernal to Hobson.[8] What I do ask here is that we think about the close connections of "East" and "West" during the heyday of the "Atlantic World," for once we do we find that during this particular period, *pace* Mr. Kipling, ever the twain shall meet.

Sometimes the connections are rendered visible in a manner analogous to that known in art as pentimento—where an earlier painting shows through another painting or at least parts thereof—as historian of China Robert B. Marks has recently pointed out.[9] For example, does the small peninsula at the westernmost tip of the Eurasian landmass become *Western Europe* as we came to know it in the early modern period without the Black Death (which spread from Asia) and the collapse of the Mongol Empire? For these factors were arguably necessary (though clearly insufficient) in shaping, indeed, perhaps even *permitting* the region's impressive fifteenth-century advance. And not to put too fine a point on it, if we would explain Western Europe's rise beginning in that century, particularly its tentative external expansion, can we realistically do so without taking full account of the huge role of Islamic, Indian, and Chinese knowledge, particularly in the realms of science, mathematics, engineering, and technology? For starters, can we talk about paper, printing, measuring devices, the equine horse collar, the Indic stirrup, gunpowder, weaponry (including rudimentary missiles, rockets, grenades, bombards, and cannons), the compass, and the lateen sail? Then, of course, there is the number zero, first developed in India sometime during the Gupta period (320–550 CE), and, while we're at it, the arch and vault from Indian Buddhist architecture as well![10]

Now I'm certainly not claiming that Europe contributed nothing of technological note over the ages: I've read my Landes and know all about eyeglasses, and even people such as Joseph Needham and Donald Lach would admit that the vast majority of the technologies transferred appeared in the West before the sixteenth century.[11] Moreover, I know enough about technology not to deprecate the creativity involved in successful technological transfer. Think for a moment what Europeans *did* with printing, gunpowder/weaponry, and the stirrup (not to mention with the arch and vault!), and, later, with another "Asian" technology: the cotton gin.[12] All I'm saying is that we can't understand the rise of Western Europe and, withal, the Atlantic World by severing these developments from developments in the rest of Europe, the rest of Eurasia, or, more, accurately, Afro-Eurasia. Indeed, according to historian Felipe Fernández-Armesto, Westerners can for some purposes be viewed as "the dregs of Eurasian history, and the salient they inhabit... the sump into which Eurasian history has drained."[13] If the Atlantic World *was* a world Europeans, Africans and Americans "made together," they made it together with peoples without.[14]

Then there are various questions relating to *mentalité*, personnel, and behavior. That is to say, can one readily, accurately, or legitimately draw hard-and-fast distinctions between voyages and voyagers to the West and voyages and voyagers to the East? Obviously, there are important distinctions to be made here, but said distinctions need greater interrogation and qualification than they are often given. This appears particularly true *early* in the early modern period when it seems anachronistic even to attempt to distinguish between discrete "Atlantic" and "non-Atlantic" or "extra-Atlantic" thrusters, particularly since most "thrusters," Atlantic or otherwise, were certainly searching for the "East." As time passed, distinctions became more clear-cut—no successful colonies of "settlement" were established in the "East" by Europeans in the early modern period—but, this said, at the broadest level, economic gain was paramount among most voyagers East and West throughout the period in question, and, more so, among those organized collectivities of Europeans (public, public/private, or private) that sponsored and financed them.[15] Take the Lords Proprietors of Carolina. The eight men to whom Charles II granted the Carolina Charter in 1663 were nothing if not *worldly*, involved over the course of their lives in financial ventures, adventures, and misadventures stretching from the Indian Ocean to West Africa to the West Indies to Hudson's Bay. In addition to investments in Tangier, the Northwest Passage, and the Royal Africa Company. Whatever, wherever their economic behavior seemed to direct them![16]

Still, right now we don't know nearly enough to speak with much precision or calibration in a comparative sense about *mentalité*, personnel, and behavior among those that ventured east and those that set out west. Or even about the numbers involved. Although the number of Europeans who migrated to Asia in the "early modern" period was far greater than many realize—some estimates run as high as 375,000 for Dutch migrants alone in the seventeenth century (with another 100,000 from "Britain")—we are only now beginning to appreciate the importance of contextualizing Atlantic developments by linking them to European expansionary initiatives elsewhere in the *world* during the period 1500–1800 CE.[17] We could begin by paying more attention, in studying the "Age of Discovery," to matters relating to who, what, where, when, why, how, and "how many." Just one tantalizing example in this regard: According to quantitative data put together by Ronald Findlay and Kevin H. O'Rourke, the value of English and Dutch imports from Asia in the middle of the eighteenth century—whatever the number of English and Dutch residents there—was greater than the value of English and Dutch imports from the Americas at that time.[18]

A cautionary note at this point before we all set sail, though: in casting our eyes outward, we must take care not to bid *bon voyage* to Europe itself. In taking the Atlantic World bit—ok, the global bit, too—it is easy to lose sight of the fact that though developments in Western Europe, West Africa, the Americas, and Asia were dramatic in the early modern period, there was still a lot going on, economically and otherwise, in other parts of Europe, too. Intra-European trade, for example, was massive (if not particularly exciting) during the period, to which the barge traffic on the Rhine and the traffic through the Danish Sound (among other indicators) amply attests. Proto-industrialization in central Europe. The so-called second serfdom further east. Trade in *la méditerranée* still going strong. And whereas roughly six thousand Scots ventured to the Americas in the seventeenth century somewhere between 30,000 and 50,000 Scots migrated to the Polish crown lands.[19] In other words, it is important always to keep in mind that all of the action hadn't left town. That said, all aboard!

Now that we're on blue water, let me come right out and say it: It is well nigh impossible somehow to hive off the Atlantic "unit" from a bigger unit: the world. This is especially true when speaking of matters material, particularly biological and economic concerns. We've already mentioned the Black Death, for example, to which we can add other disease scourges entering the "West" from the "East." Indeed, what we in the West refer to as the late medieval/early modern period can be broadly bracketed by two pandemics—bubonic plague (1347–1350) and cholera (1832)—arriving from Asia.

In matters economic, it defies logic to proceed under the assumption that the Atlantic World was a discrete economic unit when roughly 75 percent of one of its most important (and certainly celebrated) economic resources, American silver, ended up in China over the course of the early modern period (and when the Spanish *real* functioned as the international trading currency over much of Asia).[20] When the African slave trade ran largely on textiles—"long cloths," "Guinea cloths," allijars, salemporis, etc.—from India and cowry shells from the Maldives. And speaking of Indian textiles, how does a dyed-in-the-wool Atlanticist explain the appeal of Indian "calicoes" which dominated the English textiles market (as well as the appeal of Indian "guinea cloth" in the West Indies and British North America) in the late seventeenth and early eighteenth centuries?[21] What about the equally dominant position in Europe during this same period of silk imports from the "East?" And, of course, what about the fabled spice trade—pepper, cinnamon, cloves, nutmeg, mace—drugs and "apothecary," ceramics, porcelain, coffee, tea, and, later in the period, various other articles of chinoiserie?[22]

The international trade in rice provides yet another powerful case in point. Most of the world's rice, of course, has always been grown and eaten in Asia, and most trading in rice has been intra-Asian. Prior to the sixteenth century, most of the rice that *was* traded in the West—not that much, actually—came from India and the Middle East, but between roughly the middle of the sixteenth century and the middle of the nineteenth century demand in the West was met largely by Western suppliers, first from northwestern Italy and Spain, but, beginning in the eighteenth century, from American suppliers in South Carolina, Georgia, and Brazil as well. By the end of the eighteenth century, rice was becoming commodified in the West, and once transport costs had declined sufficiently as to allow cheap rice from South Asia and, later, Southeast Asia to penetrate Western markets, Western suppliers were increasingly eased out of the most lucrative parts of the rice-export trade. Political economist David MacPherson noted the commodification of rice in the West and the shift—at that time, only at the margin—toward Asian suppliers as early as 1795, pointing out that rice was the first "necessary" sent in significant quantities to the West from Asia, all previous trade consisting of articles and products "rather of ornament and luxury than of use." [23] By the 1860s Asian rice had inundated the West, and Western suppliers had been knocked out of all of the main markets in the Atlantic world by cheap rice from Bengal, Java, Lower Burma, Siam, and Cochinchina.[24]

But what about the early modern period itself? Cannot that period at least be considered a cut-and-dried, case-closed "Western" phase of the Western rice trade? Well, yes and no. When considering that period, it is important to keep in mind that rice was a crop of Asian origin produced via technology developed to a considerable extent in Asia by a labor force, the American portion of which was acquired in West Africa in exchange in large part for South Asian goods and products (cowries and textiles, most notably).[25] Even here, then, lots of hemorrhaging from the Atlantic, lots of mixing, blending, blurring of "East" and "West."

In addition to articles of trade, what about traders themselves? We all know about the famous European companies in Asia—the Portuguese East India Company, the English East India Company, and the V.O.C.—as well as the English Levant Company, the *Compagnie des Indes Orientales* (among other French companies), the Swedish East India Company, the Ostend Company, a Danish company, and others emanating from Prussia, Russia, and Spain. Islamic Turks, Levantine Jews, and Armenians also traded throughout Europe (and sometimes in West Africa, too) during the period in question, and various indigenous middlemen—brokers, bankers, and the like (known in South

Asia as banions, shroffs, dubashes, etc.)—worked closely with Europeans in Asia as well.[26] While we're on the subject of trade, it should be noted that "East" and "West" shared many of the same commercial institutions and mechanisms—commenda contracts, bills of exchange, debt instruments, trade associations, spot markets, etc.—and worked out viable ways of doing business (or "cross-cultural exchange," as Curtin puts it) together.[27] Just to be snide, let me add as an aside that in his famous early account, *Suma Oriental*, written between 1512–1515, the Portuguese apothecary/accountant/traveler Tomé Pires stated (in at least one version of his famous account) that the merchants of Cambay in western India were better at commerce than were the Italians themselves! [28] So there.

Pushing ahead—Eastward Ho, one might say—how can one consider the Atlantic World a discrete unit after 1571, the Manila Galleon, and all that?[29] Unless, that is to say, one is prepared to redefine China as an Atlantic power, a project which Gavin Menzies has been trying to promote, mercifully with little success to date.[30] And if the Atlantic and the non-Atlantic worlds are so distinct, why did the treaties ending the nearly incessant warfare among European powers in the early modern period—Breda, Ryswick, Utrecht, Aix-la-Chapelle, Paris, etc.—typically contain important provisions relating to Asia?[31] Invoking the last of these, the Peace of Paris, brings to mind another important matter: the *Indian* dimensions of the French and Indian War. I think it not merely plausible, but reasonable to argue that in the long run the French surrender at Pondicherry in January 1761—effectively removing the French as a presence in India—may have been one of the most significant results of that whole conflict. It certainly helped to facilitate the creation of the "Second British Empire," although I must admit that I don't see the need for, much less value in dividing said empire into phases I and II. In this regard—I'm on a roll now—Britain's opening up of the Philippines' trade during the Seven Years' War and the collapse of the V.O.C.'s trade monopoly on Java as a result of Asian military action during the "American" Revolution helped to usher in profound changes in Asian trade patterns, changes which were later reinforced by Stamford Raffles, who was Lord Minto's secretary when Minto seized Java in the name of Britain in 1811. After the seizure of Java, Raffles was named Lieutenant-Governor by Minto, and became the key person in charge there between 1811 and 1816, during which period he put into place a number of liberal reforms (by the way, Raffles was born on a ship off of the coast of Jamaica, and, in fall 2005, when I began working on this piece on *Atlantic history*, I was holding the Raffles Professorship in *Southeast Asian history* at the National University of Singapore, which further underscores my overarching point).[32] And for yet another powerful "coincidence": Lord Charles Cornwallis of Yorktown fame, after passing Go(a!), rebounded nicely in India, where as Governor General and Commander in Chief between 1786 and 1793, he earned an estimable reputation as a reform-minded administrator. After returning to England, he was later Viceroy of Ireland, and one of the negotiators of the Treaty of Amiens, before being reappointed Governor General of India in 1805. He died in India on October 5 of that same year.[33]

Thus far I've been making the case in this chapter that the so-called Atlantic World should not be treated as a discrete unit during the period 1500–1800 CE. Northwestern European political entities were expanding outward during this period, creating global empires in the process. At the same time, other "Old World" empires were expanding all across and around the Eurasian landmass: Russia, the Ottomans, Safavid Iran, Mughal India, and China. In some areas these empires butted up against one another, which led to conflict. At the same time, however, these empires (or at least parties located therein) traded peacefully with one another, at times directly, at other times through intermediaries. Indeed, stepping back a bit, one finds that the so-called early modern period was one of those intermittent historical eras of relatively open trade across and around the Eurasian landmass. As Philip Curtin among others has pointed out, one such period occurred "in the Han-Parthian-Roman period in the early Christian era," and another during what might be called the Tang-Abbassid period during the seventh and eighth centuries[34] Yet another such period occurred during the height of Mongol power between c. 1250–1350 CE—the period of Janet Abu-Lughod's first "world system"—and, then again, as Europe expanded outward by sea to link up with what K.N. Chaudhuri referred to as the "emporia trade" of Asia in the period after 1500.[35]

Speaking of these emporia reminds me (again, as a bit of an aside): the final point in my aforementioned 2002 critique of Atlantic history *qua* field related to the tendency by proponents to overestimate the place of Europe in things during the period 1500–1800 CE. At that time, I invoked the work of a variety of scholars, most notably, those associated with the so-called California School, to make the case that "Asia" was economically far more dynamic, wealthy, and vibrant during the early modern period than many writers had previously believed, with the most advanced regions in Asia—the lower Yangzi delta, most notably—by many standards on par with, if not ahead of the most advanced regions in northwestern Europe during much of this period.[36] Although the California School cannot yet claim total victory here—indeed, I myself don't completely buy into parts of its argument, particularly that part purporting to explain the reasons for Asia's relative fall and Europe's relative rise c. 1750–1800—even the most ardent Eurocentrics in the house, assessing the state of the debate in 2008, would concede that scholars associated with the California School have demonstrated pretty conclusively that whatever differentials in wealth and living standards existed between Asia and Europe in the early modern period were probably trivial.[37]

On the face of it, it seems implausible to link Northwestern Europe's external expansion, Eurasian empires, and relatively open trade. Relatively open trade? During the age of mercantilism? Again, we're talking big picture here, and, with this in mind, it makes sense to invoke Abu-Lughod again. The conceptual schema she lays out in *Before European Hegemony: The World System* A.D. *1250–1350* with reference to the Mongol period is suggestive for later ones as well, including the early modern period. According to Abu-Lughod the (loosely integrated) thirteenth-century world system was comprised of eight interacting and partially overlapping "trade circuits" encompassing much of Europe, the Middle East, north and northeast Africa, and Asia. In some ways her circuits resemble Venn diagrams, depicting, as they do, a series of historical (trade) sets, which have some, but not all, elements in common. The common areas might be considered (trade) intersections, but the entire series can be spanned without any breaks. According to Abu-Lughod, this system, for a variety of reasons, gradually broke down after about 1350—others argue that the breakdown she sees may be overstated—but it may repay our time to think a bit about how a similar, but much more extensive system of circuits was reconstituted in the period from 1450 to 1800 CE or thereabouts.[38]

This system, though not yet quite global, was for the first time *approaching* true "world-system" status in a literal sense by the end of this period. By 1800, the entire world, again, for the first time, had pretty much been incorporated into the mental maps—the metageographies, as it were—of navigators and intellectuals alike, and trade orbits were becoming increasingly far-flung.[39] In the middle of this period, say 1650 or 1700, one finds modifications of, and extensions to the circuits found by Abu-Lughod several hundred years' earlier, but much of her system is still recognizable. The most notable change, of course, is a new circuit encompassing the "Atlantic World" we know and love—with a trans-Pacific extension in Manila, the principal importance of which was to link American silver to China, and, thereby, to Chinese goods. Another major change was what might be called the Vasco da Gama circuit linking Western Europe and West Africa to "extended" Indian Ocean emporia (all the way to Japan and Formosa) via the Cape of Good Hope. Although Asianists (particularly those associated with the California School) reject the notion that this circuit revolutionized Asian trade—not for them Panikkar's implicitly Eurocentric notion of an "epoch of Vasco da Gama"—it was nonetheless important in creating new links and relationships.[40]

There are other smaller changes in Abu-Lughod's system. The Mediterranean circuit extends further west and south. The North Sea world has emerged as a circuit. The Eurasian overland circuit is qualitatively different (and now facilitated largely by Armenian traders). The Arabian Sea/Northeast Africa-Red Sea circuits incorporate more of East Africa. The Asian circuits are larger, and several new circuits have emerged in Africa: the trans-Saharan circuit, and a variety of smaller circuits linking up coastal areas in Africa with the interior. Speaking of Africa, it is important to recognize that sub-Saharan Africa by this time can be said to have three "coasts: the Atlantic, the Indian Ocean, and the Sahara itself, with traders and trade centers operating on the "coastlines" of all three. And, finally, a continental circuit or two may have encompassed broad parts of the Americas.[41]

The upshot of all of this circuitry was a historically rapid increase in world trade during the early modern period. As Kevin H. O'Rourke and Jeffrey Williamson among others make clear, world trade grew significantly faster than did world population in this period, testimony to the relative openness—in a functional sense at least—of the "system."[42] The "system." I've used "system" and "world-system" quite a bit in the last few paragraphs, but, for the record, let me stress that I'm not pushing a full-blown, reified "world-system" in a Wallersteinian sense. I'm not at all about cores, semi-peripheries, peripheries, and external arenas, let alone about Frankian satellites and metropoli.[43] All I'm trying to convey in the discussion above is that it is possible to distinguish certain broadly patterned trade routes and trade relationships in the period 1500–1800 CE, and, if one is so inclined (and I am), one can legitimately refer to them as circuits, orbits, etc., that were related to one another in different ways and to varying degrees.

To say here that I am not calling for a Wallersteinian form of "world-systems" analysis is not meant to disparage either Wallerstein or the many scholars in the historical social sciences, particularly historical sociology who still operate within this framework. In fact, I've always had a soft spot in my heart for approaches—various Marxist and neo-Marxist approaches, for example—with a predilection or "preferential option" for seeing things as inter-related, as parts of a greater whole. If I can't buy into the Wallersteinian framework, it's not because it's completely unhelpful as a heuristic, but because I prefer in this case an alternative framework drawn from the literature on the "articulation of productive modes." This literature can be rather abstruse at times (to put it mildly), but, employed cautiously and metaphorically, it can help us, I believe, to understand and interpret the relationship in the early modern period between the Atlantic and the World.

To put things in brutally simple and somewhat stylized form: to Marxists, a mode of production refers to the relationship between the producers of some economic output, on the one hand, and the owners of the means of production, on the other. In classical Marxism, modes of production are seen as following one another in successive stages from various pre-capitalist "modes"—primitive communalism, slavery, feudalism—to capitalism, and, in time (and with a leap of faith) to socialism. The European founders of Marxism generally wrote as though *world* history would unfold more or less as it did in Europe, with areas everywhere proceeding in time through the various productive modes in the same linear sequence, indeed, in the same linear manner as had Europe. To be sure, Marx, Engels, Luxemburg, Hilferding, Bukharin, Lenin, and other so-called classical Marxists were sensitive to complexities arising from so-called transitions between discrete modes, but the basic sequence of the scheme outlined above was not seriously questioned.[44]

Over the past two generations, however, many neo-Marxists, particularly those focusing on what used to be called the Third World, found this basic scheme unsatisfactory. They found that the theoretical options available to them in categorizing the economies of developing countries that were in close contact with fully capitalist economies—those options being pre-capitalist, transitional, or fully capitalist—did not adequately explain the "facts on the ground." More specifically, these writers—and here I'm lumping together scholars with somewhat diverse views such as Giovanni Arrighi and P.P. Rey, and, to some extent, Colin Leys as well—believed that different production modes often existed simultaneously, without necessarily being part of any linear "transition" to capitalism, and without necessarily being in contradiction.[45] Rather, such modes interacted or *articulated* with one another in different ways and with varying consequences. In most cases, though, these writers saw one or another pre-capitalist form—whether slavery or some type of indigenous tributary mode or kin-based mode—being harnessed in such a way to as to subsidize, underpin, and support capitalist actors and sectors in the exploitation and expropriation process in one or another part of the Third World. This linkage *cum* subsidization/support process—seen as an unequal and asymmetrical one—became widely known in the literature as the articulation of production modes.[46]

So how does this literature help us in understanding the Atlantic/World? In my view, the key lies in the concept of articulation, for in the early modern period the unitary "Atlantic World" clearly articulated with other circuits and orbits around the globe. And this articulation process—what might be called the spatial articulation of trade circuits, or, speaking more broadly, *exchange* circuits—manifested itself in different ways and with varying consequences, all of which in principle at least are worthy of study in their own right. In this scheme, the Indian Ocean trade, the Manila Galleon, the Silk Road—not to mention the exchange circuits of the Mediterranean, Africa, central and eastern Europe, and the North Sea—are all conjoined in appropriate ways to goings on in and along the Atlantic Basin per se. If we adopted this approach, of course, we would need, among other things, to modify David Armitage's useful trichotomy by adding to the concepts Circum-Atlantic, Trans-Atlantic, and Cis-Atlantic history the concept of, let's call it *Conjuncto-Atlantic* history.[47]

In so doing, we could link up with other questions and other historiographies to offer a broader, richer, amplified view of Atlantic dynamics. What, for example, were the differential effects of the spatial articulation of trade circuits on the various actors and entities involved therein? Did such effects change over time? If so, how? Were the dominant areas in the Atlantic World, particularly those in northwest Europe, supported and subsidized by the process of articulation—as might be presumed—or were matters more complicated? Or, perhaps in some cases such as East Asia (or at least the lower Yangzi) even reversed? Obviously, answering such questions goes beyond the scope of this chapter. In any case, we still lack the empirical evidence regarding some of these circuits to speak with much confidence about the articulation process(es) in which they were involved. Nonetheless, I for one am convinced that this is the direction in which Atlanticists—at least some Atlanticists—need to move. For *whatever* the answers to the above questions, they would be based, properly in my view, on the linkage of processes occurring *in* the Atlantic with those *of* the Atlantic (even if *extra*-Atlantic in a strict geographical sense). In other words, Manila, Canton, the Moluccas, Malacca, Calicut, Surat, Kashgar, Samarkand, the Maldives, Mocha, and Cairo—as well as Venice, Danzig, and Cologne—were all implicated in the making of Atlantic history rather than worlds apart.

Almost all attention thus far has been on matters material, particularly on matters economic. The inter-related circuits mentioned above refer specifically to trade, too, but such circuits are to a greater or lesser degree applicable to other types of exchanges—biological, technological, and scientific exchanges, most obviously, but extending to the philosophical/ religious realm as well. The spread of Islam from its birthplace on the Arabian peninsula to other parts of Afro-Eurasia during the early modern period, and the (more modest) spread of Catholicism to (parts of) the Philippines, to cite two famous examples. Jerry Bentley's impressive study *Old World Encounters* documents many other examples of such transfers and exchanges in the philosophical/religious realm.[48] Although many social theorists over the years have made the case that certain religious traditions are more conducive to economic growth than are others—Weber, Tawney and all that—I don't want to go there, at least not here. What I *would* like to do in the remainder of this chapter, however, is briefly to discuss some exciting work in economic theory that sheds light on the way in which broad exchanges arising from the spatial articulation of *trade circuits* during the early modern period might have played a significant role in facilitating sustained economic growth both in the Atlantic World and elsewhere. And this is just one example, I believe, of the potential explanatory power of a more expansive and more relational approach to analyzing the Atlantic World.

Whereas I've drawn in the section above from several critical traditions in economics, at the end of the day I return, by no means begrudgingly, to the standard bourgeois economic mold. In so doing, we find that over the past twenty years or so economic growth theory has been transformed. Without getting into the intricacies of the transformation—essentially a shift away from Robert Solow's model emphasizing labor and capital accumulation and technical progress to "new growth theory" models associated with economists such as Nobelist Robert Lucas, Gene Grossman and Elhanan Helpman, and Luis Rivera-Batiz and Paul M. Romer—I shall call attention to some important work done by Rivera-Batiz and Romer that is relevant to our discussion.

In a hugely influential 1991 paper entitled "Economic Integration and Endogenous Growth" (and in subsequent extensions), Rivera-Batiz and Romer developed a so-called endogenous model of technological change—Solow had assumed the importance of technological change without ever adequately explaining how such change came about—that focused on economic integration as the key.[49] Developments that break down economic isolation and facilitate economic integration are particularly important to their model, not primarily in the Ricardian or neo-Ricardian sense of integration perforce bringing into play efficiency-enhancing factors relating to comparative advantage, but because with integration, particularly the integration of diverse areas and peoples from advanced societies, comes not merely flows of new goods but, more importantly, of new ideas. And the trade-induced flow of new ideas—which flow, according to Rivera-Bariz and Romer, is heavily influenced by institutions and public policy—is crucial to the cross-border (or even cross-civilizational) diffusion of new technology and thus often to technological progress and, to the fortunate, the endogenization and institutionalization of economic growth. Although Rivera-Bariz and Romer are laying out a general framework here, it is important—and, for our purposes most revealing—to note that in their now classic 1991 *QJE* paper they cite the exchange of ideas via the Silk Road as an example *par excellence* of the trade-induced concatenation of cross-cultural knowledge bases that is at the heart of their theory of integration and endogenous growth.[50] An effect of the spatial articulation of trade circuits, in other words.

What I have tried to do here is to stretch and open up the concept of Atlantic history a bit. The approach associated with the concept is arguably the most exciting development to have coursed through early-American-history circles in the last generation. It has helped to link up or at least to begin an ongoing conversation among scholars working on hitherto largely independent fields, and it has enriched our understanding of the complex, intricately imbricated relationship among various and sundry parts of Western Europe, West Africa, and the Americas during the early modern period. This has unintentionally led to the relative neglect of other important approaches—the hemispheric history approach that Jack Greene among others has recently been calling for, for example—and, even more seriously from my perspective, it has had the perverse effect of separating, if not isolating the Atlantic "unit" from all other "units" in the early modern period.[51] The global links and connections to which I have called attention here should be seen as an earnest attempt to convince Atlanticists to move "a little beyond," as the transcendentalists might put it, and to broaden their canvas, thereby justifying the use of a slash between the words "Atlantic" and "World." [52]

Acknowledgments

This chapter is based largely on an earlier piece, "Atlantic World or Atlantic/World?" *William and Mary Quarterly* 3d ser., 63 (October 2006): 725–742. The author would like to thank the *WMQ* for permission to use materials published in that journal.

NOTES

1. Bailyn, "The Idea of Atlantic History," *Itinerario* 20 (1996): 19–44. Note my use of quotation marks around the term "early modern" in the text. This complicated term is not readily, much less seamlessly transferable beyond the West.

2. In this regard it is interesting to note that Routledge began a "Seas in History" series a few years' back.

3. Martin W. Lewis and Kären E. Wigen, *The Myth of Continents: A Critique of Metageography* (Berkeley and Los Angeles: University of California Press, 1997); Wigen, "Introduction," *American Historical Review* 111 (June 2006): 717–721.

4. Coclanis, Drang Nach Osten: Bernard Bailyn, the World-Island and the Idea of Atlantic History, "*Journal of World History* 13 (Spring 2002): 169–182, especially p. 176. Also see Coclanis "Atlantic World or Atlantic / World?" *William and Mary Quarterly*, 3rd sep., 63 (2006): 725–742.

5. Daniel K. Richter, *Facing East from Indian Country: A Native History of Early America* (Cambridge: Harvard University Press, 2001).

6. Andrew M. Watson, *Agricultural Innovation in the Early Islamic World: The Diffusion of Crops and Farming Techniques, 700–1100* (Cambridge and New York: Cambridge University Press, 1983).

7. On the "idol of origins," see Marc Bloch, *The Historian's Craft*, trans. Peter Putnam (Manchester: Manchester University Press, 1954), pp. 29–35.

8. Marshall G.S. Hodgson, *Rethinking World History: Essays on Europe, Islam, and World History*, ed. Edmund Burke III (Cambridge and New York: Cambridge University Press, 1993); Martin Bernal, *Black Athena: The Afroasiatic Roots of Classical Civilization*, 3 vols. (New Brunswick, N.J.: Rutgers University Press, 1987–2006); John M. Hobson, *The Eastern Origins of Western Civilisation* (Cambridge and New York: Cambridge University Press, 2004).

9. Robert B. Marks, *The Origins of the Modern World: A Global and Ecological Narrative* (Lanham, Maryland: Rowman & Littlefield, 2002), pp. 7–8.

10. For informed discussions of the Eastern roots of these and other technologies and innovations, see in particular Joseph S. Needham's ongoing *Science and Civilisation in China* series (Cambridge: Cambridge University Press, 1954-), esp. Vol. I, and Donald F. Lach's *Asia in the Making of Europe* series (Chicago: University of Chicago Press, 1965-), Vol. I, Book I.

11. David S. Landes, *The Wealth and Poverty of Nations: Why Some are so Rich and Some are so Poor* (New York: W.W. Norton, 1998). Also see Lach, *Asia in the Making of Europe*, Vol. I, Book I, pp. 81–84.

12. On the Asian—Indian and Chinese in particular—role in the development of the cotton gin, see Angela Lakwete, *Inventing the Cotton Gin: Machine and Myth in Antebellum America* (Baltimore and London: Johns Hopkins University Press, 2003), pp. 5–8, 11–16 esp.

13. Fernández-Armesto, *Pathfinders: A Global History of Exploration* (New York: W.W. Norton, 2006), p. 121.

14. The phrase "made together" is drawn from Mechal Sobel, *The World They Made Together: Black and White Values in Eighteenth-Century Virginia* (Princeton, N.J.: Princeton University Press, 1987).

15. Coclanis, "ReOrienting Atlantic History: The Global Dimensions of the 'Western' Rice Trade," in *The Atlantic in Global History, 1500–2000*, eds. Jorge Cañizares-Esguerra and Erik R. Seeman (Upper Saddle River, N.J.: Pearson/Prentice-Hall, 2006), pp. 111–127.

16. See Coclanis, "ReOrienting Atlantic History." Also see Coclanis, "Global Perspectives on the Early Economic History of South Carolina," *South Carolina Historical Magazine* 106 (April-July 2005) 130–146.

17. See Coclanis, "*Drang Nach Osten*," p. 176. Note that Bailyn goes with a lower estimate in *Atlantic History: Concepts and Contours* (Cambridge: Harvard University Press, 2005), p. 134, note 44.

18. Ronald Findlay and Kevin H. O'Rourke, "Commodity Price Integration, 1500–2000," in *Globalization in Historical Perspective*, eds. Michael D. Bordo, Alan M. Taylor, and Jeffrey G. Williamson, National Bureau of Economic Research Conference Report (Chicago: University of Chicago Press, 2003), pp. 13–62, esp. pp. 19–21.

19. Waldemar Kowalski, "The Placement of Urbanised Scots in the Polish Crown Lands during the Sixteenth and Seventeenth Centuries," in *Scottish Communities Abroad in the Early Modern Period*, ed. Alexia Grosjean and Steve Murdoch (Leiden, Netherlands: Brill, 2005), pp. 53–103, esp. pp. 63–64.

20. Dennis O. Flynn and Arturo Giráldez, "Spanish Profitability in the Pacific: The Philippines in the Sixteenth and Seventeenth Centuries," in *Pacific Centuries: Pacific and Pacific Rim History Since the Sixteenth Century*, eds., Dennis O. Flynn, Lionel Frost, and A.J.H. Latham (London and New York: Routledge, 1999), pp. 23–37; Andre Gunder Frank, *ReOrient: Global Economy in the Asian Age* (Berkeley: University of California Press, 1998), pp. 139–149; Marks, *The Origins of the Modern World*, pp. 79–82; K.N. Chaudhuri, *Trade and Civilisation in the Indian Ocean: An Economic History from the Rise of Islam to 1750* (Cambridge and New York: Cambridge University Press, 1985), pp. 97, 215–216.

21. Coclanis, "ReOrienting Atlantic History"; Chaudhuri, *Trade and Civilisation*, pp. 18–19, 82, 97; Prasannan Parthasarathi, "Rethinking Wages and Competitiveness in the Eighteenth Century: Britain and South India," *Past and Present* 158 (February 1998): 79–109; Marks, *The Origins of the Modern World*, pp. 96–101. On the role of cowry shells in the slave trade, also see Jan S. Hogendorn and Marion Johnson, *The Shell Money of the Slave Trade* (Cambridge and New York: Cambridge University Press, 1986); Frank Perlin, "Money-Use in Late Precolonial South Asia and the World Trade in Currency Media," in Perlin, '*The Invisible City': Monetary, Administrative and Popular Infrastructures in Asia and Europe, 1500–1900* (Aldershot, Hampshire, Great Britain: VARIORUM/Ashgate, 1993), pp. 141–149.

22. See, for example, Holden Furber, *Rival Empires of Trade in the Orient, 1600–1800* (Minneapolis: University of Minnesota Press, 1976), pp. 230–263 esp.; Chaudhuri, *Trade and Civilisation*, pp. 63–97, 182–202; Philip D. Curtin, *Cross-*

Cultural Trade in World History (New York and Cambridge: Cambridge University Press, 1984), pp. 136–157; Arun Das Gupta, "The Maritime Trade of Indonesia: 1500–1800," in *India and the Indian Ocean, 1500–1800*, eds. Ashin Das Gupta and M.N. Pearson (Calcutta: Oxford University Press, 1987), pp. 240–275; Anthony Reid, *Southeast Asia in the Age of Commerce, 1450–1680*, 2 vols. (New Haven: Yale University Press, 1988–1993), Vol. Two, pp. 1–43 esp. Also see, Lach, *Asia in the Making of Europe*, Vol. I, Book One, pp. 91–142; Vol. II, Book I, p. 55.

23. David MacPherson, *Annals of Commerce, Manufactures, Fisheries, and Navigation...*, 4 vols. (London: Printed for Nichols and Son, 1805), 4: 362.

24. Coclanis, "Southeast Asia's Incorporation into the World Rice Market: A Revisionist View," *Journal of Southeast Asian Studies* 24 (September 1993): 251–267; Coclanis, "Distant Thunder: The Creation of a World Market in Rice and the Transformations It Wrought," *American Historical Review* 98 (October 1993): 1050–1078; Coclanis, "ReOrienting Atlantic History."

25. Coclanis, "Distant Thunder"; Coclanis, "ReOrienting Atlantic History."

26. See, for example, Curtin, *Cross-Cultural Trade in World History*, pp. 136–206; Chaudhuri, *Trade and Civilisation in the Indian Ocean*, pp. 63–118, 182–228; Frederic Mauro, "Merchant Communities, 1350–1750," in *The Rise of Merchant Empires: Long-Distance Trade in the Early Modern World, 1350–1750*, ed. James D. Tracy (New York and Cambridge: Cambridge University Press, 1990), pp. 255–286.

27. See the works cited in note 26 above.

28. Tomé Pires, *Suma Oriental... 1512–1515*, trans. Armando Cortesao, The Hakluyt Society, Second Series, no. 89 (London: The Hakluyt Society, 1944), pp. 41–42.

29. See Dennis O. Flynn and Arturo Giráldez, "Born with a 'Silver Spoon': The Origin of World Trade in 1571," *Journal of World History* 6 (Fall 1995): 201–221; Flynn and Giráldez, "Cycles of Silver: Global Economic Unity through the Mid-Eighteenth Century," *Journal of World History* 13 (Fall 2002): 391–427; Peter A. Coclanis, "Pacific Overtures: The Spanish Lake and the Global Economy, 1500–1800," *Common-Place* 5 (January 2005).

30. On the purported Chinese discovery of America, see Gavin Menzies, *1421: The Year China Discovered America* (New York: William Morrow, 2003).

31. Coclanis, "ReOrienting Atlantic History."

32. Coclanis, "*Drang Nach Osten*," p. 179–18; Anthony Reid, "A New Phase of Commercial Expansion in Southeast Asia, 1760–1850," in *The Last Stand of Asian Autonomies: Responses to Modernity in the Diverse States of Southeast Asia and Korea, 1750–1900*, ed. Anthony Reid (New York: St. Martin's Press, 1997), pp. 57–81. On the surrender of Pondicherry by the French, see Fred Anderson, *Crucible of War: The Seven Years' War and the Fate of Empire in British North America, 1754–1766* (New York: Alfred A. Knopf, 2000), pp. 417–419. For the basic chronology of Raffles' life, see *Dictionary of National Biography*, 16: 604–608.

33. See *Dictionary of National Biography*, 4: 1159–1166.

34. Curtin, *Cross-Cultural Trade in World History*, pp. 90–108, esp. p. 105; Chaudhuri, *Trade and Civilisation in the Indian Ocean*, pp. 34–62; Kenneth

McPherson, *The Indian Ocean: A History of People and the Sea* (Delhi and New York: Oxford University Press, 1993), pp. 76–136; Milo Kearney, *The Indian Ocean in World History* (London and New York: Routledge, 2004), pp. 31–76.

35. Janet L. Abu-Lughod, *Before European Hegemony: The World System* A.D. *1250–1350* (New York: Oxford University Press, 1989); Kearney, *The Indian Ocean in World History*, pp. 77–102; Chaudhuri, *Trade and Civilisation in the Indian Ocean*, pp. 98–136 esp.; Peter A. Coclanis, *Time's Arrow, Time's Cycle: Globalization in Southeast Asia over la Longue Durée* (Singapore: Institute of Southeast Asian Studies, 2006), pp. 26–34.

36. Scholars associated with the "California School" include, among others, Kenneth Pomeranz, R. Bin Wong, James Z. Lee, and Robert B. Marks, as well as "honorary" alumni such as Andre Gunder Frank and James M. Blaut.

37. Coclanis, *"Drang Nach Osten,"* pp. 180–181.

38. Abu-Lughod, *Before European Hegemony*, pp. 3–40 esp. For a visual representation of the eight circuits, see p. 34, Figure 1. On the persistence of parts of her "world system," see Frank, *ReOrient*, pp. 128–130, and my argument in this piece.

39. David Armitage, "Is There a Pre-History of Globalization?" in *Comparison and History: Europe in Cross-National Perspective*, eds. Deborah Cohen and Maura O'Connor (New York and London: Routledge, 2004), pp. 165–176, esp. pp. 169–170.

40. K.M. Panikkar, *Asia and Western Dominance; A Survey of the Vasco da Gama Epoch of Asian History, 1498–1945* (London: George Allen & Unwin, 1953).

41. Curtin, *Cross-Cultural Trade in World History*, pp. 26–28. On the contours of the trans-Saharan trade, see Ralph A. Austen, "Marginalization, Stagnation, and Growth: The Trans-Saharan Caravan Trade in the Era of European Expansion, 1500–1900," in *The Rise of Merchant Empires*, pp. 311–350. The likelihood of such continental circuits seems apparent in light of the work of Alan Taylor and others. For an introduction to the "continental" approach, see Taylor, *American Colonies*, Penguin History of the United States (New York: Penguin, 2001), and the essays by Andrés Reséndez, Elizabeth A. Fenn, James F. Brooks, and Taylor in the section "Continental Possessions" in the *Journal of the Early Republic* 24 (Summer 2004): 159–188. Also see Paul W. Mapp, "Atlantic History from Imperial, Continental, and Pacific Perspectives," *William and Mary Quarterly*, 3d ser., 53 (October 2006): 713–724.

42. Kevin H. O'Rourke and Jeffrey G. Williamson, "After Columbus: Explaining Europe's Overseas Trade Boom 1500–1800," *Journal of Economic History* 62 (June 2002): 417–456, esp. Table 1, pp. 419–421. Also see Findlay and. O'Rourke, "Commodity Market Integration, 1500–2000."

43. See Immanuel Wallerstein, *The Modern World-System*, 3 vols. thus far (New York: (New York: Academic Press, 1974–1989); Andre Gunder Frank, *World Accumulation, 1492–1789* (New York: Monthly Review Press, 1978).

44. On so-called classical Marxism—works by Marxists writing around the time of the Second International (1889–1914)—see, for example, Anthony Brewer, *Marxist Theories of Imperialism: A Critical Survey*, 2d ed. (London and New York: Routledge, 1990), pp. 25–72, 88–135.

45. See Giovanni Arrighi and John S. Saul, *Essays on the Political Economy of Africa* (New York: Monthly Review Press, 1973); Arrighi, *The Geometry of Imperialism: The Limits of Hobson's Paradigm*, trans. Patrick Camiller (London: New Left Books, 1978); P.P. Rey, *Colonialisme, néo-colonialisme et transition au capitalisme* (Paris: Maspero, 1971); Rey, *Les alliances de classes* (Paris: Maspero, 1973); Colin Leys, "Capital Accumulation, Class Formation and Dependency—The Significance of the Kenyan Case," *The Socialist Register, 1978*, eds. Ralph Miliband and John Savile (New York: Monthly Review Press, 1978), pp. 241–266. For a more recent formulation of Leys' position, see Leys, "African Capitalists and Development: Theoretical Questions," in *African Capitalists in African Development*, eds. Bruce J. Berman and Colin Leys (Boulder and London: Lynne Rienner Publishers, 1994), pp. 11–38.

46. See Brewer, *Marxist Theories of Imperialism*, pp. 225–259.

47. David Armitage, "Three Concepts of Atlantic History," in *The British Atlantic World*, eds. David Armitage and Michael J. Braddick, The British Atlantic World (Basingstoke, Hampshire and New York: Palgrave Macmillan, 2002), pp. 11–27.

48. Jerry H. Bentley, *Old World Encounters: Cross-Cultural Contacts and Exchanges in Pre-Modern Times* (New York: Oxford University Press, 1993). On such encounters during the period between 1500 and 1800, see Geoffrey C. Gunn, *First Globalization: The Eurasian Exchange, 1500–1800* (Lanham, Maryland: Rowman & Littlefield, 2003).

49. Luis A. Rivera-Batiz and Paul M. Romer, "Economic Integration and Endogenous Growth," *Quarterly Journal of Economics* 106 (May 1991): 531–555.

50. Rivera-Batiz and Romer, "International Trade with Endogenous Technological Change," *European Economic Review* 35 (May 1991): 971–1004; Rivera-Batiz and Romer, "The Origins of Endogenous Growth," *Journal of Economic Perspectives* 8 (Winter 1994): 3–22; Rivera-Batiz and Romer, "Economic Integration and Endogenous Growth: An Addendum," *Quarterly Journal of Economics* 109 (February 1994): 307–308. On the reference to the Silk Road, see the 1991 *QJE* paper cited in note 49, pp. 546–547. For an excellent, empirically-based discussion of the role of the Silk Road in promoting endogenous economic growth, see Debin Ma, "The Great Silk Exchange: How the World was Connected and Developed," in *Pacific Centuries*, eds. Flynn, Frost, and Latham, pp. 38–69.

51. Jack P. Greene, "Comparing Early Modern American Worlds: Some Reflections on the Promise of a Hemispheric Perspective," *History Compass* 1 (2003) [online]. Also see Jorge Cañizares-Esguerra, "Some Caveats about the 'Atlantic' Paradigm," *History Compass* 1 (2003) [online]; Fernández-Armesto, *The Americas: A Hemispheric History* (New York: The Modern Library, 2005).

52. See Charles Capper, "A Little Beyond: The Problem of the Transcendentalist Movement in American History," *Journal of American History* 85 (September 1998): 502–539.

INDEX

CPSIA information can be obtained at www.ICGtesting.com
Printed in the USA
BVOW081145250313

316367BV00002B/86/P